The Rinehart Guide
to Grammar and Usage

The Rinehart Guide to Grammar and Usage

Bonnie Carter

Craig Skates

University of Southern Mississippi

HOLT, RINEHART AND WINSTON, INC.
New York   Chicago   San Francisco   Philadelphia
Montreal   Toronto   London   Sydney   Tokyo

Editor-in-Chief   Susan Katz
Senior Acquisitions Editor   Charlyce Jones Owen
Developmental Editor   Kate Morgan
Senior Project Manager   Françoise Bartlett
Senior Production Manager   Nancy Myers
Art Director   Louis Scardino
Text Design   Caliber Design Planning
Cover Design   Albert D'Agostino

Library of Congress Cataloging-in-Publication Data

Carter, Bonnie.
   The Rinehart guide to grammar and usage / Bonnie Carter, Craig Skates.

   Includes index.
   1. English language—Grammar—1950–   2. English language—
Usage.   I. Skates, Craig Barnwell.   II. Title.
PE1112.C27   1988
428.2—dc 19

ISBN 0-03-013619-9

Requests for permission to make copies of any part of the work should be mailed
to: Permissions, Holt, Rinehart and Winston, Inc., 111 Fifth Avenue, New York,
NY 10003.

Printed in the United States of America
Published simultaneously in Canada

8 9 0 1   016   9 8 7 6 5 4 3 2 1

Holt, Rinehart and Winston, Inc.
The Dryden Press
Saunders College Publishing

Preface to the Instructor

The skill of writing depends not only on practice and effort but also on an understanding of our language's structures, the conventions acceptable to readers, and the techniques for revising. *The Rinehart Guide to Grammar and Usage* provides the information that can build and improve the skills of all writers—from those with little experience to those who write with ease. It is thorough, but not intimidating; detailed, but not overwhelming.

The guide can serve several purposes. It is a reference book for writers who need guidance on such matters as specific usages, conventional practices, and appropriate formats. It is a textbook for writing courses—both basic and advanced courses. It is also a book for people who want to develop skills alone at an individualized pace.

Students with no foundation in the essentials—the words, phrases, and clauses that make up our language—cannot understand the advice of teachers, cannot make sense of correction guides in textbooks, and cannot use an index. These students can profit from the information in Part I, "Building Sentences: Words, Phrases, Clauses."

Students with some mastery of the basics can use the various sections of the book in whatever order is appropriate. The book is arranged from the simple to the complex, from smaller units to larger. However, one can enter the sequence at any place and can exclude inappropriate sections.

Throughout, the guide emphasizes the interconnection of writing and revising. Writing is a complicated process in which the writer is constantly thinking, writing, changing, adding, and deleting. Therefore, revising cannot be thought of as a separate step; instead, it is a continual part of writing. Typically, the first way a thought is put on paper is not the way it will appear later. A composition evolves gradually through stages to an acceptable form. Writers face the problem of how to transform a statement or passage to make it clearer, more effective, more emphatic, more appropriate. Without dogmatically dictating solutions, the guide covers various ways prose can be transformed into a satisfactory product. Techniques for revising appear all through the text.

Numerous examples and exercises reinforce the information. To emphasize that writing is not the exclusive domain of composition classes, these examples and exercises reflect a broad range of subjects—history, science, psychology, business, engineering, literature—and a variety of popular interests—school, food, entertainment, pets, issues, childhood, family. Many different kinds of sources are represented—newspapers, magazines, scholarly journals, books, movies, and television. Some material is serious, some light or humorous. Some material is academic, some popular. The examples and exercises have been chosen to reflect the versatility and variety of writing in our lives.

To emphasize that writing and revising usually involve more than working with disconnected sentences, over fifty of the exercises in Parts I through IV are full paragraphs or full compositions—prose similar to the kind a writer must revise in a real composition. Realistically, many of these exercises also involve correcting several kinds of errors as well as combining and restructuring sentences. In addition, many assignments call for students to compose paragraphs and full compositions of their own.

For polishing prose, users can turn to Part IV, where they will find how word and structure choice unite to create style. Here are suggestions for choosing words that will make writing more specific, more concrete, more exact, more appropriate, less tedious, and less pretentious. Here also are suggestions for choosing structures—structures that are varied, interesting, and even dramatic; structures that are not cumbersome, hard to read, wordy, or weak. In addition, the text provides practice in using figurative language and in working with sound and rhythm to add stylistic polish. Chapters 34 and 35 provide a brief but comprehensive discussion of the writing process, complete with a full, annotated student composition showing first through final drafts.

The "Glossary of Usage and Commonly Confused Words" and the "Glossary of Grammatical, Rhetorical, and Literary Terms" are both reference tools. Questions about word choice and usage and questions about the meaning of technical terminology can be answered quickly and easily by consulting these guides.

An Answer Key to Text Exercises is available. For a complimentary copy of this teaching aid, contact your local sales representative or write to: English Editor, Holt, Rinehart and Winston, 111 Fifth Avenue, New York, NY 10003.

We wish to thank the following colleagues for their comments and advice: Steve Adams, Northeast Louisiana University; Joy Allameh, Eastern Kentucky University; Kristine Anderson, Southern Technical Institute; Conrad Bayley, Glendale Community College; Jane Bouterse, Texarkana College; Henry Brown, Midwestern State University; Alma Bryant, Fort Valley State College; James Bynum, Georgia Tech; Peggy Cole, Arapahoe Community College; Deborah Core, Eastern Kentucky University; James Creel, Alvin Community College; Joseph Davis, Memphis State University; Ralph Dille, University of Southern Colorado; Charles Dodson, University of North Carolina; Linda Doran, Volunteer State Community College; Joseph Dunne, St. Louis Community College at Meremac; Elizabeth Fifer, Lehigh College; Eleanor Garner, George Washington University; George Haich, University of North Carolina—Wilmington; Charles Hall, Memphis State University; David Higgins, Cameron University; Gertrude Hopkins, Harford Community College; Edward Kline, University of Notre Dame; Cheryl Koski, Louisiana State University; Ruth Laux, Arkansas Technical University; Russell Long, Tarleton State University; Andrea Lunsford, University of British Columbia; Robert Lynch, New Jersey Institute of Technology; Beverly McKay, Lenoir Community College; Sam Phillips, Gaston College; Edward Reilly, St. Joseph's College; John Reuter, Florida Southern College; Dave Roberts, University of Southern Mississippi; Michael Rossi, Merimack College; Charles Sphar, Delmar College; Jo Tarvers, University of North Carolina—Chapel Hill; John Taylor, South Dakota State University; George Trail, University of Houston; Daryl Troyer, El Paso Community College; Gloria Tubb, Jones County Junior College; Richard Vandeweghe, University of Colorado at Denver; Laura Weaver, University of Evansville; Jack White, Mississippi State University;

Marie Wolf, Bergen Community College; and Peter Zoller, Wichita State University.

We thank the staff at Holt, Rinehart and Winston who made *The Rinehart Guide to Grammar and Usage* possible. In particular, we are indebted to DeVilla Williams, who introduced us to the company and got the project started; to Kate Morgan, our developmental editor, who made sure we responded to our audience and our reviews; to Nancy Myers and Lou Scardino, who contributed much to the book's production and design; and especially to Francoise Bartlett, senior project manager, whose expertise, dedication, and patience transformed the manuscript into a book. Our greatest debt is to Charlyce Jones Owen, who not only gave us the chance to write this book but also, as senior acquisitions editor, guided and encouraged us through every step. Finally, we thank our former professor, Marice C. Brown, who taught us that grammar is worthy of study. To all, in Shakespeare's words, "thanks, and thanks, and ever thanks."

October 1987   B.C.
                                                                           C.S.

Preface to the Student

No doubt you have heard a good many warnings about the importance of grammar and writing skills to your future. And perhaps you have become tired of listening. Before you dismiss the subject, however, consider for a moment why people are always insisting that you develop your ability to write. Consider what our world would be, and specifically what you would be, without the written word.

Writing makes possible human culture as we know it. Without writing, we could not codify the laws that create stable government. Without writing, there would be no education, because we could not hand down through the ages knowledge of science, medicine, art, history, and philosophy. Business and commerce would falter without the written records of transactions. Indeed, the entire culture of the civilized world rests upon writing.

On an individual level, writing skills usually parallel achievement. For example, a person who cannot read and write lives on the fringes of society, without access to the most ordinary information that literate people take for granted. A person with only rudimentary writing skills is locked out of the professional world and into the lower levels of society and the economy. A person with good writing skills has opportunities—both social and professional.

Clearly, then, learning to write well is one of the most important steps you can take toward personal achievement. Through writing, you can learn to express your feelings and thus to understand yourself. Through writing, you can learn to discipline your mind and thus to think clearly. Furthermore, the ability to write good compositions can make the difference between success and failure in school. In addition, good writing is one of the most valued skills in business, industry, and professional fields. Thus, to improve your writing skills is to improve your potential for success.

The Rinehart Guide to Grammar and Usage is a complete overview of the conventions of grammar, punctuation and mechanics, style, and usage. Whether you are an experienced writer or only a beginner, this guide provides the information necessary to develop your skills. Part I, "Building Sentences: Words, Phrases, and Clauses," is a good overview of grammatical components and of the terminology you will need to use the rest of the guide efficiently. For example, suppose you are unsure whether to put a comma or a semicolon after *began* in the sentence *Even after the rain began no one left the stadium.* If you know that *even after the rain began* is an adverb clause, looking up its correct punctuation will be easy. Or suppose you do not know whether to write *My grandmother gave the old car to my brother and I* or *My grandmother gave the old car to my brother and me.* If you know that the problem is one of pronoun case, you can find the answer very quickly.

At some point in the process of revising a paper, you must remove any structural or grammatical mistakes that obscure your prose, distract your reader, or reflect poorly on your command of the language. Thus, Part II, "Revising Sentences: Structural and Grammatical Errors," helps you recognize sentence errors and remedy them. Part III, "Following Conventions: Punctuation and Mechanics," is a guide to another important part of revision—ensuring the correctness of punctuation marks (such as commas, colons, and semicolons) and of mechanical marks (such as italics, capital letters, and apostrophes). Correctness in punctuation and mechanics not only demonstrates your knowledge of the conventions of standard written English but also helps produce clarity in prose. Part IV, "Improving Prose: Style," helps you choose words that are clear, specific, direct, and inoffensive. It also suggests ways for structuring prose in order to achieve variety. Again, the emphasis is on revision.

In Part V, "The Writing Process," the guide covers the process of writing compositions—getting ideas, making important decisions about purpose and audience, choosing a structure, writing paragraphs, and revising. In addition, a composition-in-progress (Chapter 35) shows how one student writer moved through all of the stages of the writing process.

The "Glossary of Usage and Commonly Confused Words" is an

alphabetical list of such information as the difference between *all ready* and *already, disinterested* and *uninterested, can* and *may*. It also answers such questions as whether *data* is singular or plural and whether to write *between you and I*. The "Glossary of Grammatical, Rhetorical, and Literary Terms" lists and defines terms that may be new or confusing to you—terms like *coherence, fused sentence, squinting modifier, idiom, non sequitur, antithesis,* and *protagonist*.

A guide is a handy reference; you should have no difficulty finding in it the material you need. If you are using this text in an English class, your instructor can help you learn some of the key terms for locating the information you need. Remember, however, that you will not always have an instructor to guide you; then, you must be able to locate information by yourself. Thus, you should learn to find information quickly and easily by understanding the book's organization and content. Look carefully at the Table of Contents to see what material is available and where it is located. Make sure you understand the correction symbols and the numbering system in the book. Pay close attention to cross references that refer you to other related sections of the text. Learn to use the index and the glossaries when looking for solutions to problems.

The guide contains all the information you need for writing in school and most of what you need for writing in the professional world. If you use the book effectively, you may be surprised by how much your writing skills improve—and with them, your confidence in yourself and your future.

October 1987   B.C.
                                                                  C.S.

Contents

■ **Part II**

Revising Sentences: Structural and Grammatical Errors   77

■ Part III

Following Conventions: Punctuation and Mechanics   173

Part V

The Writing Process   335

Building Sentences: Words, Phrases, Clauses

Every human language is a system of predictable patterns: words fit together to form phrases; phrases join to form clauses; clauses create sentences. This system of patterns is called "grammar." An understanding of the grammatical system of English can provide the analytical skills needed to control language, to ensure that it communicates clearly. Thus, to improve writing, you should understand the way words, phrases, and clauses combine to express ideas.

1

Nouns

One way to identify nouns is by applying the common definition, "Nouns are words that name persons, places, or things." Although the definition is rather limited, it does contain a key word—*name*. Anything in the physical and mental worlds can be named with a noun.

PEOPLE: Susan, doctor, singer, family

PLACES: ocean, Canada, home, campus

THINGS: popsicle, shoe, fingernail, crater

QUANTITIES: pound, quart, inch, dollar

SENSES: sound, smell, taste, feel

FEELINGS: hope, disappointment, anxiety, peace

OCCURRENCES: earthquake, wedding, party, contest

ACTIONS: handshake, smile, leap, wink

Another way to identify nouns is by recognizing their characteristic positions and functions.

- Nouns follow the articles *a, an,* and *the*.

  a field   the light
  an apple   the car

- Nouns appear in phrases after descriptive words called "modifiers."

  a muddy field   the bright light
  a red apple   the new car

- Nouns join with prepositions to form prepositional phrases.

  through a field   behind the light
  in an apple   under the car

- Nouns join with verbs to form sentences.

  A field lay between the house and the lake.

  She ate only an apple a day.

  The light was brilliant.

  His most prized possession was his car.

  In addition to these positions and functions, nouns have the following characteristic forms.

Proper and Common—the distinction that controls capitalization of nouns

Singular and Plural—the forms that indicate number and determine the agreement of subjects and verbs

Possessive—the forms that express ideas such as ownership and measurement

1a Proper and Common Nouns

Proper nouns are official names, such as names of people, organizations, geographical locations, holidays, languages, and historical events. Proper nouns begin with capital letters. *Common nouns,* all other nouns, are usually not capitalized unless they appear as the first word in a sentence.

PROPER NOUNS	COMMON NOUNS
Pete Rose	athlete
General Foods	company
Episcopal Church	church
United Kingdom	country
Saks	store
Okefenokee	swamp
Thanksgiving	holiday
English	language

 EXERCISE 1

For each common noun listed, give a corresponding proper noun.

EXAMPLE: building   Pentagon

1. political party
2. religion
3. family member
4. governmental body

5. historical figure   8. river
6. holiday   9. club
7. city   10. war

1b   Singular and Plural Nouns

Nouns have *number*—that is, they are either singular or plural. Singular nouns refer to one person, place, or thing; plural nouns to more than one. Disregarding number can lead to errors in agreement of subject and verb—errors that are considered very serious in formal prose. (See Chapter 10, "Subject-Verb Agreement.")

(1) Forming plurals of simple nouns

Most nouns form their plurals with the addition of *-s* or *-es*, sometimes with a slight adjustment in spelling, such as changing *y* to *i* or doubling a consonant.

Singular	Plural
week	weeks
government	governments
dime	dimes
box	boxes
church	churches
quiz	quizzes
destiny	destinies
hero	heroes

Some nouns, such as those following, form their plurals in unpredictable ways.

Singular	Plural
leaf	leaves
foot	feet
mouse	mice
child	children
salmon	salmon
stimulus	stimuli
criterion	criteria

Whenever you are not sure whether a noun's plural undergoes a spelling change or has an unpredictable form, you should consult a dictionary.

(2) Forming plurals of compound nouns

Compound nouns are made up of two or more words functioning as a single noun. The compound may be written as separate words (*half dollar*); it may be hyphenated (*man-of-war*); or it may be written as a single word (*holdup*). The plurals of compound nouns are formed in several different ways.

- First word is plural.

    sisters-in-law

    runners up

- Last word is plural.

    pocket knives

    go-betweens

- Both words are plural.

    women astronauts

    gentlemen farmers

- Either part is plural.

    spoonfuls *or* spoonsful

    attorney generals *or* attorneys general

Since it is often difficult to predict the plural of a compound noun, you should check a dictionary whenever you are unsure of the correct form.

☐ EXERCISE 2

Find the nouns, both common and proper, in the following sentences. Identify each as singular or plural.

1. The police are investigating the rash of robberies on the west side of town.
2. A cyclone once caused 300,000 deaths in Bangladesh.
3. The traditional gift for a sixtieth wedding anniversary is a diamond.
4. The Mohave Desert has unusual varieties of cacti.
5. Vitamin D, important for bone development, is derived from sunlight.

6. Bristlecone pines, which grow in the White Mountains, are thought to be the oldest trees in the world.
7. A young eel is known as an elver.
8. The ecology of the lake has been upset by an abundance of algae.
9. Reindeer are capable of running thirty miles an hour.
10. The newspaper has had three editors-in-chief in the last year.

☐ EXERCISE 3

Give the plural form (or forms) for each singular noun listed. If you have any doubt about a correct form, you should consult a dictionary.

1. shrimp
2. passerby
3. wolf
4. day
5. candy
6. cupful
7. bypass
8. crisis

9. index
10. synopsis
11. antenna
12. box
13. ox
14. maid-of-honor
15. major general

1c Possessive Nouns

Nouns have *possessive forms,* which indicate a variety of meanings, such as

OWNERSHIP:	my <u>sister's</u> house (house belonging to my sister)
AUTHORSHIP:	<u>Ibsen's</u> plays (plays by Ibsen)
SOURCE:	the <u>mayor's</u> permission (permission from the mayor)
MEASUREMENT:	a <u>year's</u> leave (leave of a year)
DESCRIPTION:	<u>men's</u> dormitory (dormitory for men)

(1) Forming possessives of singular nouns

The possessives of singular nouns are formed by the addition of an apostrophe + s ('s).

SINGULAR	SINGULAR POSSESSIVE
year	year's
condition	condition's

| James | James's |
| Surgeon General | Surgeon General's |

An apostrophe alone (') forms the possessive of a proper noun with enough syllables and "hissing" consonants to make the addition of an apostrophe + s ('s) sound peculiar.

SINGULAR	SINGULAR POSSESSIVE
Xerxes	Xerxes'
Massachusetts	Massachusetts'

(2) Forming possessives of plural nouns

Possessives of plural nouns are formed in two ways. Plural nouns that end in *s* add an apostrophe (') only.

PLURAL	PLURAL POSSESSIVE
doctors	doctors'
institutions	institutions'
fire fighters	fire fighters'

Plural nouns that do not end in *s* add an apostrophe + *s* ('s).

PLURAL	PLURAL POSSESSIVE
children	children's
mice	mice's
Associated Alumni	Associated Alumni's

For a more detailed discussion of possessive forms, see 26a, "Apostrophes to Indicate Possession."

 EXERCISE 4

In the following sentences, change each *of* or *for* phrase to a possessive noun.

EXAMPLE: The border guard examined the visa of every tourist. → The border guard examined every tourist's visa.

1. The face of Medusa turned people to stone.
2. The waterfront of San Francisco attracts many visitors.
3. Medicine sometimes affects the stamina of the patient.
4. The seismograph measured the intensity of the earthquake.
5. The new shop specializes in games for children.
6. The success of the athletes at the games surprised the sports world.

7. He lost his pay for a whole week.
8. The court appointed a guardian for the child.
9. The birthplace of Brahms was destroyed in a World War II air raid.
10. The psychologist studied the attitudes of hostages toward their captors.

2

Pronouns

The word *pronoun* means literally "for a noun"; and, in fact, pronouns do occur in most of the same positions as nouns and noun phrases.

NOUN: Students can have identification cards made at the sports arena.

PRONOUN: You can have identification cards made at the sports arena.

NOUN PHRASE: I left your coat with the attendant at the door.

PRONOUN: I left your coat with someone at the door.

NOUN PHRASE: The collie ate the whole turkey.

PRONOUN: The collie ate what?

Often, pronouns substitute for previously stated nouns or noun phrases, called *antecedents*.

Voters did not turn out today. They were deterred by the weather.

The curry was so hot that few people could eat it.

A taxpayer whose returns are audited should hire an accountant.

Although they make up a relatively small class of words, pronouns are in constant use. Notice that of the two passages that follow, the one without pronouns sounds unnatural.

WITHOUT PRONOUNS

Emily Dickinson is regarded as a great American poet. Even though Emily Dickinson lived in seclusion, Dickinson's poems have universal significance: Dickinson's poems concern the relationship between the inner self and the outer world. Dickinson regarded the relationship between the inner self and the outer world as tragic. Dickinson examined the relationship between the inner self and the outer world with irony and wit.

WITH PRONOUNS

Emily Dickinson is regarded as a great American poet. Even though she lived in seclusion, her poems have universal significance: they concern the relationship between the inner self and the outer world. She examined this relationship, which she regarded as tragic, with irony and wit.

Even though they all serve in noun positions, pronouns function in different ways. Based on these functions, pronouns fall into five classes: personal, demonstrative, relative, interrogative, and indefinite.

2a Personal Pronouns

There are seven *personal pronouns,* each with different forms for different uses.

I, me, my, mine	it, its
you, your, yours	we, us, our, ours
he, him, his	they, them, their, theirs
she, her, hers	

The personal pronouns are classified by person, number, gender, and case.

- *First person singular (I)* refers to the speaker; *first person plural (we),* to the speaker and another person or group. *Second person (you)* refers to the person(s) spoken to, and *third person (he, she, it, and they),* to the person(s) or thing(s) spoken about.
- *Number* refers to whether the pronoun is singular (one) or plural (more than one).
- *Gender* is the sex represented by third-person singular pronouns: masculine (*he*), feminine (*she*), neuter (*it*).

- *Case* involves the various forms a pronoun takes according to its use in a sentence. For example, *they* is a subject form (*They* are my friends). *Them* is an object form (Don't call *them*). *Their* is a possessive form (*Their* house is on Main Street). Case forms and their uses are discussed in Chapter 14, "Case of Nouns and Pronouns."

The *-self/-selves* personal pronouns

In addition to case forms, personal pronouns also have compound forms, made by adding the suffixes (endings) *-self* or *-selves: myself, yourself, himself* (not *hisself*), *herself, itself, ourselves, yourselves, themselves* (not *theirselves*). These forms are used in two ways.

- As reflexives, the *-self/-selves* pronouns function as objects that rename the subjects of sentences: We enjoyed ourselves.
- As emphatics, the *-self/-selves* pronouns repeat, for emphasis, the words and phrases they refer to: She races the boat herself.

☐ EXERCISE 1

Improve the prose of the following passage by substituting personal pronouns for nouns and noun phrases.

Lady Godiva, wife of Earl Leofric, lived in England in the 1000s. As the legend goes, Lady Godiva asked the Earl to reduce the taxes of Coventry. Earl Leofric agreed if Lady Godiva would ride naked through the streets. To avoid embarrassment, Lady Godiva asked the people of Coventry not to watch Lady Godiva's ride. All the people of Coventry complied with Lady Godiva's wishes except Tom the Tailor. Tom the Tailor peeped through a shutter and was instantly struck blind.

2b Demonstrative Pronouns

The only *demonstrative pronouns* are *this* and *that*, along with their corresponding plurals, *these* and *those*. A demonstrative can be used alone to point out that something is relatively near to or far from the speaker.

This certainly has been a better year than that. [*This* year is the present year; *that* is past.]

I prefer these to those. [*These* are closer to the speaker than *those*.]

A demonstrative can also precede a noun and function as a determiner to indicate that something has been previously mentioned.

> Dieters should avoid beef, pork, and lamb when dining out, since these meats are high in both calories and fat. [*These meats* refers to beef, pork, and lamb.]

> In the last game of the season, the coach threw a chair at the referee; that tantrum cost him his job. [*That tantrum* refers to the coach's behavior.]

☐ EXERCISE 2

Use demonstrative pronouns to improve the following passage. Be sure that any demonstrative without a noun immediately following it refers clearly to a previous noun.

> Manners seem a thing of the past. I drew the previous conclusion about manners when a friend arrived an hour late for dinner, brought an uninvited guest, and never apologized. The incident with the late friend was followed by others: a bank teller slamming a window in my face, a driver refusing to yield the right-of-way, a store clerk ignoring my questions. The experiences with my friend, the bank teller, the driver, and the clerk indicate the unfortunate breakdown of a valuable tradition—being polite.

2c Relative Pronouns

The *relative pronouns* are as follows.

> who,* whom* (referring to people)
>
> which, what (referring to things)
>
> that, whose* (referring to either people or things)

Since their function is to introduce dependent adjective clauses (see 7c.2), the relative pronouns often allow writers to combine sentences and eliminate choppy prose.

> CHOPPY: I voted for the candidate. He promised the least.

> IMPROVED: I voted for the candidate who promised the least.

---

* These forms represent different cases: subjective *(who)*, objective *(whom)*, and possessive *(whose)*. See Chapter 14, "Case."

CHOPPY: Julian arrived in a limousine. He had rented it at great expense.

IMPROVED: Julian arrived in a limousine, <u>which</u> he had rented at great expense.

CHOPPY: Only one creature recognized Ulysses. It was his dog.

IMPROVED: The only creature <u>that</u> recognized Uysses was his dog.

The relatives *who, which,* and *what* sometimes appear with the suffix *-ever.*

<u>Whoever</u> raises the most money wins the trip.

Discuss first <u>whichever</u> question seems easiest to you.

He said <u>whatever</u> came to his mind.

EXERCISE 3

Identify the relative pronouns in the following passage.

An enjoyable hobby that does not involve any talent or expense is collecting what I call "sign bloopers." The term refers to any sign that is misleading or unintentionally humorous. For example, here are two from my own collection:

Sign on door of high school: "Please use other door. This door is broke."
Sign in lounge: "We reserve the right to refuse service to everyone."

Anyone who has a notebook and pencil can start a collection. Furthermore, anyone whose mind is alert to the written word can accumulate quite a few prized items in a short while. Most bloopers appear in hand-lettered signs, which are common in family-owned businesses and places where employees want to give temporary instructions. Two more bloopers that I have collected can illustrate.

Sign in diner: "No chicks please."
Sign in tax collector's office: "Motor vehicles use other line."

2d Interrogative Pronouns

The interrogative pronouns (*who, whom, whose, which,* and *what*) introduce questions that ask for information, rather than a yes or no answer. (For the distinction among *who*, *whom*, and *whose*, see 14c.)

Who painted the ceiling of the Sistine Chapel?

Whose idea was it to tell stories on the way to Canterbury?

Which house was Liberace's?

What did Arthur call his sword?

2e Indefinite Pronouns

Some pronouns, called *indefinite,* do not require antecedents and need not refer to specific people or things. Indefinite pronouns can be completely general, such as those in the following two sentences.

Anyone can raise tropical fish.

To an adolescent, everything seems a crisis.

In addition, indefinites can refer to nouns or noun phrases already named or about to be named.

Numerous needleleaf trees grow in the Southeast, but few are as graceful as the loblolly pine.

Many of the North American totems depict birds and fish.

Also, antecedents are required for two indefinite pronouns, *each other* and *one another* (called *reciprocal pronouns*). *Each other* refers to two persons or things; *one another*, to more than two.

The two participants debated each other for an hour.

The four directors communicate with one another by telephone.

The indefinite pronouns include the following.

all	everybody	no one
another	everyone	nothing
any	everything	one
anybody	few	one another
anyone	many	other
anything	more	others
both	most	several

each	much	some
each other	neither	somebody
either	nobody	someone
	none	something

☐ EXERCISE 4

Locate the pronouns in the following passage and identify their types.

Who gives us the best advice about nutrition? The advice we get is often contradictory and leaves us thoroughly confused. For example, some advisors condone vitamin supplements; others advise against them. According to some authorities, meat is nutritionally indispensable. However, many studies suggest that it contributes to coronary problems and cancer. Nutritional controversies also rage over salt, sugar, fiber, and fat. These substances are usually recommended for our diets, but in different quantities—sometimes liberal, sometimes limited. When the authorities don't agree, what are we to do? We can only await new studies that may provide answers.

☐ EXERCISE 5

Use pronouns to improve the following passages by eliminating repetition and choppy sentences.

1. Leaf-cutter ants use leaves to create a fertilizer for the ants' basic food, a fungus. Leaf-cutter ants cultivate the fungus in underground "gardens."
2. Agatha Christie knew a great deal about poisons. Christie's knowledge of poisons helped Christie with fictional murders.
3. A tornado is a drift of down-spiraling clouds shaped like a funnel. The funnel can revolve at 200 to 500 miles an hour. As the tornado gathers force and touches land, the tornado sucks up objects and debris. Objects and debris increase the density of the funnel.
4. Many people are compulsive buyers. These people buy many things. These people do not need the things. Things require expense, time, and effort. Therefore, compulsive buyers often become slaves of compulsive buyers' habits.
5. The television program conveyed a message. The message of the program was directed to girls. The program encouraged girls to pay attention to mathematics. If girls are unable to master mathematics, girls will be excluded from half of all college majors.

3

Adjectives and Adverbs

Adjectives and adverbs are modifiers—that is, they describe, limit, or qualify some other word or words. Sometimes modifiers are not part of the basic sentence structure; they flesh out the skeletal structure but do not change it. For example, if the underlined modifiers were deleted, the structure of the following sentence would be unaltered.

> Suddenly I came over a steep rise and saw a panoramic sweep of brilliantly blue water and alabaster sand.

Other times modifiers are not merely descriptive additions but part of the basic sentence structure. For example, if the underlined words in the following sentences were deleted, the structures would be unfinished.

> The water is cold.
>
> Grady seemed angry.
>
> The court declared the law unconstitutional.
>
> The auditor is here.

3a Adjectives

Adjectives modify nouns and a few pronouns to express attributes such as quality, quantity, or type. The most characteristic positions of adjectives are these.

- Before nouns (and occasionally pronouns)

  <u>rusty</u> scissors

  <u>flexible</u> plastic

  <u>new</u> one

- After *very*

  very <u>rusty</u>

  very <u>flexible</u>

  very <u>new</u>

- After forms of the verb *be*

  The scissors are <u>rusty</u>.

  This plastic is <u>flexible</u>.

  That one is <u>new</u>.

Another way to identify adjectives is to look for typical suffixes (endings). The most characteristic adjective suffixes are the comparative and superlative endings.

<u>-ER</u> AND <u>-EST</u>: shorter, shortest; younger, youngest; brighter, brightest
(For information on appropriate comparative and superlative forms, see 15b.)

Other adjective suffixes include

<u>-OUS</u>: pompous, religious, callous

<u>-ISH</u>: foolish, boyish, kittenish

<u>-IC</u>: artistic, rustic, fantastic

<u>-IVE</u>: reclusive, expensive, repulsive

<u>-IAN</u>: Brazilian, authoritarian, totalitarian

<u>-ABLE</u>: believable, removable, noticeable

<u>-FUL</u>: spiteful, useful, careful

<u>-Y</u>: wealthy, frilly, leafy

☐ EXERCISE 1

Insert adjectives to modify the nouns in the following sentences.

1. Around the house were hills, forests, and meadows.
2. We entered the lobby from a stairway.
3. The waiter served tea from a pot.
4. The job led her to consider a change.

5. A bonfire shed a light on the beach.
6. The announcer spoke with a dialect.
7. His library was filled with maps.
8. The interviewer's attitude grated on my nerves.
9. Moss covered the worms in the can.
10. The boat had a sail made of a shirt.

3b Adverbs

Adverbs modify adjectives, adverbs, verbs, and whole clauses. Consequently, many different groups of words are classified as adverbs.

- Most adverbs are made by adding the suffix *-ly* to adjectives: *boldly, smoothly, actively, usefully, outrageously, gracefully, unbelievably.*

- Other, less common adverb suffixes are *-ward* and *-wise: backward, southward, lengthwise, clockwise.*

- One group of adverbs includes words formed by adding *some, any, every,* or *no* to words such as *how, place, way,* and *where: somehow, someplace, anyway, anywhere, anyhow, everywhere, nowhere.*

- Another group is made up of words that can also be prepositions: *in, out, up, down, over, under, inside, outside,* and so forth. These adverbs usually express place or direction: locked *inside*, went *out*, look *down*.

- A small but very widely used group of adverbs includes *now, then, soon, still, last, here, there, far, always, never, once, twice*— expressions of time, place, distance, and frequency.

- Some adverbs also function as interrogatives: *when, where, why,* and *how.*

- A special group of adverbs, the qualifiers, serve to intensify or restrict an adjective or adverb: *very, quite, really, too, rather, hardly, somewhat.* The qualifiers and the words they modify make up adjective and adverb phrases: *very* upset, *somewhat* humid, *rather* suddenly.

- Conjunctive adverbs function as sentence modifiers. They are used in prose as transition between sentences and paragraphs. This group includes words such as *furthermore, moreover, also, instead, consequently, therefore, thus, nevertheless, however, still.* (For a more complete list, see TRANSITIONAL EXPRESSION in "Glossary of Grammatical, Rhetorical, and Literary Terms.")

☐ EXERCISE 2

Write sentences containing the following types of adverbs.

1. an adverb made by adding -*ly* to an adjective
2. an adverb made with the suffix -*ward*
3. a qualifier modifying an adverb
4. a qualifier modifying an adjective
5. an adverb that can also be a preposition

☐ EXERCISE 3

Identify the modifiers in the following sentences as adjectives or adverbs.

1. The value of the new stock jumped dramatically.
2. The old town had a rather efficient sawmill; nevertheless, the economy was distressed.
3. The company now reluctantly accepts full responsibility.
4. Abruptly, the local newspaper quit printing the controversial cartoon.
5. The white Persian kittens were extremely fat.
6. The painting graphically portrayed the cruel war.
7. Sometimes anti-inflammatory drugs can permanently damage an athlete.
8. The obviously professional thieves carried out a lucrative theft.
9. The pedantic professors discussed their views on genetic engineering.
10. The contributions of Edward R. Murrow are very important to contemporary journalism.

3c Adjective and Adverb Degree

A characteristic of adjectives and adverbs is that they can express *degree*. The *positive* form is the simple form of a modifier; the *comparative* form is used to make a comparison between two items; the *superlative* is used to make a comparison among three or more items.

> POSITIVE: The lake is big.
>
> COMPARATIVE: Sardis is the bigger of the two lakes.
>
> SUPERLATIVE: Superior is the biggest of the Great Lakes.

(1) Adjective forms

Most one-syllable adjectives and many two-syllable adjectives have -*er*/-*est* forms to show degree.

POSITIVE:	short	fast	shallow	funny
COMPARATIVE:	shorter	faster	shallower	funnier
SUPERLATIVE:	shortest	fastest	shallowest	funniest

Some two-syllable adjectives use *more* and *most* to show degree.

POSITIVE:	obscene	careful	spacious
COMPARATIVE:	more obscene	more careful	more spacious
SUPERLATIVE:	most obscene	most careful	most spacious

Adjectives of three or more syllables use *more* or *most* to show degree.

POSITIVE:	innocent	conventional
COMPARATIVE:	more innocent	more conventional
SUPERLATIVE:	most innocent	most conventional

The comparative and superlative forms of some adjectives are irregular.

POSITIVE:	good	bad	many/much	far
COMPARATIVE:	better	worse	more	farther/further
SUPERLATIVE:	best	worst	most	farthest/furthest

Adjectives may also be compared with *less* and *least*.

POSITIVE:	important	intelligent
COMPARATIVE:	less important	less intelligent
SUPERLATIVE:	least important	least intelligent

(2) Adverb forms

Adverbs with the same positive forms as adjectives usually have the *-er/-est* forms.

POSITIVE:	near	slow	early
COMPARATIVE:	nearer	slower	earlier
SUPERLATIVE:	nearest	slowest	earliest

Most adverbs, particularly those derived from adjectives, require *more/most*.

POSITIVE:	fully	suddenly	deeply
COMPARATIVE:	more fully	more suddenly	more deeply
SUPERLATIVE:	most fully	most suddenly	most deeply

The comparative and superlative forms of some adverbs are irregular.

POSITIVE:	well	badly	little	far
COMPARATIVE:	better	worse	less	farther/further
SUPERLATIVE:	best	worst	least	farthest/furthest

Adverbs may also be compared with *less* and *least*.

POSITIVE:	graciously	smoothly
COMPARATIVE:	less graciously	less smoothly
SUPERLATIVE:	least graciously	least smoothly

For a discussion of the appropriate use of comparative and superlative forms, see 15b.

 EXERCISE 4

Show the comparative and superlative degrees of the following adjectives and adverbs. If you are unsure of a form, you should look up the word in a dictionary.

1. weak
2. abruptly
3. rudimentary
4. heavy
5. friendly

6. little
7. thoughtfully
8. nervous
9. conspicuously
10. fast

4

Verbs and Verb Phrases

Verbs are often defined as words that state action, occurrence, or existence. This definition, however, does not adequately convey the importance of verbs in communication; they make up the most versatile and intricate word class in the language. Their characteristic forms, positions, and functions combine to provide an enormous range of meaning and a variety of subtle distinctions. Therefore, the effective use of language requires mastering the verb system.

Basic Forms—the standard verb forms and their uses
Auxiliaries and Verb Phrases—the possible combinations of forms
Person and Number—the relationship of the verb to its subject
Tense—the appropriate use of basic forms and auxiliaries to indicate time
Progressive Forms—the various forms that indicate action in progress
Voice—the forms that indicate whether the subject acts or is acted upon
Mood—the forms that indicate the attitude of the speaker or writer toward what is being said

4a Basic Forms

English verbs have different forms for different functions. Using those forms correctly is essential to acceptable writing since failure to do so can result in nonstandard English. Suppose, for instance, that you use the wrong verb forms in sentences such as *They had ran out of money* or *Every student go to registration with the perfect schedule in mind*. Although readers will understand what you mean, they will seriously question your competence and thus your ideas. If you want your readers' respect and attention, you must use the forms appropriate to standard English.

All verbs and verb phrases include one of the basic forms. Three of these forms––base, past, and past participle—are often called the *three principal parts*. As the charts illustrate, regular verbs make their past forms and past participles by adding −*d* or −*ed* to the base; irregular verbs do not follow this predictable pattern. (For a list of irregular verbs and their principal parts, see IRREGULAR VERB in "Glossary of Grammatical, Rhetorical, and Literary Terms.")

In addition to the three principal parts, two other forms exist for all verbs, both regular and irregular: the −*s* form, made by adding −*s* or −*es* to the base, and the present participle, made by adding −*ing* to the base. Thus, all verbs (except *be*, which is treated separately) can be said to have a total of five possible forms.

Examples of Regular Verbs

Base	−s Form	Past	Past Participle	Present Participle
assume	assumes	assumed	assumed	assuming
drag	drags	dragged	dragged	dragging
dry	dries	dried	dried	drying
enjoy	enjoys	enjoyed	enjoyed	enjoying
fix	fixes	fixed	fixed	fixing
imitate	imitates	imitated	imitated	imitating
laugh	laughs	laughed	laughed	laughing
pat	pats	patted	patted	patting
remind	reminds	reminded	reminded	reminding
wish	wishes	wished	wished	wishing

Examples of Irregular Verbs

Base	−s Form	Past	Past Participle	Present Participle
begin	begins	began	begun	beginning
bet	bets	bet	bet	betting
cut	cuts	cut	cut	cutting
draw	draws	drew	drawn	drawing
eat	eats	ate	eaten	eating
grow	grows	grew	grown	growing
hide	hides	hid	hidden	hiding
leave	leaves	left	left	leaving
think	thinks	thought	thought	thinking
write	writes	wrote	written	writing

vb
4a

☐ EXERCISE 1

Fill in the following chart. If you are unsure of a correct form, you can find it in the dictionary.

Base	−s Form	Past Form	Past Participle	Present Participle
EX. lift	lifts	lifted	lifted	lifting
1. work				
2. forbid				
3. cost				
4. prove				
5. break				
6. spin				
7. ride				
8. shred				
9. slay				
10. burn				
11. lead				
12. beat				
13. burst				
14. creep				
15. study				

Basic forms of *be*

The verb *be* does not follow the patterns of other verbs; it has eight forms, including three for the present and two for the past.

Base	−s Form	Past	Past Participle	Present Participle
be	am is are	was were	been	being

☐ EXERCISE 2

Fill in the blanks with the verb forms called for. Use your dictionary whenever you are not sure of a correct form.

1. The sea gull _____ into the water. (past of *dive*)
2. Fate has _____ him a cruel blow. (past participle of *deal*)
3. The execution could not be _____. (past participle of *delay*)
4. The camper _____ on the cold ground all night. (past of *lie*)
5. The consumer _____ the price for advertisements. (*−s* form of *pay*)
6. The stations are _____ interference. (present participle of *get*)
7. The stock has _____ listed in *Dunn & Bradstreet* for the past year. (past participle of *be*)
8. The employees have been _____ all night. (present participle of *work*)
9. The troops _____ the battlefield. (past of *flee*)
10. He _____ to play halfback. (*−s* form of *try*)
11. The new movie theater will _____ open next week. (base form of *be*)
12. The project has _____ a number of setbacks. (past participle of *have*)
13. The wine is _____ aged in oak barrels. (present participle of *be*)
14. The map will _____ you the shortest route. (base form of *show*)
15. The catalog _____ only American-made products. (past form of *list*)

4b Auxiliaries and Verb Phrases

Frequently, the verb in a sentence is not a single word but a phrase made up of two or more words. In a verb phrase, the last word is called the *main verb* and is always the base form, the present participle, or the past participle. All preceding words in the phrase are called *auxiliaries*.

> Intense heat <u>does</u> not affect the paint.
>
> The orchestra <u>has been</u> rehearsing.
>
> The wallet <u>might have been</u> stolen.

There are four categories of auxiliaries that combine with one another and with main verbs to create a variety of structures and subtle shades of meaning.

(1) *Be* auxiliary

The *be* auxiliary appears in one of eight forms (*am, is, are, was, were, be, being, been*) and is always followed by the present or past participle.

> AUXILIARY + PRESENT PARTICIPLE OF LEAVE: He <u>is leaving</u>.

> AUXILIARY + PAST PARTICIPLE OF FIRE: I <u>was fired</u> today.

(2) *Have* auxiliary

The *have* auxiliary appears in one of four forms (*have, has, had, having*) and is always followed by a past participle.

> AUXILIARY + PAST PARTICIPLE OF FORGET: I <u>have forgotten</u> the combination.

> AUXILIARY + PAST PARTICIPLE OF BREAK: The quarterback <u>had broken</u> his ankle.

(3) Modal auxiliaries

The *modal* auxiliaries are so named because they influence the "mood" of verbs by expressing ideas such as ability, advisability, necessity, and possibility. For example, the verb *complete* takes on slightly different meanings when accompanied by different modal auxiliaries.

> ABILITY: The crew <u>can complete</u> the job in one week.

> OBLIGATION: You <u>should complete</u> the investigation before you begin the report.

> NECESSITY: We <u>must complete</u> the remodeling by June.

> POSSIBILITY: I <u>may complete</u> the course in time for graduation.

The common modal auxiliaries are *will, would, can, could, shall, should, may, might,* and *must*. These auxiliaries are followed by the base form of either the main verb, the *be* auxiliary, or the *have* auxiliary.

> AUXILIARY + BASE FORM OF ARRANGE: The director <u>will arrange</u> a meeting.

> AUXILIARY + BASE FORM OF BE AUXILIARY: She <u>might be living</u> in Paris.

> AUXILIARY + BASE FORM OF HAVE AUXILIARY: I <u>could have taken</u> three courses this summer.

(4) *Do* auxiliary

The *do* auxiliary appears in one of three forms (*do*, *does*, *did*) and is always followed by the base form of the main verb. This auxiliary is unique in that it cannot combine with other auxiliaries.

> AUXILIARY + BASE FORM OF REVEAL: The studies <u>do reveal</u> current trends.
>
> AUXILIARY + BASE FORM OF BLOOM: The tree <u>did</u> not <u>bloom</u> this year.

☐ EXERCISE 3

Rewrite the following sentences, changing the verb in order to add the auxiliaries indicated.

EXAMPLE: We finished the work before dark. (must) →We must finish the work before dark.

1. Their shop sells homemade quilts. (will)
2. The general led a successful coup. (can)
3. The chefs prepare an excellent chocolate mousse. (have)
4. The museum has sold the painting. (may)
5. The newspaper reported the murder. (did)
6. He played the stock market. (should)
7. The hotel made a profit. (has)
8. A conference on pollution takes place in August. (is)
9. We will leave by Friday. (have)
10. A library staff has assembled the collection. (been)

☐ EXERCISE 4

Write sentences containing verb phrases in the combinations of auxiliaries and main verbs listed.

EXAMPLE: modal auxiliary + *have* auxiliary + past participle of *see* →You <u>should have seen</u> the game last night.

1. modal auxiliary + base form of *sell*
2. *have* auxiliary + past participle of *go*
3. *be* auxiliary + present participle of *live*
4. *be* auxiliary + past participle of *call*
5. modal auxiliary + *be* auxiliary + present participle of *sleep*
6. modal auxiliary + *have* auxiliary + past participle of *know*
7. *do* auxiliary + base form of *deny*
8. *have* auxiliary + *be* auxiliary + present participle of *read*

9. modal auxiliary + *have* auxiliary + *be* auxiliary + past participle of *see*

10. modal auxiliary + *have* auxiliary + *be* auxiliary + present participle of *work*

4c Person and Number

In a sentence, the noun or pronoun used as the subject determines both the person and the number of the verb. The term *person* refers to whether the subject of the verb is speaking, spoken to, or spoken about.

- First person includes *I* and *we*.

   Subject is speaking.

   I work in the afternoons.

   Subject is speaking for self and another or others.

   We signed up for the workshop.

- Second person includes *you*, whether one person or more.

   Subject is spoken to.

   You forgot about our lunch date.

- Third person includes all nouns and pronouns except *I*, *we*, and *you*: *he, she, it, they, everyone, anyone, train, mountains, mathematics, Joan, birds, success*, and so forth.

   Subject is spoken about.

   He attended the Naval Academy.

   She majored in genetics.

   It is the best apartment building in town.

   They overcharged me at the bookstore.

   Everyone enjoyed the game.

   The birds are migrating now.

The term *number* refers to singular (one) and plural (more than one). In the third person of the present tense, the number of the subject affects the form of its verb: the third person singular ends in an −*s*; the third person plural does not. (See Chapter 10, "Subject-Verb Agreement.")

- Singular subject and singular verb

    The <u>program</u> <u>has</u> been cancelled.

    <u>Something</u> <u>is</u> wrong with my car.

- Plural subject and plural verb

    The <u>programs</u> <u>have</u> been cancelled.

    Many <u>things</u> <u>are</u> wrong with my car.

☐ EXERCISE 5

Identify the person (first, second, or third person) and the number (singular or plural) of the subject and verb in each of the following sentences.

1. Capital punishment is a hotly debated subject.
2. This week I am taking a course in motor mechanics.
3. The doctor has a long history of drug abuse.
4. Every year you improve your typing speed.
5. For next summer, we have planned a trip to Europe.
6. He has spent hours in the library.
7. Dogs have a strong sense of territory.
8. Everything indicates a wiring problem.
9. Few oppose the new insurance system.
10. You must keep your seats during intermission.

4d Tense

Tense indicates something about the verb's time frame. For example, present tense usually states constant or repetitive actions. Past tense shows that an action was completed in the past. Future tense can express future events. Present perfect can suggest that an action begun in the past is not yet complete. Thus, the tenses express differences in time. Nevertheless, you should remember that tense is not equivalent to time and that the meanings expressed by the tenses can overlap. The same idea, for instance, can often be expressed in either the present or the future tense.

> PRESENT TENSE: **Intense heat causes the surface to crack.**

> FUTURE TENSE: **Intense heat will cause the surface to crack.**

The following chart shows the range and variety of meanings that can be expressed by the three simple tenses (present, past, and future) and the three perfect tenses (present perfect, past perfect, and future perfect).

Simple Tenses

Formation	Uses	Examples
Present		
−*s* form in third person singular; base form everywhere else	expressions of present time with certain verbs, especially those referring to the senses	I hear a car in the driveway.
	statements of fact	The Amazon empties into the Atlantic.
	expressions of repetitive action	My father walks two miles a day.
	references to works of art and literature	In the *Mona Lisa*, the woman smiles enigmatically.
	expressions of future time	The races start tomorrow.
Past		
past form	expressions of past occurrences	
	• single actions	The Rams won the game.
	• repetitive actions	She drove only sports cars.
	• conditions	The experiment was a success.
Future		
will + base form and sometimes *shall* + base form*	expressions of future time	The store will open in May.
	expressions of the results in condition/result relationships	If the barometric pressure drops drastically, the mayonnaise will separate.

*In current usage, *shall* and *will* often suggest different meanings. *Shall we go?* is an invitation—"Would you like to go?" *Will we go?* asks "Are we going?" *Shall* also occurs in set expressions (*we shall overcome*), in laws and resolutions (*the court shall set the fine*), and in heightened prose (*we shall never surrender*).

Perfect Tenses

Formation	Uses	Examples
Present Perfect		
have/has + past participle	expressions of occurrences completed at some unspecified time in the past	He <u>has sung</u> at the Met.
	expressions of action begun in the past and continuing up to the present	We <u>have</u> always <u>gone</u> to Vermont in the summers.
Past Perfect		
had + past participle	expressions of past action (A) occurring before some other past action (B)—"A happened before B happened."	The troops <u>had reached</u> the river when the message arrived.
Future Perfect		
will + *have* + past participle	expressions of action (A) that will occur before or by the time of another future action (B)—"A will have happened before B happens."	We <u>will have left</u> by the time he arrives.

☐ EXERCISE 6

Identify the tense of each verb and verb phrase in the following sentences.

1. They have planned the museum's textile exhibit carefully.
2. He collected all Glenn Gould's recordings of Bach.
3. The freighter travels down the Mississippi to New Orleans every spring.
4. Trisodium phosphate will remove grease and heavy stains.
5. He had hoped for one victory on the PGA tour.
6. The veterinarian now does dental work on dogs.
7. The erosion will have caused an irreversible problem by next year.
8. In Goethe's drama, Faust sold his soul to Mephistopheles.
9. He had not applied for the job before the deadline.
10. The dancers have practiced pirouettes for two hours.

vb
4e

☐ **EXERCISE 7**

Write a sentence using each verb in the tense indicated. Include enough detail in each sentence so that the tense seems appropriate. In other words, avoid writing sentences such as *I see, I ran, I will tell you,* and the like.

EXAMPLE: Past perfect tense of *leave*
    The train <u>had left</u> a half hour before I reached the station.

1. present tense of *clean*
2. past tense of *ride*
3. future tense of *type*
4. present perfect tense of *select*
5. past perfect tense of *hope*
6. future perfect tense of *complete*

4e Progressive Forms

The six tenses have *progressive forms* that indicate actions in progress. A progressive verb is made with a form of the verb *be* followed by a present participle (an *−ing* form of the verb). The following chart explains the progressive forms and their uses.

Progressive Forms

Formation	Uses	Examples
Present		
am/is/are + present participle	expressions of action currently in progress	Crowds <u>are lining</u> the streets.
	expressions of future time	He is sailing Monday.
Past		
was/were + present participle	expressions of action in progress in the past	I <u>was watching</u> television when the power went out.
Future		
will be + present participle	expressions of action that will be in progress in the future	James <u>will be traveling</u> with a rock group for the rest of the year.
	expressions of future action that is not continuous	She <u>will be arriving</u> at noon.

**vb
4e**

Perfect Tenses

Formation	Uses	Examples
Present Perfect *have/has* + *been* + present participle	expressions of continuous past actions still occurring or occurring until recently.	The committee has been considering the issue all week.
Past Perfect *had* + *been* + present participle	expressions of past action (A) in progress until another past action (B) occurred—"A had been happening before B happened."	He had been lifting weights daily before his doctor advised restraint.
Future Perfect *will* + *have* + *been* + present participle	expressions of continuous future action (A) that will be complete at some other future time (B)—"A will have been progressing by the time of B."	He will have been pitching for fifteen years by the time the season ends.

☐ EXERCISE 8

In the following sentences, identify the tense of each progressive verb form.

1. The agency is now considering candidates for director.
2. Red wines from France's Rhone region were selling well.
3. After the new guidelines are established, the commission will be rating movies on a scale of one to four.
4. Before the recession, the company had been growing rapidly.
5. In May the factory will have been using robots for six months.
6. Psychics have been predicting earthquakes in Tennessee.
7. Experts are restoring the building to its original state.
8. The hurricane had been moving toward Texas when it suddenly reversed its course.
9. At sunrise the barges were crossing the river.
10. The city has been issuing bonds for school construction for the past ten years.

EXERCISE 9

Write sentences using each of the following verb forms. Include enough detail so that readers can see why each verb is appropriate to its sentence.

EXAMPLE: had given

I had given the painting away before I found out how valuable it was.

1. catch	5. had hurt	8. were sleeping
2. burns	6. was drawing	9. had been drinking
3. is fighting	7. has been selling	10. will learn
4. rode		

4f Voice

Some verbs can be expressed in either active or passive voice. In *active voice,* the subject acts or in some way controls the action of the verb.

> An auditor checked the figures.
>
> Snow covers the mountains.
>
> We should have renovated our house years ago.
>
> The studio is filming the movie in Alaska.

In *passive voice,* the subject receives the action. The actor or agent, if named, appears in a prepositional phrase beginning with *by* or *with.* No matter how many words the verb phrase contains, the last two words are always a form of *be* and a past participle.

> The figures were checked by an auditor.
>
> The mountains are covered with snow.
>
> Our house should have been renovated years ago.
>
> The movie is being filmed in Alaska.

Active voice sentences have this pattern.

ACTOR	VERB	RECEIVER OF ACTION
My mother	managed	the store.

Passive voice sentences begin with the receiver of the action and have this pattern.

RECEIVER OF ACTION	A FORM OF BE	PAST PARTICIPLE	BY OR WITH	ACTOR
The store	was	managed	by	my mother.

Often in passive voice, the agent is not named, and the *by* or *with* phrase is omitted.

> ACTIVE: Three masked men <u>robbed</u> the bank.
> PASSIVE: The bank <u>was robbed</u> by three masked men.
> PASSIVE: The bank <u>was robbed</u>.

> ACTIVE: The horse <u>threw</u> the rider over the fence.
> PASSIVE: The rider <u>was thrown</u> over the fence by the horse.
> PASSIVE: The rider <u>was thrown</u> over the fence.

> ACTIVE: Trash <u>littered</u> the streets.
> PASSIVE: The streets <u>were littered</u> with trash.
> PASSIVE: The streets <u>were littered</u>.

For a discussion of when to avoid passive voice, see pages 320–321.

☐ EXERCISE 10

Identify the verbs in the following sentences as active or passive.

1. The tour leader was lecturing the group in the Library of Congress.
2. The proposition was explained to the marketing representives.
3. The radio advertisement is not attracting buyers.
4. Airlines offer reduced fares to people over sixty-five.
5. The bank has notified the company by telephone.
6. The essays in the collection are all written by scientists.
7. Clam chowder is always served on Friday.
8. The courier must deliver the package by five o'clock.

☐ EXERCISE 11

Change the following passive voice sentences to active.

EXAMPLE: The dents in the car were made by hail stones. → Hail stones made the dents in the car.

1. Nutritional problems are sometimes overlooked by doctors.
2. Few memberships have been accepted by the club.
3. In *The Pride of the Yankees,* Lou Gehrig was played by Gary Cooper.
4. Gas production has been hampered by control laws.
5. The hillsides were blanketed with wild flowers.

☐ EXERCISE 12

Change the following active voice sentences to passive and delete the resulting *by* phrase.

EXAMPLE: The citizens elect a President every four years. → A President is elected every four years.

1. Witnesses saw the suspect driving a red convertible.
2. The school named her Outstanding Teacher of the Year.
3. You can purchase tickets two weeks in advance.
4. The company publishes the book only in paperback.
5. People expect doctors to be infallible.

4g Mood

The mood of a verb is determined by whether the idea it expresses is a fact (indicative mood), a command (imperative mood), or a matter of desire or possibility (subjunctive). In English, the three moods are expressed through special verb forms.

(1) Indicative mood

The indicative mood is used to make statements and ask questions. This mood has six tenses, shown in the following chart. (For a full treatment of tense in the indicative mood, see the charts in 4d.)

Singular	*Plural*
Present	
It grows.	They grow.
Past	
It grew.	They grew.
Future	
It will grow.	They will grow.
Present Perfect	
It has grown.	They have grown.
Past Perfect	
It had grown.	They had grown.
Future Perfect	
It will have grown.	They will have grown.

(2) Imperative mood

The *imperative mood* is used to give commands. The omitted but understood subject of all imperative verbs is the singular or plural *you.* In addition, for all verbs except *be,* the imperative is the form used with *you* in the present tense.

POSITIVE	NEGATIVE
Close the door.	Do not/Don't close the door.
Answer the memo.	Do not/Don't answer the memo.
Order the sirloin.	Do not/Don't order the sirloin.

The imperative of the verb *be* is always *be* for positive commands and *do not/don't be* for negative commands.

POSITIVE	NEGATIVE
Be serious.	Do not/Don't be serious.
Be an observer.	Do not/Don't be an observer.
Be adventurous with money.	Do not/Don't be adventurous with money.

(3) Subjunctive mood

In current English, the *subjunctive mood* has limited use, appearing only in a few idioms (set expressions) of blessing or farewell; in dependent clauses expressing hypothetical situations or conditions contrary to fact; and in dependent clauses of demand, recommendation, wish, or need. The forms of subjunctive verbs (other than *be*) are the same as the forms of the indicative except in one respect: the −s is not added in the third-person singular present tense.

SUBJUNCTIVE: **Heaven forbid.**

INDICATIVE: **Heaven forbids.**

With *be,* the present tense subjunctive is always *be;* the past tense subjunctive is always *were.*

SUBJUNCTIVE: **We demand that the accused be tried in a court of law.**

INDICATIVE: **The accused is tried in a court of law.**

SUBJUNCTIVE: **Even if the movie were free, I would not see it.**

INDICATIVE: **The movie was free, but I did not see it.**

Idiomatic Expressions

The subjunctive is present in a few idioms that historically have been used to express farewells and blessings.

SUBJUNCTIVE: God <u>bless</u> you.

INDICATIVE: God <u>blesses</u> you.

SUBJUNCTIVE: Peace <u>be</u> with you.

INDICATIVE: Peace <u>is</u> with you.

SUBJUNCTIVE: Long <u>live</u> the queen.

INDICATIVE: The queen <u>lives</u> long.

Dependent Clauses Expressing Hypothetical Situations or Conditions Contrary to Fact

The subjunctive is used in clauses introduced by conjunctions such as *if, as if,* and *as though* to express hypothetical situations or conditions contrary to fact.

SUBJUNCTIVE: <u>If</u> a left turn signal <u>were installed</u>, traffic flow would improve.

INDICATIVE: <u>When</u> a left turn signal <u>was installed</u>, traffic flow improved.

SUBJUNCTIVE: She felt <u>as though</u> she <u>were dreaming</u>.

INDICATIVE: She knew she <u>was dreaming</u>.

SUBJUNCTIVE: <u>If</u> I <u>were</u> you, I would not smoke.

INDICATIVE: I <u>am</u> not you, but I don't think you should smoke.

Dependent Clauses of Demand, Recommendation, Wish, or Need

The subjunctive occurs in *that* clauses naming demands, recommendations, wishes, and needs.

SUBJUNCTIVE: We demand <u>that</u> the terms of the contract <u>be met</u>.

INDICATIVE: The demands of the contract <u>are met</u>.

SUBJUNCTIVE: He moved <u>that</u> the meeting <u>be adjourned</u>.

INDICATIVE: The meeting <u>is adjourned</u>.

SUBJUNCTIVE: The committee recommended <u>that</u> he <u>submit</u> a proposal.

INDICATIVE: He <u>submits</u> a proposal.

SUBJUNCTIVE: I wish I <u>were</u> good at math. [*That* is understood after *wish*.]

INDICATIVE: I <u>am</u> good at math.

SUBJUNCTIVE: It is urgent <u>that</u> the police department <u>enforce</u> zoning regulations.

INDICATIVE: The police department <u>enforces</u> zoning regulations.

☐ EXERCISE 13

Determine whether the mood of each underlined verb is indicative, imperative, or subjunctive.

1. Stalin <u>planned</u> to liquidate some of his political associates.
2. The constitution requires that a majority <u>be</u> present to vote.
3. To keep your terrarium from souring, <u>add</u> broken charcoal.
4. The dreadful extravaganza <u>will cost</u> about ten million.
5. Two free throws <u>were made</u> in the final minute.
6. <u>Describe</u> what you see in the ink blots.
7. Most Asian countries insist that a visitor <u>receive</u> cholera injections before entry.
8. If I <u>were</u> in Italy during August, I would avoid Venice.
9. The sprinklers <u>have been running</u> all weekend.
10. It is imperative that she <u>have</u> privacy.

5

Verbals and Verbal Phrases

A verbal is a present participle (*winning*), a past participle (*won*), or an infinitive (*to win*) functioning in a sentence as something other than a verb. A verbal may function as

A NOUN: Winning was all that mattered to him. [subject of sentence]

AN ADJECTIVE: Teams are rated by the number of games won. [adjective modifying *games*]

AN ADVERB: We were surprised to win. [adverb modifying *surprised*]

A verbal phrase is a verbal plus any words that complete its meaning.

Winning the game was all that mattered to him. [verbal + object]

Teams are rated by the number of games won within the conference. [verbal + modifier]

We were surprised to win so easily. [verbal + modifier]

5a Infinitives and Infinitive Phrases

Infinitives are the *to* forms of verbs (*to go, to think, to seem*). These verbals appear alone or in phrases and may function as adverbs, adjectives, and nouns.

As Adverbs

The audience rose to cheer the performance. [modifying *rose*]

This exercise machine is difficult to use. [modifying *difficult*]

The river flows too slowly to do much damage. [modifying *slowly*]

To return to my question, is the government interfering in another country's affairs? [modifying the rest of the sentence]

As Adjectives

Many writers have a tendency to use too many commas. [modifying *tendency*]

A poison to kill fire ants is now available. [modifying *poison*]

As Nouns

To invest successfully in oil requires the instincts of a good gambler. [subject of *requires*]

Darwin believed natural selection to be important in the origin of plants and animals. [object of *believed*]

The delegates argued about how to cast the votes. [object of *about*]

The "sign" of the infinitive, *to,* is omitted after certain verbs like *let, make, hear, see,* and *feel.*

Let the record show that only four people were present.

We saw her steal the necklace.

After other verbs, like *help* and *have,* the *to* sign is optional.

The company helps you develop a safe but profitable portfolio. (or "helps you to develop")

Have them call for reservations. (or "have them to call")

☐ EXERCISE 1

Combine the following pairs of sentences by changing the second sentence in each pair to an infinitive phrase.

EXAMPLE: Listen to your voice on a tape recording. You can find out how you sound to other people. → To find out how you sound to other people, listen to your voice on a tape recording.

1. The plant must install equipment. The equipment must limit the pollutants emitted.
2. The jockey uses a crop. The crop gives a horse special signals.
3. Galileo designed the sector. The sector aids draftsmen.

4. At night the hippopotamus leaves the water. At night the hippopotamus feeds on land.

5. Packwood and Brinson Inc. has been hired. Packwood and Brinson Inc. will design the museum.

6. The United States uses artificial satellites. The satellites obtain weather information.

7. The tourists visited Argentina. The tourists will see Buenos Aires.

8. Hannibal's military genius helped him. Hannibal defeated armies much larger than his.

9. The Argonauts sailed with Jason. The Argonauts searched for the Golden Fleece.

10. The scientists use a particle accelerator. The scientists study atomic particles such as neutrinos.

5b Gerunds and Gerund Phrases

Gerunds are present participles (*walking, believing, feeling*) functioning as nouns. Like other verbals, gerunds may appear alone or in phrases.

> Selling beer without a license is illegal. [subject of *is*]
>
> The patient had lost his hearing because of a childhood illness. [object of *had lost*]
>
> Mendel devoted his time to studying genetics. [object of *to*]

☐ EXERCISE 2

Identify the gerunds and gerund phrases in the following sentences.

1. By marrying a Persian princess, Alexander the Great encouraged intermarriage.

2. Looking too far into the future can be frightening.

3. A typewriter's bell prevents typing past the right margin.

4. *All the King's Men* describes the making of a powerful southern politician.

5. Amoebas reproduce by fission, or splitting apart.

6. Many experts consider jogging the best aerobic exercise.

7. A current fad among amateur photographers is developing film.

8. Fred Astaire gave dancing an athletic grace.

9. Poundmaker, a Cree Indian chief, led an uprising against the Canadian government.

10. Sunlight, temperature, precipitation, soil condition, plants, and animals—all these elements go into forming a "natural community."

5c Participles and Participial Phrases

The two basic forms of *participles* are

- The present participle (the *-ing* form of a verb)—*walking, thinking, singing*
- The past participle (the form that can follow *have* in a verb phrase)—*walked, thought, sung*.

Participles, alone or in phrases, can act as adjectives to modify nouns or pronouns that perform or receive the verbal's action.

> Containing more than 40,000 entries, the encyclopedia provides an enormous range of information. [present participle modifying *ency-clopedia;* "encyclopedia contains"]

> The celebration, bordering on hysteria, was monitored by the police. [present participle modifying *celebration;* "celebration borders"]

> Surrounded by adoring fans, he felt beseiged. [past participle modifying *he;* "he was surrounded"]

> The museum, established in 1980, is funded by a foundation. [past participle modifying *museum;* "museum was established"]

☐ EXERCISE 3

Combine each pair of sentences by changing the second to a participial phrase. Position the participle carefully so that it clearly refers to the word it modifies.

EXAMPLE: Vivaldi's works included instrumental compositions and operas. Vivaldi's works were admired by Bach. → Admired by Bach, Vivaldi's works included instrumental compositions and operas.

1. The book describes current medical discoveries. The discoveries are revolutionizing cancer treatment.
2. The people filled the street in front of the Capitol. The people were protesting the law.
3. The tour goes to forty destinations. The destinations include ten stops in China.
4. A virus injects its genetic material into a cell. The virus compels the cell to make more viruses.
5. We purchased a charcoal grill. The charcoal grill was designed for a commercial restaurant.
6. The first European explorers found that many Indian tribes farmed the land. European explorers arrived in South America.

7. Authorities continued searching for three members of a family. The family was missing after a twister ripped apart their house.
8. At one time Thebes was the most powerful city-state in all Greece. Thebes supposedly was founded by Cadmus.
9. Tutankhamen's tomb contained a coffin of solid gold. The coffin is now located in the Cairo Museum.
10. In *Tom Sawyer,* Mark Twain wrote about Hannibal, Missouri. Twain called Hannibal, Missouri, St. Petersburg.

5d Absolute Verbal Phrases

An *absolute construction* is one with no direct connection to any particular element in its sentence. Instead, the absolute construction modifies the entire sentence in which it appears. Usually, these constructions are familiar expressions containing participles and infinitives: *generally speaking, speaking of. . . , to tell the truth, to sum up.*

> ABSOLUTE PHRASE: Speaking of friends, Susan let me use her credit card when I was broke.

> ABSOLUTE PHRASE: To tell the truth, my vacation was more work than my job.

Absolute verbal phrases may begin with a noun or pronoun that acts as the subject of a participle that follows—a structure sometimes called a *nominative absolute.*

> ABSOLUTE PHRASE: His fortune squandered on women and horses, he went to work as a valet.

> ABSOLUTE PHRASE: The boy stared into space, his face white with terror. [The participle *being* is understood: *his face being white with terror.*]

Less common is the absolute infinitive with a subject.

> ABSOLUTE PHRASE: The drawing will be held July 1, the winner to be announced at the July Fourth celebration.

The absolute verbal phrase containing a subject is somewhat formal and usually explains causes or adds details to sentences.

- Explaining causes:

> The seas being rough, we put into harbor.

> Three fires having been reported in the area, the police suspected arson.

<u>Examinations completed</u>, students fled campus like people escaping the plague.

- Adding details:

She stood in the middle of the room, <u>her fists clenched and her eyes flashing defiance</u>.

The gunfighter of Hollywood westerns was casually sinister—<u>guns slung low on his hips, hat cocked rakishly over one eye, steps measured and slow</u>.

The bus, <u>its motor coughing and sputtering</u>, lurched along for a mile or so and then died.

 EXERCISE 4

Which of the following sentences contain absolute phrases?

1. Attaching itself to a shark, the remora gets both transportation and protection.
2. The weather being cool and dry, they suggested an old-fashioned hayride.
3. To make a long story short, the only fish we caught swam into the boat when it capsized.
4. Strictly speaking, the tomato is not a vegetable.
5. Suddenly we saw the dog, his hackles raised and his teeth bared for attack.
6. To escape the noise of the dormitory, I began studying in the library.
7. Soaring through the clouds, the little plane looked much like a graceful seagull.
8. We searched for the location of the town, the map spread out before us.
9. I awoke slowly, my head pounding, my eyes burning with fever.
10. To conclude, the program cannot survive without federal funds.

EXERCISE 5

Identify each verbal phrase in the following sentences. Then classify the phrase as an infinitive, gerund, participial, or absolute phrase.

1. The athlete has our gratitude for representing our country so well in the Olympics.
2. A peninsula jutting out from the northeast corner of France, Brittany was once an independent state.
3. Use the expression "Very truly yours" to close a particularly formal letter.

4. My head nodding and eyelids drooping, I struggled in vain to pay attention to the speaker.

5. To praise the computer as the answer to all financial problems is ridiculous.

6. Sometimes crying about a problem is the first step toward facing it.

7. The eagle rose higher and higher, soaring in ascending circles.

8. The publication contains all the maps relating to the Lewis and Clark expedition.

9. When cheating on taxes becomes excessive, more money must be put into enforcement.

10. The three-barred cross, also known as the Russian cross, is a symbol of the Russian Orthodox Church.

11. This combination of chemicals has the potential to explode.

12. It is important for members of our diplomatic corps to know foreign languages.

13. Cargo fits in containers shaped to conform to the airplane's interior.

14. Some reporters, going beyond the boundary of reasonable questions, threaten an individual's privacy.

15. The excavation, completed last year, uncovered a Roman street.

6

Function Words

Nouns, verbs, adjectives, and adverbs make up the greater part of our vocabulary and convey most of the semantic meaning of sentences. However, meaning also depends on *function words*: prepositions, conjunctions, determiners, and expletives. These words create structure. If the function words are removed from a sentence, all that is left is a list of unrelated vocabulary items.

> WITH FUNCTION WORDS: Under the canopy sat a man and a woman waiting for the bus.
>
> WITHOUT FUNCTION WORDS: canopy sat man woman waiting bus

You might think of the vocabulary items as bricks and of the function words as the mortar that holds them together: both are necessary to build meaning.

6a Prepositions and Prepositional Phrases

A *prepositional phrase* contains a preposition and its object, usually a noun, noun phrase, or pronoun. The following list includes some of the most common prepositions. Although most are one word, some (called *phrasal prepositions*) are two and even three words.

above	against	at
across	around	away from
after	as	because of

before	in front of	over
beneath	in spite of	past
between	into	since
by	like	through
by means of	near	toward
down	of	under
during	off	until
except	on	up
except for	onto	with
for	out	within
from	outside of	without
in		

Prepositional phrases usually function like adjectives to modify nouns, noun phrases, and pronouns or like adverbs to modify verbs, verbals, and adjectives.

- Modifying Nouns and Pronouns

    snake in the grass

    my grandmother on my father's side

    one of her courses

    boats in the harbor and on the lake

- Modifying Verbs and Verbals

    ran through the alley

    had been sleeping behind the hedge

    staying in San Antonio

    hitting the ball between the light poles and over the fence

- Modifying Adjectives

    optimistic about the future

    conscious of our discomfort

    lost since Monday

    open after noon and before midnight

In addition to their use as modifiers, prepositional phrases can also function like nouns. Occasionally, a prepositional phrase appears as the subject at the beginning of a sentence. But more often, the phrase appears after the verb.

- Functioning as Subjects and Objects

  <u>After Thursday</u> will be too late.

  The creature emerged from <u>behind the snowbank.</u>

☐ EXERCISE 1

Identify the prepositional phrases in the following sentences.

1. Because of the music, this advertisement about cigarettes appeals to young people.
2. In the nineteenth century, American literature broke away from British tradition.
3. We were happy about their arrival and ecstatic over their departure.
4. For thousands of years, monks have used chant as a part of their sacred liturgy.
5. In the mornings before ten will be convenient.

6b Conjunctions

Conjunctions are grammatical connectors that link sentence elements. Without conjunctions, we could not express relationships between ideas. For instance, we could not attribute causes or effects. We would have difficulty expressing consequences or signaling time sequences. We could not indicate alternatives, parallels, or contrasts. As the following passage shows, prose without conjunctions is grammatical but disjointed.

WITHOUT CONJUNCTIONS

We rarely think in terms of meters/liters. We are accustomed to inches/pounds. There has been an effort to change to the metric system. The changeover has met strong opposition. We are familiar with a foot. We can estimate length fairly accurately in feet. We can easily stride off a distance to measure it in yards.

The addition of conjunctions makes clear the relationships of the ideas.

WITH CONJUNCTIONS

We rarely think in terms of meters <u>and</u> liters <u>because</u> we are accustomed to inches <u>and</u> pounds. <u>Although</u> there has been an effort to change to the metric system, the changeover has met strong opposition. We are <u>so</u> familiar with a foot <u>that</u> we can estimate length in feet fairly accurately, <u>and</u> we can easily stride off a distance to measure it in yards.

(1) Coordinating conjunctions

Coordinating conjunctions are so named because they connect words, phrases, and clauses that are grammatically coordinate, or equal in structure. Some coordinators can join any structures that are grammatically equal—two or more nouns, verbs, adjectives, prepositional phrases, adverb clauses, independent clauses, and so forth.

and	but
or	nor
yet	

CONNECTING NOUNS: I'll order fish <u>or</u> chicken.

CONNECTING VERBS: We did not eat <u>nor</u> sleep for five days.

CONNECTING ADJECTIVES: The singer was loud <u>but</u> off-key.

CONNECTING PREPOSITIONAL PHRASES: The road runs through the valley <u>and</u> up the mountain.

CONNECTING CLAUSES: He was a stern man, <u>yet</u> he was patient.

Two of the coordinating conjunctions connect only independent clauses.

for	so

The conductor stopped abruptly, <u>for</u> the cellist had begun to snore.

The English language does not have many inflections, <u>so</u> it does not have a flexible word order.

☐ EXERCISE 2

Use coordinating conjunctions to combine the pairs of sentences. Join either words, phrases, or clauses.

1. You can work out on the Nautilus machines. On the other hand, you can work out on the free weights.

2. Politicians came to the meeting in Chicago. Financiers came to the meeting in Chicago.
3. There are nearly fifty legal grounds for divorce. The majority of American suits are filed for cruelty.
4. Alec Guinness appeared in *The Bridge on the River Kwai*. He appeared in *Lawrence of Arabia*.
5. The sky is crystal clear. The moon is almost full.

(2) Correlative conjunctions

A special type of coordinating conjunction consists of a pair of words or phrases that work together to connect elements within a sentence or to produce a compound sentence. As with all coordinating conjunctions, those elements connected by *correlatives* must be of equal grammatical structure—two nouns, two verbs, two adjectives, two independent clauses, and so forth. Two sets of correlatives connect elements within clauses.

both . . . and

not . . . but

CONNECTING ADJECTIVES: An adequate hospital should provide <u>both</u> in-patient <u>and</u> out-patient care.

CONNECTING NOUNS: The problem is <u>not</u> the hardware <u>but</u> the software.

Three sets of correlatives can connect two clauses as well as elements within independent clauses.

not only . . . but also

either . . . or

neither . . . nor

CONNECTING ADJECTIVES: The stove is <u>not only</u> compact <u>but also</u> fuel efficient.

CONNECTING PREPOSITIONAL PHRASES: Paper is made <u>either</u> by a mechanical process <u>or</u> by a chemical process.

CONNECTING NOUNS: <u>Neither</u> Melville <u>nor</u> Hawthorne is as popular with students as Poe is.

CONNECTING CLAUSES: <u>Not only</u> did the Egyptians distinguish between planets and stars, <u>but also</u> they devised a 365-day calendar.

(3) Subordinating conjunctions

Subordinating conjunctions introduce dependent clauses and express relationships such as cause, contrast, condition, manner, place, and time. Some commonly used subordinators are listed here.

after	except that	than
although	if	unless
as	in case	until
as if	in that	when
as though	now that	whenever
because	once	where
before	since	while
even though	so that	

The following examples suggest the versatility of subordinate clauses, but for a more complete discussion, see 7c.1, "Adverb Clauses."

MODIFYING A VERB: You should act as though you are accustomed to such elegance.

MODIFYING AN ADJECTIVE: I am sure that he has forgotten the appointment.

MODIFYING A CLAUSE: When the movie began, the theater was empty.

☐ EXERCISE 3

Combine the pairs of sentences by using subordinating conjunctions.

EXAMPLE: I did not pay my bill for two months. So the phone company disconnected my telephone.→ The phone company disconnected my telephone because I did not pay my bill for two months.

1. The plane descended. We saw the Washington Monument.
2. Prehistoric humans did no cultivating. They were forced into nomadic life.
3. Father grew older. He became less and less able to farm without help.
4. I was only twelve. But I could fly a P51 Mustang.
5. Their favorite restaurant was an outdoor cafe. They had both worked there ten years before.

(4) Comparative conjunctions

A special type of subordinating conjunction has two parts—for example, *so . . . that* and *as . . . as*. These conjunctions usually introduce clauses of measurement or degree; that is, they introduce ideas that express how much or to what extent. The following are the most common *comparatives*.

- as . . . as

    She is not <u>as</u> clever <u>as</u> I thought she was.

- so . . . that

    Paul was <u>so</u> scared <u>that</u> he was shaking.

- such . . . that

    He is <u>such</u> a nice man <u>that</u> people take advantage of him.

- A comparative form of an adjective or adverb . . . *than*

    The river is clean<u>er</u> <u>than</u> it was last year.
    This pump works <u>more</u> efficiently <u>than</u> the old one did.

- A superlative form of an adjective . . . *that*

    His Thunderbird was the fanci<u>est</u> car <u>that</u> I had ever seen.
    The game is the most <u>complicated</u> that the company has designed.

☐ EXERCISE 4

Use a comparative conjunction and a clause to specify degree in each of the following sentences.

EXAMPLE

ORIGINAL: The area is subject to flooding. (How subject is it to flooding?)

REVISED: The area is so subject to flooding that no one should build a house there.

1. The drink was bitter. (How bitter was it?)
2. They are close friends. (How close are they?)
3. The picnic was enjoyable. The dance was enjoyable. (Which one was more enjoyable?)
4. The skater performed poorly. (How poorly did she perform?)
5. This race track is fast. (How fast is it?)

**func
6c**

☐ **EXERCISE 5**

Use conjunctions to combine the sets of sentences. You can choose coordinating, correlative, subordinating, or comparative conjunctions—whichever is appropriate.

EXAMPLE

ORIGINAL: The computer program is efficient. It makes editing simpler. It eliminates retyping.

COMBINED: The computer program is efficient because it makes editing simpler and eliminates retyping.

1. The presidential seal shows the American eagle clutching arrows in one talon. The eagle is clutching an olive branch in the other.
2. Nuclear plants produce electricity without air pollution. Nuclear fission has several disadvantages.
3. Bob Marley died in 1981. He is considered the creator of the best Jamaican Reggae music.
4. The moon's revolution is irregular. The irregular revolution is due to the fact that its orbit is elliptical.
5. The camera is versatile. The camera comes with a telephoto lens. It also comes with a wide-angle lens.
6. The little fishing village becomes populated in the summer. It is populated like a bustling city.
7. *Tropic of Cancer* was published. Then Henry Miller became a famous figure. He also became a controversial figure.
8. This organism flourishes in fresh water. It also flourishes in brackish water.
9. The street was hot. It burned my feet through my shoes.
10. Plants do not live alone. Animals do not live alone.

6c Determiners

Determiners signal that a noun will follow, if not immediately, then shortly. Some words are always determiners.

- The articles—*a, an, the*

    A new theory about dinosaurs has been proposed.
    Where did you hide the chocolate chip cookies?

- Some possessive pronouns—*my, her, its, our, your, their, whose*

  Her German accent sounds authentic.

  Whose music did they play?

- An indefinite pronoun—*every*

  Every item was marked down 50 percent.

In addition, some nouns and pronouns frequently function as determiners.

- Possessives: *his, everyone's, Kathy's, today's,* and so on

  DETERMINER: Leading the discussion is his responsibility.

  PRONOUN: The responsibility is his.

- Demonstrative pronouns: *this, that, these, those*

  DETERMINER: You must pack these provisions for the trip.

  PRONOUN: The necessary provisions are these: food, water, and first-aid equipment.

- Indefinite pronouns: *each, every, either, neither, all, some, many, much, any, few, more, less,* and so on

  DETERMINER: Few inventors achieve success.

  PRONOUN: Of the thousands of inventors, few achieve success.

- Interrogative pronouns: *which, what*

  DETERMINER: We could not determine which virus was present.

  PRONOUN: A virus was present, but we could not determine which.

- Cardinal numbers—*one, two, three,* and so on

  DETERMINER: The terrorists showed pictures of four hostages.

  NOUN: There were six hostages, but the terrorists showed pictures of only four.

☐ EXERCISE 6

Identify the determiners in the following sentences.

1. Our instructor sent his first story to *Harper's*.
2. December's weather has ruined the fruit crops.
3. Every spring, a heavy rain causes floods in that section of town.
4. Which kinds of cars will people buy this year?
5. The three projects helped eliminate the downtown traffic snarl.
6. Only an inadequate bank account kept him from a life of luxury.

6d Expletives

The two *expletives, it* and *there,* are "filler words" that introduce clauses and allow the real subjects to be delayed until after the verbs or verb auxiliaries. *There* usually introduces a clause with a noun or noun phrase as the subject.

> SUBJECT FIRST: **A phone is ringing.**
>
> SUBJECT DELAYED: **There is a phone ringing.**
>
> SUBJECT FIRST: **A notice from the bank is on your desk.**
>
> SUBJECT DELAYED: **There is a notice from the bank on your desk.**

When the real subject of a clause is an infinitive or a *that* clause, beginning with the expletive *it* sounds more natural than beginning with the subject.

> SUBJECT FIRST: **To call is important.**
>
> SUBJECT DELAYED: **It is important to call.**
>
> SUBJECT FIRST: **That the dam will break is unlikely.**
>
> SUBJECT DELAYED: **It is unlikely that the dam will break.**

The expletive *it* has an additional function—to introduce constructions that have no real subject.

> **It is raining.**
>
> **It is noisy in here.**

CAUTION: The words *it* and *there* are not always expletives. *There* can function as an adverb; *it* is frequently a pronoun. Compare the following pairs of sentences:

> EXPLETIVE: **There are three horses in the paddock.**
>
> ADVERB: **Three horses are there in the paddock.**
>
> EXPLETIVE: **It is dangerous to jog after eating.**
>
> PRONOUN: **Jogging after meals is dangerous. It should be avoided.**

☐ EXERCISE 7

In the following passage, indicate whether each *there* is used as an expletive or an adverb. Also, indicate whether each *it* is used as an expletive or a pronoun.

There are two effective aids to kicking the cigarette habit. First, it helps to motivate yourself by thinking of all the bad effects of smoking—such as wrinkles, coughs, expense, and diseases. You can even tape the list to your bathroom mirror. There you will see it every morning when shaving or putting on makeup. Second, it is advisable to avoid environments like bars and coffee houses, environments that tempt people to smoke.

7

Clauses and Sentences

A *clause* is a grammatical construction with both a subject and a predicate. The subject consists of at least one noun (or noun substitute) and all its modifiers. The noun or noun substitute is called the *simple subject;* the simple subject with all its modifiers is called the *complete subject.* The *predicate* consists of at least one verb and all its modifiers and completing words. As the following examples show, the predicate makes an assertion about its subject.

SUBJECT	PREDICATE
Travis	**defended the Alamo.**
Everyone in the elevator	**panicked.**
The convention	**will be in Des Moines next year.**

When the subject and predicate express a complete idea, the clause is called a *sentence.* Although the number of clauses and sentences possible in the language is infinite, their structures fall into a limited number of patterns. Learning to recognize these patterns will give you more control over structuring sentences.

7a Clause Patterns

In all clause patterns, the subject is a noun (or noun substitute) plus any modifiers. What distinguishes the patterns from one another is not the structure of the subject but rather the structure of the predicate. The predicate structure is determined by the type of verb it contains—intransitive, transitive, or linking.

Intransitive Verb Pattern

Technically, an *intransitive* verb is complete by itself and is the only element needed in the predicate structure.

SUBJECT	+	INTRANSITIVE VERB
The doctor		smiled.
The prisoner		has escaped.
They		were leaving.

Frequently, however, the pattern is fleshed out by an adverbial modifier following the verb.

> The doctor smiled <u>sheepishly</u>.
>
> The prisoner has escaped <u>through a tunnel</u>.
>
> They were leaving <u>before the party was over</u>.

Transitive Verb Patterns

All *transitive verbs* require direct objects. In addition, some transitive verbs allow indirect objects, and some allow object complements. As a result, there are three transitive verb patterns.

(1) SUBJECT	+	TRANSITIVE VERB	+	DIRECT OBJECT
The FBI		investigated		him.
A local press		has published		her memoirs.
Energy shortages		would change		our lifestyles.

In this pattern, the subject performs the verb's action, and the direct object receives or is affected by the verb's action. One characteristic of this pattern is that it may be converted to the passive voice (see 4f). In this conversion, the direct object moves to the subject position, where it still receives the verb's action.

> ORIGINAL: **The mayor favors lower taxes.**
>
> PASSIVE: **Lower taxes are favored by the mayor.**

> ORIGINAL: **The Coast Guard searched the ship.**
>
> PASSIVE: **The ship was searched by the Coast Guard.**

(2)

SUBJECT	+	TRANSITIVE VERB	+	INDIRECT OBJECT	+	DIRECT OBJECT
The company		has awarded		the investors		a dividend.
Our courts		cannot deny		a felon		due process.
My mother		knitted		me		a wool sweater.

An indirect object appears between the verb and the direct object. You can identify a word or phrase as an indirect object by this simple test: the word or phrase can be preceded by the prepositions *to, for,* or occasionally *of* and moved to follow the direct object.

ORIGINAL: The controller gave the pilot instructions.

TEST: The controller gave instructions to the pilot.

ORIGINAL: The invention made him a fortune.

TEST: The invention made a fortune for him.

ORIGINAL: The professor asked us only one question.

TEST: The professor asked only one question of us.

Some transitive verbs that commonly allow indirect objects are *give, make, tell, show, bring, send, sell,* and *offer.*

(3)

SUBJECT	+	TRANSITIVE VERB	+	DIRECT OBJECT	+	OBJECT COMPLEMENT
The city council		declared		the water		unsafe.
The fog		will make		travel		dangerous.
We		consider		the tomato		a vegetable.
The critics		have pronounced		the play		a flop.

An object complement can be either an adjective *(unsafe, dangerous)* or a noun *(a vegetable, a flop).* When the complement is an adjective, it modifies the direct object: *unsafe water, dangerous travel.* When the complement is a noun, it renames the direct object: *the tomato = a vegetable, the play = a flop.*

Transitive verbs that commonly allow an object complement are *make, consider, call, elect, appoint, declare, name,* and *choose.* In this pattern, the object complement completes the meaning of the verb. Without the complement, the verb often means something different.

WITH COMPLEMENT: The reporter called Jack a crook.

WITHOUT COMPLEMENT: The reporter called Jack.

WITH COMPLEMENT: **I kept the letter secret.**

WITHOUT COMPLEMENT: **I kept the letter.**

Linking Verb Patterns

A *linking verb* requires a subject complement to complete its meaning. The complement modifies or renames the subject of the clause. With most linking verbs, the subject complement is an adjective (predicate adjective) or a noun (predicate nominative). With the verb *be,* however, the complement may be an adjective, a noun, a possessive, or an adverb of time or place. Thus, most linking verbs have two possible patterns, but *be* has four.

(1) SUBJECT	+ LINKING VERB	+ ADJECTIVE SUBJECT COMPLEMENT
Most of the guests	were	obnoxious.
The surface	feels	rough.
He	grew	restless.

In this pattern, the subject complement is a predicate adjective that completes the meaning of the verb and modifies the subject. You can test the pattern by making a noun phrase with the subject and the subject complement.

ORIGINAL: **The horse was lame.**

TEST: **the lame horse**

ORIGINAL: **The medicine tastes bitter.**

TEST: **the bitter medicine**

Although this pattern is a very common one, it occurs with only a limited number of verbs: *be,* verbs with a meaning similar to *be (seem, appear, become, grow, remain),* and verbs that refer to the senses *(taste, look, smell, sound, feel).*

(2) SUBJECT	+ LINKING VERB	+ NOUN SUBJECT COMPLEMENT
This typewriter	is	an Olympia.
Stacy	became	a jockey.
They	have remained	friends.

In this pattern, the subject complement is a noun, a predicate nominative, that completes the meaning of the verb and names or refers to the subject. You can test the pattern by this method: subject = complement.

ORIGINAL: This move is a serious mistake.

TEST: this move = a serious mistake

ORIGINAL: Your candidate appears the loser.

TEST: your candidate = the loser

Only a very few verbs occur in this pattern; the most common are *be, become, remain, seem,* and *appear.*

(3) SUBJECT	+ BE	+ POSSESSIVE SUBJECT COMPLEMENT
That motorcycle	is	Karen's.
The fault	was	mine.
The loss	would be	everyone's.

In this pattern the subject complement is either a possessive noun or pronoun. You can test the pattern by making a noun phrase from the possessive and the subject. When the subject complement is a personal pronoun, you may have to change its form to test the construction.

ORIGINAL: The plans are theirs.

TEST: their plans

ORIGINAL: The Jaguar was Kathleen's.

TEST: Kathleen's Jaguar

(4) SUBJECT	+ BE	+ ADVERB SUBJECT COMPLEMENT
A police officer	is	outside.
The meeting	will be	tomorrow.
The game	was	at 7:30.

The adverb subject complement can be either a simple adverb or a prepositional phrase acting as an adverb. This complement locates the subject of the clause in time or space. You can usually test the pattern by making a noun phrase with the subject and the adverb complement. In the resulting noun phrase, the modifier follows the noun.

ORIGINAL: The election is next month.

TEST: the election next month

ORIGINAL: The fly is in my soup.

TEST: the fly in my soup

When the adverb complement is a word that ordinarily functions as a preposition, the test will not work. For example, you cannot convert *The barricade is down* to *the barricade down*. You can, however, tell that *down* is an adverb complement since it indicates the location of the barricade.

EXERCISE 1

Each of the following sentences conforms to one of the clause patterns listed here. Match each sentence with the pattern of its structure.

(a) SUBJECT + INTRANSITIVE VERB
(b) SUBJECT + TRANSITIVE VERB + DIRECT OBJECT
(c) SUBJECT + TRANSITIVE VERB + INDIRECT OBJECT + DIRECT OBJECT
(d) SUBJECT + TRANSITIVE VERB + DIRECT OBJECT + OBJECT COMPLEMENT
(e) SUBJECT + LINKING VERB + ADJECTIVE SUBJECT COMPLEMENT
(f) SUBJECT + LINKING VERB + NOUN SUBJECT COMPLEMENT
(g) SUBJECT + BE + POSSESSIVE
(h) SUBJECT + BE + ADVERB SUBJECT COMPLEMENT

1. In 1846, Thoreau spent one night in jail.
2. Leaf-cutter ants can strip a tree bare in a day.
3. The Internal Revenue office is downstairs.
4. The Islam religion is strictly monotheistic.
5. Gerald Ford was the first nonelected Vice President.
6. Freshly grated nutmeg tastes superior to the commercially ground variety.
7. For America's national symbol, Benjamin Franklin proposed the turkey.
8. Three ounces of lean beef give an individual 169 calories.
9. The Interior Department considers the peregrine falcon an endangered species.
10. Chess became an obsession to Rex.
11. The asparagus seems unsuited for gardens in south Florida.
12. During the winter, the South Pole is dark twenty-four hours a day.
13. Since last month, the stock market has been up.
14. Copyrights now last for the life of an author plus fifty years.
15. Every year the Academy of Television Arts and Sciences awards the best dramatic series an Emmy.
16. Many connoisseurs consider the prepared mustards of Dijon or Dusseldorf best.

17. The refrigerator is one of the biggest users of energy in the home all year round.
18. Vanilla seems the most popular ice-cream flavor in this area.
19. American industry can learn from the success of Japanese industry.
20. Edison called his research laboratory at Menlo Park an "invention factory."

7b Independent Clauses

Independent clauses (sometimes called *main clauses*) may stand by themselves as sentences.

SUBJECT	PREDICATE
The book	examines human cruelty.
The ideas	are not pessimistic.
A hostile crowd	had gathered.
Serbian assassins	waited.

In addition, independent clauses can be joined to produce compound sentences.

The book examines human cruelty, but the ideas are not pessimistic.

A hostile crowd had gathered; the Serbian assassins waited.

7c Dependent Clauses

Like independent clauses, *dependent clauses* (also called *subordinate clauses*) have subjects and predicates. But unlike independent clauses, they cannot stand alone as sentences, and they usually begin with an introductory word that signals dependence.

INTRODUCTORY WORD	SUBJECT	PREDICATE
because	lead	causes tarnishing
that	we	call Baalbeck
if	their tires	are underinflated

Since they are not complete in themselves, dependent clauses must be attached to independent clauses:

Pewter articles no longer contain lead because lead causes tarnishing.

The town <u>that we call Baalbeck</u> was known to the Greeks as Heliopolis.

Drivers waste gasoline <u>if their tires are underinflated</u>.

Dependent clauses function in sentences as modifiers or as nouns and are generally classified as adverb clauses, adjective clauses, and noun clauses.

(1) Adverb clauses

The most versatile of dependent clauses is the adverb clause, which can modify verbs, adjectives, adverbs, and whole clauses. In fact, any dependent clause that does not act as a noun or modify a noun can safely be called an *adverb clause*.

Adverb clauses are introduced by subordinating conjunctions to express relationships such as time, cause/effect, purpose, condition/result, contrast, place, and manner. Most of the subordinating conjunctions can be grouped according to these relationships.

TIME

when, whenever, while, after, before, as, just as, as soon as, until, since, ever since, once, as long as

The British blockaded Germany <u>when World War II broke out</u>.

<u>As soon as a dolphin is born</u>, the mother pushes it to the water's surface for its first breath of air.

CAUSE/EFFECT

because, since, now that, once, as, in case

<u>Because some years produce better wines</u>, experts often judge quality by the vintage year.

In Nebraska, most farmers must install irrigation systems <u>in case rainfall is under 10 inches a year</u>.

PURPOSE

in order that, so that

We left the tour group <u>in order that we could visit some small villages</u>.

The star hired teenagers to mob the airport <u>so that his arrival would get publicity</u>.

CONDITION/RESULT

if, unless, once, provided that, whatever, whoever, whichever, whether or not, no matter what (which, how, when, who, where), assuming that

Please check the color-coded map <u>if you do not know the correct subway line</u>.

<u>No matter what critics say</u>, O. Henry is a popular writer.

CONTRAST

although, even though, even if, though, except (that), whereas

<u>Even though the superhighways have made travel faster</u>, they have also made it less scenic.

The Aztec capital was as large as a European city, <u>although the Indians neither domesticated animals nor used wheels</u>.

COMPARISON

as . . . as, so . . . as, so . . . that, more . . . than, most . . . that, than

The Royal Canadian Mounted Police are <u>as</u> effective in reality <u>as they are in legend</u>.

The Imperial Hotel in Tokyo was <u>so</u> well built <u>that it survived the destructive 1923 earthquake</u>.

PLACE

where, wherever

We saw nothing but litter <u>where the fair had been</u>.

The migrant workers went <u>wherever jobs were available</u>.

MANNER

as, as if, as though, just as, just as if

She walked with her shoulders squared and head erect <u>as though life were her adversary</u>.

The Celtics played <u>as if the championship were at stake</u>.

☐ EXERCISE 2

Combine the following pairs of sentences by making the second one an adverb clause that shows the meaning indicated in the parentheses.

EXAMPLE: **The students at Lincoln High School were in seventh-period classes. The fire alarm went off. (time)** → The students at Lincoln High were in seventh-period classes when the fire alarm went off.

1. Overcrowding gets worse every year. India's enormous population keeps growing rapidly. (cause / effect)
2. This state judges criminals insane. They cannot distinguish right from wrong. (condition / result)
3. Wegener formally proposed the theory of continental drift in 1912. Others had suggested the idea as early as 1629. (contrast)
4. Dante's poetry helped establish the common language of Italy. Chaucer's writings helped establish English. (manner)
5. The Allies kept the plans for the invasion of Normandy a secret. They could deceive the Germans about the true landing site. (purpose)
6. The archer was accurate. Every arrow hit the gold center. (comparison)
7. In the familiar version, Little Red Riding Hood escapes the wolf. In the original version, she does not. (contrast)
8. I used to catch colds every winter. Then I began taking massive doses of vitamin C. (time)
9. You will be able to transform paper into planes and kites. You read the book on origami. (condition / result)
10. Snakes weren't a real worry at the camp site. Snakes are fairly sluggish in the dry season. (cause /effect)

(2) Adjective clauses

Adjective clauses modify nouns and pronouns. These clauses are often called *relative clauses* because they are introduced by relative pronouns *(who/whom/whose, which, that)* or relative adverbs *(when, where, why)*. Unlike a subordinating conjunction, which merely connects an adverb clause to a main clause, a relative introducer functions within an adjective clause as a noun or an adverb. Also, the relative introducer follows and refers to the word or phrase being modified.

One fifth of the water that runs off the earth's surface is carried by the Amazon.

Afghanistan is a land-locked country whose strategic location has affected its history.

Ellen Terry, who played all of Shakespeare's heroines, was a celebrated actress for almost fifty years.

A tax on tea brought about the Boston Tea Party, which triggered the Revolutionary War.

In Connecticut, November is the month when the wild animals and insects retreat to shelter.

Sometimes an adjective clause appears without a relative introducer.

The playwright he emulates is Tennessee Williams.

The robots they manufacture are installed in chemical plants.

In such cases, the introducer is understood to be *that*.

The playwright [that] he emulates is Tennessee Williams.

The robots [that] they manufacture are installed in chemical plants.

The adjective clause is sometimes set off with commas and sometimes not, depending on its relationship to the noun it modifies. For a discussion of how to punctuate adjective clauses, see 21d.1. For a discussion of when to use *who/whom* and *whoever/whomever,* see 14c.

☐ EXERCISE 3

Combine each pair of sentences by converting the second sentence of the pair to an adjective clause.

EXAMPLE: Destructive waves are caused by undersea earthquakes or hurricanes. The waves sweep in from the ocean. → Destructive waves that sweep in from the ocean are caused by undersea earthquakes or hurricanes.

1. The hotel was designed for the very rich. The very rich can afford unlimited luxuries.
2. During a thunderstorm, you should avoid dangerous locations. Dangerous locations are significantly higher than their surroundings.
3. The trilogy by Tolkien tells of a ring. The ring's wearer can control the world.
4. The computer has a graphics index. The graphics index will file and retrieve pictures.
5. Goya's "black paintings" are painted directly on the walls of his house. Goya's "black paintings" depict scenes nightmarish and grotesque.
6. On September 2, 1945, World War II ended. On September 2, 1945, the Japanese signed the "instrument of surrender."

7. A Frisbee is named for the Frisbie Bakery. At the Frisbie Bakery, pie tins resembling the plastic disk were used.

8. Orthodox physicians drove Dr. Mesmer from practice in Vienna. Dr. Mesmer developed hypnotism.

9. The fullback played the entire game. The fullback's ankles were both taped.

10. The counterfeiters made the money on a photocopy machine. The counterfeiters were very unprofessional.

(3) Noun clauses

Noun clauses function in the same ways that all nouns do—as subjects, objects, and complements. These clauses are introduced with a variety of words, most of which begin with *wh-*.

> *that, who, whom, whose, which, what*
>
> *whoever, whomever, whatever, whichever, however*
>
> *whether, where, when, how, if*

Noun Clauses as Subjects

A noun clause can occur as a subject at the beginning of a sentence, but that position is not very common.

> What parents believe is usually what children reject.
>
> Whatever you decide is acceptable to me.

A more natural position for a noun clause used as a subject is at the end of the sentence. In the following examples, *it* is an expletive and the noun clause is a delayed subject. (See 6d, "Expletives.")

> It is unlikely that a satisfactory solution will ever be found for disposing of nuclear waste.
>
> It doesn't matter what you study.

Noun Clauses as Direct Objects

Noun clauses probably appear most frequently as direct objects after verbs like *say, believe, think, decide, propose, hope,* and *prove*—usually verbs that name some sort of mental activity.

> The scientist calculated that a million black holes exist in our galaxy.
>
> The group proposed that San Francisco ban the building of more skyscrapers in downtown.

Sometimes the subordinator *that* is left out, although it is understood by a reader.

> Ecologists hope [that] the whooping crane can be saved.

> Buddhists believe [that] monks should live a life of poverty.

Noun Clauses as Objects of Prepositions

When the noun clause appears as the object of a preposition, the clause usually begins with *whether, how, what, whatever, whoever,* or some other interrogative word.

> A controversy has arisen among anthropologists over <u>whether cannibalism has ever existed in a cultural context</u>.

> After improving the telephone, Edison turned his attention to <u>how one might permanently record sound</u>.

> When he received his "visions," Edgar Casey was totally unconscious of <u>what went on around him</u>.

Noun Clauses as Subject Complements

Sometimes, after the verb *be,* noun clauses function as subject complements (predicate nominatives) to rename the subject.

> The new pesticide is <u>what caused the citrus blight</u>.

> The problem was <u>that Edward the Confessor died without an heir</u>.

> The candidate will be <u>whoever can afford to run</u>.

❑ EXERCISE 4

Identify the noun clauses in the following sentences.

1. A Gold Record Award goes to whichever record sells one million units.
2. What made *Bridge on the River Kwai* an interesting film was its complex characters with both good and bad traits.
3. Scientists believe there may be millions of insects not yet classified.
4. Procrastinators put off until later whatever doesn't have to be done immediately.
5. It is not clear when the composer will finish the music for the new ballet.
6. The new supervisor will be whoever has the best sales record.
7. What interested me most was the exhibition on the history of flight.
8. A part of the legend of Hercules is that under Hera's jealous influence, Hercules killed his wife and children.

9. The British scientists discovered that Piltdown man's skull had the jawbone of a modern ape.
10. From the information in the book, we can draw conclusions about what the early settlers thought.

(4) Elliptical clauses

In an *elliptical clause,* one or more words that can be readily supplied by the reader are dropped from the complete structure. The most common omissions in elliptical clauses are a relative pronoun *(that, which,* or *whom),* the subject and a form of *be,* and a previously stated verb or predicate.

> Most economists believe [that] the bond market is improving.
>
> Dylan Thomas died at age thirty-nine while [he was] on an American tour.
>
> The Appalachian National Scenic Trail is longer than any other hiking trail in the country [is long].
>
> As a rule, private colleges charge more tuition than public colleges [charge].
>
> Bats of some species roost in colonies of millions; others [roost], in solitude.

❑ EXERCISE 5

Identify the elliptical clauses in the following sentences, and supply the missing words in each.

EXAMPLE: I bought the camera while visiting Japan.
        I bought the camera while [I was] visiting Japan.

1. Perseus was given a brass shield as bright as a mirror.
2. Fluorescent lights give more light at a lower energy cost than incandescent bulbs with the same wattage.
3. Some stars burn their hydrogen fuel so fast they explode as supernovas.
4. While analyzing the data on the printout, the astronomers discovered the existence of background radiation.
5. Courtney played with seven different baseball leagues; Chiti, with four.

❑ EXERCISE 6

In the following sentences, underline the independent clauses once and the dependent clauses twice. Indicate whether the dependent clauses are functioning as nouns, adjectives, or adverbs.

1. Travelers can bring home $300 worth of duty-free goods whenever they return from abroad.
2. Many Germans believe that their divided country will someday be reunited.
3. The principal river in the United States is the Mississippi, whose chief literary interpreter was Mark Twain.
4. Robots are now being installed in factories, where they can make almost any manufactured product.
5. They argued over whether they should go to the beach or to the mountains.
6. A recent study estimated that illiteracy costs the United States approximately $500 billion a year.
7. Woodrow Wilson suffered a stroke just as he was striving to popularize his ideas for a league of nations.
8. Once people are in a hypnotic trance, they can focus their attention on one thing and ignore distractions.
9. Some abbreviations that are acceptable in technical reports may not be appropriate in formal essays.
10. You can reduce fuel costs provided that you insulate your house adequately.
11. In the legend, whoever could solve the riddle of the Sphinx would be spared her vengeance.
12. The fact that *Fidelio* is the only opera composed by Beethoven gives it special significance.
13. Before the German people followed Hitler into World War II, they had suffered a severe depression.
14. In order that his son could win bicycle races, Dunlop developed the pneumatic tire.
15. The fight ended as abruptly as it had begun.
16. Although Dracula died with a stake through his heart in the first film, the monster has reappeared in many sequels.
17. Scientific study can increase what is known about athletic performance.
18. *The New Yorker,* which was founded in 1925, was first edited by Harold Ross.
19. It is likely that a raccoon raided the kitchen.
20. The sculptor whom we commissioned sued us when we rejected his work.

7d Kinds of Sentences

Independent clauses appear alone or in combinations—with other independent clauses or with dependent clauses. One method of classifying sentences is based on the number and kinds of clauses in a single construction. According to this classification system, there are four categories of sentences: simple, compound, complex, and compound-complex.

(1) Simple sentence

A *simple sentence* is made up of only one independent clause. The sentence may contain modifiers and compound elements (for example, compound subjects and verbs); but it may not contain more than one subject-predicate structure.

> Cigarette <u>smoke</u> <u>contains</u> carbon monoxide.
>
> <u>The Rhone</u> <u>flows</u> south through France and then <u>empties</u> into the Mediterranean.
>
> Brought up from the minors in 1956, <u>Stuart</u> <u>became</u> one of only four men to hit thirty or more home runs in each major league.

(2) Compound sentence

A *compound sentence* is made up of two or more independent clauses. The primary ways to coordinate independent clauses are with commas and coordinating conjunctions *(and, but, or, for, nor, so, yet)* and with semicolons.

> For centuries, Brittany was an independent state, but now the area is part of France. [independent clause + independent clause]
>
> Socrates wrote nothing; his thoughts are known only through the works of Plato and Xenophon. [independent clause + independent clause]
>
> The restaurant was dark, the air was filled with smoke, and the music was deafening. [independent clause + independent clause + independent clause]

(3) Complex sentence

A *complex sentence* is made up of one independent clause and one or more dependent clauses—adverb, adjective, or noun.

> Although most rifle experts have 20/20 vision, pistol experts are often very nearsighted. [dependent adverb clause + independent clause]
>
> The game involves three contestants who spin a roulette wheel. [independent clause + dependent adjective clause]

Dr. Strangelove concerns a psychotic general who believes that Communists are poisoning America's water with flouride. [independent clause + dependent adjective clause + dependent noun clause]

(4) Compound-complex sentence

A *compound-complex sentence* is made up of two or more independent clauses and one or more dependent clauses.

London's Great Exhibition, which opened in 1851, was designed to show human progress; it brought together in the "Crystal Palace" industrial displays remarkable for their day. [dependent adjective clause within independent clause + independent clause]

Alchemists believed that they could change lesser metals into gold, and although they failed, they helped establish the science of chemistry. [dependent noun clause within independent clause + dependent adverb clause within independent clause]

The fathom once was the distance that a Viking could encompass in a hug; a gauge was the distance that lay between the wheels of a Roman chariot; an acre was an area that could be plowed in one day by a team of two oxen. [independent clause + dependent adjective clause + independent clause + dependent adjective clause + independent clause + dependent adjective clause]

▢ EXERCISE 7

Identify each clause in the following sentences as independent or dependent. Then determine whether each sentence is simple, compound, complex, or compound-complex.

1. Opponents of government aid argue that if the government gives money to a group, that group may insist on control.
2. Some fishermen locate schools of fish by devices similar to those used for detecting enemy submarines.
3. Plastic machine parts run silently, yet they need little or no oiling.
4. Although the fans booed and threw lemons, Babe Ruth hit one of the longest homers that has ever been recorded.
5. We arrived in Germany on June 27, and one of the first things that we did was head for the Mosel to taste wines and eat fresh trout.
6. The director says that however the actors interpret their roles is acceptable to him.
7. To tell the truth, most of the funds have already been spent.
8. We were not told of the decision to replace the manager; however, we had suspected it.

9. To prevent piracy, manufacturers of computer programs have spent much time developing systems that have "copy protection."

10. Giddons, who wrote his first novel at age twenty, had made his reputation by age thirty; but he accomplished nothing after he turned forty.

 EXERCISE 8

Combine each of the following sets of sentences to create the kind of sentence indicated. If you have trouble punctuating the combined sentences, see Chapter 21, "Commas," and Chapter 22, "Semicolons."

EXAMPLE: She grew tired of the incessant gossip. She slipped quietly off from the group. (simple) → She grew tired of the incessant gossip and slipped quietly off from the group.

1. The programmers worked for twenty-one hours without a break. They managed to complete the project on time. (complex)

2. Helium appears in natural gas deposits. Helium appears in the atmosphere. (simple)

3. The last chapter summarizes the evidence. He supports the evidence. His critics attack the evidence. (complex)

4. Heiroglyphics sometimes read from left to right. Usually, they read from right to left or top to bottom. (compound)

5. Pterodactyls could fly. They were not birds. They were reptiles. (compound-complex)

6. Speed reading is practical for easy material. Slower reading is more effective for complex, challenging works. (compound)

7. The horse stood on muscular legs. The legs supported a deep, full chest. The legs supported massive haunches. (complex)

8. Ms. Bloom reported the missing funds. Ms. Bloom had stolen the money herself. (complex)

9. My great-grandfather was one of ten children. My great-grandmother was one of seven. (compound)

10. John Culhane was an aggressive skater. In one game he met his match. A burly defenseman bumped him to the ice five times. (compound-complex)

 EXERCISE 9

The prose in the following passages is choppy, and the relationship between ideas is not always clear. Improve the passages by varying the sentence types to include simple, compound, and complex sentences.

1. Readers often have trouble understanding supernatural stories. The action may truly take place. The action may take place only in the narrator's mind. For example, the narrator of Poe's "The Fall of the House of Usher" verges on insanity. Readers do not know the truth about the strange events. The events take place in a gloomy mansion. The events take place in a decayed mansion. In Henry James' "The Jolly Corner," Brydon sees a ghost. Brydon pursues the ghost. Brydon thinks the ghost is physically real. But the reader wonders. Is the ghost real? Is the ghost a symbol of Brydon's inner being?

2. I have always loved Thanksgiving. I love turkey and dressing. I love family dinners. At family dinners, relatives get together. They eat, drink, and laugh. After dinner, they relax. They watch football games. They swap stories. I also love Thanksgiving for another reason. It is not commercialized. For instance, salesclerks don't dress up like pilgrims. People don't feel obligated to buy presents. Parents aren't frantically looking for the last Pocahontas doll in town. Thanksgiving is the ideal holiday. It brings families together. It doesn't cost much money.

Revising Sentences: Structural and Grammatical Errors

When you write, you must concentrate on matters such as content, organization, purpose, and audience. Naturally, incorrect constructions are likely to appear in early drafts of a composition. Therefore, before you complete a final draft, you must read your work carefully and revise any sentences that contain structural or grammatical errors. Careful revision will help ensure clear and logical prose.

8

Sentence Fragments

A *sentence fragment* is a group of words punctuated like a complete sentence but lacking the necessary structure—at least one independent clause. The following passage shows how confusing sentence fragments can be.

> Humans accept death as their certain destiny. In nature, however, everything does not die. The hydra, a freshwater, tube-shaped creature. The hydra's body cells regenerate every two weeks. Giving it an unlimited life expectancy. Except for predators and diseases, some fish might never die. Because they never stop growing. In a sense, the amoeba doesn't die. It simply divides. And thus not only survives but also multiplies.

This passage includes six complete sentences, which express complete thoughts, even out of context.

> Humans accept death as their certain destiny.
>
> In nature, however, everything does not die.
>
> The hydra's body cells regenerate every two weeks.
>
> Except for predators and disease, some fish might never die.
>
> In a sense, the amoeba doesn't die.
>
> It simply divides.

In contrast, the passage's four fragments seem meaningless out of context.

> The hydra, a freshwater, tube-shaped creature.
>
> And thus not only survives but also multiplies.

Giving it an unlimited life expectancy.

Because they never stop growing.

In a few special instances, fragments do not handicap communication.

- Dialogue: "Now," thought William. "Now."
- Deliberate stylistic effects: The play catches everyone and everything in its swirl. Rather like a tornado.
- Answers to questions: When? Only ten years from now.
- Interjections: Oh! Well.
- Advertising: The best hardware for your best software.
- Idioms: The sooner the better. So much for that.

As a general rule, however, you should write in complete sentences and avoid fragments. If, while revising, you do find an accidental fragment, you must eliminate it in one of two ways.

Join the fragment unaltered to a sentence.
Rewrite the fragment as some other kind of structure.

8a Dependent Clause Fragments

A dependent clause contains a subject and a predicate and begins with a subordinating word such as *since, if, because, although, who, which, that.* (See 7c, "Dependent Clauses.") When punctuated as a complete sentence, a dependent clause is considered a fragment.

FRAGMENT: Registration was a nightmare. Although I did get the courses I wanted.

REVISED BY JOINING: Registration was a nightmare, although I did get the courses I wanted.

REVISED BY REWRITING: Registration was a nightmare. I did, however, get the courses I wanted.

FRAGMENT: At age twenty-six, Jefferson began Monticello. Which he did not complete until he was sixty-eight.

REVISED BY JOINING: At age twenty-six, Jefferson began Monticello, which he did not complete until he was sixty-eight.

REVISED BY REWRITING: At age twenty-six, Jefferson began Monticello; but he did not finish it until he was sixty-eight.

frag
8b

☐ EXERCISE 1

Eliminate the fragment in each group of words by two methods.
(a) joining the fragment to the complete sentence
(b) rewriting the fragment as some other kind of structure

1. Mel Tillis, the country music star, has no trouble singing. Although he stutters when he speaks.
2. While arthritis rarely threatens life. It can be a frustrating, painful experience.
3. As we were strolling casually along a tree-lined boulevard. We were approached by a man begging for money.
4. The company was plagued with both personnel and equipment problems. Which finally resulted in bankruptcy.
5. Noise places strain on the mind. Because it interferes with speech and hearing.

8b Phrase Fragments

A phrase is a group of related words that does not contain a subject and a predicate. Ordinarily, no phrase should appear alone as a complete sentence.

(1) Verbal phrases as fragments

A verbal is a participle *(riding, ridden)* or an infinitive *(to ride);* it is not a main verb. A verbal phrase consists of a verbal plus any related words, such as objects and modifiers *(riding the horse, ridden furiously, to ride the horse furiously).* (See Chapter 5, "Verbals and Verbal Phrases.")

> FRAGMENT: Manufacturers will hold a trade fair in St. Louis next month. The fair to promote new sports equipment.

> REVISED BY JOINING: Manufacturers will hold a trade fair in St. Louis next month to promote new sports equipment.

> REVISED BY REWRITING: Manufacturers will hold a trade fair in St. Louis next month. The event will promote new sports equipment.

> FRAGMENT: The surface bubbles were discovered by engineers. Checking the gas lines across the river bottom.

**frag
8b**

REVISED BY JOINING: **The surface bubbles were discovered by engineers checking the gas lines across the river bottom.**

REVISED BY REWRITING: **Engineers checked the gas lines across the river bottom and discovered bubbles breaking the surface of the water.**

(2) Verb phrases as fragments

A verb phrase contains a main verb (not a verbal) and any modifiers, objects, and complements of that verb. (See Chapter 7, "Clauses and Sentences.") A verb phrase fragment lacks a subject.

FRAGMENT: **Students must register by June 1. Or pay a late fee of fifty dollars.**

REVISED BY JOINING: **Students must register by June 1 or pay a late fee of fifty dollars.**

REVISED BY REWRITING: **Students who do not register by June 1 must pay a late fee of fifty dollars.**

FRAGMENT: **The department's bloodhound has trailed 165 missing people. And has found 85 percent of them.**

REVISED BY JOINING: **The department's bloodhound has trailed 165 missing people and has found 85 percent of them.**

REVISED BY REWRITING: **The department's bloodhound has trailed 165 missing people; she has found 85 percent of them.**

(3) Noun phrases as fragments

A noun phrase is a group of related words containing a noun and modifiers of that noun. A noun phrase fragment lacks a predicate, that is, a verb with any modifiers or completing words.

FRAGMENT: **Spider-Man's strength and climbing ability came from a remarkable source. The bite of a radioactive spider.**

REVISED BY JOINING: **Spider-Man's strength and climbing ability came from a remarkable source: the bite of a radioactive spider.**

REVISED BY REWRITING: **Spider-Man's strength and climbing ability came from a remarkable source. He was bitten by a radioactive spider.**

(4) Prepositional phrases as fragments

**frag
8b**

A prepositional phrase is a construction made up of a preposition (*at, on, after, over, behind, because of,* and so on) and a noun phrase as its object.

> FRAGMENT: I quit smoking last Christmas. Because of a chronic cough.
>
> REVISED BY JOINING: I quit smoking last Christmas because of a chronic cough.
>
> REVISED BY REWRITING: I quit smoking last Christmas. At that time, my cough had become chronic.

☐ EXERCISE 2

Eliminate the fragment in each group of words by either joining the fragment to the complete sentence or rewriting the fragment as some other kind of structure.

1. He lost a million dollars in just a few months. His cocaine habit ruining his financial judgment.
2. The car is a network of computer controls. Controls for improving performance and maintenance.
3. They bought color-coordinated exercise suits. With the intention of getting into shape.
4. Our agency has promoted the development of synthetic fuels. Fuels to eliminate a dependence on oil.
5. The slogan is often worn on a button. Or displayed on a bumper sticker.
6. The professor was trying to explain computer speeds. Speeds such as milliseconds, microseconds, and nanoseconds.
7. Pedestrians had to dash through the spray of the lawn sprinkler. Or walk around it, out into the road.
8. I hit at the third pitch. Grazing the ball as it hurtled past.
9. Athletes should drink water frequently. Before, during, and after sports activities.
10. The record for completed passes was held by Rupert Gonzales. The first college quarterback to be drafted this year.

☐ EXERCISE 3

Rewrite the following passage to eliminate sentence fragments.

The bicycle has been used in wars since 1870, but rarely by the United States. The French first trying bicycles for scouting expeditions in the Franco-Prussian War. In 1875 when Italians tried maneuvers on bicycles. Because of the pneumatic tire, reduced weight, and the ability to be folded up. By World War I, European troops used bikes extensively on the front lines. When World War II broke out, soldiers on bicycles frequently seen in Europe and Asia. Yet American troops traveled by ships, planes, trucks, and trains. In Europe, soldiers used bicycles to destroy railroads and bridges behind German lines. And to move supplies when the motors of trucks and jeeps broke down. Bicycles, which helped the Japanese move through thick jungles to take over Malaya and Singapore. During the Vietnam War, the Viet Cong used bicycles to carry supplies. Because bicycles make little noise and seldom broke down. Perhaps American troops with their dependence on modern technology overlooked an effective vehicle— the bicycle.

frag
8b

9

Comma Splices and Fused Sentences

If you connect two independent clauses with only a comma, you create a *comma splice,* so called because the clauses are "spliced" together. If you run the clauses together without a conjunction or proper punctuation, you create a fused (or run-on) sentence.

> COMMA SPLICE: **Pickpockets have become a serious problem, tourists should be especially alert in crowded areas.**

> FUSED SENTENCE: **Pickpockets have become a serious problem tourists should be especially alert in crowded areas.**

Neither of these constructions is acceptable in standard written English. Thus, if you find comma splices and fused sentences in your writing, you must revise them by one of five options. The relationship of the two clauses frequently determines which option is best. When several options will work, you can choose the one that produces the emphasis you prefer.

9a Revision with a Comma and a Coordinating Conjunction

Comma splices and fused sentences can often be revised by connecting the clauses with both a comma and a coordinating conjunction (*and, but, or, nor, for, so, yet*). This option works well when the clauses do not contain much internal punctuation and when you can express the proper relationship between the clauses with one of the conjunctions.

COMMA SPLICE: Winter lasts six months in Wyoming, life gets hard at 20 to 40 degrees below zero.

FUSED SENTENCE: Winter lasts six months in Wyoming life gets hard at 20 to 40 degrees below zero.

REVISED: Winter lasts six months in Wyoming, <u>and</u> life gets hard at 20 to 40 degrees below zero.

cs/fs
9b

COMMA SPLICE: My dormitory room is supposed to house two people comfortably, actually it has only enough space for a six-year-old child.

FUSED SENTENCE: My dormitory room is supposed to house two people comfortably actually it has only enough space for a six-year-old child.

REVISED: My dormitory room is supposed to house two people comfortably, <u>but</u> actually it has only enough space for a six-year-old child.

9b Revision with a Semicolon

A semicolon works well when the clauses in a comma splice or fused sentence do not have a relationship easily expressed by one of the coordinating conjunctions.

COMMA SPLICE: The novel is remarkable, Mr. Wright has written over 50,000 words without once using the letter *e.*

FUSED SENTENCE: The novel is remarkable Mr. Wright has written over 50,000 words without once using the letter *e.*

REVISED: The novel is remarkable; Mr. Wright has written over 50,000 words without once using the letter *e.*

The semicolon is especially appropriate when the second independent clause begins with a transitional expression such as one of the following:

also	furthermore	on the other hand
as a result	however	regardless
consequently	in conclusion	sometimes
finally	in fact	still
first	in other words	then
for example	moreover	therefore
	nevertheless	thus

(For other transitional expressions, see TRANSITIONAL EXPRESSION in "Glossary of Grammatical, Rhetorical, and Literary Terms.")

Do not confuse these words and expressions with coordinating conjunctions, which have no more than three letters (*and, but, or, nor, for, so, yet*). Transitional expressions are not grammatical conjunctions that join two clauses but rather conjunctive adverbs and adverb phrases that are part of the second clause. Notice how the conjunctive adverb *however* can move about in its clause.

> COMMA SPLICE: They discovered that the library ceiling contained asbestos, <u>however</u>, the school could not afford to have the material removed.

> REVISED: They discovered that the library ceiling contained asbestos; the school could not, <u>however</u>, afford to have the material removed.

> REVISED: They discovered that the library ceiling contained asbestos; the school, <u>however</u>, could not afford to have the material removed.

A coordinating conjunction cannot move about in a sentence but must remain between the clauses it connects.

> CORRECT SENTENCE: They discovered that the library ceiling contained asbestos, <u>but</u> the school could not afford to have the material removed.

> IMPOSSIBLE SENTENCE: They discovered that the library ceiling contained asbestos; the school could not, <u>but</u> afford to have the material removed.

A semicolon can also be used with a coordinating conjunction when the first clause has internal punctuation.

> COMMA SPLICE: Standing on the pier, her blond hair blowing in the wind, she looked frail, innocent, and vulnerable, she was actually planning a robbery.

> REVISED: Standing on the pier, her blond hair blowing in the wind, she looked frail, innocent, and vulnerable; <u>yet</u> she was actually planning a robbery.

9c Revision with a Colon

Occasionally, one independent clause is followed by another that explains or amplifies it. In this very special case, you can join the two clauses with a colon.

COMMA SPLICE: The economics of the country caused the 1848 revolution, harvests and commerce were at a low.

REVISED: The economics of the country caused the 1848 revolution: harvests and commerce were at a low.

9d Revision with a Dependent Clause or Phrase

Often you can correct a comma splice or fused sentence by changing one of the independent clauses to a dependent clause or phrase. This correction is a good solution when you want to indicate a special relationship—a relationship such as time, place, condition/result, cause/effect, contrast, and so forth.

FUSED SENTENCE: Sometimes I craved fried foods floating in grease then I ate in the school cafeteria.

REVISED WITH A DEPENDENT CLAUSE: When I craved fried foods floating in grease, I ate in the school cafeteria.

REVISED WITH A PHRASE: Craving fried foods floating in grease, I ate in the school cafeteria.

This correction also works well when the two independent clauses have a noun or noun phrase in common.

COMMA SPLICE: We desperately need zoning laws, the construction of unsightly commercial buildings could be prevented by zoning laws.

REVISED WITH A DEPENDENT CLAUSE: We desperately need zoning laws, which could prevent the construction of unsightly commercial buildings.

REVISED WITH A PHRASE: We desperately need zoning laws to prevent the construction of unsightly commercial buildings.

9e Revision by Creating Two Sentences

You can effectively revise many comma splices and fused sentences by creating two separate sentences—particularly when you want a

cs/fs
9e

major break between the clauses. This revision is especially useful when the two clauses are long or when you want to emphasize each clause.

> COMMA SPLICE: Unlike most of my friends, I cannot abide watching those silly, mindless situation comedies, for one thing, I resent having the laugh track tell me when to be entertained.

> REVISED: Unlike most of my friends, I cannot abide watching those silly, mindless situation comedies. For one thing, I resent having the laugh track tell me when to be entertained.

☐ EXERCISE 1

Revise each comma splice or fused sentence by using the option indicated in brackets.

1. A weekend guest should send a house gift to the hosts it should be neither expensive nor comic. [comma and coordinate conjunction]
2. Columbus mistook a group of manatees for mermaids, in fact, a blubbery manatee looks like Grover Cleveland with a moustache. [semicolon]
3. What the people want is clear, they want maximum government services and minimum taxes. [colon]
4. The pizza parlor refused to take our order, we had requested a pizza with one-third pepperoni, one-fourth ground beef, and five-twelfths ham. [dependent clause]
5. Struggling with the English language, he was frustrated by the pronunciation of *though, bough,* and *through,* no logic seemed to help. [two sentences]

☐ EXERCISE 2

Revise each comma splice and fused sentence by one of the options described in 9(1) through 9(5). Choose an option that produces an effective sentence.

1. Sweat is extremely important, it is the primary way the body cools itself.
2. In Paris, the first week of fashion shows is "closed," admittance is limited to professional buyers, the invited press, and privileged clients.
3. Bibliographies are arranged topically, chronologically, or alphabetically, however, the alphabetical arrangement is the most common.
4. My friend has little time to study the stock market consequently, he has invested in a mutual fund.
5. Compulsive gambling is a psychiatric disorder, few treatment centers exist.

6. Sometimes the operations manuals are too technical for students, then the lab assistants must interpret the instructions.
7. Some areas of Texas got two inches of rain, most of the state got only a trace.
8. Fiercely competing for audiences, the soap operas are shooting on location in exotic settings, in addition, the shows are featuring unrealistic plots involving international crime, natural disasters, and travel in outer space.

cs/fs
9e

☐ EXERCISE 3

Revise the following passages to eliminate comma splices and fused sentences.

1.   You can travel easily in Paris by taxi. Taxis are plentiful, there are numerous stands. You can go to the "Tête de Station," obviously, you should take the first taxi in line. Some private cars serve as taxis, however, before taking them, you should settle the price. The easiest way to get a taxi is through your hotel concierge or porter whoever summons the taxi should get a one franc tip.

2.   Studying for most objective tests is very different from studying for essay tests. Objective tests usually require only a knowledge of facts, however, essay tests also require the ability to interpret.

To study for objective tests, I put each fact to be learned on a 3×5 card then I arrange the cards in logical order. When I learn a fact, I put that card into a separate stack. Gradually, the "learned stack" becomes larger and larger, finally, it contains all the cards, and I am ready for my test.

My method for essays tests is very different. I go through my textbook taking notes, then I combine them with my class notes. From this composite set of notes, I make an outline. Next, I try to predict possible test questions and group appropriate headings from my outline under the questions, therefore, I am able to assemble information into meaningful units. Also, I can practice analyzing the information I must use on the test.

In short, studying for an objective test is like getting ready for a trivia match, however, studying for an essay test is like preparing a debate.

10

Subject-Verb Agreement

Achieving subject-verb agreement involves choosing the verb form appropriate for the subject. In general, the choice depends on person, number, and tense.

- *Person* refers to whether the verb's subject is speaking, spoken to, or spoken about.

> FIRST PERSON: The subject is I or we.
>
> SECOND PERSON: The subject is you.
>
> THIRD PERSON: The subject is any noun or pronoun except I, we, or you.

- *Number* refers to singular (one) and plural (more than one).
- *Tense* is the verb feature that indicates time. (See 4d.)

(1) Agreement with all verbs except *be*

With all verbs except *be,* subject-verb agreement requires that the verb form end in an -*s* in the third person singular of the present and present perfect tenses. (The -*s* form of the verb is not used for other persons and tenses.)

Present Tense

PERSON	SINGULAR	PLURAL
FIRST:	I upset him.	We upset him.
SECOND:	You upset him.	You upset him.
THIRD:	Anything upsets him.	All things upset him.

Present Perfect Tense

PERSON	SINGULAR	PLURAL
FIRST:	I have upset him.	We have upset him.
SECOND:	You have upset him.	You have upset him.
THIRD:	Something has upset him.	Several things have upset him.

s/v agr
10a

(2) Agreement with the verb *be*

The verb *be* has three different forms in the present tense and two different forms in the past tense. The person and number of the subject determines which form is correct.

Present Tense

PERSON	SINGULAR	PLURAL
FIRST:	I am a chemist.	We are chemists.
SECOND:	You are a chemist.	You are chemists.
THIRD:	My aunt is a chemist.	My aunts are chemists.

Past Tense

PERSON	SINGULAR	PLURAL
FIRST:	I was a chemist.	We were chemists.
SECOND:	You were a chemist.	You were chemists.
THIRD:	My aunt was a chemist.	My aunts were chemists.

When the subject of a sentence is simple and appears next to its verb, subject-verb agreement usually presents no problems. But some subjects are tricky. As you edit your writing, watch for constructions such as the following that can cause agreement problems.

10a Intervening Words Between Subject and Verb

Often the subject of a sentence is followed by an adjective phrase or clause that contains a noun. Be careful to make your verb agree with the true subject and not with a noun that follows the subject.

> One of those video game machines appears everywhere I go. [*One* is the subject, not *machines;* and thus the verb is singular.]

> A collection of glass animals was artfully arranged on the table. [*Collection* is the subject, not *animals;* and thus the verb is singular.]

> Crates of exotic citrus fruit were rotting on the dock. [*Crates* is the subject, not *fruit;* and thus the verb is plural.]

10b Subjects Joined by *And*

When a sentence has two or more subjects joined by *and,* the verb usually takes the plural form.

> The governor and the attorney general <u>drive</u> limousines.
>
> <u>Sun and wind</u> <u>cause</u> skin burn.
>
> <u>McDonald's, Wendy's, and Burger King</u> <u>have been waging</u> commercial warfare.

CAUTION: This convention does not apply to subjects joined by phrases such as *as well as, together with, in addition to.*

> The governor, as well as the attorney general, <u>drives</u> a limousine.
>
> <u>Hot sun</u> together with strong wind <u>causes</u> severe skin burn.
>
> <u>McDonald's,</u> in addition to Wendy's and Burger King, <u>has been waging</u> commercial warfare.

Exceptions to the *and* convention are as follows.

- When *each* or *every* precedes subjects joined by *and,* the verb is singular.

> Each governor and each attorney general <u>was assigned</u> a limousine.
>
> Every hamburger chain and every fried chicken franchise <u>has been engaged</u> in commercial warfare.

- When the subjects joined by *and* refer to a single person, thing, or idea, the verb is singular.

> <u>Red beans and rice</u> <u>is</u> a popular Cajun dish.
>
> My best friend and confidant <u>has betrayed</u> me.

10c Subjects Joined by *Or/Nor*

When the subjects of a sentence are joined by *or* or *nor* (or *either . . . or, neither . . . nor*), the verb agrees with the subject closer to it. If the closer subject is singular, the verb is singular; if the closer subject is plural, the verb is plural.

> Neither the boxwood nor <u>the roses</u> <u>have survived</u> the ice storm.
>
> Neither the roses nor <u>the boxwood</u> <u>has survived</u> the ice storm.

CAUTION: This practice can cause awkward constructions, particularly with the verb *be* when the subjects are in different persons: *Either Steve or I am in charge.* Although this sentence is technically correct, you may want to avoid awkwardness by using two clauses instead of one: *Either Steve is in charge, or I am.*

☐ EXERCISE 1

Choose the correct verb for each sentence, making sure that it agrees with its subject. The problems involve compound subjects and words intervening between subjects and verbs.

1. Either the bonds or the real estate _____ (is/are) sufficient collateral for the loan.
2. An assortment of diamonds, emeralds, and sapphires _____ (gleams/gleam) from the pendant.
3. Her coach and mentor _____ (was/were) the only person she consulted.
4. On a tool bit, the clearance and relief angles, which are ground on the bit, _____ (determines/determine) the quality of the work.
5. France, along with Germany and Italy, _____ (produces/produce) most European wines.
6. The second major section of the balance sheet, the liabilities, _____ (lists/list) the debts that the company must pay.
7. Organization and planning _____ (is/are) the key requirements for a successful recording session.
8. Clouds of red clay dust _____ (has/have) settled on the fields.
9. The students or the professor _____ (has/have) confused the examination date.
10. My roommate, together with three friends, _____ (is/are) giving me a birthday dinner.

10d Indefinite Pronouns as Subjects

Singular verbs are required with most indefinite pronouns such as *everyone, everybody, anyone, one, no one, each, either, neither,* and so on. Frequently, prepositional phrases follow these indefinites, and sometimes a writer mistakes the preposition's object for the verb's subject. Make sure the verb is governed by the subject, not by the object of a preposition.

> <u>Everyone</u> in the group <u>reads</u> music.
>
> <u>Neither</u> of the vehicles <u>has</u> new tires.
>
> <u>Each</u> of the articles <u>was published</u> in 1985.

With some indefinite pronouns, such as *all, any, most, none,* and *some,* the context determines the number. If the pronoun refers to a plural noun that is countable *(books, chairs, ships),* the verb is plural. If the pronoun refers to a noun that is not countable *(information, noise, art),* the verb is singular.

> COUNT/PLURAL: <u>Most</u> of the residents <u>were</u> elderly.
>
> NONCOUNT/SINGULAR: <u>Most</u> of the confusion <u>was</u> over.

> COUNT/PLURAL: <u>Some</u> of the pages <u>were missing</u>.
>
> NONCOUNT/SINGULAR: <u>Some</u> of the laughter <u>was dying</u>.

Some people prefer that *none* always occur with a singular verb, even when it refers to a plural, countable noun: <u>None of the paintings was sold</u>. Nevertheless, most contemporary writers prefer a plural verb in these circumstances: <u>None of the paintings were sold</u>.

10e Relative Pronouns as Subjects

When a relative pronoun *(that, which, who)* is the subject of a clause, its verb agrees with the pronoun's antecedent—the word or phrase that the pronoun stands for.

> The Phantom is powered by <u>engines</u> <u>that</u> <u>deliver</u> 17,900 pounds of thrust. [<u>engines</u> <u>deliver</u>]

> Her celebrated <u>collection</u> of photographs, <u>which</u> <u>documents</u> Christmas in rural America, is on display during December. [<u>collection</u> <u>documents</u>]

When the relative pronoun is preceded by *one of those* . . . or *one of the* . . . the verb is plural.

> He is <u>one of those students</u> <u>who</u> always <u>study</u> early. [<u>students</u> <u>study</u>]

When the relative pronoun is preceded by *the only one of . . .* the verb is singular.

> He is the only one of the students who always studies early. [one studies]

 EXERCISE 2

Choose the correct verb for each sentence, making sure it agrees with its subject—an indefinite or a relative pronoun.

1. Neither of the labor leaders _____ (was/were) willing to negotiate further.
2. Winston Brown is one of those journalists who _____ (satirizes/satirize) politics.
3. None of the instruction manuals fully _____ (explains/ explain) the procedure.
4. Each of the techniques reviewed in this report _____ (requires/require) further research.
5. Pair ice-skating is the only one of the Olympic events that _____ (suggests/suggest) romantic love.

10f Subjects of Linking Verbs

Very often a linking verb connects a singular subject with a plural complement or a plural subject with a singular complement. (See subject complements, pp. 61–63.) Regardless of the number of the complement, the verb still agrees with its subject.

> My chief entertainment was the old movies on television.
>
> The old movies on television were my chief entertainment.

10g Subjects That Follow Verbs

Verbs agree with their subjects even when normal sentence order is inverted and the subjects are delayed.

> There are three reasons for the mistake.
>
> There is a good reason for the mistake.
>
> Covering the wall were dozens of ancestral portraits.
>
> Covering the wall was a medieval tapestry.

☐ EXERCISE 3

Choose the correct verb for each sentence, making sure it agrees with its subject. The problems involve linking verbs and subjects that follow verbs.

1. The main expense _____ (was/were) supplies, such as balsam, droppers, and Bunsen burners.
2. In the 1940s, all along the highway _____ (was/were) Burma-Shave signs.
3. There _____ (has/have) been six accidents at this intersection in three months.
4. My parents' main concern _____ (is/are) my grades.
5. Hanging in her closet _____ (was/were) three fur-lined coats.

10h Collective Nouns and Amounts as Subjects

A collective noun refers to a group that forms some sort of unit, for example, *team, class, audience, enemy, orchestra, panel, crew, family, club.* When these nouns refer to the group as a whole, they take a singular verb; when they refer to the individual members of the group, they take a plural verb.

> Parliament sits in majestic houses along the Thames. [*Parliament* refers to the governing body as a unit.]

> Parliament disagree on the tax issue. [*Parliament* refers to the individuals within the group since a unit cannot disagree with itself.]

> The team is on the court. [*Team* refers to the group as a unit.]

> The team are taking their practice shots. [*Team* refers to the individuals within the group since each team member must take practice shots by himself or herself.]

A plural verb with a collective noun (*team are*) sounds peculiar to most people and is therefore uncommon. Instead, writers usually prefer to pair a plural verb with a subject that is obviously plural.

> The members of Parliament disagree on the tax issue.

> The players are taking their practice shots.

When the subject refers to a unit amount, a kind of lump sum, the verb is singular; when the subject refers to several units, the verb is plural.

Four days seems a reasonable time.

Four days were marked off on the calendar.

Five acres is enough land for a truck farm.

Five acres are under cultivation.

When the word *number* is the subject and is preceded by *the,* its verb is singular; when preceded by *a,* its verb is plural.

The number of students taking workshops has increased.

A number of students have signed up for the workshop.

Sometimes with amounts, either a singular or a plural verb is appropriate.

Three truckloads of gravel was (or were) needed to fill the hole.

☐ EXERCISE 4

Choose the correct verb for each sentence, making sure the verb agrees with its subject—a collective noun or an amount.

1. The jury _____ (disagrees/disagree) with public opinion.
2. The number of accidents _____ (has/have) decreased since the new drunk-driving laws have been in effect.
3. Nine weeks _____ (is/are) a sufficient time to complete the exit ramps.
4. The crew _____ (is/are) wearing their new uniforms.
5. Six tons of crushed shells _____ (was/were) used in the project.

10i Titles and Proper Names as Subjects

Titles and proper names are considered singular, regardless of whether the words in them are singular or plural.

The United States is a republic.

Fifty Ways to Cook Hamburger does not sell well in gourmet food stores.

Hot Springs attracts tourists all year round.

10j Foreign Nouns as Subjects

Some nouns borrowed from foreign languages have retained their foreign plurals and do not "look" plural to an English speaker. If you are not sure about the number of a foreign noun, consult an up-to-date, standard dictionary. There you will find, for example, that *genera* is the plural form of *genus; bases,* the plural of *basis;* and *media,* the plural of *medium.*

Data is probably the most commonly used of these foreign nouns because it frequently occurs in technical literature. Traditionally, *datum* is the singular form and *data* is the plural.

> The data were gathered over a six-month period.

However, you rarely encounter the singular *datum;* and increasingly, *data* is being used by technical writers as a noncountable noun like *information.*

> The data was gathered over a period of six months.

10k Subjects Ending in *-ics*

A number of words in English end in *-ics: linguistics, physics, mathematics, economics, ceramics, statistics, ballistics, athletics, aerobics, gymnastics, calisthenics, acoustics, politics, ethics,* and so on. When referring to a body of knowledge, a field of study, or an activity, a noun ending in *-ics* requires a singular verb. When referring to the activities of an individual, the same noun requires a plural verb.

> Politics is one of the major industries in this country.
> His politics make me nervous.

> Calisthenics is required in the qualification trials.
> Calisthenics are simple gymnastic exercises.

10l "Words" as Subjects

A word cited as the word itself must be marked in one of two ways: enclosed in quotation marks or underlined (counterpart of italic type). Whether singular or plural, a word used as a word requires a singular verb.

> "Fiddlesticks" <u>was</u> my grandmother's favorite expression.
>
> In law, *person* <u>means</u> either a human being or an organization with legal rights.
>
> *People* <u>is</u> a plural noun.

EXERCISE 5

Choose the correct verb for each sentence, making sure it agrees with its subject—a title, a proper name, a foreign noun, a noun ending in *-ics,* or a word used as a word.

1. *Six Years with Cecil* _____ (is/are) a new novel by Sarah Hughes.
2. "Politics _____ (make/makes) strange bedfellows."
3. Sometimes, the media _____ (seem/seems) to revel in tragedy.
4. The acoustics in the new auditorium _____ (is/are) not good.
5. *Cattle* _____ (has/have) no singular form.
6. Ballistics, which _____ (is/are) the study of projectiles, has become a highly intricate discipline.
7. The bases of the argument _____ (seems/seem) to be rather petty.
8. Niagara Falls _____ (is/are) a breathtaking sight.
9. When I was a child, "The Three Little Pigs" _____ (was/were) my favorite story.
10. In most of the junk mail I receive, "free gifts" _____ (appears/appear) at least ten times.

EXERCISE 6

Correct any errors in subject-verb agreement in the following passage.

I don't know about other people, but the only one of life's rules that have no exceptions is this: the other lane or line always move faster than the one you are in.

Let's take, for example, my drive into town every morning. There are studies in "lane theory" that suggests that the left lane is preferable because people usually keep right. When I leave my house in the mornings, I pull into the closer lane: the left. For a few minutes I cruise along at a rapid pace. Suddenly in front of my car is about fifty drivers moving at 20 miles per hour. At this point cars in the right lane begins zipping past me like jackrabbits. I move quickly into the right lane, which slow immediately to a near halt. And so on it goes until I arrive at my destination, exhausted and frustrated.

Or take my weekly visit to the grocery store. After I've collected my groceries, I start evaluating the check-out lines. There is three things I consider: Does the check-out person move fast? How full is the baskets of the customers? How many people are in the line? Then I make a choice. Sometimes all the factors is in my favor: the person at the register is hustling, and three people with only a few purchases are ahead of me. But does my deliberations pay off? No. The first person in line has an item that is not priced, so someone working in the store walk down eight aisles, find the item price, and return to report. The second of the three customers want to write a check for $3.20 on a bank in another country, and the manager must be called to stare at the check and the customer for five minutes. The third customer has a large envelope full of coupons to sort through. As it turns out, six people with seventy-five dollars worth of groceries apiece gets through the line next to me while I have been standing in mine.

And let's take banks. At the drive-in window, I always get behind one of those people who is doing the daily deposits of businesses. Inside the bank, I get behind a crowd who is obtaining travelers' checks, wrapping coins into paper cylinders, or wiring money to Canada.

Since I cannot escape my fate, I am going to change my habits. I will leave home in the morning a half hour early and put books in my purse to read while standing in lines.

11

Incorrect Verb Forms

Problems with verb forms occur most commonly for three reasons.

1. Because a writer does not know the correct principal parts of irregular verbs and thus writes a verb such as *had went* for *had gone*
2. Because a writer transfers the sounds of speech to writing and drops a letter, producing a verb such as *use to* for *used to*
3. Because a writer confuses a verb with a word that closely resembles it, using *loose,* for example, instead of *lose*

The wrong verb form may not always obscure meaning. If you make the errors just described, a reader will possibly understand what you mean but will judge you uneducated—or at the very least, careless. Therefore, when revising your prose, you should make sure you have used verbs and their forms correctly.

11a Incorrect Principal Parts of Verbs

The principal parts of verbs include three forms.

1. Base form: used in the present tense and with some auxiliary verbs (e.g., *cure, does cure, will cure, should cure*)
2. Past form: used in the past tense (*cured*)
3. Past participle: used with *have* in perfect verbs (e.g., *have cured, had cured, will have cured*) and with *be* in passive verbs (e.g., *is cured, were cured, can be cured*)

101

vb
form
11a

Problems do not ordinarily arise with the principal parts of regular verbs because both the past and past participle forms are made by adding *-d* or *-ed* to the base. (See 4a.)

BASE FORM	PAST FORM	PAST PARTICIPLE FORM
believe	believed	believed
investigate	investigated	investigated
succeed	succeeded	succeeded
work	worked	worked

Most problems with principal parts arise with irregular verbs, which have unpredictable past and past participle forms. (See IRREGULAR VERB in "Glossary of Usage and Commonly Confused Words.")

BASE FORM	PAST FORM	PAST PARTICIPLE FORM
bet	bet	bet
begin	began	begun
choose	chose	chosen
come	came	come
drive	drove	driven
think	thought	thought

If you are not sure of the standard parts of a verb, look that verb up in a dictionary. Any standard desk dictionary lists the principal parts of irregular verbs, and some list even the principal parts of regular verbs. If no principal parts are given, you may assume that the verb is regular.

☐ EXERCISE 1

List the past and past participle forms of the following verbs. If you are not sure of a form, you should look the verb up in a dictionary.

Base	*Past Form*	*Past Participle Form*
1. dive		
2. dream		
3. let		
4. cleave		
5. bid		
6. spin		
7. prove		
8. spring		
9. sing		
10. pit		

11b Dropped -s/-es and -d/-ed Verb Endings

Two important verb endings are *-s/-es* and *-d/-ed*. The *-s/-es* occurs with all verbs in the present tense singular, except those whose subjects are *I* and *you*. The *-d/-ed* occurs with regular verbs to form the past tense and past participle. In conversation, speakers sometimes drop these endings, producing verb forms such as the ones in the following sentences.

-s DROPPED: "He exist on potato chips and sodas."

-es DROPPED: "She sometimes miss the bus."

-d DROPPED: "We use to go to New Orleans every year."

-d DROPPED: "Tom drank a quart of ice tea."

-ed DROPPED: "They box the equipment yesterday."

In writing, however, you must retain the *-s/-es* and *-d/-ed*, regardless of whether you would pronounce them. Dropping these important endings will result in incorrect verb forms:

INCORRECT: That reporter always ask personal questions.

CORRECT: That reporter always asks personal questions.

INCORRECT: The players are suppose to practice every day.

CORRECT: The players are supposed to practice every day.

INCORRECT: You cannot successfully reheat bake potatoes.

CORRECT: You cannot successfully reheat baked potatoes.

EXERCISE 2

In the following passage, add *-s/-es* and *-d/-ed* endings on verbs and verb forms where necessary.

I have a friend who insist that she never sleeps over three hours a night and thinks she is suppose to sleep about eight hours. Since I use to have the same problem, I suggested a few steps she might take before she waste money on a sleep-therapy course that cost $300.

First, anyone rest better when completely relax. Therefore, an insomniac should stop worrying about sleep because worry increase tension. Second, if a sleepless person resist eating spicy foods (such as barbeque potato chips and pizza), sleep will be more peaceful. Also, going to bed at a fix time helps develop a rhythm and makes it easier to fall asleep. In case everything else fail, there are always sheep to count.

11c Verbs Confused with Similar Words

Some verbs closely resemble other words in spelling, pronunciation, or meaning. For example, *affect* is often confused with *effect* because the two words look and sound so much alike; however, they have very different uses. *Affect* is usually a verb, meaning "to influence." *Effect* is usually a noun, meaning "a result." As a verb, *effect* means "to cause to occur."

> **Barometric pressure can <u>affect</u> our emotional states.**
>
> **We studied the <u>effect</u> of barometric pressure on emotions.**

Imply and *infer* are often confused because their meanings overlap somewhat. *Imply* usually means "to suggest, without stating directly"; *infer* usually means "to draw a conclusion." Thus, a speaker or writer implies; a listener or reader infers.

> **The announcer <u>implied</u> that the game was fixed.**
>
> **I <u>inferred</u> from the announcer's remark that the game was fixed.**

The verbs *lie* and *lay* are troublesome for several reasons. They look and sound much the same: each is a three-letter word beginning with *l*. They have a principal part in common: the base form of *lay* is the past form of *lie* (*lay, laid, laid; lie, lay, lain*). In addition, their meanings are closely related. *Lay* means "to put or place"; *lie* means "to rest or recline."

> **Don't <u>lay</u> wet towels on the furniture.**
>
> **Don't <u>lie</u> in the sun too long.**

Regardless of the source of confusion—spelling, pronunciation, or meaning—you can solve the problem by looking up a troublesome verb in a dictionary. There you will find the principal parts, the meaning, and sometimes notes on usage. Furthermore, the following pairs of words are discussed in the "Glossary of Usage and Commonly Confused Words."

accept, except	burst, bust
advice, advise	censor, censure
affect, effect	complement, compliment
aggravate, irritate	comprise, compose
bring, take	convince, persuade

device, devise	lose, loose
emigrate, immigrate	orient, orientate
ensure, insure	precede, proceed
hanged, hung	prosecute, persecute
imply, infer	raise, rise
lay, lie	set, sit
lend, loan	use, utilize

 EXERCISE 3

Look up the following pairs of words in the "Glossary of Usage and Commonly Confused Words" at the end of this textbook. For each word, write a sentence that illustrates its meaning.

1. advise/advice
2. censor/censure
3. device/devise

4. ensure/insure
5. lie/lay
6. sit/set

 EXERCISE 4

Choose the correct verb for each sentence.

1. The Vietnam War had a profound _____ (affect/effect) on the generation of the 1960s.
2. The weak connection caused the transmitter to _____ (lose/loose) power.
3. The "Delta" refers to the region that _____ (lays/lies) between the Mississippi and the Yazoo rivers.
4. _____ (Lie/Lay) this quilt across the foot of the bed.
5. By her facial expression, she _____ (implied/inferred) more than she actually said.

 EXERCISE 5

In blanks in the following passage, insert the correct past and past participle forms of the verbs called for. Pay particular attention to irregular verbs and verbs easily confused with other words. Also, be sure to retain the -d/-ed ending on verbs like *used* (*to*).

Last Saturday, a crowd of several hundred gathered to watch the demolition of the old Edgewater Beach Hotel, a structure that had _____ (stand) for more than a hundred years. In the nineteenth century, the Edgewater had _____ (be) a gathering place for the idle rich. In the twentieth, it had _____ (see) elderly couples reliving their youth, teenagers attending basketball tournaments, and even the wrath of Hurricane Camille. Last Saturday, the demolition crew was _____ (suppose) to destroy it so that a new Sears store could be _____ (build) in its place.

On Friday the crew had _____ (set) the charges. And on Saturday the crowd gathered to cheer for the Edgewater, expecting in some vague way that she might defy this onslaught as she _____ (use) to defy tourists, teenagers, and hurricanes for decades.

The crew _____ (put) on their hard hats, _____ (wave) the crowd back to a safe distance, and _____ (detonate) the charges. Nothing _____ (happen). The Edgewater _____ (stand) fast. The crowd _____ (cheer) madly.

For three hours, the crew _____ (reset) the charges. A strange hush _____ (lay) over the crowd. No one _____ (leave). Finally, the crew _____ (signal) again. The levers _____ (go) down. The Edgewater _____ (shudder), then _____ (shook), but _____ (stand). A great roar _____ (burst) from the crowd. Then people _____ (begin) to sing "We shall overcome." But they had _____ (forget) the deadly certainty of technology.

The crew _____ (dive) in again. And after hours of labor, they _____ (blow) down the Edgewater. She _____ (sink) into a pile of rubble.

12

Pronoun Reference

A pronoun's antecedent is the person, thing, or idea to which the pronoun refers. Normally, a pronoun takes its meaning from its antecedent.

> The French flag is called the "Tricolor" because it has three vertical bands of different colors. [The pronoun *it* stands for the antecedent *the French flag.*]
>
> Nathaniel Currier issued his first two prints in 1835. [The pronoun *his* stands for the antecedent *Nathaniel Currier.*]

When you revise, you should make sure that the reference of each pronoun is absolutely clear. The following discussion covers the common problems of pronoun reference.

12a Implied Reference

When a pronoun refers to a noun antecedent that is not stated but merely implied, the result is called an *implied reference*. In the following sentence, for example, the appropriate antecedent of *one, horse,* is not stated.

> IMPLIED REFERENCE: At first, horseback riding scared me because I had never been on <u>one</u>.

The sentence can be revised by providing a clear antecedent or by removing the pronoun.

CLEAR ANTECEDENT: At first, I was scared to ride <u>a horse</u> because I had never been on <u>one</u>.

REMOVAL OF PRONOUN: At first, horseback riding scared me because I had never ridden before.

In the next sentence, the possessive *Homer's* is functioning as a modifier, not as a noun, and therefore cannot serve as the antecedent of *he*.

IMPLIED REFERENCE: In Homer's poems, <u>he</u> recounts the events of the Trojan War.

An antecedent can be provided, or *he* can be eliminated.

CLEAR ANTECEDENT: In <u>his</u> poems, <u>Homer</u> recounts the events of the Trojan War.

REMOVAL OF PRONOUN: Homer's poems recount the events of the Trojan War.

12b Broad Reference

"Broad reference" is the use of a pronoun to refer to ideas expressed in preceding clauses or sentences. Although broad reference is sometimes clear to readers, it can cause confusion. For example, in the following passage, a reader cannot be sure which of the facts are referred to by the pronoun *this*.

BROAD REFERENCE: The space above the spout of a boiling kettle of water is filled with a gas called "water vapor," or "steam." The visible cloud above this space is not steam but droplets of water formed when the gas cools. <u>This</u> is called "condensation."

You can easily avoid this kind of broad reference by supplying a noun or noun phrase that describes the idea referred to.

REVISED: The space above the spout of a boiling kettle of water is filled with a gas called "water vapor," or "steam." The visible cloud above this space is not steam but droplets of water formed when the gas cools. <u>This droplet formation</u> is called "condensation."

Another kind of broad reference involves a dependent clause that begins with *which*.

BROAD REFERENCE: Next semester, personal computers can be connected to the university system, <u>which</u> will reduce the amount of equipment students will need to work at home.

The pronoun *which* seems to refer to *university system* but, in fact, refers to the entire idea expressed by the preceding clause: "Next semester, personal computers can be connected to the university system." The sentence should be revised to provide a clear antecedent for *which* or to remove the pronoun.

CLEAR ANTECEDENT: Next semester, personal computers can be connected to the university system—an <u>arrangement which</u> will reduce the amount of equipment students will need to work at home.

REMOVAL OF PRONOUN: Next semester, personal computers can be connected to the university system in order to reduce the amount of equipment students will need to work at home.

12c Indefinite *You, They,* and *It*

In conversation, speakers frequently use *you, they,* and *it* indefinitely—that is, to refer to people or things in general. This kind of reference, however, is not acceptable in formal writing.

INDEFINITE YOU: <u>You</u> can inherit certain diseases.

REVISED: People can inherit certain diseases.

INDEFINITE THEY: In Houston <u>they</u> have thousands of acres of parks.

REVISED: Houston has thousands of acres of parks.

INDEFINITE IT: <u>It</u> states in the Declaration of Independence that everyone is created equal.

REVISED: Jefferson states in the Declaration of Independence that everyone is created equal.

☐ EXERCISE 1

In the following sentences, correct any errors in implied, broad, or indefinite pronoun reference.

1. The fabric can be cleaned, but it must be done by a professional.
2. Keep the steps simple, and do not combine them. This simplifies the job of converting the steps into a chart.
3. In many states, they do not require a test for the renewal of a driver's license.
4. It says in the article that the number of "reentry" students is increasing rapidly.
5. One way to give pills to a dog is to hide them in hot dogs, which is called the "hollow-weenie" method.

12d Ambiguous Reference

Reference is "ambiguous" when a pronoun has more than one possible antecedent. A pronoun should refer unmistakably to one antecedent.

> AMBIGUOUS REFERENCE: **When the fire fighters met with the city council members, they outlined the problems.**

In this sentence, *they* can refer to *fire fighters,* to *city council members,* or to both. The sentence must be revised to eliminate the ambiguity.

> REVISED: **The fire fighters, who outlined the problems, met with the city council members.**

> REVISED: **The fire fighters met with the city council members, who outlined the problems.**

> REVISED: **At the meeting, the fire fighters and the council members outlined the problems.**

Another type of ambiguous references involves one antecedent for either of two possible pronouns.

> AMBIGUOUS REFERENCE: **Of all the candidates, she was most impressed by him.**

The sentence can mean either that "she" or that "he" was the candidate. The sentence can be revised to convey either meaning.

> REVISED: **She thought he was the most impressive of the candidates.**

> REVISED: **She, of all the candidates, was most impressed by him.**

12e   Mixed Uses of *It*

The word *it* is used in several ways.

- As a personal pronoun referring to a noun or noun phrase previously mentioned

> As soon as I saw that Corvette, I knew I wanted it. [*It* refers to *that Corvette.*]

- As an expletive—a function word that begins a sentence and delays the subject

> It is dangerous to sleep in the sun. [*It* is an expletive; *to sleep in the sun* is the subject.]

- With *do,* as a predicate substitute

> If you really want to go to law school, you should do it. [*Do it* stands for part of the predicate, *go to law school.*]

When the uses are mixed in the same sentence or in sequential sentences, the result is an awkward structure.

> AWKWARD MIXED USE
>
> Our financial adviser suggests that we sell our house since it [personal pronoun] has become a drain on our budget. It [expletive] is hard, however, to let go of a place with beautiful memories; and we really don't want to do it [predicate substitute].

For clarity's sake, the passage should be rewritten to eliminate mixed use of *it.* In the following revised version, *it* is used twice as a personal pronoun, referring to *house.*

> REVISED
>
> Our financial adviser suggests that we sell our house since it has become a drain on our budget. The house is so full of beautiful memories, however, that we don't want give it up.

☐ EXERCISE 2

In the following sentences, correct any errors in ambiguous pronoun reference and in the mixed uses of *it.*

1. My job at Jiffy Car Wash was to take the hub caps off the wheels and wash them.

2. When they presented Max with the award for outstanding athlete, it was obvious that he expected to win it.
3. I threw my radio against the window and shattered it.
4. The chef told the head waiter that his job was not to flatter customers.
5. He wrote the song "Take My Love or Take a Bus." It said in the interview that it was for a country-and-western band that he wrote it.

12f Remote Reference

A pronoun must be close enough to its antecedent to make the reference instantly clear. For example, in the following passage, a sentence intervenes between the pronoun *they* and its antecedent *fairies.*

REMOTE ANTECEDENT

Fairies—small, magical creatures—appear in most of the folklore of the Middle Ages. During that time, belief in magic exerted a strong influence on human behavior. They might be mischievous, helpful, or fearsome; but always they interfered in the daily lives of the folk.

The pronouns are so remote from their antecedent that the reference is unclear. The problem can be solved easily by repeating the noun antecedent.

REVISED

Fairies—small, magical creatures—appear in most of the folklore of the Middle Ages. During that time, belief in magic exerted a strong influence on human behavior. Fairies might be mischievous, helpful, or fearsome; but always they interfered in the daily lives of the folk.

12g Titles as Antecedents

Titles of papers are not part of the text and cannot be the antecedents of pronouns.

NO ANTECEDENT

Glaciers

They are rivers of ice, with movement measured in inches per day instead of miles per hour. . . .

You must repeat a title or a part of it, no matter how close the pronoun is to the title.

**ref
12g**

REVISED

Glaciers

Glaciers are rivers of ice, with movement measured in inches per day instead of miles per hour. . . .

☐ EXERCISE 3

Revise the following passage to ensure that all pronoun references are clear.

The Typewriter Keyboard

The most conventional one is called "Qwerty," after the first six keys of the third row from the bottom. It was designed in 1873 to slow typists down, because the keys stuck if they went too fast.

Sticking keys are no longer a problem, and a better system is needed. Patented in 1936, the Dvorak-Dealy keyboard reduces fatigue and increases speed, which makes it more efficient. The most commonly used keys are on the second row from the bottom—vowels and punctuation on the left, consonants on the right. This reduces the distance that the fingers must cover. In fact, with the Dvorak-Dealy system, typists' fingers travel about one mile a day; with the Qwerty system, they move their fingers about eighteen miles a day.

With the increase in computer use, more and more people are learning to type. Perhaps if manufacturers would offer the Dvorak-Dealy system as an alternative keyboard, it would be possible that someday all typists would change to it.

13

Pronoun-Antecedent Agreement

A pronoun must agree in number with its antecedent—that is, the noun or noun phrase that the pronoun refers to. A singular antecedent requires a singular pronoun; a plural antecedent, a plural pronoun.

SINGULAR ANTECEDENT/ SINGULAR PRONOUN:	<u>The Amethyst</u> is usually purple or bluish-violet; <u>it</u> is a semiprecious stone made from a variety of quartz.
PLURAL ANTECEDENT/ PLURAL PRONOUN:	<u>Amethysts</u> are usually purple or bluish-violet; <u>they</u> are semiprecious stones made from a variety of quartz.

When revising, be sure that the pronouns agree with their antecedents. In most cases, you simply find the antecedent and check to see whether it matches the pronoun in number. In cases where the number of the antecedent is not obvious, the following guidelines will help you choose the appropriate pronouns.

114

13a Antecedents Joined by *And*

Usually, antecedents joined by *and* require a plural pronoun.

> PLURAL PRONOUN: The wombat and the bandicoot carry their young in pouches.

In two instances, however, antecedents joined by *and* require a singular pronoun.

1. When the antecedents refer to a single person, place, thing, or idea

> SINGULAR PROUNOUN: The judge and executioner eyed his victim impassively.

2. When *each* or *every* precedes the compound

> SINGULAR PROUNOUN: Each hot spell and each rainstorm took its toll on my dwindling vegetable garden.

> SINGULAR PRONOUN: Every retired bronc rider and calf roper in the Southwest had paid his entry fee.

13b Antecedents Joined by *Or/Nor*

When singular antecedents are joined by *or/nor,* the pronoun is singular; when plural antecedents are joined by *or/nor,* the pronoun is plural.

> SINGULAR PRONOUN: The field judge or the back judge blew his whistle.

> PLURAL PRONOUN: Neither the Russians nor the Chinese sent their delegations.

When one antecedent is singular and the other plural, the pronoun agrees with the nearer antecedent. To avoid an awkward sentence, place the plural antecedent nearer the pronoun.

> AWKWARD: Neither my grandparents nor my mother would sign her name to the petition.

> REVISED: Neither my mother nor my grandparents would sign their names to the petition.

13c Indefinite Pronouns and Sexist Language

Singular pronouns are used to refer to indefinite antecedents (such as *anyone, everyone, everybody, everything, no one, none, each, either*). (See 2e.)

> SINGULAR PRONOUN: **We tested everything in the area for its radiation level.**

In casual conversation, speakers often use a plural pronoun to refer to *everyone* and *everybody,* since these indefinites suggest plurality.

> INFORMAL USAGE: **Everyone in the auto-repair clinic must provide their own vehicle.**

But this construction is not acceptable in formal prose. *Everyone* is singular; therefore the pronoun *their* does not agree with its antecedent. One solution is to rewrite the sentence in the plural. In this case, the noun following *their* (*vehicles*) must also be plural: more than one participant, more than one vehicle.

> PLURAL NOUN AND PRONOUN: **Participants in the auto-repair clinic must provide their own vehicles.**

Another solution is to make the pronoun singular, but this option presents yet another problem. In the past, writers used a masculine pronoun to refer to both males and females. (See 32f, "Sexist Language.")

> OUTDATED USAGE: **Everyone in the auto-repair clinic must provide his own vehicle.**

Today, the use of a masculine pronoun for both men and women is considered sexist language. If you use *he/him/his* for both sexes, you stand to offend some readers—an offense that could cost you credibility, assistance, or even a job. Thus, if you don't like the plural option, you would be wise to use both a masculine and a feminine pronoun.

> SINGULAR PRONOUNS: **Everyone in the auto-repair clinic must provide his or her own vehicle.**

Remember, however, that frequent use of both the masculine and feminine pronouns in a single passage is awkward and wearisome. When possible, revise by switching to plurals or eliminating pronouns.

AWKWARD: Everyone in the auto-repair clinic must provide his or her vehicle so that he or she can work individually with instructors. The clinic, however, will furnish the tools needed by everyone for his or her hands-on training.

REVISED: Everyone in the auto-repair clinic must provide a vehicle so that individual instruction will be possible. The clinic, however, will furnish all the tools needed for hands-on training.

pn agr 13e

13d Generic Nouns and Sexist Language

Sexist language can be a problem when nouns are used generically to refer to all members of a group—*the astronaut* can refer to all astronauts, *the writer* to all writers, *the swimmer* to all swimmers, *the police officer* to all police officers. Even though these generic nouns refer to more than one person, they require singular pronouns. Formerly, writers used *he/him/his,* which were supposed to refer to both sexes. Today, the use of masculine pronouns to refer to both males and females is unacceptable. (See 32f, "Sexist Language.")

OUTDATED USAGE: The astronaut must begin his training long before a flight.

You can make such a sentence acceptable in three ways.

1. Include both the feminine and masculine singular pronouns.
2. Rewrite the sentence with plural nouns and pronouns.
3. Eliminate the pronoun altogether.

SINGULAR PRONOUNS: The astronaut must begin his or her training long before a flight.

PLURAL PRONOUN: Astronauts must begin their training long before flights.

NO PRONOUN: The astronaut must begin training long before a flight.

13e Collective Nouns as Antecedents

Collective nouns—such as *audience, jury, orchestra, committee, family*—are singular when they refer to a group as a unit and plural when they refer to the individual members in the group. Therefore, depending on their meanings, collective nouns may require singular or plural pronouns.

GROUP AS A UNIT: The family incorporated itself for tax purposes.

INDIVIDUAL MEMBERS: The family are squabbling over their grandfather's estate.

If *the family are* sounds peculiar to you—as it does to many people—you can always supply a subject that is clearly plural.

PLURAL SUBJECT: The members of the family are squabbling over their grandfather's estate.

☐ EXERCISE 1

Rewrite the following sentences to make pronouns and antecedents agree and to avoid sexist language.

1. Each salesperson and each manager must submit their job description annually.
2. Neither the faculty members nor Dean Harper gave their approval to the new curriculum.
3. Everyone on board the ship had saved money for more than five years to pay for their passage.
4. A civil engineer should make sure that he has a thorough knowledge of architectural history.
5. When the jury delivered their verdict, reporters raced from the courtroom.
6. Did the popcorn or the pretzels have its ingredients listed on the package?
7. Both the angler fish and the stargazer have "lures" to attract its prey.
8. Every citizen should keep informed about how their tax money is spent.
9. A nurse under stress may do their job inefficiently and unsafely.
10. The Cadillac or the Buick is supposed to have their transmission fixed today.

☐ EXERCISE 2

Edit the following passage to ensure that pronouns and antecedents agree.

Because Shakespeare wrote for his audience, we can learn much about his plays by looking at the people who attended the Globe Theater.

The average theatergoer did not question the social or political system, in which everyone knew their place. They had inherited a belief in an ordered universe. And yet that order was threatening to collapse. Both the aristocrat and the commoner in Shakespeare's day began to think that his ordered world might be shattered.

This conflict was partially responsible for the excellence of Shakespeare's work. Theodore Spencer suggests that great tragedy is written in periods when a person's patterns of behavior and their beliefs are threatened. Probably neither the theatergoers nor Shakespeare realized how soon their social order would collapse. But they were aware of the conflict. And in the conflict were some of the components of Shakespeare's remarkable plays.

☐ EXERCISE 3

Revise the following passage to eliminate sexist language. Make sure that in your revision each pronoun agrees with its antecedent.

The Cooperative Education Program allows the student to alternate his academic study with periods of work related to his major. Trained advisors assist the student in securing employment that will provide him with practical work experience as well as financial aid to support his education. Any student with an overall GPA of 2.50 is eligible to enter the program after he has completed forty-five hours. An applicant should submit the names of four character references, including at least one member of the business community, who must write his assessment of the student's employment potential.

14

Case of Nouns and Pronouns

Nouns and pronouns have *case;* that is, they have different forms for different functions. All nouns and most pronouns have two cases: common and possessive. A few pronouns, however, have three: subjective, objective, and possessive.

Two Cases

COMMON: president, week, Ann, it, you, everybody

POSSESSIVE: president's, week's, Ann's, its, your/yours, everybody's

The *common* forms are used for all noun and pronoun functions except possession.

> The president abstained. [subject]
>
> The meeting is this week. [subject complement]
>
> They named the cat Ann. [object complement]
>
> I used to have a watch, but I broke it. [direct object]
>
> Sam gave you the tickets. [indirect object]
>
> The rule applies to everybody. [object of preposition]

The *possessive* forms express ideas such as ownership, measurement, authorship, and origin or source: *president's power, week's pay, Ann's poems, your phone.*

Three Cases

SUBJECTIVE: I, he, she, we, they, who, whoever

OBJECTIVE: me, him, her, us, them, whom, whomever

POSSESSIVE: my/mine, his, her/hers, our/ours, their/theirs, whose

The subjective forms are used as subjects and subject complements (or predicate nominatives). Also, since appositives have the same case as words they rename, appositives to subjects and subject complements are in the subjective form.

> We fed the animals a high-protein diet. [subject]
>
> The first guest to arrive was she. [subject complement]
>
> The finalists, Hoffman and he, compete next week. [appositive renaming subject]

The objective forms are used as objects, appositives to objects, and subjects and objects of infinitives.

> The voters will never elect him. [direct object]
>
> The new hospital gave them hope. [indirect object]
>
> I felt the painting looking at me. [object of preposition]
>
> The decision affects only two people, my daughter and me. [appositive renaming direct object]
>
> My manager wanted me to hire them. [subject and object of infinitive]

The *possessive* forms are used to express source, authorship, and ownership: *her request, whose novel, their Mercedes.*

In addition to case, some pronouns have forms made with the suffixes *-self* and *-selves: myself, yourself, himself, herself, itself, ourselves, yourselves, themselves.* These forms are used in two ways.

- **As reflexives**

Reflexives are objects that rename subjects.

> She corrected herself.
>
> The winners congratulated themselves.
>
> I was ashamed of myself.

- **As emphatics**

Emphatics are pronouns that repeat, for emphasis, the nouns or pronouns they refer to.

> The owner himself waited on tables.
>
> You must write the letter yourself.
>
> They catered the party themselves.

Use of incorrect pronoun case does not ordinarily cause misunderstanding for the reader. Nevertheless, if you do use the wrong case, your writing can seem juvenile and nonstandard. Therefore, when you revise your papers, check the case of pronouns carefully. The following guidelines should help you choose the appropriate forms.

14a Case in Compound Constructions

Compounding in no way affects the case of a pronoun. When in doubt about which case is appropriate, simply drop all other elements in the compound. Then you can readily determine the correct form.

> The Senator hired Mary and _____ (I or me). [You would write *The Senator hired me,* not *The Senator hired I.* Thus, the correct sentence is *The Senator hired Mary and me.*]

> Both his brother and _____ (he or him) attended Yale. [You would write *He attended Yale,* not *Him attended Yale.* Thus, the correct sentence is *Both his brother and he attended Yale.*]

In a compound appositive, a pronoun's case depends on the use of the word that the appositive renames: an appositive renaming a subject or subject complement is in the subjective case; an appositive renaming an object or object complement is in the objective case.

> The centers, Hackett and he, were benched for fighting. [*Hackett and he* renames the subject, *centers.* Thus, the pronoun is in the subjective case.]

> The cabin was built by three people—Craig, Ray, and me. [*Craig, Ray, and me* renames *people,* the object of the preposition *by.* Thus, the pronoun is in the objective case.]

Compounds that often cause mistakes contain pronouns in the first person singular: *between you and I* and *Carl and myself.* Always use *me* as the object of any preposition, regardless of the context.

> INCORRECT: Just between you and I, the credit union is in financial trouble.

> CORRECT: Just between you and me, the credit union is in financial trouble.

The pronoun *myself* is properly used only as a reflexive or an emphatic (see p. 121). Never use *myself* when the subjective or objective case is called for.

INCORRECT: Brett and <u>myself</u> had dinner at Antoine's.

CORRECT: Brett and <u>I</u> had dinner at Antoine's.

INCORRECT: The coach saw Lee and <u>myself</u> at the party.

CORRECT: The coach saw Lee and <u>me</u> at the party.

☐ EXERCISE 1

For each sentence, choose the pronoun in the appropriate form.

1. According to the *Old Farmer's Almanac,* which my father and _____ (I, me) rely on, March 5 will be flannel-pajama weather.
2. In the Chinese restaurant, Luke and _____ (I, myself) got the same fortune cookie message: "Big Luck to Big Tippers."
3. My grandmother divided her property between _____ (he, him) and _____ (I, me).
4. The credit for the team's performance must go to two people, the coach and _____ (he, him).
5. The attendant told Mr. Ford and _____(she, her) that the flight had been delayed.

14b Pronoun Case After *Be*

In conversational English, most people use pronouns in the objective case as complements of *be.*

INFORMAL: It's <u>me</u>.

INFORMAL: That's <u>him</u>.

Although the objective case is appropriate in conversation, the subjective case is required in formal writing.

FORMAL: The first dignitary presented at state occasions was always <u>he</u>.

FORMAL: The only medical doctor in the county was <u>she</u>.

☐ EXERCISE 2

In each sentence, choose the form of the pronoun appropriate in formal writing.

1. It wasn't _____ (I, me) who recommended the course.
2. The best violinist in the orchestra is _____ (she, her).

3. The employee who most often used the microfiche machine was _____ (he, him).
4. It was _____ (they, them) who wrote the script.
5. They discovered that it was _____ (I, me) who had called.

14c *Who/Whom* and *Whoever/Whomever*

The form *whom* is rare in spoken English, but in written language it is expected. Therefore, when you write, you should observe the case distinctions between *who/whoever* (subjective case) and *whom/whomever* (objective case).

To use the forms correctly, you must determine the pronoun's use in its own clause—whether independent or dependent. You can make this determination by the following method.

1. Isolate the pronoun's clause.
2. If the clause is inverted, put the parts in normal order (subject + verb + other elements).
3. Substitute pronouns to see which fits. If *he, she,* or *they* fits, use *who* or *whoever.* If *him, her,* or *them* fits, use *whom* or *whomever.*

A few sample sentences will illustrate the method.

> Who/whom did you contact?
> You did contact who/whom?
> You did contact him.
> Whom did you contact?

> These are the recruits (who/whom) we think will go to OCS.
> Who/whom will go to OCS.
> They will go to OCS.
> These are the recruits who we think will go to OCS.

> The newspaper always attacks (whoever/whomever) the governor appoints.
> The governor appoints whoever/whomever.
> The governor appoints her.
> The newspaper always attacks whomever the governor appoints.

☐ EXERCISE 3

Insert *who, whoever, whom,* or *whomever* in each of the following sentences. (Remember to base your decision on the use of the pronoun in its own clause.)

1. The conference will be attended by those _____ teach psychology in senior colleges.
2. The position should be filled by someone _____ our clients will trust.
3. Show this pass to _____ is at the gate.
4. He is the actor _____ they say the director slapped.
5. The delegation met with the Prime Minister, _____ they assumed was in a position to make decisions.
6. Do you know someone _____ we can ask?
7. You can get through a class reunion by saying "You look fantastic!" to _____ you don't remember.
8. My grandmother knew a man _____ groomed Teddy Roosevelt's horse.
9. _____ stole my car now owns a gas guzzler that breaks down every fifteen miles.
10. _____ did he say wrote that novel?

14d Case in Elliptical Clauses

Dependent clauses introduced by *than* or *as* are often elliptical— that is, some parts are not stated but understood (see 7c. 4). When an elliptical clause contains a pronoun, you might have to fill in the missing parts to determine the pronoun's case. For example, suppose you were trying to decide whether to use *she* or *her* in the following sentence: *Her parents seemed younger than.* . . . Completing the sentence will tell you which form is correct.

> ELLIPTICAL: **Her parents seemed younger than she.**
>
> COMPLETE: **Her parents seemed younger than she seemed.**

In some elliptical clauses, either subjective or objective case is possible. Be sure to choose the pronoun form that conveys the intended meaning.

> ELLIPTICAL: **The skiing lessons helped Joan more than I.**
>
> COMPLETE: **The skiing lessons helped Joan more than I helped Joan.**

ELLIPTICAL: The skiing lessons helped Joan more than <u>me</u>.

COMPLETE: The skiing lessons helped Joan more than <u>they helped me</u>.

ELLIPTICAL: Her friends annoy me as much as <u>she</u>.

COMPLETE: Her friends annoy me as much as <u>she annoys me</u>.

ELLIPTICAL: Her friends annoy me as much as <u>her</u>.

COMPLETE: Her friends annoy me as much as <u>they annoy her</u>.

☐ EXERCISE 4

Supply the correct pronouns in the following sentences. If either the subjective or objective case is possible, explain why.

1. Anyone in the department can edit the report as well as _____ . (I/me)
2. A monarchy is not an appropriate government for people such as _____ . (they/them)
3. She writes about Jefferson as well as _____ . (he/him)
4. Mr. Thames, rather than _____ , should present the award. (she/her)
5. We understood their ideas better than _____ . (they/them)

14e Possessive Case with Gerunds

A gerund is the *-ing* form of a verb functioning as a noun (see 5b). In formal prose, nouns and pronouns acting as determiners for gerunds must be in the possessive case: *my singing, Frank's passing, their whispering*. In conversation, you might say, "I don't mind him spending the money." But you should write, "The public objected to his spending money on state dinners"—because it is the spending that the public objects to, not him. *His* identifies whose spending it was.

INFORMAL: I was tired of <u>Jim</u> copying my homework.

FORMAL: I was tired of <u>Jim's</u> copying my homework.

INFORMAL: The security office objected to <u>them</u> parking in the fire lanes.

FORMAL: The security office objected to <u>their</u> parking in the fire lanes.

❑ EXERCISE 5

In the following sentences, change nouns and pronouns to the possessive case where necessary.

1. My teacher insists on me typing all the essay tests.
2. I am bored with him constantly whining about life's injustices.
3. We are concerned over the project getting funded.
4. The State Department objected to them traveling to Libya.
5. I appreciated the driver letting me change lanes.

❑ EXERCISE 6

Revise the following passages to correct any errors in noun or pronoun forms.

1.   Whenever my neighbors get a new dog, they get a terrier who they always name Fido. This habit is almost as old-fashioned as my father naming his dog Rover. One man who I know called his dogs clever names like Go Away and Let Go. Between you and I, these silly names would embarrass any decent, self-respecting dog. Then, there are the American Kennel Club members, to who we are indebted for such names as Jo-Ni's Red Baron of Crofton, Sir Lancelot of Barvan, and St. Aubrey Dragonora of Elsdon.

    My brother and me have a solution to all this nonsense. We favor names like Sam and Jake for our dogs. You can't find more sensible names than them, and sensible animals deserve sensible names.

2.   We began the study in fall 1985 at the University Sleep Center. The subjects were divided into two groups—one monitored by Dr. Patricia Goldin and myself, the other by a team of Austrian researchers. The participants who Dr. Goldin and me worked with were all under thirty years of age. None of the subjects objected to us monitoring them breathing during deep and twilight sleep. The subjects who we monitored recorded their breathing habits during waking hours. Dr. Goldin divided the collected data between the Austrian team and I for analysis.

15

Incorrect Adjective and Adverb Forms

Adjectives and adverbs are modifiers—that is, they describe and qualify other elements of sentences. Adjectives modify nouns and pronouns; adverbs modify verbs, adjectives, other adverbs, and whole clauses. (See also 3a and 3b.) Many adjectives and adverbs have characteristic forms. Confusion or misuse of these forms will produce nonstandard English.

15a Confusion of Adjectives and Adverbs

Be careful not to substitute adjectives for adverbs. A few adjectives and adverbs (such as *fast, early, late*) share identical forms. However, the adjective and adverb forms of most modifiers are different. In fact, many adverbs are formed by adding *-ly* to adjectives. For example, *serious* and *perfect* are adjectives; *seriously* and *perfectly* are adverbs.

ADJECTIVE SUBSTITUTED FOR ADVERB: We talked serious about our future.

CORRECT USE OF ADVERB: We talked seriously about our future. [*seriously* modifying *talked*]

CORRECT USE OF ADJECTIVE: We had a serious conversation about our future. [*serious* modifying *conversation*]

ADJECTIVE SUBSTITUTED FOR ADVERB: He recited the speech perfect.

CORRECT USE OF ADVERB: He recited the speech perfectly. [*perfectly* modifying *recited*]

CORRECT USE OF ADJECTIVE: His speech was perfect. [*perfect* modifying *speech*]

**ad
15a**

You probably have little difficulty with modifiers such as *serious/seriously* and *perfect/perfectly*. However, because of a conflict between conversational and written English, a few pairs of modifiers are particularly troublesome.

awful/awfully	**most/almost**
bad/badly	**real/really**
good/well	

The adjective forms of these modifiers should be used after linking verbs such as *feel, taste,* and *sound.*

INCORRECT ADVERB FORM: I feel badly.

CORRECT ADJECTIVE FORM: I feel bad.

If you have problems with any of these troublesome modifiers, look them up in "Glossary of Usage and Commonly Confused Words" at the end of this book. There they are defined, and their appropriate uses are discussed and illustrated.

☐ EXERCISE 1

Choose the correct adjective or adverb for each sentence. When in doubt about the correct choice, look the options up in the Glossary.

1. The linguini tastes _____. (good, well)
2. I feel _____ about the mistake. (bad, badly)
3. The health farm is a _____ expensive resort. (real, really)
4. It _____ always rains during our annual rodeo. (most, almost)
5. The child reads exceptionally _____. (good, well)
6. The steak was _____ burned. (bad/badly)
7. If we are going to perform well, we must practice _____. (regular, regularly)
8. She spoke so _____ that I could not hear her. (quiet/ quietly)

9. The employees felt _____ about the layoff. (bitter/
bitterly)

10. Our test was _____ hard. (awful/awfully)

15b Inappropriate Comparative and Superlative Forms

A characteristic of adjectives and adverbs is that they can express degree: the comparative is used to compare two items; the superlative is used to compare more than two items. These degrees are expressed either by the -er and -est endings or by *more* and *most.* (See 3c.)

POSITIVE: The roast beef is cheap.

COMPARATIVE: The roast beef is cheaper than the sirloin.

SUPERLATIVE: The roast beef is the cheapest item on the menu.

POSITIVE: The sunsets here are beautiful.

COMPARATIVE: The sunsets here are more beautiful than those in the East.

SUPERLATIVE: The sunsets here are the most beautiful in the world.

Do not use the comparative form to refer to more than two items or the superlative to refer to only two.

INCORRECT COMPARATIVE: Jones is the more interesting of all the lecturers.

REVISED: Jones is the most interesting of all the lecturers.

INCORRECT SUPERLATIVE: We should buy the fastest of the two printers.

REVISED: We should buy the faster of the two printers.

Avoid double comparisons—the use of *more* or *most* with another comparative or superlative modifer. Sentences containing double comparisons sound childlike or uneducated.

DOUBLE COMPARISON: This summer is more hotter than the last.

REVISED: This summer is hotter than the last.

**ad
15c**

DOUBLE COMPARISON:	The <u>most unusualest</u> piece in the collection was an ebony necklace.
REVISED:	The <u>most unusual</u> piece in the collection was an ebony necklace.

Some adjectives, called *absolutes,* cannot logically express degree. For example, one thing cannot be "more first" than another nor "more infinite": something is either first or not, either finite or infinite. About other adjectives, however, there is disagreement. Some people claim that perfection, uniqueness, and correctness can be approximated. Thus, one thing can be "more perfect," "more unique," or "more correct" than another. Other people apply strict logic: something is either "perfect" or "imperfect," "unique" or "not unique," "correct" or "incorrect."

Since many readers disapprove of the comparison of absolutes, you should avoid the usage. You can always insert "more nearly" before the adjective.

QUESTIONABLE COMPARISON:	The second portrait is a <u>more perfect</u> likeness than the first.
REVISED:	The second portrait is a <u>more nearly perfect</u> likeness than the first.

☐ EXERCISE 2

In the following sentences, correct any errors in the comparative and superlative forms of adjectives and adverbs.

1. German shepherds are the more dependable of all the popular guide dogs for the blind.
2. The Smithsonian is the most complete of the two museums.
3. The grass on the front lawn is deader than that on the back.
4. The new missile is more faster than its predecessor.
5. The mainest thing to remember is that the clutch doesn't work.

15c Inappropriate Demonstratives

The demonstratives (*this, that, these,* and *those*) can function not only as pronouns but also as determiners—*this concept, that tablet, these entries, those mistakes.* Only two problems are usually associated with these modifiers.

- The incorrect use of *them* in place of *these* or *those*

    INCORRECT: Them shoes were half price.

    REVISED: Those shoes were half price.

- The incorrect use of *these* instead of *this* before a singular noun like *kind, sort, type*

    INCORRECT: These kind of flowers bloom twice a year.

    REVISED: This kind of flower blooms twice a year.

    REVISED: These kinds of flowers bloom twice a year.

☐ EXERCISE 3

Revise the following passage to correct any adjective or adverb errors.

It used to be real hard for me to leave a party. I would have the most hardest math test the next day and need to study, but I couldn't find a polite way to leave. Every time I was the first person to go, people would say they felt badly that I did not have a good time or that I should wait to hear their new guitar. These kind of remarks drove me crazy.

For a while, I tried two excuses. The best one was that I had to leave to let my dogs out of the house. The worst was that a spell of nausea had overtaken me very sudden. But no one took them excuses serious.

The silly thing is that most of the time, people don't actually care when I leave. They are merely being nice. So now I simply leave rapid before anyone notices that I am gone.

16

Dangling and Misplaced Modifiers

The function of modifiers is to describe other words—to qualify, limit, intensify, or explain them. Thus, modifiers and the words they describe form a close relationship, which must be immediately clear to readers. When a modifier is not clearly related to any other word in its sentence, it is called *dangling*.

> DANGLING PHRASE: To have a successful camping trip, the right equipment must be packed.
>
> REVISED: To have a successful trip, campers must pack the right equipment.
>
> DANGLING CLAUSE: When covered with a fine white ash, the chicken should be placed on the grill.
>
> REVISED: When the coals are covered with a fine white ash, the chicken should be placed on the grill.

When a modifier seems to relate to the wrong element in a sentence, it is called misplaced.

> MISPLACED PHRASE: He led me to a corner table with a sneer.
>
> REVISED: With a sneer, he led me to a corner table.
>
> MISPLACED CLAUSE: We cooked fresh vegetables on an old wood stove that we had picked that morning.
>
> REVISED: On an old wood stove, we cooked fresh vegetables that we had picked that morning.

133

Both types of faulty modification can create awkward and confusing constructions. Therefore, when you revise your writing, watch for dangling and misplaced modifiers, and rewrite to eliminate them.

16a Dangling Modifiers

Although any modifier can dangle, the problem occurs most commonly with verbal phrases and elliptical clauses. (See Chapter 5 and 7c.4.)

(1) Dangling verbals: participles, infinitives, and gerunds

When functioning as a modifier, a verbal phrase must refer logically to some word that is the agent of the verbal's action. When no such word appears in the sentence, the verbal phrase is said to dangle. Although a dangling verbal phrase can appear in the middle or at the end of a sentence, it is usually introductory. In the introductory position, a verbal must modify the subject of the following clause—that is, the agent of the verbal's action must be the subject of the clause. You can revise dangling verbals in two ways.

- **Supply an agent for the verbal's action.**
- **Restructure the sentence to eliminate the verbal phrase.**

DANGLING PARTICIPLE: Scoring a touchdown in the last four seconds, the game was won 6–0.

REVISED BY SUPPLYING AGENT: Scoring a touchdown in the last four seconds, the team won the game 6–0.

REVISED BY ELIMINATING VERBAL: The team won the game 6–0 with a touchdown in the last four seconds.

DANGLING PARTICIPLE: Having worn the coat, it was impossible to return it.

REVISED BY SUPPLYING AGENT: Having worn the coat, I could not return it.

REVISED BY ELIMINATING VERBAL: I could not return a coat that I had already worn.

DANGLING INFINITIVE: To restore the damaged wood, a special chemical was used.

REVISED BY SUPPLYING AGENT: To restore the damaged wood, they used a special chemical.

REVISED BY ELIMINATING VERBAL: A special chemical restored the damaged wood.

DANGLING INFINITIVE: The course of the lava is charted in order to predict the danger.

REVISED BY SUPPLYING AGENT: Scientists chart the course of the lava in order to predict the danger.

REVISED BY ELIMINATING VERBAL: A chart of the lava's course predicts the danger.

DANGLING GERUND: By minimizing keyboards, home computers were made more "user friendly."

REVISED BY SUPPLYING AGENT: By minimizing keyboards, designers made home computers more "user friendly."

REVISED BY ELIMINATING VERBAL: The reduced size of keyboards made home computers more "user friendly."

DANGLING GERUND: In deciding the case, illegally obtained evidence was used.

REVISED BY SUPPLYING AGENT: In deciding the case, the judge used illegally obtained evidence.

REVISED BY ELIMINATING VERBAL: The judge's decision was based partially on illegally obtained evidence.

A few participles and infinitives are not considered dangling, even though they do not modify a specific noun. Always common expressions (such as *considering, assuming, excluding, to conclude, to tell the truth*), these verbals introduce and modify whole sentences.

SENTENCE MODIFIER: Considering the expense, the trip isn't worth it.

SENTENCE MODIFIER: Excluding the major personalities, most television actors don't make much money.

SENTENCE MODIFIER: To tell the truth, an independent candidate would have a good chance.

dm
16a

☐ EXERCISE 1

Rewrite the following sentences to correct the dangling verbal phrases.

1. Enough French can be learned to ask common questions by using a conversation guide.
2. Caught in a rip current, it is important for a swimmer not to panic.
3. To see well on the water, sunglasses dark enough to hide the eyes should be worn.
4. Beating Milwaukee, a well-deserved trophy was won by the Celtics.
5. It was necessary to buy an atlas to understand the terrain of Wales.
6. By awarding $10,000 in scholarships, potential nurses will be encouraged.
7. In working effectively for a candidate for governor, adequate funds must be available.
8. Blowing from the north, the bay was kicking up white caps from the wind.
9. To learn more about the Loch Ness monster research, annual reports of the Loch Ness Phenomena Investigation Bureau can be studied.
10. To be an effective chip, most experts say that it must operate in either parallel or serial mode.
11. By blending Hollywood glamor and soul music, the direction of American music has been changed by Motown.
12. Based on this growing interest, the department has become more specialized.
13. The snake's mouth was open in an attempt to bite.
14. After ascending the English throne, French became the language of government.
15. To avoid confusion, it is necessary to organize the balance sheet properly.

(2) Dangling elliptical clauses

In an elliptical clause (see 7c.4), the subject and a form of the verb *be* are sometimes omitted. If an elliptical dependent clause is correctly constructed, its omitted subject is the same as the subject of the main clause.

ELLIPTICAL: While attending Radcliffe, she began her autobiography. [*She was* is omitted after *while.*]

ELLIPTICAL: Although responsible for the crash, the air controller refuses to accept any blame. [*The air controller is* is omitted after *although.*]

An elliptical clause dangles when the omitted subject is not the same as the subject of the main clause. You can correct a dangling clause in two ways.

- Make the subject of the main clause the same as the omitted subject of the elliptical clause.
- Rewrite the sentence to avoid the ellipsis.

DANGLING CLAUSE:	While living in Tahiti, rich tropical settings were painted by Gauguin.
REVISED BY MATCHING SUBJECTS:	While living in Tahiti, Gauguin painted rich, tropical settings.
REVISED TO AVOID ELLIPSIS:	In Tahiti, Gauguin painted rich, tropical settings.
DANGLING CLAUSE:	If dissatisfied with a product, a complaint should be made.
REVISED BY MATCHING SUBJECTS:	If dissatisfied with a product, the consumer should complain.
REVISED TO AVOID ELLIPSIS:	The consumer who is dissatisfied with a product should complain.

☐ EXERCISE 2

Revise the following sentences to eliminate dangling elliptical clauses.

1. Once redecorated, there was a pleasant atmosphere in the office.
2. Although annoyed by his attitude, his argument was convincing.
3. When repeating the story, a few details were added to make it more gruesome.
4. While making the meringue, the pie should be set aside to cool.
5. If enrolling in the class, it is recommended that you know Fortran.

16b Misplaced Modifiers

A modifier can be positioned so that it seems to modify the wrong word or phrase. It is possible to misplace any sort of modifier—a word, a phrase, or a clause.

(1) Misplaced words

mm

16b

The most commonly misplaced words are "qualifiers," such as *only, nearly, simply, almost, even,* and *just.* In speech, these words (regardless of what they modify) are usually placed before the verb. In written English, however, you should place qualifiers immediately before (or as near as possible to) the words they modify.

> MISPLACED: I only ordered a bowl of soup.
>
> REVISED: I ordered only a bowl of soup.

> MISPLACED: The students just pay one-third of the cost.
>
> REVISED: The students pay just one-third of the cost.

Misplacement of words other than qualifiers often leads to ambiguity.

> AMBIGUOUS: Follow the instructions for installing the antenna carefully. [*Carefully* can modify either *follow* or *installing.*]
>
> REVISED: Follow carefully the instructions for installing the antenna. [*Carefully* modifies *follow.*]
>
> REVISED: Follow the instructions for carefully installing the antenna. [*Carefully* modifies *installing.*]

(2) Misplaced prepositional phrases

Prepositional phrases should be placed as near as possible to the words or elements they modify since placement affects the meaning of sentences.

> The researchers studied aggressive behavior in Washington. [*In Washington* modifies *behavior.*]
>
> The researchers in Washington studied aggressive behavior. [*In Washington* modifies *researchers.*]

Misplacing a prepositional phrase can produce a sentence that is unclear or even silly.

> MISPLACED: The computer contained the voting statistics we had collected on a disk.
>
> REVISED: The computer contained on a disk the voting statistics we had collected.

> MISPLACED: Heinrich planned to conquer France on his deathbed.
>
> REVISED: On his deathbed, Heinrich planned to conquer France.

(3) Misplaced clauses

Like words and phrases, dependent clauses should refer clearly and logically to the words that they modify. In some sentences, you can move misplaced dependent clauses near the words they modify. In other sentences, you may have to rewrite to eliminate the misplaced clauses.

> MISPLACED: The archeologists found at the site a ceramic pot they had been digging in for two years. [Clause modifies *pot.*]

> CLAUSE MOVED: The archeologists found a ceramic pot at the site they had been digging in for two years. [Clause modifies *site.*]

> MISPLACED: Because of his allergies, he could not drive a tractor in a hayfield that was not air-conditioned. [Clause modifies *hayfield.*]

> CLAUSE ELIMINATED: Because of his allergies, he could not drive an un-air-conditioned tractor in a hayfield. [*Un-air-conditioned* modifies *hayfield.*]

(4) Squinting modifiers

"Squinting" modifiers are misplaced in such a way that they can modify either the preceding or the following elements.

> SQUINTING: The courses he teaches frequently have been cancelled. [*Frequently* modifies either *teaches* or *have been cancelled.*]

> REVISED: The courses he frequently teaches have been cancelled. [*Frequently* modifies *teaches.*]

> REVISED: The courses he teaches have been cancelled frequently. [*Frequently* modifies *have been cancelled.*]

> SQUINTING: They told him after the meeting to submit a proposal. [*After the meeting* can modify *told* or *to submit.*]

> REVISED: After the meeting, they told him to submit a proposal. [*After the meeting* modifies *told.*]

> REVISED: They told him to submit a proposal after the meeting. [*After the meeting* modifies *to submit.*]

❏ EXERCISE 3

Rearrange or rewrite the following sentences to eliminate the misplaced and squinting modifiers.

1. We went to a movie about a criminal that was considered controversial.
2. The campers had hiked to the end of the island without any water.
3. Mrs. Jones decided to hang two swords that had belonged to her father on the wall.
4. The soap opera that we watch often has characters suffering from amnesia.
5. McLemore wrote that the computer would probably arrive on Tuesday in a letter.
6. The fisherman decided on the dock to clean the fish.
7. A therapy session will be held for students who have crises from 5:00 to 7:30 P.M.
8. The Nobel Prize winner for chemistry almost received enough money to retire.
9. The sailboat moving through the water slowly came into view.
10. As an adult golden retriever, I expect him to be a well-mannered house dog and companion.
11. Johnson tried always to have a lot of money in his account.
12. The police officer who was summoned immediately arrested the suspect.
13. The author said that he opposed taxation on property in the first chapter.
14. The computer only has one disk drive.
15. My instructor gave the class notes on how to design a title page that I now had to consult.

❏ EXERCISE 4

Revise the following passage to eliminate dangling and misplaced modifiers.

By wearing Western clothes to events like football games and movies, a strange, out-of-place look is created. Western dress is natural only while working around horses and cattle.

For a ranch hand, cowboy clothes are practical. Using a cowboy hat for a variety of everyday needs, life can be simplified. When wearing the hat, the sun cannot burn the skin. Filled with water, drinking cups are made. Riders can also use hats to urge their horses to move faster.

Long and narrow for a good reason, riders wear specially shaped boots. Because of this shape, a stirrup can be used with ease. Boots also protect the wearer from snake bites, covering the lower leg.

Knotted around their necks, ranch hands wear bandanas. To protect noses and mouths from dust, a bandana can be tied around the face. Tied around their hats, riders can keep them from blowing away. By wearing wet bandanas on their heads, heat can be eliminated. Also, if needed, bandanas can be tourniquets.

Western shirts have a practical design. A person who works on a ranch often needs to rope a wild steer. The broad shoulders of the shirt provide room for easy movement. Also, with a tapered body, the ranch hand doesn't catch a shirt on the horns of an angry steer. And finally, snaps instead of buttons are used on a shirt that pop open in case a horn gets stuck in it.

Being familiar with the purpose of Western clothes, they look silly on people who have never seen a horse. In fact, wearing cowboy boots and a Stetson hat to a football game is as ridiculous as wearing penny loafers and a blazer to herd cattle.

17

Shifts

A "shift" is an unnecessary change from one kind of construction to another—for example, from present to past tense, from active to passive voice, from an indirect to a direct quotation. Any kind of shift hampers communication by focusing the reader's attention on the syntax rather than on the message. Thus, when revising, watch for shifts that you may have created in early drafts when you were concentrating on ideas rather than grammatical structure.

17a Shifts in Verb Tenses

Because of the variety of possible contexts, it is difficult to make rules about the sequence of verb tenses. Nevertheless, any tense shifts must be logical so that the reader can follow the movement of your prose. (See 4d, "Tense.")

(1) Present and past tenses

Sometimes, the first sentence in a passage establishes a time context—either present or past. Once established, the time should not shift illogically between the present and past tenses.

> MIXED TIME: **My brother <u>collects</u> [present] used furniture, not antiques. He <u>thinks</u> [present] that the prices of antiques <u>are</u> [present] so high that used furniture <u>is</u> [present] a good buy.**

Also, he enjoyed [past] repairing and refinishing bargains that he picked up [past] in places like auctions and garage sales.

CONSISTENT PRESENT TIME: My brother collects used furniture, not antiques. He thinks that the prices of antiques are so high that used furniture is a good buy. Also, he enjoys repairing and refinishing bargains that he picks up in places like auctions and garage sales.

CONSISTENT PAST TIME: My brother collected used furniture, not antiques. He thought that the prices of antiques were so high that used furniture was a good buy. Also, he enjoyed repairing and refinishing bargains that he picked up in places like auctions and garage sales.

(2) Perfect tenses

The perfect tenses allow a writer to record layers of time—to show the relationship between the time of one occurrence and the time of another. In general, you use the present perfect and past perfect tenses as follows.

- Use the present perfect tense (*have/has* + past participle) along with present tense or time.
- Use the past perfect tense (*had* + past participle) along with past tense or time.

MIXED TIME: Obviously, the architect's travels have influenced [present perfect] his work. All his designs reflected [past] the houses he has visited [present perfect] in Tokyo.

CONSISTENT PRESENT TIME: Obviously, the architect's travels have influenced [present perfect] his work. All his designs reflect [present] the houses he has visited [present perfect] in Tokyo.

CONSISTENT PAST TIME: Obviously, the architect's travels had influenced [past perfect] his work. All his designs reflected [past] the houses he had visited [past perfect] in Tokyo.

The future perfect tense (*will* + *have* + past participle) is rarely used; the simple future (*will* + base form) is usually adequate.

The future perfect is appropriate, however, when the context includes another future time expressed by a present tense verb or by an adverb of time, not by a future tense verb.

> MIXED TIME: The game will have begun [future perfect] by the time we will arrive [future].

> REVISED: The game will have begun [future perfect] by the time we arrive [present].

> REVISED: The game will have begun [future perfect] by dark.

17b Shifts with *Can/Could* or *Will/Would*

Conversational English allows a casual use of the auxiliaries *can, could, will,* and *would.* But in written English, the conventions for the use of these words are rather strict. In general, follow these guidelines.

- Use *can* with *will* and *could* with *would.*
- Use *can* and *will* with present tense and time.
- Use *could* and *would* with past tense and time.

> SHIFTED: If I could borrow a car, I will go to the dance.

> CONSISTENT: If I could borrow a car, I would go to the dance.

> CONSISTENT: If I can borrow a car, I will go to the dance.

> SHIFTED: Jaffe predicts [present] that current trends could double the shortage in ten years.

> CONSISTENT: Jaffe predicts [present] that current trends can double the shortage in ten years.

> CONSISTENT: Jaffe predicted [past] that current trends could double the shortage in ten years.

> SHIFTED: If the trees are cut down [present], the house would lose its charm.

> CONSISTENT: If the trees are cut down [present], the house will lose its charm.

> CONSISTENT: If the trees were cut down [past], the house would lose its charm.

17c Shifts in Mood

The indicative is the verb mood most common in prose. But sometimes, for special meanings, you use the imperative or the subjunctive mood. (See 4g.2 and 4g.3.) You can mix moods when the logic of
a passage demands the shift, but an unnecessary or illogical shift
results in awkward prose.

> SHIFTED: If I <u>were</u> [subjunctive] an honor student and I <u>was</u> [in-
> dicative] ready to graduate, I would apply to a medical
> school.

> CONSISTENT: If I <u>were</u> [subjunctive] an honor student and I <u>were</u> [sub-
> junctive] ready to graduate, I would apply to a medical
> school.

> SHIFTED: In one day, <u>eat</u> [imperative] no more than 30 milligrams
> of cholesterol, and you <u>should drink</u> [indicative] no
> more than 4 ounces of alcohol.

> CONSISTENT: In one day, <u>eat</u> [imperative] no more than 30 milligrams
> of cholesterol, and <u>drink</u> [imperative] no more than
> 4 ounces of alcohol.

> CONSISTENT: In one day, you <u>should eat</u> [indicative] no more than 30
> milligrams of cholesterol, and you <u>should drink</u> [indica-
> tive] no more than 4 ounces of alcohol.

17d Shifts in Voice

The term *voice* refers to whether the subject of a sentence performs
the action (active voice) or receives the action (passive voice). (See
4f.) You should not shift, without good reason, between active and
passive voice— particularly within a sentence. A shift in voice usually
results in an awkward and cumbersome sentence.

> SHIFTED: In the eighteenth century, Noah Webster
> <u>set out</u> [active] to make American English
> independent from British English; and
> through his books, great influence <u>was</u>
> <u>exerted</u> [passive] on the language.

> CONSISTENT ACTIVE VOICE: In the eighteenth century, Noah Webster
> <u>set out</u> to make American English independ-

ent from British English; and through his books, he <u>exerted</u> great influence on the language.

☐ EXERCISE 1

Revise the following sentences to correct shifts in verb tense, auxiliaries, mood, and voice.

1. The dictionary lists the most common part of speech first, and the most frequent meaning is given as the first definition.
2. In Spanish, *macho* is an adjective meaning "manly"; *machismo* was a noun that meant "masculinity."
3. If the diver were equipped with the new tank, he can stay underwater for eight hours.
4. The litigants will have spent thousands of dollars before an agreement will be reached.
5. In emergencies, pause, and then you should take a couple of deep breaths.
6. By providing a puppy with the proper atmosphere, you can promote good habits; and then trainability can be established.
7. If I can go to bed earlier, I would get more done during the day.
8. In reviews, critics usually point out when actors had overplayed scenes.
9. The doctor suggested that lowering my salt intake will reduce hypertension.
10. In Orwell's *1984,* the government plans an official Newspeak dictionary, which was supposed to free the world of words like *justice, morality,* and *science.*

17e Shifts in Number

The term *number* refers to singular (one) and plural (more than one). You should not shift carelessly between singular and plural nouns that should have the same number. You can correct shifts in number in either of two ways.

- Match singular nouns with singular nouns and plural nouns with plural nouns.
- Eliminate the noun that causes the shift.

> SHIFTED: <u>Students</u> must report their grade point <u>average</u>.
>
> REVISED: <u>Students</u> must report their grade point <u>averages</u>.

SHIFTED: Frequently, a person exercises to relieve stress. As a result, people sometimes become psychologically dependent on excessive exercising.

REVISED: Frequently, people exercise to relieve stress and, as a result, sometimes become psychologically dependent on excessive exercising.

**shft
17f**

17f Shifts in Person

The term *person* refers to first person (*I, we*), second person (*you*), and third person (all other pronouns and all nouns). Shifts in person usually involve *you* and a noun. You can revise these shifts by using *you* consistently. However, when you refer to a group of people in general, revising in the third person is the better solution.

SHIFTED: Off-campus students should use the bus system because you get frustrated trying to park every day.

REVISED IN THIRD PERSON: Off-campus students should use the bus system because they get frustrated trying to park every day.

REVISED IN SECOND PERSON: If you live off campus, you should use the bus system because you will get frustrated trying to park every day.

☐ EXERCISE 2

Revise the following sentences to correct any shifts in person and number.

1. Don't submit your manuscripts in ornamental binders; students should put their manuscripts in plain folders or boxes.
2. A traveler should consult several guides. Travelers who do no research are sure to miss many opportunities.
3. These four courses require a one-hour lab.
4. You will find the microcomputer especially valuable when you prepare proposals. The writer can easily pull together previously stored data.
5. At first, math teachers objected to the student use of pocket calculators. Now, however, a math teacher usually sees the value of one.

17g   Shifts Between Direct and Indirect Discourse

In direct discourse, the exact words of a speaker or writer appear in quotation marks: *Truman said, "If you can't convince them, confuse them."* In indirect discourse, the words of a speaker or writer are not reported exactly, and the quotation marks are omitted: *Truman said that if you can't convince people, you should try to confuse them.* A shift from one type of discourse to the other can create an awkward, unbalanced sentence.

> SHIFTED: **The reporter said, "I would rather write about steeplechases than football games," but that his editor would not approve.**

The reporter's words should be stated in either direct or indirect discourse.

> DIRECT DISCOURSE: **The reporter said, "I would rather write about steeplechases than football games, but my editor wouldn't approve."**

> INDIRECT DISCOURSE: **The reporter said that he preferred to write about steeplechases rather than football games but that his editor would not approve.**

17h   Shifts in Sentence Structure

Probably the most common shifts in sentence structure occur in "mixed constructions" that state reasons and definitions. These structures usually begin with an expression such as the following.

> **"The reason is because. . . ."**
>
> **"Something is when. . . ."**
>
> **"A place is where. . . ."**

Because definitions state that one thing is equivalent to another, a noun or noun construction should appear on both sides of the verb *be*. In other words, the *be* verb should be followed by a noun, noun phrase, or noun *that* clause and not by an adverb clause beginning with *because, when,* or *where*. The relationship between the subject and the predicate should be one of equality and not one of cause, time, or place. You can revise shifted structures in two ways.

- Place a noun, noun phrase, or noun clause after the *be* verb.
- Rewrite the sentence with a verb other than a form of *be*.

SHIFTED: The reason tuition increased was because enrollment dropped.

REVISED WITH NOUN CLAUSE: The reason tuition increased was that enrollment dropped.

REVISED WITH VERB CHANGE: Tuition increased because enrollment dropped.

SHIFTED: A malapropism is when a person misuses a word humorously.

REVISED WITH NOUN PHRASE: A malapropism is the humorous misuse of a word.

REVISED WITH VERB CHANGE: A malapropism results when a person misuses a word humorously.

SHIFTED: Farm clubs are where players train for the major leagues.

REVISED WITH NOUN PHRASE: Farm clubs are training grounds for the major leagues.

REVISED WITH VERB CHANGE: At farm clubs, players train for the major leagues.

Another kind of sentence shift occurs when a writer loses control of the structure in midsentence and mixes incompatible parts. These shifts can result not only in awkward sentences but also in sentences that make no sense.

The various ways in which structures can be mismatched are not entirely predictable. Most mismatches occur in rough drafts written in haste; you should, therefore, read drafts carefully in order to revise any shifts in structure. Also, if you have trouble revising structural shifts, review Chapter 7, "Clauses and Sentences."

MISMATCHED SUBJECT AND PREDICATE: Fraternities that were banned on campus were an issue loudly debated.

REVISED: The banning of fraternities on campus was an issue loudly debated.

SENTENCE WITH NO SUBJECT:	Currently, with the lack of security, causes financial losses from computer crime.
REVISED:	Currently, the lack of security causes financial losses from computer crime.
MISMATCHED MODIFIER:	Maturity is the stage that a person accepts responsibility.
REVISED:	Maturity is the stage at which a person accepts responsibility.

☐ EXERCISE 3

Revise the following sentences to correct the shifts in direct/indirect discourse and in sentence structure.

1. The Renaissance was when people began to emphasize classical art and culture.
2. Garbage as an energy source is a capacity to save money.
3. The reason for the boycott was because the company charged too much rent.
4. The lady protested indignantly, "What do you mean, you won't take dogs" and that her Fifi would never stay in a kennel.
5. Women, growing in numbers in the police force, the improvement has produced results.
6. The reason he quit his job was because he wanted to move to Florida.
7. The reduction of the car's weight is an idea that will reduce gasoline use.
8. She feels that by working at two jobs would make enough money to buy a motorcycle.

☐ EXERCISE 4

Revise any shifts in the following passage.

The American Computer Chess Championship is a contest that is sponsored annually by the Association for Computing Machinery. This contest was not really between computers but between their programmers. A programmer must spend hours getting programs ready. In fact, if you want to write a successful computer chess program, a lifetime could be spent working.

Look at the winning Cray Blitz program. The programmers estimate spent 32,000 man hours on the program. Because opening moves are important, 100,000 of these positions had been entered. Not only do they have to type in the possible moves, but also these moves had to be analyzed. You can't depend on the chess textbooks; some of the moves they recommend would not be the best move possible. Also, programmers must look at many possible moves, not just one at a time but usually about four and a half at a time.

Despite all of the effort that goes into programming chess strategy, the programs still cannot beat the best human players. So, if you create a chess program, be sure to challenge other machines and their programmers—not a human player.

18

Split Constructions

A construction is any unit of two or more words related in some way—subject and predicate, auxiliary and main verb, verb and direct object, and so on. No rule forbids splitting a construction with a modifier or modifiers, but you should be cautious. Some splits result in blurred meaning and awkward constructions.

18a Split Subjects and Predicates

Subjects and predicates cannot always appear next to each other; modifiers may interrupt the construction. Be sure, however, that the interruption is not so long that it distracts a reader. As the following examples illustrate, sentences are cumbersome and sometimes difficult to comprehend when verbs are far removed from their subjects. You can often revise a sentence with a split subject and predicate by moving the intervening element.

SPLIT: **The language, with a simple sound system of only five vowels and seven consonants, is easy to learn.**

REVISED BY MOVING INTERRUPTER: **With a simple sound system of only five vowels and seven consonants, the language is easy to learn.**

In some cases, you can restructure the sentence to position the subject and verb closer together. In the following sentence, for example, the long interruptive element can be rewritten as the predicate.

SPLIT: Our campus newspaper, which caricatures such groups as graduate students, athletes, sorority and fraternity members, and independents, is edited by two promising comedy writers.

REVISED BY REWRITING INTERRUPTER: Our campus newspaper, edited by two promising comedy writers, caricatures such groups as graduate students, athletes, sorority and fraternity members, and independents.

Another possible solution is to divide a cumbersome construction into two separate sentences.

SPLIT: Shopping malls, which have grown from clusters of shops to elaborate structures with fountains, exotic plants, restaurants, and theaters, have led the American consumer to associate buying with entertainment.

REVISED AS 2 SENTENCES: Shopping malls have grown from clusters of shops to elaborate structures with fountains, exotic plants, theaters, and restaurants. These extravagant centers have led the American consumer to associate buying with entertainment.

18b Split Verbs and Complements

Sometimes a modifier separates a verb from its direct object or subject complement—an element that completes the verb's meaning. When a verb and its completer are separated unnecessarily, the interruptive element should be moved to another place in the sentence.

SPLIT: The marathoner injured, during the last race, his left foot.

REVISED BY MOVING MODIFIER: The marathoner injured his foot during the last race.

SPLIT: No one knows, although some historians estimate about 5,000, exactly how many soldiers the Germans lost on D-Day.

REVISED BY MOVING MODIFIER: **Although some historians estimate about 5,000, no one knows exactly how many soldiers the Germans lost on D-Day.**

18c Split Verbs

The verbs in many sentences are not single words but phrases: *would improve, will be moving, has been profiteering, could have been debated.* Frequently adverbs occur between the parts of a verb phrase. In fact, sometimes the natural place for an adverb seems to be within, rather than before or after, a verb phrase.

> The issue was hotly debated.

> Experts are now predicting a rise in prices.

Furthermore, when the verb phrase is accompanied by *not,* you have no choice but to split the construction.

> The new drug will not produce any side effects.

If you do split a verb phrase, take care not to split it awkwardly with a long modifier, especially a prepositional phrase or a clause.

SPLIT: **Women are, in the future, going to make up a large share of the labor force.**

REVISED BY MOVING MODIFIER: **In the future, women are going to make up a large share of the labor force.**

SPLIT: **A conversion will, when the plates are in metric measurement, give the needed dimensions.**

REVISED BY MOVING MODIFIER: **A conversion will give the needed dimensions when the plates are in metric measurement.**

18d Split Infinitives

An infinitive is the *to* form of a verb: *to go, to understand, to hear, to be.* Sometimes an infinitive is split because of the normal patterns of the language.

NORMAL SPLIT: We expect our membership <u>to</u> more than <u>double</u> next
year.

Other times an infinitive is split because to place a modifier anywhere else in the sentence would create an awkward construction or
change the intended meaning.

SPLIT INFINITIVE: They met <u>to</u> quickly <u>assess</u> the damage done by
the oil spill.

AWKWARD SENTENCE: They met to assess quickly the damage done by
the oil spill.

CHANGED MEANING: They met quickly to assess the damage done by
the oil spill.

In general, however, you should avoid splitting infinitives—
particularly with long modifiers. Such splits always create awkward
constructions.

SPLIT INFINITIVE: The robot's three-pronged finger arrangement allows it <u>to</u> with a great deal
of accuracy <u>pick up</u> objects.

REVISED BY MOVING MODIFIER: The robot's three-pronged finger arrangement allows it to pick up objects
with a great deal of accuracy.

Even splitting an infinitive with a short modifier can create an awkward rhythm.

SPLIT INFINITIVE: Don Knotts' portrayal of Deputy Barney
Fife seems <u>to</u> never <u>lose</u> popularity.

REVISED BY MOVING MODIFIER: Don Knotts' portrayal of Deputy Barney
Fife seems never to lose popularity.

☐ EXERCISE 1

Revise the following sentences to eliminate awkward and unclear
split constructions.

1. If you default on mortgage payments, the lender can, according to the
   general rule of mortgage law, foreclose on your property.
2. Warm Springs, Georgia, where Franklin D. Roosevelt went to try to
   recover the use of his legs in the warm baths, is now a rehabilitation
   center.
3. Whatever the English architects imported, they changed it to, with
   great inventiveness, fit the British climate and temperament.
4. The first mechanical adding machine was, suprisingly in 1642, invented by Blaise Pascal when he was just a teenager.

5. The focus of genetic research in agriculture has been to safely increase yield and to effectively make plants resistant to disease and damage.

6. To make computer chips, engineers first draw by hand or by a computer, maps of the electrical circuit.

7. A "serendipity" is something you happen to, without looking for it, find.

8. Elvis Presley was, according to Tom Wolfe, a "Valentino for poor whites."

9. Rudolf Flesch, the author of numerous books on reading and what Flesch calls "readability," has devised a formula that measures the reading level of prose.

10. Portions of the Conewago River were unable to satisfactorily support the reproduction of trout.

☐ EXERCISE 2

Revise the passage to eliminate awkward or unclear split constructions. You may decide that some of the split constructions are acceptable.

In high school, I, with insistence from my parents, took French. I had no idea why they had at this time demanded that I learn a foreign language. No one around me spoke French. Anyway, I obediently enrolled, but there was no incentive to industriously and enthusiastically study. France was very far away, and I had in no flight of fancy any idea of ever meeting a native.

I, you might guess, did not apply myself to learning. I did, however, come to intensely love the sound of French; it can make the dullest statements sound romantic and interesting. But I after weeks and weeks of struggling could never master the *r* in the throat or the *n* or *m* in the nose. Another problem was in some spoken phrases that the French run words together. For example, *les hommes* (*the men*) when it is spoken sounds like *laysohm.*

I could manage to without difficulty learn vocabulary like *boeuf* for *beef, porc* for *pork,* and *juin* for *June.* But other words were with my limited effort much harder to learn.

The worst problem was that the nouns are masculine or feminine. *The book* (*le livre*) for some very strange reason is masculine; *the chair* (*la chaise*) for an equally strange reason is feminine.

This summer I have a chance to visit Paris, and I, with real regrets about not studying, will have to probably depend on sign language and pity from the French to survive.

19

Incomplete Constructions

In some sentences, a word or words needed for grammatical completeness may not appear. The omission does not always detract from the meaning. For example, the following sentences would be perfectly clear even if the words in brackets were omitted.

> Did you think [that] we weren't coming?
>
> The police made the arrest while [they were] on a routine inspection.
>
> Zombies have always frightened me more than werewolves [have frightened me].

Sometimes, however, an omission makes a sentence confusing.

> CONFUSING: She writes more often to her Representative than you.
>
> POSSIBLE MEANING: She writes more often to her Representative than you write.
>
> POSSIBLE MEANING: She writes more often to her Representative than she does to you.

When a reader doesn't know exactly what the writer has left out or when an omission makes the meaning unclear, the construction is not acceptable. Incomplete constructions can easily be corrected by the addition of the necessary words.

19a Omissions in Compound Constructions

Make sure that you have not omitted a necessary part of a compound expression because this omission may obscure structure or meaning.

OMISSION OF DETERMINER: **My teacher and counselor advised me to study physics.** [*My teacher and counselor* could refer to one person or two.]

REVISED TO MEAN ONE PERSON: **My teacher counseled me to study physics.**

REVISED TO MEAN TWO PEOPLE: **My teacher and my counselor advised me to study physics.**

OMISSION OF PART OF VERB: **I have never and will never be interested in the stock market.** [*Been* must follow *have.*]

REVISED: **I have never been and will never be interested in the stock market.**

OMISSION OF PART OF IDIOM: **The bright lights detract and ruin the effect of the display.** [*Detract* must be followed by *from.*]

REVISED: **The bright lights detract from and ruin the effect of the display.**

Any omitted words in the second clause of a compound sentence should be present in the first clause. Otherwise, the second clause may be ungrammatical or illogical.

OMISSION OF NECESSARY VERB: **In the past I flew everywhere; now, nowhere.** [*Flew* is in the wrong tense.]

REVISED: **In the past I flew everywhere; now I fly nowhere.**

OMISSION OF NECESSARY VERB: **Our previous vacations to Maine have been exciting; this one, very dull.** [*Have been* is the wrong number for the subject of the second clause—*one.*]

REVISED: **Our previous vacations to Maine have been exciting; this one has been very dull.**

❏ EXERCISE 1

Revise the following sentences to correct any incomplete constructions in the compound elements.

1. Many consumers are insisting and purchasing foods low in sodium, sugar, and fat.
2. The writer and director we heard speak last year in New York will be on the panel.
3. The Huntsville area was once known as an agricultural center; now, as a center for high technology.
4. The hotel has not and does not plan to charge guests for telephone calls.
5. Some states have seen an increase in unemployment; our state, a decrease.

19b Omitted *That*

That may introduce a noun clause. Frequently, as in the following example, *that* can be omitted without any loss of meaning.

> The players believed [that] they would win.

But in some sentences, the omission will cause readers to think that the subject of the noun clause is the object of the preceding verb. In such cases you must not omit *that*.

> OMISSION OF THAT: He noticed the mistake worried me. [On a first reading, *mistake* could be read as the object of *noticed.*]
>
> REVISED: He noticed that the mistake worried me.

❏ EXERCISE 2

Insert *that* in any of the following sentences where it is necessary for clarity.

1. John Brookings added the loans by the bank had been excessive.
2. The recent graduates said when they tried to get jobs, they had no success.
3. The budget cuts have proved the answer can come from financial control.
4. The students estimated they would make more money in California.
5. I read the indictment was not made public for three weeks.

19c Incomplete Comparisons

Omissions frequently occur in comparisons, and usually a reader can fill in the missing word or words with no difficulty.

> This route is as long as that one [is long].
>
> The copies from this machine are darker than those [copies are dark].
>
> The weather is hotter this week than [it was] last [week].

In some comparative constructions, however, the omissions cause the comparison to be unclear, illogical, or grammatically incomplete.

- Sometimes a reader cannot know with certainty what a writer intended.

> UNCLEAR COMPARISON: Stray dogs are friendlier to me than my roommate.
>
> POSSIBLE MEANING: Stray dogs are friendlier to me than my roommate is.
>
> POSSIBLE MEANING: Stray dogs are friendlier to me than they are to my roommate.

> UNCLEAR COMPARISON: *Gone with the Wind* is the best movie.
>
> POSSIBLE MEANING: *Gone with the Wind* is the best movie ever made.
>
> POSSIBLE MEANING: *Gone with the Wind* is the best movie I have ever seen.

- Sometimes a comparison seems illogical.

In the next example, the writer has illogically compared a technique to a contender when the intention was to compare two techniques.

> ILLOGICAL COMPARISON: His technique for throwing the discus is unlike any other contender.
>
> REVISED: His technique for throwing the discus is unlike any other contender's.
>
> REVISED: His technique for throwing the discus is unlike that of any other contender.

- Sometimes a writer leaves out the word *other,* thus illogically comparing something to itself.

For example, in the following sentence, Texas cannot produce more oil than "any state" since Texas is itself a state.

inc
19c

ILLOGICAL COMPARISON: Texas produces more oil than any state.

REVISED: Texas produces more oil than any other state.

- In informal conversation, a speaker sometimes uses *so, such,* and *too* as intensifiers like *very* or *extremely.*

INFORMAL: The lights are so bright.

INFORMAL: It is such a difficult book.

But in formal English, *so, such,* and *too* signal comparisons or measurements. A reader expects to learn the result of the "light's brightness" or the "book's difficulty." Therefore, a writer must either complete the comparison or use a true intensifier.

INFORMAL: The noise of the plane was so loud.

REVISED BY COMPLETING COMPARISON: The noise of the plane was so loud that we could not hear what was said.

REVISED BY CHANGING INTENSIFIER: The noise of the plane was extremely loud.

INFORMAL: The information was too scandalous.

REVISED BY COMPLETING COMPARISON: The information was too scandalous to print.

REVISED BY CHANGING INTENSIFIER: The information was exceedingly scandalous.

- If a sentence contains a double comparison, any words that make both comparisons complete must not be omitted.

OMISSION OF As: Aiken's autobiography is as successful, if not more successful than, Adam's.

REVISED: Aiken's autobiography is as successful as, if not more successful than, Adam's.

☐ EXERCISE 3

Make the changes necessary to eliminate any confusion that results from incomplete or illogical comparisons.

inc

19c

1. Few candidates have had their campaigns aided by so influential a supporter as Mayor Nelson.
2. The computers at the library work so slowly.
3. They installed the most sophisticated stereo equipment.
4. The Washington Monument is nearer the Mall than the Lincoln Memorial.
5. Louisiana's shrimp season begins earlier than other Gulf states.
6. The Sears Tower in Chicago is taller than any building in America.
7. The jazz performance was such a brilliant one.
8. Cheese has far more fat.
9. The volcano is as dangerous, perhaps even more dangerous than, Mt. St. Helens.
10. The damage done by the water was more serious than the wind.

☐ EXERCISE 4

Revise the following passage to eliminate incomplete constructions.

Horse racing is more harmful to horses than any sport. I once considered it exciting; but now, inhumane. I have come to realize profits are more important to owners than the horses.

Races are scheduled so often. The owners do not take into consideration the general health of the horses may be endangered by fatigue. Even bad weather does not often cause cancellation of races.

Sometimes the race track surface is too hard. Horses' legs are more fragile than many other animals. Numerous injuries are caused and result from this physical abuse. Drugging horses is crueler. I have noticed drugs like narcotics are still used at many racetracks. The horses run unaffected and unaware of pain.

Probably some owners treat their horses humanely. But others have never and will never consider the welfare of their horses to be as important, or more important than, profits.

20

Parallelism

// /
20

Sentences frequently contain lists of two or more items. Such items in a sequence must be parallel; that is, they must have the same grammatical structure. The following examples illustrate parallel sequence.

2 PARALLEL NOUN PHRASES: The best beer has both <u>nat-ural ingredients</u> and <u>natural fer-mentation</u>.

3 PARALLEL PREPOSITIONAL PHRASES: The Shakespeare company has trav-eled not only <u>to city theaters</u> and <u>to college campuses</u> but also <u>to small communities</u>.

4 PARALLEL VERB PHRASES: "Uncooperative" computers <u>have been riddled with bullets</u>, <u>burned up with gasoline</u>, <u>stabbed with screwdrivers</u>, and <u>hammered with shoes</u>.

3 PARALLEL NOUN CLAUSES: We now know <u>that sleep has at least four depths</u>, <u>that dreaming is most intense in the period of rapid eye movement</u>, and <u>that sleep deprivation is dangerous</u>.

A mixture of items with various grammatical structures is clumsy and illogical. You must be careful to make all items grammatically paral-lel whenever you write a compound structure, a series, a list, or an outline.

163

20a Parallelism in Compound Structures

/ /
20a

The two items in a compound structure must be grammatically the same: *pencil* and *paper, working* and *playing, to search* and *to find, when they read* and *when they listen.* Although the two constructions are most often linked by *and,* there are several possible connections—all requiring parallel items.

• Compounding with coordinate conjunctions (*and, but, or, nor, yet*)

The elements on either side of a coordinate conjunction must be the same grammatical construction. When they are not, you must convert one of the elements to the same structure as the other.

> NOT PARALLEL: The heat wave <u>will increase the demand</u> for electricity and <u>causing power outages</u>. [*And* joins a verb phrase to a participial phrase.]

> REVISED WITH 2 VERB PHRASES: The heat wave <u>will increase the demand</u> for electricity and <u>will cause power outages</u>.

> NOT PARALLEL: The bicycle path should be located a<u>long Route 234</u> or <u>to follow the</u> Pendleton River. [*Or* joins a prepositional phrase to an infinitive phrase.]

> REVISED WITH 2 PREPOSITIONAL PHRASES: The bicycle path should be located <u>along Route 234</u> or <u>beside the</u> Pendleton River.

• Compounding with correlative conjunctions (*not only . . . but also, not . . . but, either . . . or, neither . . . nor, both . . . and*)

The two parts of the correlative conjunctions must precede identical structures; that is, whatever element follows the first part of one of these conjunctions must also follow the second part.

> NOT PARALLEL: I will either <u>leave from National Airport</u> or <u>from Dulles</u>. [*Either* is followed by a verb; *or* is followed by a prepositional phrase.]

REVISED WITH PARALLEL VERBS: I will either leave from National Airport or leave from Dulles.

REVISED WITH PARALLEL PREPOSITIONAL PHRASES: I will leave either from National Airport or from Dulles.

NOT PARALLEL: The reporter wondered both what the lawyer had meant and should the remark be reported. [*Both* is followed by a noun clause; *and* is followed by a verb phrase.]

REVISED WITH PARALLEL NOUN CLAUSES: The reporter wondered both what the lawyer had meant and whether the remark should be reported.

NOT PARALLEL: We not only want to visit the Corcoran Gallery but also the Hirshhorn Museum. [*Not only* is followed by a verb; *but also* is followed by a noun.]

REVISED WITH PARALLEL NOUN PHRASES: We want to visit not only the Corcoran Gallery but also the Hirshhorn Museum.

- Compounding with other connecting words (*not, as well as, rather than, less than, more than, from . . . to, instead of*)

A few words create compound structures in the same way that the coordinate conjunctions do. And like the elements joined by coordinate conjunctions, the elements joined by these words must have the same grammatical structure.

NOT PARALLEL: We should advertise the carwash rather than to be overlooked by potential customers. [*Rather than* joins a verb to an infinitive.]

REVISED WITH PARALLEL VERBS: We should advertise the carwash rather than be overlooked by potential customers.

NOT PARALLEL: The reporter has covered the trial from the swearing in of the jury to when the judge sentenced the murder. [*From . . . to* joins a noun phrase to a subordinate clause.]

/ /
20b

REVISED WITH PARALLEL
NOUN PHRASES:
The reporter has covered the trial from the swearing in of the jury to the sentencing by the judge.

NOT PARALLEL:
My history teacher is guilty of telling about past events instead of an explanation of them. [*Instead of* joins a gerund phrase and a noun.]

REVISED WITH PARALLEL
GERUND PHRASES:
My history teacher is guilty of telling about past events instead of explaining them.

☐ EXERCISE 1

Find and correct any examples of faulty parallelism in compound structures.

1. The book is divided into two sections—the first focusing on individuals and the second examines generalizations.
2. We wrote a letter intended to eliminate the confusion and which was apparently not received.
3. In temperament, not how he appeared, he resembled his mother.
4. The story is not only puzzling but also disturbs the ordinary reader.
5. As a fly ball is hit, a fielder must judge where the ball will come down and how fast to run to get there.
6. Future space explorations will require flights not of days but years.
7. I would rather suffer through a boring lecture than to miss out on important information.
8. We neither have the time nor the means to learn German before our trip.
9. The book covers information from the discovery of the site to when the artifacts were displayed in the Egyptian museum.
10. The campers were either in their cabins or eating in the mess hall.

20b Parallelism in Series, Lists, and Outlines

A sequence of more than two items may appear within a sentence or in a list with one item under the other. All the items, no matter how many, must be the same grammatical structure. If they are not, you must revise the sequence by finding a structure that all the items can share.

NOT PARALLEL:	The students go to the clinic to get vitamins for anemia, for aspirins for headaches, or just counseling. [The series contains an infinitive phrase, a prepositional phrase, and a noun phrase.]
REVISED WITH SERIES OF NOUN PHRASES:	The students go to the clinic to get vitamins for anemia, aspirins for headaches, or counseling for their emotional problems.
NOT PARALLEL:	I asked the curator whether the museum was well funded, about the style of paintings it featured, and to supply the names of its patrons. [The series contains a noun clause, a prepositional phrase, and an infinitive phrase.]
REVISED WITH SERIES OF CLAUSES:	I asked the curator whether the museum was well funded, what style of paintings it featured, and if he would supply the names of its patrons.

// 20b

NOT PARALLEL: The members decided to fulfill these responsibilities:

1. Meet with parents and guardians
2. Meet with interested citizens
3. Answers to questions from the news media
4. A record of responses to telephone calls

[The list contains two verb phrases and two noun phrases.]

REVISED WITH SERIES OF VERB PHRASES: The members decided to fulfill these responsibilities:

1. Meet with parents and guardians
2. Meet with interested citizens
3. Answer questions from the news media
4. Record responses to telephone calls

In a formal outline, the items should be parallel. If the outline is a sentence outline, parallelism is no problem; every item, no mat-

/ /
20b

ter at what level, is a complete sentence. If the outline is a topic outline, you must make the items at each level the same grammatical structure. In most topic outlines, every item is a noun phrase. Thus, when you revise an outline with faulty parallelism, the two most logical options are to make all items sentences or noun phrases.

NOT PARALLEL

Slang: Its Useful Purposes
  I. Slang used to identify social groups
 II. To enliven language
III. Slang gives us new names
IV. Euphemisms for things that are unpleasant or offensive

> [Outline contains a noun phrase, an infinitive phrase, an independent clause, and a noun phrase.]

REVISED WITH PARALLEL SENTENCES

Slang Serves Useful Purposes.
  I. Social groups use slang as a sign of identification.
 II. Slang develops to enliven language, to eliminate monotony.
III. Slang gives us names for new things, such as physical objects or social movements.
IV. Slang supplies euphemisms for unpleasant or offensive actions and places.

REVISED WITH PARALLEL NOUN PHRASES

The Usefulness of Slang
  I. In-group identification
 II. Variety
III. Names for new things
IV. Euphemisms

☐ EXERCISE 2

Correct the faulty parallelism in the following sentences.

1. I find your continuing chauvinistic attitude offensive, sophomoric, and simply displays the worst taste.
2. Computers are capable of programming, remembering, scanning, and they can sort information.
3. The author is a distinguished journalist, lecturer, and has written over fifteen books.
4. The most successful adults have learned to channel their energy, to empathize with others, and they fit into a suitable society.

5. A marketing research analyst has these duties:

   designing marketing research studies
   to interpret research results
   operating a research data retrieval system
   an analyst must monitor existing products

🔲 EXERCISE 3

Fill in the blanks with words parallel to the other words in the sequences.

1. The songs have typical themes—broken hearts, lonely nights, and _____ .
2. The program traces not only how we got involved in Vietnam but also _____ .
3. A path winds through the woods, along a stream, and _____ .
4. The store sells expensive but _____ books.
5. At the school I will learn either to use the word processor or _____ .
6. He has a reputation for working hard but _____ .
7. Many people do not know what a quark is or _____ .
8. I will take a cut in pay rather than _____ .
9. _____ and when you use credit cards, you must take special care not to overextend yourself financially.
10. How you take a photograph, not _____, will determine the quality of the result.

🔲 EXERCISE 4

Revise the following passage to remove any faulty parallelism.

In football games, the job of the officials is not easy. They must be ready to react to such confusing plays as blocked kicks, fumbled snaps and catches, goal line plays, end zone plays, and whether a player is eligible. They must be aware both of when a foul occurs and where the ball is at the time of the foul.

Officials not only must know all the rules but also be able to remember them instantly. They must cope with such complicated infractions as these:

   an illegal block by the fair catch caller
   when a player runs into or either roughs the kicker or holder
   when a player bats the ball forward in the field of play or backwards
       out of the end zone
   a noncontact interference with the opportunity to catch a kick

No official can stop the game, get out the rule book, studying the details, and then calling the play.

The officials' job, though, is not just to call the plays on the field; officials must also deal with the players themselves. Players frequently play very aggressively, not in a cooperative mood. Officials must make sure that all players are under control and respecting the whistle which signals the end of a play. To ensure this control, officials must stay alert and being able to move quickly to the location of the infraction. Either the players must respond to this authority or be removed from the game.

The next time you disagree with an official or hear one booed by fans, take pity. It's hard work.

☐ REVIEW EXERCISE

Revise the following compositions to remove all grammatical and structural errors. As you read, look specifically for

fragments	comma splices
fused sentences	subject-verb agreement errors
incorrect verb forms	pronoun reference errors
pronoun antecedent	incorrect pronoun case
agreement errors	dangling or misplaced modi-
adjective-adverb confusion	fiers
shifts	split constructions
incomplete constructions	faulty parallelism

1.   King Louis XIV of France commissioned La Salle to explore the Mississippi River and claim its great valley for France. La Salle organized an expedition in Canada and started down the Mississippi River in February 1682. La Salle's expedition, like many before and after it, made not only important discoveries but also encountered many misadventures and tragedies.

When La Salle reached the mouth of the river on April 9, 1682. He then planted the French flag and proclaimed that all lands of this great river valley belonged to Louis, King of France. In his honor, he named the new lands "Louisiana."

La Salle's next job was to fortify the mouth of the river to keep other nations out. After returning to France for supplies, soldiers, and men, the plan was to sail back to the mouth of the river by way of the Gulf of Mexico. Events begun to go awry immediately, on the trip the Spanish captured one of La Salle's four ships. Then, La Salle, suffering from a near fatal illness and misled by erroneous information about winds and currents in the Gulf, sailed too far west and misses the mouth of the river. Instead, they landed at Matagorda Bay on the Texas coast.

La Salle's troubles multiplied. Attempting to make camp ashore, he lost many of his provisions when his supply ship ran aground. Local Indians attacked his camp, and also his hunting parties were harrassed. Sending one of his two remaining ships back to France, La Salle set out cross-country with a small party of twenty men, he hoped to locate the mouth of the river. Unable to find it, he returned to his camp to learn that his only remaining ship had been run aground and destroyed.

Now stranded, he set out to feel his way toward Canada. On the way, his crew was weary, and La Salle became more despondent almost to the point of madness. This caused the crew to mutiny. After an argument, they murdered La Salle's nephew and two aides. Then to conceal these murders, he was killed. They buried him in the wilderness and walked back to Canada. Only five of the men made it to Canada. On the Texas coast, the settlers, who La Salle had left behind, were wiped out by the Indians and because they got diseases. France's first attempt to settle the Gulf Coast ended in failure.

2.   I began reading those "romance novels" last summer that are sold in drugstores and quick-stop groceries. Finally, after three months, I realized both that these books all tell the same story and have the same characters.

Readers are first introduced to the heroine, who they are supposed to identify with. On page one, you see her in shabby clothing however, we know she was born an aristocrat because of her "aristocratic brow and regal bearing." As our story opens, we discover our heroines family is down on their luck. Although the young lady has been forced to work as a governess or music teacher to support an invalid mother or father. The family have rich (but haughty) relatives.

Now the hero. He, of course, is one of the rich and haughty relatives who has shunned the heroines family. But the relationship is distant enough for him to marry the heroine eventually. The hero had black hair— and plenty of it. He also has black, "mocking" eyes and with muscles that show through his clothes.

When the hero and heroine meet, this happens. She is rude to him because he is real arrogant, he is charmed by her "spirit." The plot unfolds. The heroine both despises and yearns for the hero. He, after becoming fatally smitten with her charms, "determines to have her." The reason is because she is "in his blood." In some of these kind of novels, the characters engage in steamy love scenes. In others, the author demurely notes when the heroine is near the hero, her "pulse quickens alarmingly." In the end, it's all the same. Hero marries heroine. Hero becomes doting wimp, heroine becomes rich.

After reading these literary clones, a plot of my own begun to take shape. Author of books tell same story over and over to wimpy readers; author gets rich.

PART III

Following Conventions: Punctuation and Mechanics

Punctuation and mechanics are signals that work together with words and structures to create meaning. With the aid of these signals, readers anticipate, link, separate, stress, de-emphasize, and characterize ideas according to a writer's wishes. In fact, readers rely so heavily on these marks that their misuse can distort or obscure intended meaning. Therefore, to communicate clearly, you must use punctuation marks and mechanics according to standard practice.

21

Commas

21a

The comma is the most versatile punctuation mark, with numerous and varied uses. For example, commas appear with conjunctions between independent clauses, mark introductory elements, separate items in a series, enclose nonessential information, and set off official titles. Because commas serve primarily to indicate sentence structure, their correct use is essential to clear writing.

21a Commas Between Independent Clauses Joined by Coordinating Conjunctions

Two independent clauses can be joined with a comma and a coordinating conjunction (*and, but, or, nor, for, so,* and *yet*).

> The Vice President will arrive at 9:30, and the commissioning of the battleship will begin at 10:00.

> The regular edition of the dictionary is twelve volumes, but the compact edition is only two.

> I have to maintain a C average, or my parents will make me pay for my own courses.

> The old man had never reported any income, nor had he ever had a bank account.

> All the dormitories were full, so we were housed temporarily in local motels and hotels.

174

The comma may be omitted when the independent clauses are very short and parallel in structure and when the conjunction is *and, but, or,* or *nor.*

The lights are off and the door is locked.

Regardless of length and parallelism, however, the comma is included when the conjunction is *for, so,* and *yet.* Because these conjunctions can function as other parts of speech, the comma is needed to prevent misreading. For example, in the first sentence of the following pair, *for* seems to be a preposition with *roots* as its object; in the second, the comma makes clear that *for* is a conjunction.

MISLEADING: **They went back home for their roots were there.**

CLEAR: **They went back home, for their roots were there.**

In the first sentence of the next pair, *yet* seems to be an adverb of time; in the second, *yet* is clearly a conjunction.

MISLEADING: **We didn't want to go yet we thought it was our duty.**

CLEAR: **We didn't want to go, yet we thought it was our duty.**

NOTE: When independent clauses are long or contain internal punctuation, some writers prefer to join them with a semicolon and a coordinating conjunction. (See 22c.)

If you approach the colt slowly, talking in a calm voice, you can gain his confidence; but if you move abruptly or speak sharply, he will bolt.

☐ EXERCISE 1

In the following phrase, insert commas where they are needed between independent clauses.

In the 1950s, there were a number of "quiz" shows on television. Contestants displayed a breadth of knowledge but most won very little money. Winning the game by displaying one's knowledge was the point. Now the quiz shows are gone and in their place have come "game" shows. Contestants don't need any knowledge to play yet they must have the ability to jump up and down and squeal. With this talent, they can win thousands of dollars or they can drive away in Cadillacs.

☐ EXERCISE 2

Join each of the pairs of sentences with a comma and an appropriate coordinating conjunction (*and, but, or, nor, for, so,* and *yet*).

1. Classes were dismissed at noon. By 1:00, the campus was deserted.
2. I dropped out of school temporarily to get some experience in the business world. To put it another way, I ran out of money and had to work for a while.
3. We stayed in Florida for an entire week. The sun never came out once.
4. This course has no prerequisite. It can be taken anytime during the program.
5. In the past, children of divorced parents were said to come from "broken homes." Now these children are said to belong to "single parents."

21b Commas After Introductory Prepositional Phrases, Verbals, and Dependent Clauses

An introductory or dependent clause appears at the beginning of a sentence or another clause—either independent or dependent. For a discussion of verbals, dependent clauses, and independent clauses, see Chapter 5, "Verbals and Verbal Phrases," and Chapter 7, "Clauses and Sentences."

(1) Introductory prepositional phrases

A comma usually follows an introductory prepositional phrase (a preposition and its object) or a combination of phrases.

<table>
<tr><td>PHRASE INTRODUCING A SENTENCE:</td><td>At yesterday's press conference, the coach denied the NCAA charges of recruiting violations.</td></tr>
<tr><td>PHRASES INTRODUCING A DEPENDENT CLAUSE:</td><td>The local television station announced that as a result of a recent campaign, the city government had agreed to improve the public bus service.</td></tr>
<tr><td>PHRASES INTRODUCING A SENTENCE:</td><td>After a bizarre wedding ceremony in the health spa, the couple jogged off into the sunset.</td></tr>
<tr><td>PHRASES INTRODUCING A SECOND INDEPENDENT CLAUSE:</td><td>The well-known *couturiers* once catered to the idle rich, but with so many women now in the business world, designers are taking a more practical approach to fashion.</td></tr>
</table>

If a prepositional phrase is short and does not interfere with ease of reading, the comma can be omitted.

By 1862 the pony express was no longer in existence.
At twilight we always heard the whippoorwill.

21b

☐ EXERCISE 3

In the following sentences, place commas after introductory prepositional phrases. Point out when the commas can be omitted.

1. In my family public displays of affection were discouraged.
2. During droughts the plant's roots reach deeper into the ground.
3. As an entering freshman I was intimidated by my professors, but after one semester in school I realized that most of them are helpful and not fearsome.
4. A representative of the group stated that without a good bit of government aid many area farmers would lose their farms this year.
5. By noon electricity had been restored.

(2) Introductory verbals and verbal phrases

A comma follows an introductory verbal (participle, infinitive, or gerund) or verbal phrase, regardless of its length.

PARTICIPAL PHRASE INTRODUCING A SENTENCE: Built in 1752, Connecticut Hall is the oldest building on the Yale campus.

PARTICIPLE PHRASE INTRODUCING A SECOND INDEPENDENT CLAUSE: He swung the door open; then realizing his error, he stammered and backed from the room.

INFINITIVE PHRASE INTRODUCING A SENTENCE: To avoid the crowds, I did my Christmas shopping in September.

GERUND PHRASE INTRODUCING A SENTENCE: By encroaching on the dense woods, we have greatly reduced the wild-turkey population.

Even a single introductory participle or infinitive is followed by a comma.

PARTICIPLE INTRODUCING A SENTENCE: <u>Exhausted</u>, she fell asleep on the chair.

INFINITIVES INTRODUCING A FIRST AND SECOND INDEPENDENT CLAUSE: <u>To jitterbug</u>, you must tense your arm muscles, but <u>to waltz</u>, you must relax them.

21b

☐ EXERCISE 4

In the following passage, insert commas where needed after introductory verbal phrases.

To understand the history of changes in women's athletics we must go back to 1972 and the passage of Title IX of the Education Amendments Act, which prohibits sex discrimination in federally assisted schools. Fearing the loss of federal funds schools and universities began paying some attention to women's athletics. By implementing Title IX athletic departments increased sports funds for women from 1 percent to 16 percent; and responding to the attention women increased their participation in intercollegiate athletics from 16,000 to 150,000. The difference made by Title IX was demonstrated in the 1984 Olympic Games; given the proper training women athletes excelled for the first time in our history.

(3) Introductory adverb clauses

Most introductory clauses are adverb clauses, introduced by subordinate conjunctions such as *after, although, as soon as, because, before, even though, if, once, since, unless, when, where, while.* (See 7c.1, "Adverb Clauses.") Usually, a comma separates an introductory adverb clause from the rest of the sentence.

> <u>Although hypnosis now has a recognized place in medicine</u>, the technique has its opponents.
>
> <u>Unless the student newspaper can generate more advertising</u>, readers will have to pay fifty cents per issue.
>
> <u>When a tuning fork is struck</u>, the tone remains always the same.

A comma also follows an adverb clause that introduces a subsequent clause in a sentence.

> A baby is born with the language center in the left side of the brain, but if he or she suffers brain injury very early in infancy, the language center can shift to the right side.

The power went out because <u>when I plugged in the coffee pot,</u> I overloaded the circuit.

The comma can be omitted after a short introductory clause that does not interfere with ease of reading. Nevertheless, the comma is always appropriate.

> CORRECT: <u>When it snows</u> I get depressed.
>
> CORRECT: <u>When it snows,</u> I get depressed.

21b

☐ EXERCISE 5

In the following passage, insert commas where needed after introductory adverb clauses.

> Even though the birthrate is increasing over half the population of the United States will soon be over fifty years of age. If we are to deal successfully with this new trend we must rethink our attitudes toward aging. In the past, most of us have believed that when we reach fifty we should also have reached all our goals. We cannot afford, however, to have 50 percent of our citizens without goals, without direction, without interest in the future. Life after fifty can be full of challenge and growth. But how?
>
> Where there is learning there is growth. Once we stop trying to educate only our youth and start trying to educate the entire population we will make progress. Continued learning—at all ages—is the key to a full life and to a vital citizenry. As we have always heard youth can accomplish much with education. The same is true of those no longer young.

(4) Introductory noun clauses

Normally, a noun clause used as an object or complement follows the verb and is not separated from the rest of the sentence with a comma. (See 7c.3, "Noun Clauses.")

> COMPLEMENT: People can be <u>whatever they want to be.</u>
>
> DIRECT OBJECT: The group automatically opposes <u>whomever labor supports.</u>

When the normal order is reversed and the noun clause is introductory, it is followed by a comma.

> INTRODUCTORY COMPLEMENT: <u>Whatever people want to be,</u> they can be.
>
> INTRODUCTORY OBJECT: <u>Whomever labor supports,</u> the group automatically opposes.

NOTE: Do not confuse introductory noun clauses with noun clauses used as subjects. In the following example, the noun clause is the subject of the sentence, not an introductory element. Notice that the noun clause is followed by its verb, not by another subject and verb.

<u>Whatever people want subconsciously</u> is usually what they get.

21c

☐ EXERCISE 6

Put commas after the introductory noun clauses serving as objects and complements but not as subjects.

1. Whoever wishes to enjoy a cruise must also enjoy close quarters.
2. Whatever he said his assistant echoed.
3. Whomever the governor appoints the legislature must approve.
4. Whatever the animal is trained to be it will be.
5. Whatever the omens foretold was not questioned.

21c Commas Between Independent Clauses and Clauses or Phrases That Follow

When an adverb clause or phrase follows an independent clause, the nature of the connection determines the proper punctuation.

- No comma precedes an adverb clause or phrase essential to the meaning of the sentence.
- A comma precedes an adverb clause or phrase that simply adds information or restates an idea.

ESSENTIAL PHRASE: The session began <u>after roll call.</u> [The phrase tells when the session began.]

NONESSENTIAL PHRASE: The session began promptly at 10:15, <u>after roll call.</u> [The phrase adds nonessential information.]

ESSENTIAL CLAUSE: Oyster production has been declining <u>since fresh water from the rivers upset the salinity of the Gulf in April.</u> [A *since* clause that cites time is usually essential.]

NONESSENTIAL CLAUSE: Oyster production may be increasing, <u>since influx of fresh water is now being controlled.</u> [A *since* clause that states reason is usually nonessential.]

ESSENTIAL CLAUSE: The commentator covered the event as though he were bored. [The clause is essential to indicate how the commentator covered the event.]

NONESSENTIAL CLAUSE: The commentator covered the event in a monotone, as though he were bored. [The phrase *in a monotone* indicates how the event was covered; the clause adds nonessential information.]

21d

☐ EXERCISE 7

Decide which of the following sentences contain nonessential clauses or phrases. Separate the nonessential elements from the independent clauses with commas.

1. The office will notify you at 1:00 on Wednesday.
2. The office will close at 1:00 after the employees receive Christmas bonuses.
3. We must leave for the airport before five.
4. We must leave for the airport by five before the rush-hour traffic begins.
5. This film did not succeed since the public prefers action and special effects to the study of human relationships.
6. This film is the most sentimental comedy since the days of Capra.
7. The filtered lighting made the actress look as if she were much younger.
8. The filtered lighting made the actress look twenty-five as if she had not aged since her first movie.
9. The hikers stayed in the mountains as long as their supplies lasted.
10. We might as well hike back to camp as long as we have to replenish supplies anyway.

21d Commas to Set Off Nonrestrictive Elements

A nonrestrictive element does not restrict, limit, or identify the word or phrase it follows. Commas around the nonrestrictive element indicate that its omission would not alter the meaning of the sentence.

In contrast, a restrictive element restricts, limits, or identifies the word or phrase it follows. Thus, deletion of the restrictive element would change the meaning of the sentence. No comma or other mark of punctuation should interrupt this close connection.

1) Nonrestrictive clauses and phrases

Adjective clauses and phrases follow the words they modify and may be either restrictive or nonrestrictive. As the examples illustrate, commas do not set off restrictive clauses and phrases; commas must, however, set off nonrestrictive clauses and phrases.

21d

RESTRICTIVE CLAUSE: The Warren Report summarizes the events that relate to John F. Kennedy's assassination. [The events summarized are limited to those relating to the assassination.]

NONRESTRICTIVE CLAUSE: One of the most controversial documents in our history is the Warren Report, which summarizes the events relating to John F. Kennedy's assassination. [The clause does not identify the Warren Report, which is identified by its name.]

RESTRICTIVE CLAUSE: The team needs a quarterback who can run as well as pass. [The kind of quarterback the team needs is restricted to one who can run as well as pass.]

NONRESTRICTIVE CLAUSE: Last Saturday, the most impressive player on the team was the starting quarterback, who could run as well as pass. [The clause does not identify last Saturday's starting quarterback; there can be only one.]

RESTRICTIVE PHRASE: Meat preserved in brine and vinegar is called "pickled." [Pickled meat is restricted to meat preserved in brine and vinegar.]

NONRESTRICTIVE PHRASE: "Pickled" meat, preserved in brine and vinegar, was a mainstay in the diet of American colonists. [The phrase is a nonessential definition of pickled meat.]

RESTRICTIVE PHRASE: Dr. Edwards is the professor known to his students as Scrooge. [The phrase identifies Dr. Edwards as a particular professor.]

NONRESTRICTIVE PHRASE: I didn't want to take a course from Dr. Edwards, known to his students as Scrooge. [The phrase supplies additional information about Dr. Edwards, who is identified by name.]

Occasionally, a modifier can be either restrictive or nonrestrictive, depending on what is meant. In these cases, the punctuation must correctly interpret the sentence for the reader.

RESTRICTIVE: The Greeks who loved beauty produced great art.

NONRESTRICTIVE: The Greeks, who loved beauty, produced great art.

21d

In the first example, the absence of commas indicates that *who loved beauty* identifies the Greeks. Thus, the sentence means "Only those Greeks who loved beauty produced great art." In the second, commas indicate that *who loved beauty* is additional information. Thus, the sentence means "The Greeks produced great art and they loved beauty."

In the next pair, the punctuation again interprets the meaning.

RESTRICTIVE: I gave the old car to my daughter who lives in Chicago.

NONRESTRICTIVE: I gave the old car to my daughter, who lives in Chicago.

The absence of the commas in the first sentence indicates that the writer has more than one daughter and gave the car to the one who lives in Chicago. The presence of commas in the second sentence indicates that the writer has only one daughter.

There are several clues for determining whether a modifier is restrictive or nonrestrictive.

• An element modifying a proper noun is usually nonrestrictive, since the proper name itself serves as identification.

NONRESTRICTIVE: The Dalmatian, also called the "coach dog," closely resembles a pointer.

• An element is nonrestrictive when it modifies a noun that can refer to only one possible person, place, thing, or idea.

NONRESTRICTIVE: One of our family heroes is my mother's father, who ran away with a circus.

• If an adjective clause begins with *that* (or if *that* can be substituted for an introductory *who* or *which*), the clause is restrictive.

RESTRICTIVE: The hot ashes that rained on Pompeii sealed the city for almost 1,700 years.

RESTRICTIVE: The editorial attacked students who [or *that*] supported the quota system.

- If an adjective clause has an unstated but understood introductory word, the clause is restrictive.

> Large numbers of delegates voted the way they were told to vote. [*That* is understood before *they*.]

21d

☐ EXERCISE 8

In the following sentences, enclose the nonrestrictive clauses and phrases with commas.

1. I never get to watch my favorite soap opera which comes on during my morning classes.
2. There is an old proverb that states, "Never eat at a place called 'Mom's' and never play cards with a man named 'Doc.'"
3. James Savage who was my Shakespeare professor won the bass fishing rodeo for five straight years.
4. Chicken soup sometimes called "homemade penicillin" actually has medicinal effects.
5. Students taking the word processing course must schedule laboratory time once a week.
6. Our only snow that year which fell in early March killed all the azaleas and disappointed the tourists.
7. Everyone I knew on the entire campus had gone home for the holidays.
8. Registration reminded me of the U.S. Army whose motto is "Hurry up and wait."
9. The movies I remember most vividly from childhood were animated cartoon films.
10. *Pamela* usually considered the first English novel is subtitled *Virtue Rewarded.*

(2) Appositives

An appositive renames, restates, or explains the word or words it refers to.

> I was craving a bowl of vegetable soup, my favorite food in cold weather.

When an appositive follows the words it refers to, it may be either restrictive or nonrestrictive.

> RESTRICTIVE APPOSITIVE: Antiseptic surgery was founded by the physician Lister. [*Lister* identifies the physician who founded antiseptic surgery.]

NONRESTRICTIVE APPOSITIVE: Lister, <u>a professor of surgery at Glasgow</u>
<u>University,</u> founded antiseptic surgery.
[The appositive does not identify Lister
but merely adds information about him.
He is identified by his name.]

21d

An appositive may also appear at the beginning of a sentence, just
before the word it refers to; or it may appear at the end of the
sentence, separate from the word or words it refers to. In either case,
the appositive is separated from the rest of the sentence by a
comma. (For other ways of punctuating appositives, see 23b and
24a.)

APPOSITIVE AT BEGINNING: <u>A big-boned, overweight woman,</u> Mrs. Everett nevertheless wore clothes designed for a
petite teenager. [*Woman* is an appositive to
Mrs. Everett.]

APPOSITIVE AT END: A wonderful surprise was in the envelope, <u>a</u>
<u>round-trip ticket to Washington.</u> [*Ticket* is
an appositive to *surprise.*]

Some appositives are accompanied by expressions such as *or,
namely, that is, in other words,* and so on. Normally restatements,
these appositives should be enclosed in commas.

NONRESTRICTIVE: A good diplomat must be an expert in kinesis, <u>or</u>
<u>body language.</u> [*Body language* restates *kinesis.*]

NONRESTRICTIVE: They stayed married because they had reciprocal
needs, <u>interlocking neuroses, in other words.</u> [*Interlocking neuroses* restates *reciprocal needs.*]

☐ EXERCISE 9

In the following sentences, enclose nonrestrictive appositives with
commas.

1. It doesn't hurt to believe in Santa Claus a character who brings out the
   best in all of us.
2. The musician Dylan seemed to be at odds with the poet Dylan.
3. My main complaint about the cafeteria was elementary the food.
4. A truly unusual resort Westland offers both excitement and relaxation.
5. They were looking for something to make them feel secure in the community namely prestige.

☐ EXERCISE 10

Combine each of the following pairs of sentences into one sentence by converting an independent clause to an adjective phrase, adjective clause, or appositive. Indicate restrictive elements by the absence of commas and nonrestrictive elements by the presence of commas.

21d

EXAMPLE: One of the jewels in the Triple Crown is the Kentucky Derby. The Derby is the best-known horse race in the country. → One of the jewels in the Triple Crown is the Kentucky Derby, the best-known horse race in the country.

1. Rhode Island is the smallest state in the Union. It is also an important industrial area.
2. The royal palm is a tropical tree. It resembles a pillar with a crown of leaves at its top.
3. The shallot is the best of the sauce onions. It is especially good in wine cookery.
4. Pisces is a zodiac sign. It is represented by the fish.
5. I don't like digital watches. They look like machines instead of jewelry.
6. My father has an excellent sense of direction. He can find his way through any city with ease.
7. I try to take courses from certain professors. These professors don't assign research papers.
8. The game of hockey began in the 1800s. It became the national sport of Canada by the 1900s.

☐ EXERCISE 11

Insert commas to enclose the nonrestrictive elements in the following passage.

The authenticity of Robin Hood who was a legendary English hero has been much disputed. He was popularized as Locksley a character in Sir Walter Scott's fiction. But Robin appeared long before that. A few early historians have made claims that he lived in the 1100s. Also, he was mentioned in *Piers Plowman* a work written in the late 1300s. Furthermore, one of the earliest ballad collections that has been preserved is *Lytell Geste of Robyn Hoode* which was printed in 1495.

In most sources, Robin lives in Sherwood Forest which is located in Nottinghamshire. He leads a band of colorful outlaws who spend their time robbing the rich and giving to the poor.

Probably not much of the myth is true. Yet Robin's "grave" is supposedly located in Yorkshire where his bow and arrow are exhibited.

21e Commas Between Items in a Series and Between Coordinate Adjectives

(1) Items in a series

21e

A series is a list of three or more parallel structures—for example, three or more nouns, adjectives, verb phrases, prepositional phrases, dependent clauses, independent clauses, and so on. Ordinarily, items in a series are separated by commas. (If the series items themselves contain commas, semicolons are used. See 22d.)

SERIES OF ADJECTIVES: We are looking for someone reliable, efficient, and versatile.

SERIES OF NOUN PHRASES: When in doubt about the procedure, consult the lab manual, the operational instructions, or the student assistant.

SERIES OF DEPENDENT CLAUSES: When I returned to my room I found that my roommate had eaten lunch on my bed, that one of his friends had spilled coffee on my history notes, and that another friend had borrowed my sports jacket.

SERIES OF INDEPENDENT CLAUSES: The roots absorb the water from the soil, the sapwood carries the water to the leaves, and the leaves make food for the tree.

Some writers, particularly journalists, omit the comma between the conjunction and the last element in the series. However, omission of the last comma can sometimes cause misreading.

UNCLEAR: The Grievance Committee met with three petitioners, two students and a faculty member.

The reader cannot know whether the committee met with six people or with three. But proper punctuation can make the meaning clear.

CLEAR: The Grievance Committee met with three petitioners, two students, and a faculty member. [six people, listed as items in a series]

CLEAR: The Grievance Committee met with three petitioners: two <u>students and a faculty member.</u> [three people, presented as an appositive following a colon]

In the next example, *large* seems to modify *angel fish* and *catfish*.

UNCLEAR: The aquarium in the dentist's office contained guppies, tetras, large angel fish and catfish.

But a large catfish might weigh over a hundred pounds and would not likely be in an aquarium in a dentist's office. A comma after *angel fish* solves the problem.

CLEAR: The aquarium in the dentist's office contained guppies, tetras, large angel fish, and catfish.

☐ EXERCISE 12

In the following sentences, insert commas between items in a series.

1. As a child, he liked to read stories about the American wilderness, the exploration of the frontier and the Indian wars.
2. The primary staples of their diet were cornbread chicken rice and gravy.
3. I buy clothes that are on sale washable and wrinkle-free.
4. Either the schedule was wrong the train was late or I was in the wrong terminal.
5. The elegant auction featured diamond jewelry ancient jade statues and furniture.

(2) Coordinate adjectives

Coordinate adjectives can be rearranged and can be logically connected by *and*. In the absence of *and*, commas separate coordinate adjectives.

COORDINATE: He liked to play tennis on a <u>shady, secluded</u> court.

REARRANGED: He liked to play tennis on a <u>secluded, shady</u> court.

CONNECTED WITH <u>AND</u>: He liked to play tennis on <u>a shady and secluded</u> court.

Noncoordinate adjectives, which can be neither rearranged nor connected with *and,* should not be separated by commas.

NONCOORDINATE: He liked to play tennis on an old clay court.

IMPOSSIBLE: He liked to play tennis on a clay old court.

IMPOSSIBLE: He liked to play tennis on an old and clay court.

When an adjective phrase contains both coordinate and noncoordinate adjectives, the same principle applies: commas appear in positions where *and* could be inserted.

21e

COORDINATE AND NONCOORDINATE: I was met at the door by two large, shaggy, playful Irish setters.

POSSIBLE: I was met at the door by two large and shaggy and playful Irish setters.

IMPOSSIBLE: I was met at the door by two and large and shaggy and playful and Irish setters.

☐ EXERCISE 13

In each series of modifiers, insert commas between coordinate adjectives but not between noncoordinate adjectives

1. a spacious elegant Italian provincial house
2. the first four years of school
3. a smooth delicate cheese sauce
4. a cold gray rainy afternoon
5. many happy carefree lazy summer vacations

☐ EXERCISE 14

In the following passage, insert commas between items in a series and coordinate adjectives.

When taking photographs with people as subjects, most amateur photographers do not pay enough attention to the horizon the position of the subjects or the framing. These problems can be easily solved.

First, you need to make sure that the horizon is not tilted that it does not dominate the picture and that it does not split the picture in half. Next, you need to position your subjects so that the picture seems evenly lit. You can place subjects where the sun hits them from the side you can put them in the shade against an uncluttered background or you can put them in filtered muted lighting.

Finally, check the edges of the photograph fill the whole area with what you are shooting and eliminate as much background as possible. To make your subject or subjects more interesting, you can include something interesting in the foreground: a tree branch to suggest depth a stream that leads from the foreground to the background or a fence that the eye can follow.

21f Commas in Place of Omitted Words

When consecutive clauses have parallel structure and common vocabulary, a comma can eliminate the repetition of the verb or part of the predicate.

> Rankin received 312 votes; Jenkins, 117. [The comma represents *received.*]
>
> The older sister wanted to be an actress, and the younger sister, a doctor. [The comma represents *wanted to be.*]
>
> The first question was on the prose of the eighteenth century; the second, on the poetry; and the third, on the drama. [The commas represent *was.*]

☐ EXERCISE 15

In the following sentences, use commas to indicate where verbs or parts of predicates have been omitted.

1. An African bull elephant weighs from 12,000 to 14,000 pounds; an Asian bull from 7,000 to 12,000.
2. The Brontë sisters shocked readers with their unusual stories: Emily with the eerie *Wuthering Heights;* Charlotte with the independent heroine of *Jane Eyre.*
3. The northern trade route ran from China across central Asia to Byzantium; the southern route from China to the Red Sea and overland to the Nile and northern Egypt.
4. During the day the temperature is over ninety; at night under sixty.
5. The ancestry of a purebred horse is traced through a single breed; the ancestry of a thoroughbred horse to three Arabian stallions—Darley Arabian, Godolphin Barb, and Byerly Turk.

21g Commas to Set Off Parenthetical, Transitional, and Contrastive Elements

(1) Parenthetical elements

A parenthetical element is a structure that could be enclosed in parentheses without changing the meaning of the sentence. The element can occur within a sentence and interrupt the structure abruptly, or it can appear at the end of a sentence and serve as a concluding remark.

INTERRUPTING THE SUBJECT AND VERB: The coach, according to informed sources, intends to leave after this season.

INTERRUPTING THE VERB AND OBJECT: The bank officers said, believe it or not, that they had accurately reported the assets.

INTERRUPTING THE VERB PHRASE: She was not, strictly speaking, managing the estate.

CONCLUDING REMARK: Salaries have not improved at all during the last three years, at least not as far as the clerical staff is concerned.

'
21g

☐ EXERCISE 16

In the following sentences, insert commas to set off parenthetical elements that function either as interrupters or as concluding remarks.

1. You should write a note after a job interview regardless of whether you want the job to thank the interviewer for his or her time.
2. Diary keeping at least for many people is a way of comparing dreams and realities.
3. The stereo speakers according to the instructions should be about 20 feet apart.
4. The reporter refused to reveal her sources because she wanted to protect their safety or so she said.
5. Wrinkles as a general rule are caused by the breakdown of collagen and elastin in the skin.

(2) Transitional expressions

Transitional expressions, or conjunctive adverbs, are words and phrases such as *however, therefore, for example, in conclusion, accordingly, nevertheless, in addition,* and so on. (See TRANSITIONAL EXPRESSION in "Glossary of Grammatical, Rhetorical, and Literary Terms.") These expressions link sentences and passages by pointing to what precedes or what follows. Notice how commas set off the transitional expressions in this passage.

> Houseplants available at nurseries can be expensive and, in addition, difficult to grow. Therefore, people without green thumbs are often reluctant to spend money to watch their purchases wither and die. There is, however, a solution for people who want to grow plants with little expense or effort—the avocado.
>
> The seed of a well-ripened avocado planted in porous soil will sprout and produce a good-sized plant in a few weeks. An avocado plant grown in the house will not, of course, flower or bear fruit. Nevertheless, it will provide inexpensive, luxurious, and trouble-free greenery.

21g (margin)

☐ EXERCISE 17

Use commas to set off the transitional expressions in the following passage.

> While looking at some old photograph albums that had belonged to my mother, I was struck by how carefully she had documented her life. First there was her young adulthood with friends; then there were the early years of her marriage; and finally there were the stages of her children's lives. For example I saw her at high school dances and college football games. I saw her on her honeymoon at Niagara Falls. I saw my brother and me as infants, toddlers, grammar school brats, and teenagers.
>
> Most of the pictures of course were amateurish. In addition many were blurred with age. Nevertheless that photograph album brought whole lives into focus. And more particularly it brought only the good times back. Consequently looking at the snapshots made me feel that life had been good to my mother and to her children.
>
> As a result I have determined to take more photographs. I will naturally embarrass my children by running around with a camera, leaping from behind potted palms to immortalize them with a click. They will however thank me when they grow up—just as I now thank my mother.

(3) Contrastive elements

A contrastive element begins with a word like *not, never,* or *but;* it expresses an idea that contrasts with or contradicts one that has preceded. Enclosing the contrastive element within commas emphasizes it.

> It was the beginning, not the end, of the social upheaval.

The egalitarian Shakespeare, <u>not the elitist Jonson,</u> was popular with the masses.

Our codes of conduct in those days were dictated by our peers, <u>never by our parents.</u>

The speech was informative, but tedious.

☐ EXERCISE 18

In the following sentences, enclose the contrastive elements within commas for emphasis.

1. Lately, it seems that football not baseball is the national pastime.
2. Living in Los Angeles unlike living in New York requires a car.
3. They provide guides for tours but only for walking tours.
4. The reflexive of *they* is *themselves* never *theirselves.*
5. This manual is a complete but not very readable guide to organic gardening.

21h Commas to Set Off Interjections, Words in Direct Address, and Tag Questions

Interjections, words in direct address, and tag questions modify whole clauses or sentences and are therefore set off with commas. These elements usually occur in fiction and in dialogue rather than in formal prose.

An interjection is an expression of emotion that can be punctuated as a separate sentence with a period or an exclamation point. The so-called "mild" interjection is usually separated from the rest of the sentence with a comma.

<u>Well,</u> the time has finally come to act.

<u>Goodness,</u> did the bell ring?

Words in direct address name whomever or whatever is spoken to.

Excuse me, <u>sir,</u> is this the plane to Denver?

Sit up and beg, <u>Butch.</u>

Tag questions appear at the end of statements and ask for verification.

The budget was balanced, <u>wasn't it?</u>

She did not ask for a second opinion, <u>did she?</u>

☐ EXERCISE 19

In the following speech, insert commas to set off interjections, words in direct address, and tag questions.

Ladies and gentlemen may I have your attention please. Thank you for coming tonight to hear our candidate for governor. Usually, all politicians are alike. We know how they operate don't we? They make promises they don't keep in return for our contributions—which they do keep. Well this candidate is a bit different. He's going to tell us what he might be able to do as governor. He isn't going to tell us thank goodness what he promises to do. And wonder of wonders he isn't going to ask us for any money. So friends please help me welcome this unique candidate won't you?

21i Commas in Special Contexts: in Dates, Places, Addresses; in Numbers; in Letters; with Titles of Individuals; with Quotation Marks

(1) Dates, places, and addresses

The commas in dates, places, addresses serve to isolate each item for the reader.

- Month day, year,

    She graduated on May 22, 1986, from Loyola University. [commas before and after the year when the day is given]

- Day month year

    She graduated 22 May 1986 from Loyola University. [no commas when the day precedes the month]

- Month year

    She graduated in May 1986 from Loyola University. [no commas when the day is unspecified]

- City, state,

    We surveyed the voters in St. Louis, Missouri, and in Phoenix, Arizona. [commas before and after the names of states]

- Street address, city, state zip code,

    Ship the package to 1110 East Marina Road, Dallas, TX 75201, within ten days. [comma between street address and city; comma between

city and state; no comma between state and zip code; comma between zip code and material that follows]

(2) Numbers expressing amounts

Commas indicate thousands and millions in numbers of five or more
digits. Many people also prefer commas in four-digit numbers.

21i

> In 1972 they sold 2,165 records; this year they sold 1,926,021.

(3) Salutations and closings of letters

In business letters, a colon follows the salutation.

> **Dear Ms. Steinhold:**
>
> **Dear Dr. Kimbrough:**

But in more informal, "friendly" letters, a comma follows.

> **Dear Frances,**
>
> **Dear George,**

In most business and friendly letters, the closing is followed by a
comma.

> **Fondly,**
>
> **Sincerely,**
>
> **Very truly yours,**

(4) Titles of individuals

An individual's title following his or her name is enclosed with commas.

> **Applications for the summer co-op program should be sent to
> Kathryn McLeod, travel director, or to Carl Jenkins, personnel
> director.**

In current practice, many writers do not set off *Jr.* or *Sr.* following a
name.

> **Mark D. Cromwell Jr. will direct the workshop.**
>
> **James Hillery Godbold Sr. donated the funds.**

Some people, however, prefer the commas, and a writer should
honor that preference when using their names.

> **Mr. and Mrs. James W. Marcott, Jr., hosted the reception.**

☐ EXERCISE 20

In the following letter, use commas to punctuate dates, addresses, numbers, titles, and the closing.

21i

9781 Ironwood Drive
Birmingham Alabama 35201
June 11 1987

Mr. Arnold Bennett President
Bennett and Hughes
8581 Indian Wood Road
Nashville Tennessee 37219

Dear Mr. Bennett:

On June 10 1987 we surveyed the proposed site for the bridle paths. The 10112-acre site can accommodate 23 miles of paths. The terrain seems ideal, varied but not dangerous. The area is scenic, with diverse plant life, small streams, and outcrops of rock.

We suggest that you have a feasibility study done to determine whether tourist access to the area is sufficient. We can recommend a reputable firm in Nashville, with an excellent history in feasibility and marketing studies. For information, write to

> Donald Shaw Jr.
> Adams and Cromwell
> 1919 University Place
> Nashville TN 37219

Sincerely yours

L. Brett Carter

L. Brett Carter

(5) Direct quotations

To set off a quotation from the words that identify its source, commas are positioned before opening quotation marks and inside closing quotation marks.

> "You can't expect to hit the jackpot," said Flip Wilson, "if you don't put a few nickels in the machine."

"The results of the tests are insignificant," according to Dr. Landrum.

"It was a perfect title," Dixon thought, "in that it crystallized the article's niggling mindlessness, its funeral parade of yawn-enforcing facts, the pseudo-light it threw upon non-problems." (Kingsley Amis)

21j

A comma is not appropriate when a short quotation is an integral part of the sentence structure.

Several people began to scream "Fire."

Who said that for every credibility gap, there is a "gullibility fill"?

☐ EXERCISE 21

Insert commas where appropriate to set off quotations from the words that identify their source.

1.   "Remember that as a teenager" Fran Lebowitz said "you are in the last stage of your life when you will be happy to hear that the phone is for you."

2.   According to H. L. Mencken "For every human problem, there is a neat, plain solution—and it is always wrong."

3.   The report showed that employees were very dissatisfied with the classification system. Quite a few comments addressed that subject. For example, one employee said "The job levels are totally unfair, and moving from one level up to another is virtually impossible." Another complained "The salary increments for some levels do not allow for cost-of-living raises, much less for merit raises." Many employees felt that job levels did not reflect the responsibilities of the positions. "I am an assistant to two coordinators" said one person "and my responsibilities are administrative. Yet, the Office of Personnel classifies me as a clerk-typist, and I am paid accordingly."

21j Commas to Ensure Intended Reading

In some instances, commas are necessary simply to prevent misreading. For example, in the following sentence, the comma is necessary to indicate that *can try* is not a unit.

CONFUSING: Employees who can try to car pool twice a week.

CLEAR: Employees who can, try to car pool twice a week.

In other instances, commas create stylistic effects. For example, the commas in the next two sentences are not grammatically necessary; instead, they indicate pauses and create a reading different from the usual.

> "There is no safety in numbers, or in anything else." (James Thurber)
>
> The child had never had a guardian, and never had a friend.

21k

☐ EXERCISE 22

In the following sentences, insert commas for clarity.

1. No matter how late the message was welcome.
2. To the Burgundian beer drinkers are contemptible.
3. Any unlikely event that would destroy carefully laid plans if it did occur will occur.
4. According to Murphy's Law, anything that can go wrong will.
5. Those who can perform; those who cannot criticize.

21k Inappropriate Commas

A reader is as disconcerted by the presence of an unnecessary comma as by the absence of a necessary one. In general, a comma should not be used in the following situations, except where necessary to ensure proper reading.

- A comma should not separate major sentence elements—such as subject and predicate, verb and object, items in a verb phrase, and so on.

  > INAPPROPRIATE: Several people on horseback, suddenly appeared at the bridge. [separation of subject and predicate]
  >
  > APPROPRIATE: Several people on horseback suddenly appeared at the bridge.

  > INAPPROPRIATE: Conner realized, that he wanted to go home. [separation of verb and object]
  >
  > APPROPRIATE: Conner realized that he wanted to go home.

- Ordinarily, a comma should not separate two items joined by a coordinating conjunction or correlative conjunctions unless those items are independent clauses.

  > INAPPROPRIATE: The road began at the edge of the field, and ended abruptly in the middle. [separation of compound verbs]

APPROPRIATE: The road began at the edge of the field and ended abruptly in the middle.

INAPPROPRIATE: We hoped the commission would prohibit not only channelization, but also the planting of kudzu. [separation of compound objects]

APPROPRIATE: We hoped the commission would prohibit not only channelization but also the planting of kudzu.

21k

- A comma should not separate the final adjective in a series from the following noun.

    INAPPROPRIATE: He wore a cheap, shabby, and ill-fitting, suit.

    APPROPRIATE: He wore a cheap, shabby, and ill-fitting suit.

- Ordinarily, a comma should not follow a subordinate or a coordinating conjunction.

    INAPPROPRIATE: We ate at a terrible restaurant that featured waffles and, fried seafood.

    APPROPRIATE: We ate at a terrible restaurant that featured waffles and fried seafood.

    INAPPROPRIATE: Nothing grows in that section of the yard because, there is too much lime in the soil.

    APPROPRIATE: Nothing grows in that section of the yard because there is too much lime in the soil.

- A comma should not separate an indirect quotation from the rest of the sentence.

    INAPPROPRIATE: The author said, that the historical data had been carefully researched.

    APPROPRIATE: The author said that the historical data had been carefully researched.

☐ EXERCISE 23

Remove any inappropriate commas from the following sentences.

1. The ball seemed to float toward the goal posts and, then remain stationary for several seconds.
2. The book that he assigned us, was too technical for novices.
3. My feet were sore, my back was aching, and, my head was swimming.
4. The announcement said, that the winner had been disqualified, and that the race would be rerun.

5. The realtor felt, that the property was valuable.
6. I think baton twirling is silly although, I realize it takes a good bit of skill.
7. It was a slow, lazy, meandering, stream.
8. The dancer was not only graceful, but also remarkably athletic.
9. I thought I heard someone scream, that the stadium was on fire.
10. The people who lived next door, had eight cats and six dogs.

21k

☐ EXERCISE 24

In the following composition, insert commas where they are needed, and delete commas where they are inappropriate. Some of the commas are properly placed.

Getting a summer job takes a good bit of planning, that must not be overlooked. First you must consider what kinds of jobs you are qualified for. For example if you cannot type you can rule out not only a secretarial position, but also a receptionist position which almost always involves some typing. Or if you are under twenty-one you cannot expect to land a job, that requires you to handle alcoholic drinks. In other words you must realistically assess your possibilities.

After this assessment you should consider whether there are any jobs you are simply unwilling to undertake. For example if you are not willing to work late at night on weekends and on the Fourth of July you should not apply at fast-food restaurants. No, a better job for you would be, with a local government, which would ensure you regular hours, and vacations on holidays.

When you have your abilities and preferences in mind the next step is to get yourself ready to accept responsibility. Come to terms with the fact that you cannot miss work because of late-night partying and you cannot expect other employees to do the work, that you have been hired to do. You must act, in other words like a mature responsible adult.

Once you are ready, psychologically ready to work you can begin your search. First you should check all want ads bulletin boards and radio programs that list jobs. Also you should register with the local state-employment agency for this service will not charge a fee for a job search. In addition if you can afford the cost you should apply with private employment agencies which usually charge a percentage of the first, month's salary.

The next step is, to contact people in your community who might act as references and recommend you to prospective employers. Everyone has heard that old expression, "It isn't what you know that counts; it's whom you know." It does matter of course what you know but it also matters whom you know. A phone call, or letter from someone that a prospective employer knows, can help you land the job you want.

With luck and effort you can obtain some job interviews. When you do be sure to take plenty of time to prepare for each interview: anticipate possible questions, practice answering them, learn all you can about the job and the company or agency and arrive neatly groomed in an attractive no-nonsense outfit.

Finally take Winston Churchill's advice and, "never, never, never, never give up." You may search for several weeks before getting a job or you may not find one at all. The experience you gain and the contacts you achieve however will teach you a great deal and you will probably have better luck the next summer.

21k

22

Semicolons

Semicolons are used in sentences that require marks of punctuation weaker than periods but stronger than commas. Basically, there are two positions for semicolons: between independent clauses and between items in a series that contain commas. In each position, the semicolon occurs between coordinate elements—that is, elements of the same grammatical construction.

22a Semicolons Between Independent Clauses Not Joined by Coordinating Conjunctions

Independent clauses can be joined with a comma and a coordinating conjunction (*and, but, or, nor, for, so, yet*). If the ideas in the clauses have a kind of equality, the semicolon can convey more closeness and balance than a comma and a coordinating conjunction. (See 33a.1, "Combining Independent Clauses Through Coordination.")

> A hundred years ago, 50 percent of Americans were farmers; today, only 4 percent are farmers.
>
> The left brain controls the right side of the body; the right brain controls the left side.
>
> Shakespeare's vocabulary included about 20,000 words; Milton's, about 11,000.

Although you often have a choice between joining independent clauses with semicolons or with commas and coordinating conjunctions, you should be careful not to overuse semicolons within a single passage. Semicolons are more noticeable than commas and thus should be used sparingly, lest they lose their effect.

> OVERUSED: Bluegrass music is an old-timey sound out of the hills of Virginia, Tennessee, and Kentucky; it is the most traditional form of country music. Now the bluegrass festival has become a popular entertainment; families pack picnics to spend the day listening to professionals and amateurs play. Some fans listen to the performances on the stage; others wander about enjoying the impromptu sessions on the grounds.

> REVISED: Bluegrass music—an old-timey sound out of the hills of Virginia, Tennessee, and Kentucky—is the most traditional form of country music. Now the bluegrass festival has become a popular entertainment. Families pack picnics to spend the day listening to professionals and amateurs play. Some fans listen to the performances on the stage; others wander about enjoying the impromptu sessions on the grounds.

;
22b

☐ EXERCISE 1

Combine each of the following pairs of independent clauses so that a semicolon separates the clauses.

1. The weather is very strange. We should have had a hard frost at least three weeks ago.
2. Benjamin Franklin did many experiments with lightning, and in one of them he passed an electric current through a chain of six men.
3. One of the coaches resigned. The other one was fired.
4. Paper airplanes are not airplanes at all. They should be called "paper gliders."
5. People under stress report long, complex dreams, but people with placid lives report dreams that are uneventful and uninteresting.

22b Semicolons Between Independent Clauses Joined by Transitional Expressions

Often when two independent clauses are joined, the second clause is introduced by a transitional expression such as *however, therefore, consequently, thus, in addition, for example, nevertheless, for in-*

stance, then, finally. (For a more complete list, see TRANSITIONAL EXPRESSION, "Glossary of Grammatical, Rhetorical, and Literary Terms.") Although these expressions indicate the relationship between the two clauses, they are not grammatical connectors as the coordinating conjunctions are. Therefore, in the absence of a coordinating conjunction, the semicolon is necessary between two independent clauses (whether the transitional expression is present or not).

; 22b

> At first, we feared that computers would increase unemployment; however, they have instead created more jobs.

> At first, we feared that computers would increase unemployment; they have instead created more jobs.

The difference between the transitional expressions and the coordinating conjunctions can be illustrated very simply: the transitional expressions can move around in a clause; the coordinating conjunctions cannot. Notice that in the following example the transitional expression *for example* can occur before or within the second clause.

> Each year the group publishes a list of useless words that should be banished from the language; for example, it has already tried to banish "at this point in time" and "have a nice day."

> Each year the group publishes a list of useless words that should be banished from the language; it has, for example, already tried to banish "at this point in time" and "have a nice day."

☐ EXERCISE 2

Combine each of the following pairs of independent clauses into a single sentence. Introduce the second clause with a transitional word, and punctuate the sentence correctly.

1. The academic standards in the school are extremely high. Most of the graduates receive scholarships to good colleges.
2. A "cruise control" is useful for a steady highway speed. You should use it only on level roads.
3. Cooking in front of television cameras can be embarrassing. I have seen cooks spill batter all over the stove, drop food on the floor, and cover up mistakes with bunches of parsley.
4. I want to get a roommate who makes up the bed. I filled out a questionnaire to help determine roommate compatibility.
5. The women's basketball team lost their first twelve games. They won the thirteenth game by one point.

22c Semicolons Between Independent Clauses Joined by Coordinating Conjunctions

Ordinarily a comma appears between two independent clauses joined by a coordinating conjunction (*and, but, or, nor, for, so, yet*). However, a semicolon can be used with the conjunction when the first independent clause contains commas.

> UNCLEAR: Of the 11,000 men who encamped at Valley Forge, only 8,000 came with shoes, and only 8,000 survived.
>
> REVISED: Of the 11,000 men who encamped at Valley Forge, only 8,000 came with shoes; and only 8,000 survived.

> UNCLEAR: The books effectively deal with systems and languages such as UNIX, BASIC, PASCAL, C, COBOL, but these books cost approximately twenty dollars each.
>
> REVISED: The books effectively deal with systems and languages such as UNIX, BASIC, PASCAL, C, COBOL; but these books cost approximately twenty dollars each.

When only one comma occurs in the first independent clause, a comma or a semicolon can be used with the conjunction. Either of the following versions is appropriate.

> By purchasing a month-long pass for the train, travelers can save five dollars; but a year-long pass will save ninety dollars.

> By purchasing a month-long pass for the train, travelers can save five dollars, but a year-long pass will save ninety dollars.

EXERCISE 3

Combine each of the following pairs of independent clauses into a single sentence. Join the clauses with a coordinating conjunction and the appropriate punctuation.

1. In *I Had Trouble in Getting to Solla Sollew,* the hero, burdened by the troubles of life, goes in search of a city where people have no troubles. After many adventures, he realizes no place is trouble-free.
2. Blenders, food processors, and instant food have eliminated most slicing, dicing, and pureeing. The time required for putting together a meal seems the same.
3. Executives, managers, and employees were questioned about "flextime." All replied that the system works well.

4. In 1910 most American immigrants were Italians. In 1983 America had immigrants from 183 countries, the largest group from Mexico.
5. The story of the woman with multiple personalities shows the disease's brutal cause, bizarre symptoms, and strange development. The story is not ever sensationalized.

;
22e

22d Semicolons Between Items in a Series with Internal Punctuation

Ordinarily commas separate items in a series.

> We subscribe to *Time, The New Yorker,* and *Harper's.*

If, however, the items themselves contain commas, semicolons are required to mark the separation.

UNCLEAR: The train stops in Birmingham, Alabama, Atlanta, Georgia, Charlotte, North Carolina, and Charlottesville, Virginia.

REVISED: The train stops in Birmingham, Alabama; Atlanta, Georgia; Charlotte, North Carolina; and Charlottesville, Virginia.

UNCLEAR: The most significant dates of the Civil War were April 12, 1861, July 3, 1863, April 9, 1865.

REVISED: The most significant dates of the Civil War were April 12, 1861; July 3, 1863; April 9, 1865.

UNCLEAR: The participants in the exhibit are Judi Parker, who paints in water color, Simon Rogers, who is a potter, and Peter Mondavian, who sculpts in transparent plastic.

REVISED: The participants in the exhibit are Judi Parker, who paints in water color; Simon Rogers, who is a potter; and Peter Mondavian, who sculpts in transparent plastic.

22e Inappropriate Semicolons

• A semicolon should not be placed between noncoordinate elements.

The semicolon can be used to join two independent clauses or to join a series of items containing commas. In either case, the semicolon joins grammatically coordinate elements. A semicolon should not be used to join elements that are not coordinate—for example, an independent and a dependent clause or a dependent clause and a phrase.

> INCORRECT: **Only 7 plays by Sophocles now exist; even though he supposedly wrote 124.**

> REVISED: **Only 7 plays by Sophocles now exist, even though he supposedly wrote 124.**

;
22e

• **A semicolon should not introduce a list.**

A colon or dash, not a semicolon, properly introduces a list.

> INCORRECT: **I have checked the following sources; encyclopedias, almanacs, indexes, and abstracts.**

> REVISED: **I have checked the following sources: encyclopedias, almanacs, indexes, and abstracts.**

> REVISED: **I have checked the following sources—encyclopedias, almanacs, indexes, and abstracts.**

EXERCISE 4

Complete each sentence by adding a grammatically coordinate element.

1. Tennis was once a game played by the upper classes; _____ _____ .

2. You can attend jazz festivals at the college on Sunday, June 24; on Friday, June 29; or _____ _____ .

3. Some used cars are good buys; _____ _____ .

4. Dr. Bertram Strass, a lecturer in Romance languages and literature, will speak at the meeting this week; and _____ _____ .

5. Applicants must be able to type 80 words a minute; communicate effectively, both in speech and writing; and _____ _____ .

EXERCISE 5

Revise the following sentences by inserting semicolons where needed and deleting them where inappropriate.

1. Western languages contain a prejudice against left-handedness, for example, *sinister* and *gauche* are words for "left."

2. Since 1941, the Soviet Union has restricted travel by foreigners, and since 1955, the United States has limited travel by Soviet officials.

3. We have tickets for *La Traviata* on Tuesday, July 31, *Rigoletto* on Wednesday, August 29, and *Carmen* on Saturday, September 1.

4. Flashing a wide grin; the applicant tried to hide his nervousness.

5. According to a study of more than 300 adults; men cry about once a month, but women cry five times more often.

6. The new animals in the zoo are an elephant, donated by Sri Lanka, a Bengal tiger, purchased with funds, and an aardwolf, loaned by the San Diego Zoo.

7. Sherwood Anderson named his book of stories *The Book of the Grotesques,* however; his publisher changed the title to *Winesburg, Ohio.*

8. Most people who use personal computers for jobs such as word processing, bookkeeping, or filing, don't program their computers, instead, they buy prewritten software.

9. The guide lists the major excavation sites around the world; where ongoing digs are uncovering secrets of ancient civilizations.

10. "The Star-Spangled Banner" is hard to sing; but most people don't want it changed.

◻ **EXERCISE 6**

In the following passage, insert semicolons where necessary between items in a series and between independent clauses.

People who have trouble sleeping and people who keep odd hours have seen, I'm sure, a variety of Frankenstein films on television. The monster that started this trend took shape in Switzerland in 1816 at a gathering made up of Shelley, the poet, Mary, his future wife, and Lord Byron. To get through the wet, cold winter, the three wrote ghost stories, but the only memorable work produced was Mary's *Frankenstein.* The two famous poets wrote nothing significant, Mary, however, produced a masterpiece.

Most of the Frankenstein films that appear on television bear little resemblance to the original. The book dramatizes the horror that results when human beings assume God's creative power, but most Frankenstein films dramatize silliness. You can see such ridiculous versions as *Frankenstein and the Monster from Hell,* with the doctor running an insane asylum, *Frankenstein Conquers the World,* with an overgrown monster terrorizing Tokyo, *Frankenstein's Daughter,* with a ridiculous female robot, and *Frankenstein Meets the Space Monster,* with an interplanetary robot gone amuck.

23

Colons

Although the colon is used in diverse constructions, it has only two basic purposes: to point ahead and to separate. No matter what its purpose, the colon has a formal and official tone.

23a Colons Before Lists

A colon sometimes announces that a list will follow. Usually, the list is written not as a tabulation but as a continuation of the sentence. However, in scientific, technical, and business writing, the list is often separated from the sentence and itemized down the page.

NONTECHNICAL WRITING: **Several American writers have died young without completing work they had started: F. Scott Fitzgerald, Nathanael West, and James Agee.**

In the Olympics are several events that the general public knows little about: team handball, Greco-Roman wrestling, field hockey, and water polo.

TECHNICAL WRITING: **According to sports psychologists, athletes can improve their performances by several techniques:**

1. goal setting
2. mental practice
3. relaxation

Follow this sequence to delete a column:

1. Move the cursor under the first column entry.
2. Press DEL.
3. Press COLUMN.

:
23b

In nontechnical prose, a complete sentence usually precedes a colon so that an object or complement will not be separated from its verb nor an object from its preposition. In fact, writers often precede a list with an expression like "the following" or "as follows" in order to complete the sentence.

INCOMPLETE CLAUSE BEFORE A COLON: We visited: Athens, Kusadasi, Rhodes, and Heraklion.

REVISED: We visited the following places: Athens, Kusadasi, Rhodes, and Heraklion.

INCOMPLETE CLAUSE BEFORE A COLON: The root *carn* appears in: *incarnation, carnage,* and *carnival.*

REVISED: The root *carn* appears in the following words: *incarnation, carnage,* and *carnival.*

23b Colons Before Appositives That End Sentences

An appositive renames and identifies another sentence element, as "Satchel Paige" renames "pitcher" in the following example.

A great pitcher, Satchel Paige, entered the major leagues at the age of 42.

An appositive at the end of a sentence introduced by a colon creates drama or emphasis.

Seventy years after the hoax of the Piltdown Man, a surprising new suspect has been found: Sir Arthur Conan Doyle.

The book gives practical information: how to go on long camping expeditions without expensive equipment.

All the evidence points to the same conclusion: that a vast source of oil exists in the area.

23c Colons Between Independent Clauses

Ordinarily two independent clauses are joined with a comma and a coordinating conjunction or with a semicolon. On occasion, however, the second clause explains or illustrates the first clause or some part of it. A colon between the two clauses can indicate this special relationship. In this construction, the first word of the second clause may be capitalized or not.

> Galileo discovered that Copernicus was correct: The earth was not the center of the universe.

> The most exciting shot in volleyball is the spike: one team tries to drive the ball across the net at up to 110 miles an hour.

:
23e

23d Colons Before Grammatically Independent Quotations

A grammatically independent quotation is a complete sentence or several complete sentences. Ordinarily a comma separates the quotation from the rest of the sentence, but when the quotation is especially long and when the tone is formal, a colon may separate the two.

> In a radio address on April 7, 1932, Roosevelt made a statement that still seems modern: "These unhappy times call for the building of plans . . . that build from the bottom up and not from the top down, that put their faith once more in the forgotten man at the bottom of the economic pyramid."

> In 1945 Einstein wrote optimistically: "I do not believe that civilization will be wiped out in a war fought with the atomic bomb. Perhaps two-thirds of the people of the earth might be killed, but enough men capable of thinking, and enough books, would be left to start again, and civilization could be restored."

23e Colons Between Titles and Subtitles

A colon separates a title from a subtitle.

> *The Masks of God: Creative Mythology*

Famine on the Wind: Plant Diseases and Human History
"Boomerang: The Stick That Returns"
"Timon of Athens: A Reconsideration"

23f Colons in Correspondence

The salutation of a formal letter is followed by a colon.

> Dear Mr. Berger:
>
> Dear Ms. Plavin:
>
> Dear Sir or Madam:

An attention line in a letter or on an envelope includes the word *attention* or the abbreviation *attn* plus a colon.

> Attention: Dr. Grace Fortune
>
> Attn: Mr. Peter Ravitch

Subject lines contain colons when introduced by the word *subject* or its Latin abbreviation *re.*

> Subject: Reassignment of duties
>
> Re: Request for information about computer security

In letters, colons can separate the elements of notations such as these.

> cc: John Howorth [copy to John Howorth]
>
> ACK:mn [initials of writer and typist respectively]

At the start of a memorandum, the headings are frequently followed by colons.

> To: Part-Time Employees
> From: Milton Greenberg, Personnel Director
> Date: May 3, 1988
> Subject: Overtime Work

23g Colons with Numerical Elements

In several types of numerical sequences, colons separate the parts—hours from minutes, chapters from verses, and numbers in ratios —from each other.

5:30 P.M.	Psalms 29:2
10:00 A.M.	4:3

23h Colons in Citations

Some formats for bibliography entries use colons.

Canaday, John. *Mainstreams of Modern Art.* New York: Holt, Rinehart and Winston, 1981.

Brush, L. (1979). *Why women avoid the study of mathematics: A longitudinal study* (Contract No. 400-77-0099). Washington, DC: National Institute of Education.

23i Inappropriate Colons

- A colon should not be placed between a verb and its object or complement.

    INAPPROPRIATE: Is acid rain ruining: our gardens, our lakes, our farms?

    APPROPRIATE: Is acid rain ruining our gardens, our lakes, our farms?

    INAPPROPRIATE: D. W. Griffith's most important films are: *The Birth of a Nation, Intolerance, Broken Blossoms,* and *Orphans of the Storm.*

    APPROPRIATE: D. W. Griffith's most important films are *The Birth of a Nation, Intolerance, Broken Blossoms,* and *Orphans of the Storm.*

- A colon should not be placed between *to* and the rest of an infinitive.

    INAPPROPRIATE: They are planning to: secure funds and send out a request for bids.

    APPROPRIATE: They are planning to secure funds and send out a request for bids.

- A colon should not be placed between a preposition and its object.

    INAPPROPRIATE: Please send catalogues to: Carolyn Hacker and Stephen Hastings.

    APPROPRIATE: Please send catalogues to Carolyn Hacker and Stephen Hastings.

- A colon should not be placed between an independent and a dependent clause or phrase.

> INAPPROPRIATE: I have gotten only one response to my letters: although I wrote to twenty companies.

> APPROPRIATE: I have gotten only one response to my letters, although I wrote to twenty companies.

EXCEPTION: In technical documents, the colon is frequently used after a verb or a preposition to introduce a list.

> INCOMPLETE CLAUSE BEFORE COLON: This section contains: (1) a sequence of menus for each task and function, and (2) a description of each menu.

> INCOMPLETE CLAUSE BEFORE COLON: This guide is a supplement to:
> a. DPMC/General Systems
> b. DPMC/5600
> c. DPMC/25

⬛ EXERCISE

To improve clarity in the following sentences, add missing colons, remove incorrect colons, or change existing marks to colons.

1. The first electronic computer required: 17,000 vacuum tubes, 70,000 resistors, 10,000 capacitors, and 6,000 switches.
2. Our textbook for the course is *The Americans A Social History of the United States, 1587–1914.*
3. He was dressed in the standard school attire corduroy slacks, button-down Oxford shirt, and Shetland sweater.
4. During the nineteenth century, one man stands out for the influence he had on other writers Emerson.
5. Dorothy Sayers explained the appeal of mystery novels this way "Death seems to provide the minds of the Anglo-Saxon race with a greater fund of innocent amusement than any other single subject . . . the tale must be about dead bodies or very wicked people, preferably both, before the Tired Business Man can feel really happy."
6. Language can be ranked by its acceptability into these levels
   1. standard or formal
   2. informal
   3. slang
   4. jargon
   5. nonstandard
   6. taboo or vulgar

7. I am qualified in: COBOL, FORTRAN, and UNIX.
8. The candidates grappled over issues that especially concern women, equal opportunity, equal pay, abortion, old-age security.
9. The research points to a great improvement, to an immunization against colds.
10. The best travel guides are: Michelin, the Blue Guide, and Fodor's.
11. A single basic fact governs encoding; a computer stores only numbers.
12. They are trying to grow the following vegetables, corn, tomatoes, radishes, and broccoli.
13. These extensions of the Blue Ridge Mountains are names enshrined in American folklore, the Great Smokies, the Balsams, the Nantahalas.
14. The envelope had this notation "Attention A Human Being."
15. Sometimes a copy of a book by a living author can be a collector's item *Poems* (1934), William Golding's first book, sold recently for $4,000.

:
23i

24

Dashes, Parentheses, and Brackets

Dashes, parentheses, and brackets primarily enclose information, isolating it from the rest of a sentence. But the effect of these three marks of punctuation is somewhat different. Dashes emphasize the elements they enclose. Parentheses de-emphasize interrupters and nonessential elements. Brackets usually enclose clarifications, especially in direct quotations.

☐ Using Dashes

24a Dashes to Set Off Appositives Containing Commas

Dashes set off an appositive containing commas so that a reader can tell where the appositive begins and ends. (See 21d.2.) An appositive set off by dashes may appear in the middle of a sentence, at the beginning, or at the end.

> CONFUSING: A number of the Founding Fathers, Jefferson, Madison, Adams, Hamilton, were extremely intellectual.

> REVISED: A number of the Founding Fathers—Jefferson, Madison, Adams, Hamilton—were extremely intellectual.

> CONFUSING: The pitcher can throw a variety of breaking pitches, curves, screwballs, and knuckleballs.

> REVISED: The pitcher can throw a variety of breaking pitches— curves, screwballs, and knuckleballs.

216

CONFUSING: A poet, dramatist, novelist, essayist, historian, Voltaire has been an influential figure in the history of thought.

REVISED: A poet, dramatist, novelist, essayist, historian—Voltaire has been an influential figure in the history of thought.

24b Dashes to Set Off Nonrestrictive Modifiers Containing Commas

Ordinarily commas set off a nonrestrictive modifier, whether a clause or a phrase. (See 21d.1.) When the modifier itself contains commas, however, dashes can make its boundaries clear.

Jules Feiffer—who has produced cartoons, novels, plays, and screenplays—uses humor to reflect human folly.

By the eighteenth century, riddles—written, at least—were becoming less suggestive and vulgar.

EXERCISE 1

In the following sentences, insert dashes to set off appositives and nonrestrictive modifiers that contain commas.

1. The tennis instructor, a short, skinny, agile fellow, was visibly agitated by my incompetence.
2. Karl, who had recently read *The Jewel in the Crown, Gandhi,* and *The Blood Seed,* claimed to be an expert on India.
3. Blacks, Jews, Catholics, southerners, women, people of minority groups are sought out for political endorsements.
4. The editorial, which attacked university policies on housing, meal tickets, and zoning regulations, was written by a freshman.
5. The book contains reminiscences by a wide range of people, journalists, musicians, artists, critics, and teachers.

24c Dashes to Emphasize Sentence Elements

Dashes can emphasize any kind of construction (words, phrases, or clauses) that can be set off or separated from the rest of the sentence.

We have noticed a persistent quality in the lives of famous people—confidence.

They were stealing—via computer—hundreds of thousands of dollars in goods and services.

The movie is funny—in a skewed way.

The members have basic differences with their leaders—and among themselves—on the issues.

Thoreau in *Walden* tells how he built his cabin—down to the cost of the nails.

I know she was lying—she was leaving for another reason.

Most people who read the magazine never cook anything by the recipes—they're too difficult.

24d Dashes with Interrupters

Dashes effectively set off an element that interrupts the continuity of prose, separates the essential parts of a sentence pattern, or breaks a piece of dialogue.

The author was sitting—slouching, really—on the sofa.

My aunt's minah bird—it especially loved sitting on the porch calling for Joe—had an unmistakable southern accent.

"I never knew—well, I don't suppose it matters now."

"But not—I really wouldn't call the move a mistake."

EXERCISE 2

To emphasize elements and to set off interrupters, insert dashes or change existing marks to dashes.

1. Human beings, of whom there are today close to five billion, rely primarily on plants for food.
2. On the Fourth of July we had fireworks, not sparklers or Roman candles, but a large professional extravaganza.
3. Just below Lee Highway, parallel to it, in fact, is Arlington Boulevard.
4. He was, it was now unmistakably clear, a coward.
5. The subway travelers have a high tolerance level for trash, dirt, and graffiti (or they have no alternative transportation).
6. "He's, oh, my heavens, he's already here."
7. Finally (I think it was in October, or maybe November) he went to see a doctor.
8. Eakins' portraits are honest, honest in the external details and honest in the psychological characterization.

9. The riddle was a conundrum, that is, a riddle that depends on a pun.
10. The article was about America's biggest business, food.

☐ Using Parentheses

( )
24f

24e Parentheses to Enclose Interrupters

Parentheses isolate elements that interrupt a sentence or passage. These interrupters may be single words, phrases, or even whole sentences.

> Since 1603, the royal arms of Britain have been supported by the English lion (dexter) and the Scottish unicorn (sinister).

> Monticello (pronounced *Montichel´lo* in the Italian way) was built on a Virginia hilltop Jefferson's father had left him.

When one whole sentence interrupts another, the interrupter neither begins with a capital letter nor ends with a period.

> After the Civil War, gangs of homeless burglars (they called themselves "yeggs") rode the freight trains, robbing and stealing along the way.

When a whole sentence is inserted between sentences, the interrupter begins with a capital letter and ends with a period. The final parenthesis follows the period.

> In his early youth Wordsworth was an enthusiast for the French Revolution. (He had been influenced by the ideas of Rousseau.) But as he grew older, he became increasingly conservative.

24f Parentheses to Enclose Explanations

In a neat efficient manner, parentheses can enclose explanations or illustrations that clarify ideas, terms, acronyms, and the like.

> The important numbers on a car radio relate to sensitivity (the ability to receive weak signals) and selectivity (the ability to pick up a signal out of a crowd).

> KBY CHG (Keyboard Change) allows an operator to change the keyboard arrangement.

Soldiers can earn college credit for Defense Language Institute (DLI) training.

The study showed that children (ages two to twelve) and adults (ages eighteen to fifty-five) watch television three to four hours a day.

Electromagnetic waves originate from a number of sources (solar storms, for example).

Employment is a serious problem for the most disadvantaged segments of the population (young males with little education or work experience and families headed by women).

24g Parentheses for References to Pages, Figures, Tables, and Chapters

Parentheses can enclose references to specific pages, to relevant figures or tables, or to different chapters. The following examples illustrate the two ways to make these references: inside a sentence or as a separate sentence.

A map of the river shows where each aquatic plant still grows (p. 45).

James McNeill Whistler is considered the forerunner of abstract art. (See pp. 52–76.)

The inertial reel makes seat belts lock up automatically (see the accompanying diagram).

Safes fall into two types: fire-resistant safes for records and burglar-resistant safes for money. (See figs., p. 167.)

The data in the table (columns 11 and 12) show the performance of each state in preventing high school dropouts.

24h Parentheses in Citations

In some styles of documentation, the sources used in a research paper are incorporated into the text inside parentheses.

CITATION IN TEXT: Brod (1984) calls the strain of computer technology "technostress."

The properties of the polymer were altered radically (7:24).

☐ EXERCISE 3

Use parentheses to add at an appropriate place the information specified for each sentence.

EXAMPLE: The new map-making technique for the oceans has uncovered previously unknown seamounts. [Explain that seamounts are underwater volcanoes.] → The new map-making technique for the oceans has uncovered previously unknown seamounts (underwater volcanoes).

[ ]
24i

1. Generally, two-way or three-way speakers will sound better than single-cone. [Explain that two-way is coaxial; three-way, triaxial.]
2. T. E. Lawrence published an account of his World War I adventures in *The Seven Pillars of Wisdom.* [Add that the account was published in 1926.]
3. VLSI research is helping speed up the evolution of microprocessors. [Explain that VLSI means "Very Large-Scale Integration."]
4. Disconnect the battery cable from the negative post to prevent electrical sparks if a tool slips. [Add that if you must start the engine during repairs, you should be sure to reconnect the cable.]
5. The few players who engage in serious tournament chess are mainly concerned with strategy. [Instruct readers to refer to Chapter 16.]
6. The exhibit at the Anacostia Neighborhood Museum is *Black Wings,* about black American aviators. [Add the dates July 2–August 5.]
7. New York City, which is surrounded by major tomato-growing regions, depends mainly on California and Mexico for its tomatoes. [Explain that the regions are New Jersey, Long Island, and upstate New York.]
8. The goldsmith said that for $4,200 he could design the trophy. [Add the comment "That's not a bad price."]
9. From Maine to Alabama, forests are dying. [Instruct readers to see Table 3.]
10. I am an admirer of the work of Leonard. [Add the comment "More accurately, I am a fan."]

☐ Using Brackets

24i Brackets Around Insertions in Direct Quotations

Exact quotations taken out of context often contain pronouns without clear references, terms needing explanation, or names without identification. In such situations, brackets are used to insert clarifications. The bracketed explanations may be inserted after the unclear word or phrase or may replace the unclear word or phrase.

> De Tocqueville wrote, "They [the Americans] have all a lively faith in the perfectibility of man."

or

> De Tocqueville wrote, "[The Americans] have all a lively faith in the perfectibility of man."

> The author points out, "The Countess of Lovelace [Byron's daughter] met Babbage and soon became the first computer programmer."

or

> The author points out, "[Byron's daughter] met Babbage and soon became the first computer programmer."

Another common use of brackets in direct quotations is the insertion of corrections.

> Harry Truman wrote a letter to his daughter on March 19, 1956, saying, "If you don't trust the people you love . . . you'll be the unhappiest and [most] frustrated person alive."

Sometimes a writer prefers not to correct an error yet wants readers to know that it appeared in the original. In this case, the word *sic* in brackets following the error indicates that the error appeared "thus" in the source.

> From Hyeres, Fitzgerald wrote Thomas Boyd: "Zelda and I are sitting in the Café l'Universe writing letters . . . and the moon is an absolutely *au fait* Mediteraenean [sic] moon with a blurred silver linnen [sic] cap . . . we're both a little tight and very happily drunk."

To emphasize an element in the source being quoted, a writer can italicize (or underline) the element and insert an explanation in brackets.

> According to the article, "As a society, we need to grapple with the *real* problem—which is the lack of consensus—not about public education, but over what public education should be about [italics mine]."

24j Brackets Around Insertions in Unquoted Statements

Brackets are an alternative to parentheses for explaining a word or expression in an unquoted statement.

A new round of START [strategic arms reduction talks] resumed in Geneva.

24k Brackets for Parentheses Inside Parentheses

[ ]
24l

On the very rare occasions when parentheses are required inside parentheses, brackets replace the inner set.

> Most psychologists believe that phobias are stress related. (But a recent study [1984] suggests that agoraphobia may have biological origins.)

24l Brackets for Citations

Some style guides direct writers to use brackets instead of parentheses for citations.

> According to Asimov [2], "The uncertainty principle means that the universe is more complex than was thought, but not that it is irrational."

☐ EXERCISE 4

Use brackets to add the explanations and insertions specified for each sentence.

1. According to the explanation, "Teletext magazines consist of 100 to 5,000 'frames' of graphics and information." [Explain in the previous quote that "frames" means the same thing as "video screens."]
2. Sir Herbert Read wrote of "the no-man's-years between the wars." [Indicate that these "years" are 1919–1939.]
3. According to the newspaper, "The police and 'volunter' auxiliaries surrounded the statehouse and checked identifications and otherwise harassed the protesters." [Show that it was the newspaper that misspelled *volunteer.*]
4. According to Bruce Catton, "This four-year tragedy . . . is the *Hamlet* and *King Lear* of the American past." [Indicate that by "tragedy" Catton means the Civil War.]
5. About a possible operation her father needed, Virginia Woolf wrote in a letter that "any operation however slight . . . must be bad when you'r old." [Show that it was Virginia Wolfe who misspelled *your.*]

25

Periods, Question Marks, and Exclamation Points

Periods, question marks, and exclamation points are called end (or terminal) marks because they appear primarily at the ends of complete sentences. The period most commonly occurs after sentences and abbreviations. The question mark occurs mainly after a direct question. Exclamation points are common only in advertising copy, warnings in instructions, and dialogue.

❑ Using Periods

25a Periods as End Punctuation

Periods are used after several types of complete sentences.

- After statements

  Mardis Gras is the last day before Lent.

- After commands

  To make puffed potatoes, use Idahoes or Burbanks with about 80 percent starch content.

- After indirect questions

  He asked whether we had made reservations.

- After polite requests, usually in correspondence

  Would you please send me any information you have on keeping bees.

224

- After mild interjections

   "Well. That puts a new light on things."

25b Periods in Outlines and Displayed Lists

Periods follow numbers and letters in displayed lists, unless the numbers and letters are enclosed in parentheses.

Cathedrals
 I. Types of Cathedrals
  A. Palace Churches
  B. Abbeys
 II. Famous Cathedrals
  A. French Cathedrals
  B. English Cathedrals
  C. Italian Cathedrals

The report should include the following:

1. Abstract
2. Introduction
3. Procedure
4. Discussion
5. Conclusions and recommendations

25c Inappropriate Periods

A period is not used after an abbreviation at the end of a sentence. Instead, the period after the abbreviation serves also as the period for the end of the sentence.

> INAPPROPRIATE: The ceremony began at 3:00 P.M..

> APPROPRIATE: The ceremony began at 3:00 P.M.

Periods are not used in displayed lists after words and phrases.

> INAPPROPRIATE

Improperly canned foods can spoil for four reasons:

1. growth of yeasts and molds.
2. growth of bacteria.
3. presence of enzymes.
4. process of oxidation.

APPROPRIATE

Improperly canned foods can spoil for four reasons:

1. growth of yeasts and molds
2. growth of bacteria
3. presence of enzymes
4. process of oxidation

☐ EXERCISE 1

Revise the following sentences so that the periods are used correctly.

1. The tourists always ask when they can see the ghosts that haunt the castle?
2. She said calmly, "Sorry I didn't mean to upset you."
3. Garden flowers fall into three categories:
   1. annuals.
   2. biennials.
   3. perennials
4. Chinese art was flourishing by the time of the Shang dynasty, about 1500 B.C. to 102 B.C..
5. Would you please send a transcript of my grades to the address listed below?

☐ Using Question Marks

25d Question Marks as End Punctuation

The question mark is used as end punctuation in several different constructions.

- After direct questions

  When is the off-season in Florida?

- After sentences with tag questions

  September is unusually hot, isn't it?

- After elliptical questions in a series

  Should politicians be required to reveal all the details of their private lives? Why? And to whom?

25e Question Marks Within Sentences

A question mark can emphasize a direct question that appears inside a statement. This construction is acceptable only if the question is direct and not indirect.

!
25f

UNACCEPTABLE AFTER INDIRECT QUESTION: What we can gain by further negotiation? is the first question.

ACCEPTABLE AFTER DIRECT QUESTION: What can we gain by further negotiation? is the first question.

A question mark can also express doubt about a fact such as a date, a place, a statistic, and the like.

The first edition of the novel (1918?) was banned in the United States.

The most famous of the Cleopatras (VII?) lived from 69 to 30 B.C.

☐ EXERCISE 2

Revise the sentences so that question marks are used correctly both at the ends of sentences and within sentences to show emphasis or doubt.

1. What does rattlesnake taste like.
2. Is the telephone company our servant, our partner, our master, or merely off the hook.
3. The founding fathers did believe in separation of church and state, didn't they.
4. The Trojan War (in the 1200s B.C.) was fought between Greece and the city of Troy. [Indicate that the date of the war is doubtful.]
5. How can we make retirees feel productive is not adequately discussed.

☐ Using Exclamation Points

25f Exclamation Points in Dialogue

An exclamation point is used in dialogue to indicate that the speaker is shouting or expressing intense feelings.

"Stop!" the engineer shouted. "There is a unicorn on the tracks!"

"Shut up!" she said between clenched teeth. "Just shut up!"

25g Exclamation Points with Interjections

!
25i

An interjection is an expression of emotion, such as *well, goodness, oh,* and *whew.* A mild interjection is treated as a separate sentence (followed by a period) or as part of a sentence (followed by a comma).

Well. I suppose we could reconsider the matter.

Oh, he does not understand.

When the interjection expresses strong emotion, however, it is usually treated as a separate sentence and punctuated with an exclamation point.

Well! You've said quite enough.

Whew! That car barely missed me!

25h Exclamation Points in Warnings

Exclamation points are often used in warnings to catch the reader's attention and prevent mishaps.

!!!!!!!!WARNING!!!!!!!!

DO NOT USE NEAR OPEN FLAME!!!

25i Inappropriate and Excessive Exclamation Points

Inexperienced writers sometimes try to convey enthusiasm by using exclamation points and vague words such as *great, wonderful, marvelous,* and *perfect.* This technique is ineffective and often seems juvenile. Specific details are more convincing than exclamation points, as the following two passages illustrate.

INEFFECTIVE: My favorite place to visit in winter is Rancho Mirage in the California desert. The scenery is marvelous! And the weather is great!

REVISED: My favorite place to visit in winter is Rancho Mirage in the California desert. The town is set in a lush oasis surrounded by a stark desert and rugged mountains. The temperature gets up to about 80 degrees during the day and down to about 60 degrees at night.

Another ineffective use of the exclamation point is to stress the importance of an idea. A better technique is to use words and phrases that indicate more specifically the degree of the idea's importance. Compare these sentences.

VAGUE: We must revise the nursing curriculum!

REVISED: One of our major goals should be to revise the nursing curriculum.

REVISED: Our primary concern should be the revision of the nursing curriculum.

REVISED: Until we revise the nursing curriculum, we can make no progress at all.

EXERCISE 3

Improve the following sentences by eliminating exclamation points and

(a) replacing vague words with specific details or

(b) adding words and phrases that express the importance of the ideas.

1. The party was fabulous!
2. The paper should be a five-page discussion of American transcendentalism. It must have a thesis supported by concrete details!
3. We must take steps to conserve energy!
4. Last Saturday's game was the greatest I have ever seen!
5. After spending hours at registration, I finally managed to get a perfect schedule!

26

Apostrophes

26a

Apostrophes have three functions—to form possessives, to allow contractions, and in a few contexts to precede *s* in plurals. By far the most common of the three, however, is to indicate possession.

26a Apostrophes to Indicate Possession

The grammatical term *possession* refers to such relationships as ownership, origin, and measurement—*Claudia's house, the professor's approval, a week's vacation.* Some pronouns have special possessive forms: *my/mine, our/ours, your/yours, his, her/hers, its, their/theirs, whose.* Nouns and all other pronouns are made possessive by the addition of an apostrophe plus *s* or simply an apostrophe.

The general rules for showing possession with apostrophes are as follows.

- Add *'s* to most singular nouns.

    doctor→ doctor's diagnosis

    Don Quixote→ Don Quixote's quest

    boss→ boss's office

    novel→ novel's plot

EXCEPTION: The possessive of a few singular nouns (usually proper nouns) is formed by the addition of the apostrophe only: *Moses', Anchises', Mr. Hastings', Quarles'.* The addition of an extra *s* to words that already contain *s* sounds sometimes makes pronunciation difficult *(Mr. Hastings's hat)*.

- Add **'** to plural nouns that end in *s*.

  teachers→ teachers' pay

  drivers→ drivers' training school

  six months→ six months' pay

  trees→ trees' roots

EXCEPTION: The possessive of plural nouns that do not end in *s* is formed by the addition of *'s: oxen's, children's, bacteria's, alumni's*.

- Add *'s* to singular indefinite pronouns.

  everybody→ everybody's responsibility

  someone→ someone's parking spot

  neither→ neither's fault

  another→ another's idea

- Add *'s* or **'** to the last word of a compound noun or pronoun.

  editor in chief→ editor in chief's opinion

  attorney generals→ attorney generals' decisions

  no one else→ no one else's business

- To indicate joint possession, add *'s* or **'** to the last name only.

  Lebanon and Syria→ Lebanon and Syria's disagreement

  Crick and Watson→ Crick and Watson's discovery

  juniors and misses→ juniors and misses' department

- To indicate individual possession of more than one noun, add *'s* or **'** to each name:

  the mayor and governor→ the mayor's and governor's policies

  the Falcons and Saints→ the Falcons' and Saints' schedules

☐ EXERCISE 1

Change each of the following underlined phrases to a form containing an apostrophe.

EXAMPLE: the performances by the four bands = the four bands' performances

1. the constitution of Texas

2. the food <u>for his three cats</u>
3. the beliefs <u>of everyone else</u>
4. the wishes <u>of the alumni</u>
5. the law firm <u>belonging to Duncan, Weinberg, and Miller</u>
6. the time slot of *Days of our Lives*
7. the discovery <u>made by Archimedes</u>
8. an absence <u>lasting a month</u>
9. the editorial <u>appearing in the *New York Times*</u>
10. registration scheduled <u>by it</u> [the school]
11. the offices <u>of the Department of Agriculture</u>
12. the plot <u>of the story</u>
13. the houses <u>belonging to the Smiths and to the Joneses</u>
14. the book <u>belonging to whom</u>
15. a time <u>lasting a year</u>

26b Apostrophes to Create Contractions

In contractions, the apostrophe takes the place of omitted letters, numbers, or words.

it's = it is, it has	goin' (dialect) = going
who's = who is, who has	don't = do not
they're = they are	won't = will not
I'll = I will	would've = would have
'65 = 1965	we'd = we would
rock 'n' roll = rock and roll	o'clock = of the clock

Remember that *till, though,* and *round* are all words, not contractions. Do not write *'till, 'though,* and *'round.*

26c Apostrophes to Indicate Plurals of Letters, Numbers, and Words Used as Words

An apostrophe is sometimes used before an *s* to indicate the plural form of a letter, number, or word used as such. When a plural number is clear without the apostrophe, most writers, particularly journalists and technical writers, no longer use the apostrophe.

Only GI's are eligible.

He made four A's.

You have used too many *and's*

She writes her *m's* and *n's* alike.

The 1960's [or 1960s] were turbulent years.

The country wants to buy F-16's [or F-16s].

They have owned two Audi 5000's [or 5000s].

26d Inappropriate Apostrophes

- The apostrophe never appears within a word, even though the word itself ends in *s.*

INCORRECT POSSESSIVE	CORRECT POSSESSIVE
Charle's	Charles's
Jone's	Jones's
the Raider's	the Raiders'

- For ordinary words, an apostrophe is never used to form a plural.

INCORRECT PLURAL	CORRECT PLURAL
tomato's	tomatoes
price's	prices

- Apostrophes are not used in the possessive forms of personal pronouns and in the possessive form of *who.* All personal pronouns and the pronoun *who* form possessives without the apostrophe.

INCORRECT POSSESSIVES	CORRECT POSSESSIVES
it's or its'	its
her's or hers'	hers
your's or yours'	yours
our's or ours'	ours
their's or theirs'	theirs
who's	whose

Readers are especially confused by the incorrect use of *it's* and *who's* as possessives. Remember that *it's* and *who's* are contractions for *it is* or *it has* and *who is* or *who has*; they are never possessives.

INCORRECT: Do not buy the album; it's lyrics are not worth hearing more than once.

REVISED: Do not buy the album; its lyrics are not worth hearing more than once.

INCORRECT: They discussed Planet 10, who's existence has been suggested by irregularities in the orbits of Uranus and Nep-
tune.

REVISED: They discussed Planet 10, whose existence has been suggested by irregularities in the orbits of Uranus and Nep-
tune.

EXERCISE 2

Edit the following passage for incorrect or missing apostrophes.

I edited my manuscript about Democratic conventions during the
1960s with the help of a software program named Grammatik, who's purpose is to point out possible grammatical and punctuation errors. Grammatik even makes suggestion's for correcting these errors. Its a very effective program; it doesn't overlook much. It found two *m*s in *omitted,* a
missing apostrophe in *didnt,* an unnecessary apostrophe in *her's,* several
unnecessary commas, and about seven examples of wordiness. It also
pointed out that I had used in the text fifteen *very*s and ten *however*s.
Grammatiks skills improved the accuracy of the paper. It's thorough checking surprised me. Now that Ive improved the manuscripts grammar, punctuation, and style, I need a software program to help with the content.

27

Quotation Marks and Ellipses

Although quotation marks and ellipses have several uses, these marks appear most often in quotations, reproductions of someone's exact words. Quotation marks show the beginning and end of the citation. Ellipsis marks indicate where a part or parts of the original statement have been deleted.

Using Quotation Marks

27a Quotation Marks to Enclose Direct Quotations

Direct quotations of a few sentences or lines are enclosed in quotation marks. The identifying expressions, such as *the source said* or *according to the source,* appear at the beginning, middle, or end of the quotation and are not enclosed inside the quotation marks.

> According to George Marshall, "The refusal of the British and Russian peoples to accept what appeared to be inevitable defeat was the great factor in the salvage of our civilization."

> "The refusal of the British and Russian peoples to accept what appeared to be inevitable defeat was," George Marshall maintained, "the great factor in the salvage of our civilization."

> "The refusal of the British and Russian peoples to accept what appeared to be inevitable defeat was the great factor in the salvage of our civilization," George Marshall reported in 1945.

235

Quotation marks also enclose a part of a quoted statement.

> George Marshall reported that Britain's and Russia's refusal to accept defeat in World War II was "the great factor in the salvage of our civilization."

> George Marshall pointed out that Britain's and Russia's refusal to accept "inevitable defeat" in World War II saved civilization.

" "

27b

Quotation marks are not used when a quoted passage is long, that is, more than four typed lines or more than forty words. Instead, the passage is set up as a "block," separate from the text, with each line indented. (See 41i.)

Also, quotation marks are not used with an indirect quotation, one in which the source is paraphrased.

> George Marshall pointed out that in World War II Britain and Russia saved civilization by refusing to give up.

On some occasions, a quoted passage may itself contain a quotation. If a quoted passage already contains quotation marks, double marks (". . .") surround the whole passage, and single marks ('. . .') surround the inside quote. On a typewriter, the single quotation marks are made with the apostrophe key.

> ORIGINAL: His situation reminds one of a line, a plea really, from Maurice Sendak's harrowing slapstick fantasy *Higglety Pigglety Pop!*: "There must be more to life than having everything." (Leonard Marcus)

> QUOTATION FROM ORIGINAL: Marcus points out that the child's situation reminds him of a "plea . . . from Maurice Sendak's harrowing slapstick fantasy *Higglety Pigglety Pop!*: 'There must be more to life than having everything!'"

27b Quotation Marks with Other Punctuation Marks

When closing quotation marks appear with other marks of punctuation, strict conventions govern the order.

- **Quotation marks with the period and the comma**

A closing quotation mark follows a period or comma. This rule applies even when closing quotation marks are both single and double.

The judge who handled the case referred to the problem that "most defendents are indigents without easy access to assistance."

"I've never seen a 3-D movie," she insisted.

After finishing "The Headless Cupid," he read "The Famous Stanley Kidnapping Case."

The book pointed out that "Japan is creating enormous research and industrial centers called 'technopolises.'"

" "
27b

EXCEPTION: When a parenthetical citation intervenes, the quotation mark precedes the citation, and the period follows.

Stendhal conducts "the rites of initiation into the nineteenth century" (Levin 149).

- Quotation marks with the semicolon and the colon

A closing quotation mark always precedes a semicolon or colon.

Many people in business and government use jargon and "acronymese"; in fact, they often leave ordinary people totally in the dark.

He said, "The work must be finished on time"; and he meant it.

The sign listed the scheduled performances of "Mostly Mozart": July 19, July 27, and August 2.

According to the report, "Japan is shifting to a basic research phase": no longer will Japan be dependent on borrowed findings.

- Quotation marks with the question mark, exclamation point, and dash

The quotation mark follows a question mark, exclamation point, or dash that punctuates the quoted material.

The advertisement asked, "Why give the common, when you can give the preferred?"

At the end of the game, the happy fan shouted, "Time to celebrate, man!"

He said, "No—" and was immediately interrupted.

A closing quotation mark precedes a question mark, exclamation point, or dash that punctuates the unquoted part of the sentence.

Which character says, "I am a feather for each wind that blows"?

Don't ever write an antiquated expression like "heretofore"!

"These"—he pointed to a tray of snails—"are delicious."

Sometimes both the quoted and unquoted material in a sentence are questions. In these cases, the unquoted part takes precedence, and the closing quotation mark goes before the question mark.

> What poem asks, "And by what way shall I go back"?
>
> Did you ask, "Was H. L. Mencken from Baltimore"?

On rare occasions, a sequence may include a single quotation mark, a double quotation mark, and a question mark.

> He asked me, "Which actor starred in 'The Jesse Owens Story'?"

In this example, the single quotation mark goes first because the title it encloses is not a question; the question mark goes next because the quoted material, not the unquoted, is the question; and the double quotation mark goes last to conclude the quote.

> Did he ask, "Which actor starred in 'The Jesse Owens Story'"?

In this example, the question mark must go last because the unquoted part of the sentence is a question.

☐ EXERCISE 1

Correct any quotation marks that are positioned incorrectly in relation to other marks of punctuation.

1. In none of the many novels and stories about Sherlock Holmes did he once say, "Elementary, my dear Watson".
2. Over 100 years ago, Chief Sealth of the Duwamish tribe said, "The White man must treat the beasts of this land as his brothers. What is man without the beasts?"
3. In Faulkner's story "The Bear", the hunted animal, when fatally wounded "fell all of a piece, as a tree falls."
4. How did the instruction manual say to answer the question "Is this to be installed on an MP/M system?"
5. The teacher shouted to the now intimidated student, "You cannot have forgotten the entire multiplication table!"
6. I lay awake all night wondering, "Before that enormous crowd, will I remember all the words of 'The Star-Spangled Banner'?"
7. It is redundant to write "from whence"; *whence* means "from where."
8. According to the author, Caesar was "a nobleman of surpassing prestige and authority (Kahn 56)."
9. Langston Hughes wrote about the nature of the blues: "The music is slow, often mournful, yet syncopated, with the kind of marching bass behind it that seems to say, 'In spite of fate, bad luck, these blues themselves, I'm going on!'"

27b

10. According to the guide, "The preposition *in* means 'located or being with,' but it also quite correctly means 'moving or directed inside': for example, *going in the house* or *dived in the water.*"

▢ EXERCISE 2

Incorporate the quotation into sentences according to the instructions.

QUOTATION: In dealing with the future . . . it is more important to be imaginative and insightful than to be one hundred percent "right."
(Alvin Toffler, *Future Shock*)

1. Quote the entire statement, placing "according to Alvin Toffler" at the beginning.
2. Quote the entire statement, placing "Alvin Toffler wrote in *Future Shock*" at the end.
3. Quote the entire statement, inserting "Alvin Toffler has written" after *future* and before *it.*
4. Quote the entire statement, placing "Was it Alvin Toffler who wrote" at the beginning.
5. Paraphrase all of the statement, making it into an indirect quote. Give credit to Toffler.

27c Quotation Marks in Dialogue

When a dialogue with two or more speakers is represented on paper, the exact words of the speakers are placed inside quotation marks. Ordinarily the spoken words are interrupted with comments that set the scenes, identify the speakers, and create the tone. These comments must be carefully separated from the spoken dialogue, as in the following excerpt from Joseph Conrad's "An Outpost of Progress."

> "Is this your revolver?" asked Makola, getting up.
> "Yes," said Kayerts; then he added very quickly, "He ran after me to shoot me—you saw!"
> "Yes, I saw," said Makola. "There is only one revolver; where's his?"
> "Don't know," whispered Kayerts in a voice that had become suddenly very faint.

Every change of speaker is indicated by a new paragraph with quotation marks before and after the speech. To show that one speaker continues for more than one paragraph, the closing quotation mark appears only after the last paragraph. The following example includes two paragraphs containing the words of one scientist speaking of the history of the universe. Notice the omission of the quotation mark at the end of the first paragraph.

> Glashow symbolized the time that the universe has existed by drawing a red line on the board. Pointing to a dot at one end of the line, he said, "Then you have a brief ten billion years or so when things are palatable on Earth.
>
> "After that, eventually it all winds down."

27d Quotation Marks in Titles

The way a title is marked tells a reader whether the title refers to a whole work or to only part of a larger work. Titles of collections and long works, such as anthologies and novels, are italicized (underlined); titles of short works, such as stories and poems, are enclosed in quotation marks. In general, titles appearing on the covers of published works are italicized (underlined), and titles appearing within the covers of works are enclosed in quotation marks. (For a complete discussion of italics, see 28a, "Italics/Underlining in Titles.")

SHORT STORY: "Her Sweet Jerome," from *In Love and Trouble*

SHORT POEM: "Terrence, This Is Stupid Stuff," from *A Shropshire Lad*

ESSAY: "Sootfall and Fallout," from *Essays of E. B. White*

ARTICLE: "The Mystery of Tears," from *Smithsonian*

EDITORIAL: "Facts and Figures for the President," from the *Fort Wayne News-Sentinel*

CHAPTER: "Velikovsky in Collision," from *Ever Since Darwin*

TV EPISODE: "A Sound of Dolphins," from *The Undersea World of Jacques Cousteau*

SONG: "It Ain't Necessarily So," from *Porgy and Bess*

☐ EXERCISE 3

Insert quotation marks wherever necessary in the following sentences.

1. The Haunted and the Haunters is a spine-tingling ghost story.
2. One of Ogden Nash's poems is titled At Least I'm Not the Kind of Fool Who Sobs, What Kind of Fool Am I?
3. On Muzak, Johnny Mathis was singing Winter Wonderland.
4. The essay entitled The Blues: A Poetic Form analyzed the music of twelve blues singers.
5. In the *Washington Post* Friday, the editorial, Federal Officials Shirk Duty, was particularly critical of Congress.

" "

27e

27e Quotation Marks Around Words Used in Special Ways

Quotation marks can show that words have been used in a special sense—for an ironic effect, with a twist of meaning, or as words. Also, by enclosing slang words appearing in a formal context, quotation marks can indicate a deliberate shift of style.

> She insisted that the graduates from "her" school would never do such a thing.

> The report contained the "facts" of the case.

> When people talk about the movie, they use words like "strange," "haunting," and "weird."

> The speaker owns a "fat farm" in California, which slims down rich overeaters for $2,500 a week.

☐ EXERCISE 4

Explain the reasons for the quotation marks in the following sentences.

1. On the scrabble board, the tiles spelled out "SCOWLS," "SOBS," and "POOLS."
2. The dump calls itself a "restaurant" and the mush it serves "food."
3. The child cannot pronounce "aluminum."
4. The artist was "discovered" when he was fifty years old.
5. His only "exercise" is opening and closing the refrigerator door.
6. In the off-Broadway production, there are too many "hams."
7. The essays display pragmatism and a "can do" optimism.
8. In the 1960s many people thought it more important to "feel" than to "think."

9. Membership in such "exclusive" clubs is denied to women.
10. The advertisement maintains that the film is "art."

27f Inappropriate Quotation Marks

" "
27f

- Quotation marks should not enclose the title of a composition when it appears on a title page or on the first page of a manuscript.

  INAPPROPRIATE: "A Hero for Today"

  APPROPRIATE: A Hero for Today

- Quotation marks should not enclose a nickname that is used in place of a name.

  INAPPROPRIATE: In the 1950s, "Fats" Domino was one of the big names in rock and roll.

  APPROPRIATE: In the 1950s, Fats Domino was one of the big names in rock and roll.

- Quotation marks should not enclose slang or a trite expression that is being used for lack of a more effective one.

  INAPPROPRIATE: "Last but not least," we must consider the endangered species.

  APPROPRIATE: Finally, we must consider the endangered species.

☐ EXERCISE 5

Correct any errors made in the use of quotation marks.

1. The first novel Mark Twain wrote was "The Adventures of Thomas Jefferson Snodgrass."
2. In Liverpool, a cat is a moggy.
3. The editorial, A Step Toward Success, says that the program is "an investment in future security;" however, I am not sure the program is that valuable.
4. The line "In my beginning is my end" appears in the poem *East Coker* from the book "Four Quartets".
5. Have you ever heard a turtle called a "cooter?"
6. According to Edith Hamilton, Greek mythology developed when "little distinction had been made . . . between the real and unreal".
7. Was the actor in the right place on the stage when he said, "What's here? a cup, clos'd in my true love's hand?"
8. "Don't touch the"—it was too late.

9. "Duke" Wayne had his best role when he played "Rooster" Cogburn in
   "True Grit."
10. Victory is "just around the corner" and "almost in our grasp."

☐ Using Ellipsis Marks

27g Ellipsis Marks to Show Omissions

Ellipsis marks are a sequence of spaced periods that indicate an
omission in a direct quotation. For example, suppose that you
wanted to quote only a part of the following paragraph written
shortly after the Civil War by Ulysses S. Grant in a report to President
Andrew Johnson.

> I am satisfied that the mass of thinking men of the South accept
> the present situation of affairs in good faith. The questions which
> have heretofore divided the sentiment of the people of the two sec-
> tions—slavery and state's rights, or the right of a state to secede from
> the Union—they regard as having been settled forever by the highest
> tribunal—arms—that man can resort to. I was pleased to learn from
> the leading men whom I met that they not only accepted the deci-
> sion arrived at as final but, now that the smoke of battle has cleared
> away and time has been given for reflection, that this decision has
> been a fortunate one for the whole country.

To show an omission within a single sentence, you would use three
periods with a space before, between, and after each.

> Grant wrote, "The questions which have heretofore divided
> the sentiment of the people of the two sections . . . they regard as
> having been settled forever by the highest tribunal—arms—that
> man can resort to."

If an omission involves more than a part of one sentence, you would
use four periods—the period of the last sentence quoted plus the
three spaced periods showing ellipsis.

> Grant wrote in a letter to President Johnson the following ob-
> servation about the South: "I am satisfied that the mass of thinking
> men of the South accept the present situation of affairs in good faith.
> . . . I was pleased to learn from the leading men whom I met that
> they not only accepted the decision arrived at as final but, now that
> the smoke of battle has cleared away and time has been given for

reflection, that this decision has been a fortunate one for the whole country."

Usually, ellipsis marks are not used to mark an omission at the beginning of a quotation—the absence of an initial capital letter shows that the whole passage is not included. Also, ellipsis marks are not used at the end of a quotation to show that other material follows.

. . .
27h

> In a report to President Johnson after the war, Grant wrote that Southern leaders "accepted the decision arrived at as final."

A line of spaced periods shows the omission of several paragraphs of prose or one or more lines of a poem.

> Shelley writes in "Queen Mab":
>
> Power, like a desolating pestilence,
> Pollutes whate'er it touches; and obedience,
> . . . .
> Makes slaves of men, and, of the human frame
> A mechanized automaton.

27h Ellipsis Marks to Show Interruption in Dialogue

In dialogue, ellipsis marks can show interruption of a thought or statement.

> "Well, Judge, I don't know . . ." and whatever he meant to say trailed off into silence.
>
> "That car costs forty thousand . . . uh . . . forget it."

☐ EXERCISE 6

Use ellipsis marks to show the omissions indicated.

1. According to H. L. Mencken, "To be in love is merely to be in a state of perceptual anaesthesia—to mistake an ordinary young man for a Greek god or an ordinary young woman for a goddess." [Omit all of the sentence after "anaesthesia."]

2. Edith Hamilton has written: "Five hundred years before Christ in a little town on the far western border of the settled and civilized world, a strange new power was at work. Something had awakened in the minds and spirits of the men there which was so to influence the world that

the slow passage of long time, of century and the shattering changes they brought, would be powerless to wear away that deep impress. Athens had entered upon her brief and magnificent flowering of genius which so molded the world of mind and spirit that our mind and spirit today are different." [Omit the second sentence.]

3. Leslie Fiedler writes of Faulkner's writings: "The detective story is the inevitable crown of Faulkner's work; in it (the stories in *Knight's Gambit* and *Intruder in the Dust*) many strains of his writing find fulfillment, not least his commitment to the 'switcheroo' and the surprise ending." [Omit the part of the quotation in parentheses.]

4. In "The Second Coming" Yeats writes:

> Turning and turning in the widening gyre
> The falcon cannot hear the falconer;
> Things fall apart; the centre cannot hold;
> Mere anarchy is loosed upon the world,
> The blood-dimmed tide is loosed, and everywhere
> The ceremony of innocence is drowned;
> The best lack all conviction, while the worst
> Are full of passionate intensity. [Omit lines 4, 5, and 6.]

5. At 5:30 Mountain War Time, the Atomic Age began: "At that great moment in history, ranking with the moment in the long ago when man first put fire to work for him and started on his march to civilization, the vast energy locked within the hearts of the atoms of matter was released for the first time in a burst of flame such as had never before been seen on this planet." [Omit the beginning of the quote through "civilization."]

. . .
27h

28

Italics/Underlining

Italic type slants to the right. Without this special typeface, writers preparing manuscripts by hand or with ordinary typewriters must substitute underlining for italics to distinguish such things as titles, foreign words, special names of vehicles, and words used as words. Italics or underlining can also show readers when to stress words that convey especially important ideas.

28a Italics/Underlining in Titles

Titles are always marked in some way—either with quotation marks or with underlining. Although there is no absolute agreement about which method to use, it is common practice to underline the following kinds of titles. Notice that underlining with a continuous line displays the title as a single unit and thus facilitates reading.

- Books and book-length poems

    <u>The Red Badge of Courage</u>
    <u>The Short Stories of Saki</u>
    <u>Four Screen Plays of Ingmar Bergman</u>
    <u>Don Juan</u>

- Plays and movies

    <u>Othello</u>
    <u>Crimes of the Heart</u>
    <u>Dr. Strangelove</u>

- Reports and long pamphlets

    Handbook of Utilization of Aquatic Plants

    A Nation at Risk: The Imperative for Educational Reform

- Newspapers, magazines, and journals

(The word *the* beginning a title is frequently not capitalized and not underlined.)

    the Washington Post

    the New Republic

    Art in America

    Journal of Dental Research

- Operas, symphonies, ballets, albums

    Verdi's Rigoletto

    Bach's Well-Tempered Clavier

    Horowitz at the Met

    Paul Simon's There Goes Rhymin' Simon

- Television and radio series

    The Shadow

    The Jack Benny Show

    Star Trek

    Masterpiece Theatre

- Paintings and sculpture

    Absinthe Drinkers by Degas

    Guernica by Picasso

    Sky Cathedral by Louise Nevelson

    Three Way Piece No. 2 by Henry Moore

NOTE: Punctuation that is part of a title is underlined.

    They are acting in Who's Afraid of Virginia Woolf?

Sentence punctuation that follows a title is not underlined.

    Have you ever read Babbitt?

When an apostrophe or an apostrophe plus an *s* is added to a title, the addition is not underlined.

    The Counterfeiters' plot

    Time's editorial

A few titles should not be italicized or underlined.

- Names of standard dictionaries and encyclopedias unless referred to by their formal names

  Webster's Dictionary (<u>Webster's Third New International Dictionary</u>)

  Random House Dictionary (<u>The Random House Dictionary of the English Language</u>)

  Americana (<u>Encyclopedia Americana</u>)

- Names of standard religious books

  Bible

  Koran

  Talmud

- Directories and catalogs

  Atlanta Telephone Directory

  JC Penny Catalog

- The title of a composition when it appears on a title page or at the top of the first page of a manuscript

  The Trouble with Television

  The Unforgettable Miss Sternberger

28b Italics/Underlining for Words, Numbers, and Letters Used as Words

A word used as a word is underlined or sometimes enclosed in quotation marks (see 27e). For example, you can use *dog* to mean a canine animal or to represent the word *dog*.

> The dog barked. [canine animal]
>
> <u>Dog</u> comes from Anglo-Saxon. [word]

A number can refer to a quantity or signify itself as a word.

> I bought 25 plants. [quantity]
>
> On the sign a <u>25</u> was painted in red. [word]

Letters that appear as such in a sentence always are underlined or enclosed in quotation marks.

> The British put two <u>e</u>'s in <u>judgment.</u>
>
> Southerners frequently drop an r at the end of an unstressed syllable.

28c Italics/Underlining for Sounds

When sounds are represented by words or combinations of letters, they are usually underlined.

> The music had a recurrent ta ta ta tum refrain.
>
> With a woosh-thump, the golf club sent the white ball over the fairway.

ital
28e

28d Italics/Underlining for Foreign Words

Foreign names of the scientific genus and species of animals and plants are always underlined.

> The new threat to the marsh is Hydrilla verticillata, which can choke out all other life.

Foreign words that are not considered part of the vocabulary of English are underlined.

> People assume that movies with gladiators, casts of thousands, and elaborate costumes must ipso facto be bad.
>
> On the ship we ate in the tourist-class salle à manger.

Some foreign words are in such common use that they are now considered English. For example, words such as *ex officio, ballet, connoisseur, debut,* though originally Latin and French, no longer need underlining. When you are not sure if a word of foreign origin has become part of English, check in a dictionary.

28e Italics/Underlining for Vehicles Designated by Proper Names

Traditionally, ships, aircraft, spacecraft, and trains have proper names, and those names are usually underlined.

U.S.S. Iowa	City of New Orleans
Challenger	Winnie Mae

28f Italics/Underlining for Emphasis

ital
28f

Words can be underlined for emphasis, but you should use this device in moderation. Overuse negates its impact.

> The department's expenditures are edging toward the 300-billion-dollar mark.

> She works all day as a secretary, and she still likes to type.

☐ EXERCISE

Underline any words that should be italicized.

1. The Statue of Liberty, a book by Marvin Trachtenberg, tells the fascinating story of Bartholdi's efforts to "glorify . . . Liberty."
2. Lewis and Clark brought back from their western expedition the Columbian lily (Fritillaria pudica).
3. The child kept throwing rocks into the lake—kerplunk, kerplunk, kerplunk.
4. Many people object to using the masculine pronoun he to refer to both sexes.
5. He was wearing a trenchcoat straight out of Casablanca.
6. Lequesne pronounced the finished statue his chef d′oeuvre.
7. Chess was his only love. [emphasis on *only*]
8. Stamma labeled the vertical rows of the chess board from a to h.
9. Some newspapers use pontiff as a synonym for pope.
10. Watteau's The Embarkation for Cythera is filled with angels and happy, elegant people.
11. She is supposed to be a femme fatale in The Young and the Restless.
12. Civilization has made some progress. [emphasis on *has*]
13. The word check is abbreviated + in algebraic notation.
14. Toe shoes were first used in the ballet La Sylphide.
15. On the program were Mozart's Jupiter Symphony and Rachmaninoff's Prelude in G Minor.

Hyphens and Slashes

Unlike other punctuation marks such as commas and semicolons, hyphens and slashes never signal sentence structure. Instead they function on the word level—hyphens to create compound words and slashes to show alternatives and make combinations.

☐ Using Hyphens

29a Hyphens in Compound Nouns and Verbs

Nouns and verbs consisting of two or more words are called "compounds." Some compounds are hyphenated; others are written together; still others are written separately.

safeguard	meatball	cutoff
safe hit	meat grinder	lift off
safe-conduct	meat-ax	call-off

There are a few patterns in the placement of hyphens.

- Hyphens in compounds often distinguish between parts of speech.

has-been (noun)	has been (verb)
send-off (noun)	send off (verb)
single-space (verb)	single space (noun)
black-market (verb)	black market (noun)

- Compounds made of two proper nouns or of letters plus words are hyphenated.

Franco-American	X-ray
Anglo-Saxon	B-sharp
Afro-American	U-turn

29b

- Hyphens show the dual nature of some jobs or roles.

actor-director	secretary-treasurer
player-coach	city-state
clerk-typist	restaurant-lounge

Despite these tendencies, you should use an up-to-date dictionary to be sure of acceptable hyphenation in nouns and verbs. All dictionaries do not agree, but at least they provide authority for whatever practice you follow.

EXERCISE 1

Check in a dictionary to find out whether the following should be hyphenated, fused into one word, or left as two separate words.

1. call in (v)
2. call back (n)
3. baby sitter (n)
4. baby sit (v)
5. link up (n)
6. link up (v)
7. eye opener (n)
8. eye lash (n)
9. eye drops (n)
10. machine gun (v)
11. machine gun (n)
12. self reliance (n)
13. all American (n)
14. run around (n)
15. Post Impressionism (n)

29b Hyphens in Compound Modifiers

Most compound modifiers preceding nouns are hyphenated. Thus, readers can tell at a glance that a modifier forms a single unit and a single concept. Compound modifiers that do not precede nouns are not hyphenated unless normally spelled with hyphens.

Fire destroyed the sixteenth-century building.

The architecture was sixteenth century.

The machine registers only low-frequency sounds.

The sounds should be low frequency.

I own a one-and-a-half-year-old beagle.

The beagle is one and a half years old.

The music reflects their Scotch-Irish ancestry.

Their ancestry is Scotch-Irish. [modifier normally hyphenated]

A few compound modifiers preceding nouns have no hyphens. A modifier made of an -*ly* adverb plus another word is not hyphenated.

carefully written paper

highly successful restaurant

badly designed building

Also, no hyphens are used when a compound modifier is obviously a unit, as in the case of a modifier made from a proper noun, a foreign expression, or a standard compound noun.

Red Cross office

prima facie **evidence**

child welfare payment

When two compound modifiers have the same second word (*three-column and five-column charts*), the second word need not appear twice (*three- and five-column charts*). Notice, however, that the hyphen in the first compound is retained.

whole- or half-year lease

forty- or fifty-thousand dollars

term- or whole-life insurance

10-, 12-, and 15-pitch typefaces

29c Hyphens with Some Prefixes

Most prefixes are attached directly to the base word, but *self-, ex-,* or *all-* are attached with hyphens.

self-defense	ex-champion	all-purpose
self-education	ex-clerk	all-star
self-conscious	ex-husband	all-powerful

A hyphen is used when a prefix is attached to a proper noun (easily identified by its capital letter).

non-European	pre-Columbian
mid-Atlantic	anti-Communist
neo-Platonic	un-American

Sometimes a hyphen is necessary to distinguish words that would be otherwise identical.

recover re-cover	reform re-form
prejudicial pre-judicial	extraordinary extra-ordinary

When reading is complicated by a repeated letter or by too many vowels in a row, a hyphen can separate the prefix from the base.

non-nuclear	re-use
pre-empt	pro-union
anti-inflation	semi-independent

29d Hyphens in Numbers

Hyphens appear in some spelled-out numbers. Traditionally, numbers from twenty-one to ninety-nine are hyphenated, whether they appear alone or as part of a larger number.

forty-eight ounces

twenty-second birthday

twenty-five hundred words

one hundred and fifty-six days [usually 156 days]

Some writers do not hyphenate spelled-out fractions used as nouns, but all fractions used as adjectives are hyphenated.

one-fourth [or one fourth] of those surveyed

five and two-thirds yards

Hyphens separate numbers that express a range.

during the years 1975-1981

pp. 25-96

29e Hyphens for Word Divisions at the Ends of Lines

Hyphenated words are somewhat hard to read at the ends of lines, and too many hyphens look messy. If you must hyphenate to align the right margin, follow these guidelines.

- Divide words only between syllables. If you are not sure of the divisions, either do not divide the word, or look at the main entry in a dictionary, which will indicate the correct syllabication.
- Consider pronunciation. *Chemotherapy* makes more sense divided *chemo·therapy* than *chem·otherapy; fra·ternity* seems preferable to *frater·nity.*
- Do not leave one letter on a line by itself. For example, *a·like* and *tax·i* should not be divided.
- Do not divide the last word on a page. It is inconvenient to turn the page to find the rest of the word.

In making decisions about hyphenating, always keep the reader in mind. If a hyphenated word makes reading more difficult, either do not hyphenate or solve the problem by revising the sentence.

☐ EXERCISE 2

Supply any missing hyphens in the following passage.

Millions of people are enjoying the resurgence of a 4,500 year old game. They are kicking around a golfball size object. Although kick-ball games have long been popular, this new version is different. It was invented by John Stalberger of Portland, Oregon, who, in order to rehabilitate a badly injured knee, gave soccer style kicks to a mini size ball. After Stalberger introduced his "footbag" to people at a state fair, Bruce Guettich founded the World Footbag Association. Two companies, which started producing the footbag, got in a patent controversy but made an out of court settlement. The companies' products are somewhat different. One markets a four paneled footbag; the other, a two piece version. Other companies now have similar products—one an eight dollar fire engine red bag with a devil logo. Now there are even championships in which contestants play a sort of tennis and a sort of volleyball game over a 5 foot high net.

☐ Using Slashes

29f Slashes Between Alternatives

A slash between words can show alternatives—*and/or, he/she, pass/ fail.* The mark replaces the *or* that would otherwise be needed to separate the alternatives.

> radio/television
>
> A.M./P.M.
>
> animal/vegetable

In informal or technical papers, the slash is acceptable; in formal or nontechnical papers, the *or* is preferred.

29g Slashes for Making Combinations

Combinations of words or numbers such as in compounds and sequences sometimes contain slashes.

> Dallas/Fort Worth
>
> *The MacNeil/Lehrer News Hour*
>
> 20/20 vision
>
> 4/21/81
>
> 1984/85

29h Slashes Between Lines of Poetry

A few lines of poetry can be quoted in their original form or in prose form (incorporated into a sentence, from margin to margin). When the prose form is used, slashes show the poetic line divisions.

> Byron writes in *Don Juan,* "'Tis strange, but true; for truth is always strange;/ Stranger than fiction: if it could be told,/ How much would novels gain by the exchange!"

29i Slashes for Fractions

When a fraction must be written or typed, a slash separates the numerator from the denominator: *1/3, 3/5, 5/12.*

/
29i

☐ EXERCISE 3

Wherever possible, substitute slashes in alternatives, combinations, or fractions. Assume that the context for these sentences is informal or technical.

1. The agency will provide car or bus transportation to the site of the ceremony.
2. WXTR AM or FM will have regular progress reports from the football coaches.
3. Interest rates have gone up three-tenths of a percent.
4. The Biloxi and Gulfport area is one of the fastest growing areas on the Gulf Coast.
5. If a person writes a company about a billing error, the company must acknowledge his or her letter within thirty days.

30

Abbreviations and Numbers

abbr
30a

The conventions governing the use of abbreviations and numbers depend on the context. In informal or technical papers, abbreviations and numerals are common, especially when space is limited. In formal and nontechnical papers, however, some numbers and most abbreviations are written out. The following guidelines suggest an appropriate style.

■ Using Abbreviations

30a Generally Acceptable Abbreviations

No word should be abbreviated if readers will not understand the shortened form; however, some abbreviations are immediately understood by everyone and are generally appropriate whatever the style of a paper.

- Titles and ranks

  Mr., Mrs., Ms., Dr. are abbreviated when used before a name. (Note: *Miss* is not an abbreviation.)

  Civil and military titles are abbreviated only when used before a full name, not when used before the last name alone.

ACCEPTABLE	UNACCEPTABLE
Lt. Gov. John Bird	Lt. Gov. Bird
Adm. Karl Doenitz	Adm. Doenitz
Sgt. George Dumcke	Sgt. Dumcke

Reverend and *Honorable* can be abbreviated only when they do not follow *the* and when they precede a full name.

ACCEPTABLE	UNACCEPTABLE
Rev. Donald Yanella	Rev. Yanella
the Reverend Donald Yanella	
Hon. Vernon Richards	Hon. Richards
the Honorable Vernon Richards	

When used after full names, *Jr.* and *Sr.* are abbreviated; the full words are used only on formal invitations.

ACCEPTABLE: Joseph W. Alsop, Jr.

- Degrees and certifications

Scholarly degrees are abbreviated *(B.A., M.S., Ph.D.)*. When a degree follows a name, no other title goes before the name.

ACCEPTABLE: Milton G. Saunders, Ph.D.

UNACCEPTABLE: Dr. Milton G. Saunders, Ph.D.

- Words in names of businesses

Often, names of businesses include abbreviations such as *Co., Corp., Inc., Ltd., Bros., &.* Abbreviations in the official names of businesses are acceptable in most prose. However, in the middle of a sentence, you may prefer to write out a word like *Company* or to drop an added-on abbreviation like *Inc.*

- Time designations

Such designations as A.M., P.M., *EST, CDT,* A.D., and B.C. are abbreviated. Remember that A.D. precedes a year but B.C. follows.

The Han dynasty lasted from 202 B.C. to A.D. 220.

- Acronyms and familiar initials

The full forms of initials pronounced as words (acronyms) are almost never written out *(sonar, ZIP, COBOL, Nabisco, Alcoa, NASA, snafu)*. Also, neither are the full forms of many familiar initials *(UFO, ESP, IQ, ID, R.S.V.P., IBM, FBI, NBC)*.

- Latin abbreviations

Except in extremely formal papers, abbreviations are used for some Latin expressions: *i.e., e.g., v.* or *vs., etc.*

- Geographical locations

In prose, except for *Washington, D.C., U.S.S.R.,* and *U.S.* (as an adjective but not a noun), geographical locations are seldom abbreviated.

In the addresses of formal letters, words such as *street, avenue, boulevard, road,* and *building* should be written out, unless brevity is essential. Also written out are compass directions when they are part of the street name. *49 West Farris Street.* (Compass directions are abbreviated when they follow a street name: *1237 Connecticut Avenue, NW.*) In the addresses of all but the most formal business letters, a writer may abbreviate states with the two-letter abbreviations designated by the U.S. Postal Service.

- Reference notations

Even in formal papers, abbreviations are typically used for tables, footnotes, bibliographies, and indexes: *pp. 13–26, fig. 4, 3rd ed., Vol. 1.*

30b   Punctuation and Capitalization in Abbreviations

Formerly, writers used periods after most abbreviations. Now, increasingly, some periods are being dropped. Because practices change, consult a recent dictionary to keep up with current practice. There you will find that some abbreviations contain periods *(Dist. Atty., Sept., R.S.V.P.)*, some have optional periods *(ft. or ft, lb. or lb, E.S.T. or EST)*, and some have none.

> Chemical symbols: Cu, N, Zn, Au
>
> Acronyms: NATO, UNESCO, CORE
>
> Military terms: POW, USA, GI
>
> Points of the compass: NE, NW, SE
>
> States in Postal Service abbreviations: HI, OH, AZ, OK

In general, the capitalization of an abbreviation reflects that of the full word: *GOP (Grand Old Party), Ph.D. (Doctor of Philosophy), hwy. (highway), Btu (British thermal unit).* But with a few abbreviations, capitalization cannot be predicted by the capitalization in the full word: *eV (electron volt), a.m.* or A.M. *(ante meridiem),* A.D. *(anno Domini), n.d.* or *N.D. (no date).*

❑ EXERCISE 1

Rewrite the following passage, making the abbreviations appropriate for a nontechnical paper.

During WWII, Germans used submarines, called U-boats, to enforce a naval blockade of Eng. in the Atl. The U.S. had to keep the sea lanes open for supplies and for a possible invasion. The German subs, traveling in "wolf packs," moved to the American East Coast. On Jan. 12, 1942, they opened an offensive off Cape Cod, MA, and soon after inflicted heavy destruction from Canada to Jacksonville, FL. From Jan.-Apr. 1942, almost 200 ships were sunk. Then Adm. Doenitz, the German commander, moved further south and torpedoed 182 ships in May and June. Adm. King organized small escort vessels into an interlocking convoy system to combat the German subs. The convoy system, well-equipped destroyers, and radar-equipped planes eventually controlled the sub menace.

num

30c

☐ EXERCISE 2

Rewrite the following passage, abbreviating wherever appropriate for a technical document. Some of the abbreviations you can use are given at the end of the passage; others will be familiar to you.

Many large yachts are being equipped with satellite communications that give vessels all the conveniences of modern offices. These satellite communication units have two major components—an antenna, or "above decks unit," and a control center, or "below decks unit." With the "below decks unit" are a teletype/printer and telephone hand set. All satellite communication systems must be approved by International Maritime Satellite Organization before they can be marketed. Typical of the approved satellite communication systems is the Magnavox MX Z11A. The antenna of this system has a 4-foot, 5-inch diameter, stands 4 feet, 9 1/2 inches high, and weighs 429 pounds. The teleprinter contains a 4 K memory. Buyers can get as options remote telephones and a word processor with a cathode-ray tube display.

> satellite communications = sat com
> "above decks unit" = ADU
> "below decks unit" = BDU
> International Maritime Satellite Organization = INMARSAT
> cathode-ray tube = CRT

☐ Using Numbers

30c Numbers in Nontechnical Papers

In nontechnical papers, numerals may interrupt and obstruct continuity. The clearest system is to write out numbers that can be stated in one or two words. (Hyphenated numbers are counted as one word.)

> twelve o'clock [one-word number]
>
> thirty-eight battles [one-word number]
>
> forty-five thousand miles [two-word number]

Numerals should be used for numbers that would require more than two words.

> 475 books [not *four hundred and seventy-five books*]
>
> 1,028 miles [not *one thousand and twenty-eight miles*]
>
> 3,166 units [not *three thousand one hundred and sixty-six units*]

Whether words or numerals, equivalent numbers must be consistently in the same style.

> Last year the museum held 825 paintings; this year the number has grown to 900. [not *nine hundred*]

Some numbers never appear in word form.

DATES:	17 March 1980
	January 21, 1876
EXACT AMOUNTS OF MONEY:	$51.75
	1.5 billion dollars
PAGE NUMBERS:	p. 6
	pages 19–22
SECTIONS OF BOOKS:	Chapter 15
	Volume 3
ADDRESSES:	906 Wisconsin Avenue NW
	Washington, D.C. 20016
TIME WITH A.M./P.M.:	5 P.M.
	11:30 A.M.
MEASUREMENTS AND STATISTICS:	5 feet 10 inches
	2- by 4-foot tiles
	4 hours 12 minutes
	a 72 to 75 loss
	20 percent
	32-ounce bottle
	9 for, 12 against
	13% interest

30d Numbers in Technical Documents

In business, technical, or scientific documents, numbers should look precise and noticeable. Numerals are more efficient and more emphatic than words. Compare

> On the thirty-first of August, we ordered one hundred of your fifty-pound sacks of fertilizer and sent you a check for six hundred dollars and twenty-four cents.

and

> On 31 August, we ordered 100 of your 50-pound sacks of fertilizer and sent you a check for $600.24.

Any reader would obviously prefer the second example.

Therefore in technical papers, numerals are preferred for most numbers—sometimes with the exceptions of numbers below ten and numbers that express a million and above (*five million, 900 billion*). NOTE: If the numbers below ten are in sequences with numbers above ten, the forms should be consistent—all in numerals.

> CONSISTENT: We sold from 9 to 12 copies.

> INCONSISTENT: We sold from nine to 12 copies.

Even if numbers are below ten, measurements and statistics are always expressed as numerals.

> The new model fishing boat was 23 feet long with a beam of 8 feet.

> Of the people who volunteered for the study, 9.2 percent had disqualifying medical histories.

30e Numbers That Begin Sentences

In any style paper, a numeral should not appear at the beginning of a sentence. If the numeral cannot be written as a word without awkwardness, the sentence should be rewritten to reposition the number. The following sentences are changed so that the number no longer begins the sentence.

> INCORRECT: 45 copies of the brochure were printed.

> REVISED: We printed 45 copies of the brochure.

num

30e

INCORRECT: 144 square inches make up 1 square foot.

REVISED: In square measure, 144 square inches make up 1 square foot.

INCORRECT: 690 members are in the organization.

REVISED: The organization has 690 members.

30f Adjacent Numbers

Adjacent numbers are easier to read when one number is a figure and one is a word. Most often, the first number is a word; however, if this number is large, it is frequently expressed as a numeral.

We need ten 12-foot planks.

James wrote two 20-page papers.

They bought 5,000 thirteen-cent stamps.

☐ EXERCISE 3

Revise the following passage to make the forms of the numbers appropriate for a technical style.

Sam Colt's weapons have been used extensively in battles. Although the first guns with revolving cylinders had been made three hundred years earlier, Colt got an American patent in eighteen thirty-five. He was a good salesman as well as inventor. For example, in the Seminole Indian War, he sold officers all the five-shot Colt pistols that he had and fifty eight-shot rifles. Sixteen Texas Rangers, stalked by seventy Comanches, used the Colt pistol to kill thirty of the Indians. In the Mexican War, General Zachary Taylor ordered one thousand of the pistols. Colt then developed the six-shot gun and established a factory with a production line. By eighteen fifty-seven, his factory was producing two hundred and fifty pistols a day. For the Crimean War, he supplied two hundred thousand pistols. During the Civil War, the Colt factory produced three hundred eighty-seven thousand revolvers and seven thousand rifles for the Northern army.

☐ EXERCISE 4

Revise the following passage to make the forms of the numbers appropriate for a nontechnical style.

Jane Hook is indeed a prolific mystery novelist. She has written 5 novels in the last 4 years. 3 of the mysteries are set in a hospital—a good background since Mrs. Hook was for 15 years a hospital administrator. The other 2 novels also touch on Mrs. Hook's experiences; 1 mystery is built around a psychiatric symposium, and the other has a 36-year-old nurse as the protagonist. Mrs. Hook's novels tend to be longer than the average mystery. The shortest of the 5 is 255 pages; the longest is 420 pages. This output is amazing; the author must write easily and very, very rapidly.

num

30f

31

Capital Letters

Primarily, capital letters signal the beginnings of sentences and designate proper names and official titles. The practice of capitalizing the first word of a sentence is simple and stable. But the practice of capitalizing proper names and titles is more complex; authorities disagree, and conventions change. Furthermore, a word may be capitalized in one situation but not in another. The solution to most problems of capitalization, however, can be found in a standard up-to-date dictionary or a handbook like this one.

31a Capitalization of First Words

- As a general rule, the first letter of the first word of a complete sentence is capitalized.

  Youngsters broke the security of the computer system and obliterated important information.

  The city is treating all the bronze statues in order to inhibit corrosion.

  Does Assateague Island have nude beaches?

  EXCEPTION: A sentence's first letter is not capitalized when the sentence appears inside parentheses within another sentence.

266

The school's decision surprised everyone (he was, after all, a star player).

- Capitalization of the first words in a series of elliptical questions is optional.

    Does an office this small really need a copier? Two word processors? A switchboard?

    cap
    31a

    or

    Does an office this small really need a copier? two word processors? a switchboard?

- When a quotation begins a new sentence, the first word is capitalized.

    Macbeth asks, "Will all great Neptune's ocean wash this blood clean from my hand?"

    When the quoted sentence is split, only the first word begins with a capital letter.

    "In a real dark night of the soul," Fitzgerald writes, "it is always three o'clock in the morning."

    If the quotation does not begin a new sentence, the first word is not capitalized.

    Mussolini believed that only war put "the stamp of nobility upon the peoples who have the courage to face it."

- In a sentence, an element after a colon can begin either with a capital letter or with a lowercase letter. The capital makes the construction more formal and emphasizes the material following the colon.

    The lesson we learned was this: Work helps keep juveniles out of trouble.

    Orson Welles' reputation is a mystery: he is considered a genius on the basis of one work—*Citizen Kane.*

    They were all striving for the same thing: Peace.

    The city faces a serious problem: unemployment.

- In traditional poetry, the first word of every line is capitalized even when the word does not begin a new sentence.

    But words are things, and a small drop of ink,
    Falling like dew upon a thought, produces
    That which makes thousands, perhaps millions, think.

    From Byron's *Don Juan*

- The first word in every entry in an outline is capitalized.

Japanese Military Operations in Indochina
I. Military reasons for the operations
II. Entry of the Japanese
   A. Occupation of Northern Indochina
   B. Occupation of Southern Indochina
III. Japanese wartime bases
IV. Surrender to the allied forces

- In lists, the first words are often capitalized but do not have to be. The capital letters give the items more emphasis and formality.

    The benefits include

        Life and medical insurance

        Business travel and accident insurance

        Savings and investment programs

        A retirement program

- In a letter, the first word of the salutation and the complimentary close is capitalized.

    My dear Sir: Yours truly,

    To whom it may concern: Sincerely yours,

31b Capitalization of Proper Names and Proper Adjectives

Proper nouns are the names of specific persons, places, and things—given names, surnames, place names, names of organizations, historical names, brand names, and so on. (See 1a.)

- The general rule is that proper nouns and adjectives derived from them are capitalized.

    France   French culture

    Colombia   Colombian coffee

    Jefferson   Jeffersonian ideals

    Henry James   Jamesian story

The following categories illustrate the kinds of words considered proper nouns and adjectives.

NAMES OF PEOPLE AND ANIMALS— Gerry Wieland, Jean Kindelberger,
REAL AND FICTIONAL: Tom Sawyer, Trigger, Gargantua

PLACE NAMES—NATURAL AND ARTIFICIAL:	Venus, Africa, Potomac River, Montpelier, Union Station, Statue of Liberty
ORGANIZATIONS—GOVERNMENT, BUSINESS, SOCIAL:	Department of State, Committee for Economic Development, Milwaukee Chamber of Commerce, National Council of Churches
HISTORICAL NAMES:	Elizabethan Age, Tonkin Resolution, Truman Doctrine, Battle of Wounded Knee, Renaissance
RELIGIOUS TERMS:	God; He, His, Him [referring to God in a religious context]; Buddhism; Shinto; Palm Sunday, Ramadan
NAMES IN EDUCATION:	California Polytechnic State University, Basic Writing II, World History 101, Rhodes Scholarship
AWARDS, MEDALS, PRIZES:	National Book Award, Pulitzer Prize, Good Conduct Medal, Medal of Honor
CALENDAR TERMS—DAYS, MONTHS, HOLIDAYS:	Monday, August, Veterans Day, Bastille Day
PRODUCT NAMES—TRADE NAMES AND SPECIFIC NAMES:	Renault Alliance, Ford Mustang, Soyuz T-5, Frigidaire, Ivory soap [The common term of a product's name is usually not capitalized.]
ETHNIC TERMS—RACES, NATIONALITIES, LANGUAGES:	English, Japanese, Serbian, Sioux, Indo-European
SCIENTIFIC TERMS—CLASSIFICATIONS (EXCEPT SPECIES) AND CHEMICAL ABBREVIATIONS:	*Equidae, Bovidae, Canis rufus, Alligator mississippiensis,* O [oxygen]

cap 31b

- Also capitalized are nicknames or substitutes for proper names.

OFFICIAL NAMES	SUBSTITUTES
New York City	Big Apple
Missouri	Show Me State
Earl Hines	Fatha Hines
William Warren	Grandfather (but *my grandfather*)
Mayor Barry	Mayor

- Some words derived from proper nouns are no longer capitalized; others are capitalized at times. For example, the word *maverick* (derived from the name of Senator Samuel A. Maverick of Texas) is not capitalized; the word *draconian* (derived from the Athenean lawgiver Draco) is sometimes capitalized and sometimes not. Check current practice in an up-to-date dictionary.

NO LONGER CAPITALIZED

boycott (after C. C. Boycott)

bourbon (after Bourbon County, Kentucky)

quixotic (after Don Quixote)

SOMETIMES CAPITALIZED, SOMETIMES LOWER CASE

Platonic/platonic (after Plato)

Scotch/scotch (after Scotland)

Herculean/herculean (after Hercules)

31c Capitalization of Honorifics

Honorifics are titles of honor or rank—governmental, military, ecclesiastical, royal, or professional. These titles are always capitalized when they precede names.

Senator John C. Stennis

Lieutenant General David E. Grange

Reverend Jones Hamilton

Queen Elizabeth

Dr. John Fair Lucas

Professor Glover Moore

NOTE: Some honorifics may be capitalized even when they do not precede names: President and Vice President (of the United States) and the titles of members of the cabinet, members of the Supreme Court, and heads of other nations.

President Roosevelt

Roosevelt, the President in 1941

memoirs of the President

Secretary of State Elihu Root

Root, the Secretary of State

choosing a Secretary of State

Senator, Representative, Governor, and *Lieutenant Governor* can be capitalized even when they do not precede names. Either capital or lowercase letters are correct, but be consistent throughout a composition.

Senator Bill Bradley

Bill Bradley, the Senator (or senator) from New Jersey

according to the Senator (or senator)

31d Capitalization in Titles of Written Material and Artistic Works

In the titles of any written material or artistic works, the following words are capitalized.

- The first word [When *the* is the first word of a periodical, it is sometimes dropped from the title, e.g., *Washington Post,* not *The Washington Post.*]
- The last word
- Every noun, pronoun, verb, adjective, and adverb
- Conjunctions and prepositions with five or more letters
- Any word that follows a colon, dash, or question mark
- Words in hyphenated compounds [*Well-Lighted, Twenty-Five*]

These words are not capitalized unless they are the first or last words.

- Articles [*a, an, the*]
- Conjunctions and prepositions fewer than five letters
- The infinitive marker [*to*]
- The word following a hyphenated prefix unless the word is to be stressed [*Anti-imperialism* or *Anti-Imperialism*]

  The Skin of Our Teeth

  Growing Up

  "The Life You Save May Be Your Own"

  E. T.: The Extra-Terrestrial

  Why Survive? Being Old in America

  "Toys, Pseudo-Biology and the Pursuit of Profits"

  "Faith in Self-Made Success"

  How to Succeed in Business Without Really Trying

31e Capitalization in Some Abbreviations

Times of day are written A.M. and P.M. or a.m. and p.m. In print, these abbreviations are usually in small capitals. A few other abbreviations are capitalized even though the terms they replace are not, for example *T.V.* or *TV* (for *television*), *B.A.* (for *bachelor of arts*), *R.R.* or *RR* (for *railroad*), *POW* (for *prisoner of war*), *NE* (for *northeast*), *O* (for *oxygen*), A.D. (for *anno Domini*).

31f Capitalization of *I* and *O*

The pronoun *I* is always capitalized, even when it is a part of a contraction—*I'm* or *I've*. The expression *O* is capitalized, except when spelled *ob*.

31g Inappropriate Capitals

- A common noun should not be capitalized even when it appears in a phrase that contains capitals.

INCORRECT	CORRECT
American History	American history
the State of Nebraska	the state of Nebraska
Maxwell House Coffee	Maxwell House coffee
French Poodle	French poodle

- Words referring to areas of study are not capitalized unless they are names of specific courses.

CAPITALS	NO CAPITALS
Economics 302	economics
Algebra II	algebra
Studies in British Literature	literature
Introduction to Computing	computer science

NOTE: The names of languages are proper and are always capitalized: *French, English grammar, Chinese literature.*

- Words expressing family relationships, like *aunt, uncle, grandmother,* and *grandfather,* are not capitalized unless they precede or substitute for a person's name.

CAPITALS	NO CAPITALS
Uncle Will	my uncle
Grandma Moses	your grandmother

**cap
31g**

- The words *north, south, southwest,* and so on are capitalized only when they refer to regions. They are not capitalized when they refer to compass directions.

  CAPITAL: The North won the Civil War.

  NO CAPITAL: Drive north.

  CAPITAL: The first Europeans to explore the Southwest were the Spaniards.

  NO CAPITAL: The area lies southwest of here.

- Seasons are not capitalized unless they are personified.

  CAPITAL: "Come, gentle Spring! ethereal Mildness! come."

  NO CAPITAL: You plant the seeds in the spring.

- Generally, *earth* and *moon* are not capitalized. Only when these words are used in connection with named planets (and without *the*) are they capitalized.

  CAPITAL: Mercury and Venus are closer to the sun than Earth is.

  NO CAPITAL: The earth is the fifth largest planet.

  CAPITAL: The distance of Earth from Moon is 238,857 miles.

  NO CAPITAL: In an eclipse, the moon is too small to hide the sun.

❑ EXERCISE

In the following sentences, correct any incorrect capitalization.

1. As early as 1500, the English Bulldog was bred to bait bulls.
2. The president attacked the "demagoguery" of the speech made by the Communist speaker.
3. A Federal indictment was issued by U.S. attorney J. Frederick Motz.
4. The Bulgarian Government was accused of condoning drug trafficking.
5. A majority of republicans joined the democrats in support of a resolution sponsored by a senator from Maine.

6. The Commission recommended that High School students study English, Math, Science, Computer Science, and Foreign Languages.

7. The east-west conflict was aggravated by the unexpected announcement of increased Military spending.

8. Husbands and Wives may file a Tax Return jointly.

cap
31g

9. This Summer, the Chester public library announced that three Personal Computers could be checked out and taken home.

10. A pamphlet entitled "Life Insurance: Facts You Need to Know" explains the three basic types of Life Insurance policies.

11. The chief psychoactive ingredient in Marijuana *(Cannabis Sativa)* is delta-9-tetrahydrocannabinol, or thc.

12. Silver coins have gradually disappeared; during the Winter of 1970, the Government removed all silver from the Half Dollar.

13. The St. Lawrence seaway extends from the Atlantic ocean to the Western end of Lake Superior and allows ocean carriers to enter the midwest.

14. In the first Moon landing, Armstrong and Aldrin collected 48.5 Lbs. of rock and soil.

15. Have you seen "Go Tell It on the Mountain," a tv adaptation of James Baldwin's Novel?

16. The Association has registered 661 varieties of trees; a holly is the smallest, and a sequoia is the largest.

17. "To make his magic, fiction, look real," Nabokov has said, "The artist sometimes places it . . . within a definite, specific historical frame."

18. For lunch we ate chicken cooked in a Dutch oven, French fries, and a salad with Russian dressing.

19. The constitution provided for a census every ten years to determine the number of Representatives who would go to congress from each state.

20. "Beauty: a Combination from Sappho" is a translation by Rossetti of a lyric composed in the sixth century b.c.

◻ REVIEW EXERCISE

Correct the punctuation and mechanics in the following passages.

1.   Horror films long a popular genre explore the supernatural the inexplicable and the evil all to terrify viewers relentlessly. The first attempts at provoking fear were not true horror films all the mystery was logically explained at the finish. In three classic films however no rational explanation is offered or even can be.

     In 1930 Universal studios made a film about a blood drinking count, who could return from the dead Dracula. In this film directed by Tod Browning vampires travel the globe the dead live the innocent die and the irrational seems real. Audiences can find little comfort even a stake through Draculas heart cannot stop the malignant forces.

The next important horror film was directed by James Whale a british stage director. This film Frankenstein became a classic with it's brilliant performance by Boris Karloff as it's horrifying but tragic monster. The plot of the film 1931 is familiar. The brilliant Dr. Frankenstein succeeds in creating a living creature out of piece's of the dead. After killing the doctors assistant the monster escapes from the castle. Like Dracula this monster kills the innocent, and has been resurrected periodically in sequels.

The only other horror films that have ever rivaled Dracula and Frankenstein in importance are the films about Wolf Man. Introduced to the screen by Henry Hull the first werewolf film was The Werewolf of London 1934. The figure of a werewolf or lycantrope derived from the legends of central Europe where people had long heard tales of a man who changed to a wolf at every full moon, and stalked and killed victims through the night. In the future we will probably continue to see films containing these classic horror film monsters who's mysterious illogical existance continues to fascinate us.

2.   When Columbus landed in Cuba the natives told him about "a sort of grain called maiz." In the New World corn, or maize, had long been a staple crop. And it still is. Today the U.S.s per capita consumption of corn or food derived from corn is more than 3 lbs a day and the U.S. grows so much corn it can export a 3rd of the crop. Corn has been an extremely reliable crop no famine has ever decimated the U.S. as wheat and potato famines have decimated other country's.

As a food corn lends itself to wide variety. When Cortes entered Mexico in 1519 tortillas formed the basis of the Mexican diet. South Americans also prepared tamales, the equivalent of the european meat pie and chinese spring roll. Early American settlers survived partly on hominy grits succotash and cornpone all derived from corn. It was even possible to make maize beer but this drink was never as popular in America as it was in Peru and Brazil. somewhat later the richer American People could afford wheat the poorer ones ate a lot of cornmeal mush and johnnycakes.

Today we still eat all these ancient dishes, however in addition we depend heavily on meat, that comes from animals nourished by corn. We drink whiskey, made from fermented corn. And we use corn oil cornstarch and corn sweetener in innumerable products.

Improving Prose: Style

A writing "style" results from a number of details: vocabulary, sentence length, sentence patterns, figures of speech, sound and rhythm. Often these details are spontaneous choices—a reflection of the writer's personality, education, and experience. But reliance on spontaneous decisions will not always produce effective writing. Developing a good prose style requires thoughtful choices of words and structures.

32

Choosing Words

The English language has borrowed extensively from other languages. The result is an enormous vocabulary of some million words, many with similar meanings. *Roget's Thesaurus,* for example, lists almost 100 synonyms for *insane* and over 150 synonyms for *destroy.* From this abundance, writers choose the words that best fit intended meaning and individual styles.

32a General and Specific Words

General words refer to classes or categories *(magazine)*; specific words refer to particular members of a class or category *(Newsweek)*. Whether a word is general or specific is sometimes relative. For example, *media* is more general than *magazine,* and *last week's Newsweek* is more specific than *Newsweek*. The following lists illustrate a gradual progression from general to specific.

sports	food	clothes
↓	↓	↓
baseball	Italian food	pants
↓	↓	↓
the White Sox	pasta	blue jeans
↓	↓	↓
the White Sox game Friday	fettuccini	Levis

Normally, writers balance the general with the specific because both interact in the way we think. We may reason by induction, moving from specific instances to generalizations, or by deduction, applying general principles to specific instances. However, too many general words or too many specific details can hide the point or message. Compare the following.

> GENERAL: **Kindergartens benefit children by allowing interaction in an educational environment.**
>
> SPECIFIC: **Susie enjoyed playing with Mary on the jungle gym at Happy Time School.**

If the message is that children benefit socially by playing and working together in kindergarten, the general example belabors the point, while the specific example misses it. When you write, try to mix general and specific words—general words for summing up and explaining; specific words for supporting, detailing, and substantiating.

**wds
32b**

☐ EXERCISE 1

Rewrite the following passages to make the generalities more specific whenever appropriate. You may invent any specific details necessary to enliven the prose.

1. One incident involved a student found carrying a deadly weapon on the school premises. The problem was handled by the proper authorities, who expelled the student and referred him to a court. The person in charge of the occurrence said that the learning environment could not tolerate such dangerous behavior and that the perpetrator should be rehabilitated, not just punished by removal from the scene.

2. The team was ranked high in the polls early in the year. As the season began, the team started off by losing several games. Evidently, those working with the players did not do a good job. The players had problems that were not solved by any of the measures taken. The team continued to lose, and at the end of the disastrous season, the staff made plans to improve the situation next year.

32b Abstract and Concrete Words

Abstract words denote ideas, qualities, feelings—anything that has no physical existence. Concrete words denote specific realities—anything that can be seen, touched, heard. Although both kinds of words appear in most prose, an overreliance on abstract terms masks meaning and bores readers. For example, instead of an abstract discussion of the problem of frustration, readers would learn more from a description of one or more frustrating incidents—a traffic jam, a computer that refuses to compute, a test unrelated to lectures or reading assignments.

A good way to see the difference between abstract and concrete terms is to pair the two in sentences like the following.

wds
32c

> **Happiness is a cancelled 8:00 class on a cold, rainy morning.**
>
> **Luxury is the smell of leather upholstery in a new Ferrari.**
>
> **Panic is realizing that next Wednesday's test is this Wednesday.**

In each of these sentences, the quality of the abstract word is made real by the concrete and familiar example.

Prose that is full of abstractions tends to be impersonal and vague. If too many abstract words appear in your prose, you can substitute or add concrete facts, instances, and examples that will enliven, enrich, and clarify your meaning.

☐ EXERCISE 2

Pick five of the following abstractions and supply a concrete representation.

EXAMPLES: terrorism ————→ the hijacking of the *Achille Lauro*
restraint ————→ refusing a chocolate eclair because of a diet

1. fright
2. pollution
3. ambition
4. poverty
5. optimism

6. relaxation
7. power
8. invigoration
9. speed
10. difficulty

32c Denotation and Connotation

The denotation of a word is the word's meaning independent of any emotional association. The word *penguin* denotes a flightless marine bird; the word *piano* denotes a familiar keyboard instrument. In addition to a denotation, a word may have a connotation—the emotional response the word evokes in readers. Readers may associate a word with something favorable or unfavorable, something plain or fancy, something ordinary or special. To most readers, *fat* seems more unfavorable than *overweight, suave* fancier than *sophisticated, ancestry* more special than *family.*

It is very important to select words carefully for the right denotation and the most appropriate connotation. A word with an inappropriate connotation may ruin the effect. However, an incorrect denotation will not even communicate the right meaning.

(1) Dictionary meaning

Choosing a word with the right denotation means being sure of its dictionary meaning. Although writers usually depend on their everyday, working vocabulary, they may on occasion use words recently acquired or found in a thesaurus or dictionary. If you use words not yet fully mastered, be cautious. Archie Bunker got laughs by saying, "You're invading the issue"; and Dizzy Dean was famous for remarks like "The players went back to their respectable bases." Except for a comical effect, however, such mistakes (malapropisms) are unacceptable.

(2) Context

A word's proper context may be as important as its meaning. Words with the same denotation do not always fit in the same context. Suppose that you want to use the word *duress.* You know the word means "pressure." In addition, you need to know that the context for *duress* is much more limited than that for *pressure.* You can write, "The pressure was tremendous." You cannot write, "The duress was tremendous." *Duress* usually follows *under:* "I went under duress." Therefore, to use a word with authority, be sure of its explicit meaning and context before you choose it. Many dictionaries are helpful in supplying information about appropriate contexts of words. (See Appendix B, "Dictionary Use.")

(3) Associations

Writers sometimes must choose between words with approximately the same denotation but different connotations, or associations—for example, between *laziness* and *languor, yard* and *lawn, work* and *toil.* Some words are fairly neutral; others evoke associated ideas or feelings. To most readers, *home* will seem more personal and secure than *house; peril* more serious and more imminent than *danger; zealot* more fanatical than *enthusiast;* and *naked* more stark than *nude.* Writers, like advertisers, must consider how readers will respond to word choice.

☐ EXERCISE 3

Discuss the effect that each word in the parentheses would have on the sentence as a whole.

1. As the kayak rushed uncontrollably through the white water, I felt as if I were being (thrown, rocketed, cast, hurled) into space.
2. The fans (swarmed, flocked, gathered, thronged) around the winning baseball players.
3. To escape to a more exciting world, Tom reads only spy (books, novels, thrillers, adventures).
4. The initial deposit can be as low as $250, and depositors earn market rates on all balances no matter how (tiny, little, small, puny).
5. Someone had hurriedly (written, printed, lettered, scrawled) "wash me" in the dust (enshrouding, covering, blanketing, coating) the truck.

☐ EXERCISE 4

Change any words that are inappropriate to the context or that have the wrong associations.

If you are toiling to become fit, you can try several schemes to lose poundage and to gain robustness. First, limit the time you spend ogling TV or availing yourself of video games. Whenever feasible, get out of the house and frolic, walk, or jog. Second, avoid sumptuous repasts. Eat plenty of legumes and fruit. Little food and lots of exercise will give birth to results.

32d Formal and Informal Words

Each time you write, you should decide how formal or informal your style will be. In general, formal style, found in much academic and business writing, has an impersonal, detached tone. Informal style sounds conversational, as though the writer were speaking directly to the reader. The more informal a writing style, the more conversational it seems. The degree of formality or informality is determined in large part by the vocabulary. Some kinds of words tend to be formal, and others, informal.

1. Familiar, everyday words seem more informal than words less frequently used. Also, words derived from Anglo-Saxon are usually less
   formal than words derived from Greek and Latin.

INFORMAL	FORMAL
lucky	fortunate
get	receive
buy	purchase
work	labor
crazy	demented
fat	corpulent

   **wds
   32d**

2. Clipped forms and acronyms are more informal than the full words.

CLIPPED	FULL
pro	professional
ad	advertisement
phone	telephone
deli	delicatessen
quote	quotation
photo	photograph
hi-fi	high fidelity
TV	television

3. Native words are less formal than foreign terms.

NATIVE	FOREIGN
therefore	ergo
without	sans
folkways	mores
masterpiece	magnum opus
atmosphere	ambience or milieu
caution	caveat

4. The personal pronouns are more informal than the pronoun *one*.

I, you, he, she	one

5. Contractions are informal.

can't	cannot
isn't	is not
I'm	I am

6. Slang is informal—some of it, very informal. Before you use slang, be sure of the taste of your readers. If you anticipate any chance of disapproval, avoid slang words and find substitutes such as the following.

SLANG	SUBSTITUTE
cop	police officer
wheels	car
bucks	dollars
booze	alcoholic drink
bank on	expect
get wise to	become informed
a bummer	a bad experience

wds
32d

Occasionally slang can add a touch of lightness, vividness, or humor to prose. In some contexts, "beat a rap" sounds better than "avoid a penalty"; "bug a telephone" is clearer than "equip a telephone with a microphone"; "razzmatazz" is more interesting than "a flashy display." And sometimes a slang word seems to be the most efficient way of saying something: "computer nerd" is better than "a person who forgets the social amenities in an obsession for computers"; "yuppie" is a shortcut to saying "a young urban professional is moving up in the world."

Expressions like *with it* or *into* (something) have both a literal and a slang meaning. Quotation marks around an expression of this kind prevent misreading by alerting readers to its use as slang. Do not, however, use quotation marks as an apology; slang that needs justification should be avoided.

☐ EXERCISE 5

Do any words in the following passages have inappropriate connotations or incorrect denotations? Are any words inappropriately informal or formal? If you are unfamiliar with any of the words, use a dictionary.

1.   There are few aficionados of checkers. Most people think of checkers as a game for small fries. But this game can bring jollity and challenge even to the intelligentsia. Players can toil for years trying to divine the moves and can cram from hundreds of tomes that contain the lore of checkers masters. The competition at times gets fierce; it's no place for sissies with butterflies. One game played by virtuosos lasted seven hours and thirty minutes only to end in a draw.

2. You'll love the yummy cuisine you can find all over New Orleans—
especially the seafood. The oysters in an elegant café like Antoine's can be
the pièce de résistance of a lavish supper—something that will really fill
the bill. Whenever you're looking for a bellyful of sumptuous chow, you
might consider the trout Véronique at the elegiac Hotel Ponchartrain or
the shrimp rémoulade at the nifty Arnaud's.

32e Clichés

Clichés are expressions, perhaps once vivid but now stale and boring
from overuse. A cliché conveys a superficial thought—if indeed it
conveys any thought at all. In fact, it usually detracts from the point
and instead directs a reader's attention to the writer's inadequacies.

Unfortunately, there is no guide to clichés in a dictionary. Instead, to recognize them, writers must depend on experience and
learn to question the effectiveness of overly familiar expressions.
One clue for identifying clichés is that they often contain repeated
sounds.

tried and true	takes the cake
black and blue	no great shakes
worse for wear	rhyme or reason
betwixt and between	rise and shine
super duper	

Another clue for recognizing clichés is that they are frequently comparisons, such as metaphors and similes. (See 33d.) But instead of
being fresh and interesting, these comparisons have become overly
familiar and boring.

> out in left field
> chip on his shoulder
> dropped like a hot potato
> as cool as a cucumber
> like a bolt from the blue
> right in there pitching

NOTE: Sometimes several clichés together form a mixed metaphor,
an expression that begins with one overused metaphor and shifts
into another or several.

> We were out on a limb; but since we knew we were playing with fire
> and had all our eggs in one basket, we continued the struggle.

Some clichés neither contain repeated sounds nor express
comparisons. They are merely combinations that for some reason
catch on and then are repeated again and again.

agonizing defeat	cruel fate
crushing blow	a bang-up job
stifling heat	one in a million
hardened criminal	rude awakening
not half bad	

You can, of course, use a cliché that has exactly the right meaning. But you would be wise to follow the lead of William L. Shirer and
let the reader know you are not using the expression naively. In his
autobiography, *Twentieth Century Journey,* Shirer remarks of his
adventures as a foreign correspondent, "To say that 'there is no substitute for experience' may be indulging in a stale cliché, but it has
much truth in it."

☐ EXERCISE 6

**Identify the clichés in the following passage and substitute a more
vivid expression.**

The ball was snapped into the hands of the eagerly awaiting quarterback, who then handed off quick as a wink to the halfback. Like greased
lightning, the halfback sprang through a gaping hole in the line. Lo and
behold, this brilliant performance was cut off in midstream by fate in the
form of a tackler big as all outdoors. The tackler cut down the runner with
such ferocity that the ball popped loose into the waiting hands of an offensive lineman who lumbered 20 yards into the end zone, thus snatching
victory from the jaws of defeat.

32f Sexist Language

Until fairly recently, masculine pronouns *(he, his, him)* were used to
refer to either sex. Now writers and publishers try to avoid language
that refers to the male as representative of the human race. You can
avoid the masculine pronouns that refer to both men and women by
rewriting. There are several sensible solutions.

1. Make the noun antecedents of the pronouns plural.

> SEXIST: Each student must bring his own blue book.
>
> NEUTRAL: The students must bring their own blue books.

2. Change the masculine pronoun to an article.

> SEXIST: Everyone was struggling with his assignment.
>
> NEUTRAL: Everyone was struggling with the assignment.

3. Change the sentence structure to the passive form, if the result is not a weak construction. (See 33c.2, "Weak passives.")

> SEXIST: Each entrant must submit his application by April.
>
> NEUTRAL: The application must be submitted by April.

**wds
32f**

Also, masculine nouns used to represent humanity can, even unintentionally, exclude women. You need not go to the extreme of writing "huperson" instead of "human" or "freshperson" instead of "freshman," but you should, whenever possible, substitute neutral nouns for sexist ones.

SEXIST	NEUTRAL
mankind	human race or people
early man	early humans
the working man	working people
the common man	ordinary people
manpower	personnel
chairman	chair or moderator
foreman	supervisor
mailman	mail carrier or postal worker
fireman	fire fighter
Congressmen	members of Congress

Another type of sexist language isolates men and women in special roles. To avoid stereotyping men and women, you should not refer to doctors, bosses, pilots, and professors as men and to nurses, secretaries, assistants, and teachers as women. Nor should you use expressions that elevate the masculine and disparage the feminine: *a man's world, a masculine mind, girlish tastes, the fair sex,* and *ladies' chatter.* Also, avoid unnecessarily pointing out that a woman fills a typically male role *(a lady executive, a woman astronaut, a female athlete)* or that a male fills a typically female role *(a male dancer, a male nurse, a man hair stylist).*

In the interest of fairness, use parallel terms to refer to the sexes. *Man* is parallel to *woman. Boy* is the equivalent of *girl,* and *gentleman* of *lady.* It is not parallel to write "the lady and the man" or "men and girls." "A man and his wife" is also not parallel; "a husband and wife" or "a couple" is preferable.

**wds
32g**

◻ **EXERCISE 7**

Identify any sexist language in the following passage and make substitutions.

Sales brochures can be a great value to a salesman. They are useful for distribution to potential customers who ask him about his company or its products. If the brochure looks professional and sophisticated, the salesman can give it to one of the girls at the front desk to ensure that he will get to see the right man in the company.

32g Euphemisms

For profane or obscene words inappropriate in polite company, we substitute expressions called *euphemisms.* These expressions allow us to communicate without embarrassment either to the writer or to the reader. Also, we sometimes soften references to being retarded, old, crippled, or fired with euphemisms such as *exceptional, senior, disabled,* or *released from a job.* However, euphemisms that deliberately distort or glorify are dishonest and pretentious. For example, a government that supports assassination might call it "neutralization"; a jeweler who sells rhinestones might advertise "faux diamonds"; a person who deals in pornography might describe the books and movies as "adult." Whenever possible in your writing and editing, you should substitute direct expressions for euphemisms that distort reality. The list that follows suggests some possible substitutions.

EUPHEMISMS	DIRECT EXPRESSIONS
correctional facility	prison
previously owned cars	used cars
developing nations	poor nations
depopulate	kill
golden years	old age
revenue enhancements	taxes

mobile manor	trailer park
interred	buried
nonpassing grade	failing grade
preneed arrangements	funeral arrangements
underachiever	academic failure
landscape architect	gardener
sanitary engineer	garbage collector
horticultural surgeon	tree trimmer
credit analyst	bill collector
destination adviser	tour guide
eligibility technician	welfare clerk

**wds
32h**

☐ EXERCISE 8

Identify the euphemisms in the following passage. When you think they are deceptive or pretentious, make substitutions.

When your beloved lifetime companion, having passed through the golden years, reaches the time to pass onward to the final resting place, consider the facilities of the Bow Wow Perpetual Interment Memorial Garden. We offer the full gamut of prearrangement option plans for such eventualities. A ceremoniously frocked mortician will deliver individualized obsequies for each doggie you lose. Come visit the resting places and slumber chambers for your dear beloved departed companions.

32h Jargon and Technical Words

Jargon has two meanings—one, the specialized vocabulary of a group such as lawyers, psychologists, or baseball players; the other, the obscure vocabulary of writers who use language to confuse, confound, or impress readers. The discussion here will focus only on specialized, or technical vocabulary; excessively confusing language is discussed in 32i.

The constant increase of jargon and technical language has expanded English to an enormous size. Computer programmers may write about matrix orthogonalization techniques, bi-directional interface, and patching. Sociologists may use words like *anomie, differential association,* and *nuclear families.* In fact, specialized jargon can reduce length and strengthen precision. For example, it is more efficient to write "hot line" than "direct line of communication between leaders during crises to lessen the danger of nuclear war." It is more precise to write "debug" than "isolate and remove mistakes from a computer routine." But when jargon fails to save space and add clarity, it becomes a disadvantage. It is just as efficient and clear to write *exit* as it is to write *egress.* In most contexts, the following "plain" words convey the same meaning as the jargon.

**wds
32h**

Jargon	Plain English
vitreous	glassy
comestibles	food
allotropic	different
dichotomized	divided in two
poikilothermic	cold-blooded
incursion	invasion
Kriegspiel	wargame
confrontation management	riot control

Thus, some jargon can be replaced with perfectly acceptable words that anyone would understand. With an option, choose the ordinary expression; unnecessary jargon adds a burdensome weight. Even if jargon is acceptable in your discipline, use it cautiously, and never use specialized or technical terms for readers in another discipline.

☐ EXERCISE 9

Identify the jargon in the following sentences and substitute plain English. Use a dictionary whenever the meaning of words is unclear.

1. They had maximized the decibel level of the radio; people several blocks away could hear the music.
2. The police officer apprehended the subject at the scene of the perpetration; the robbery of the bank had just occurred.
3. I hereby and irrevocably appoint Bennet Fairley as my sole and exclusive agent persuant to all matters pertaining to my profession as a professional football player.
4. Because the drug currently has a low incidence of adverse reactions, doctors are now prescribing it freely.
5. The helicopter will be held in a state of readiness to extract the VIPs at 1330 hours.

32i Gobbledygook

There is a widespread movement in government and business to eliminate gobbledygook, also called jargon, bureaucratic language, double-talk, officialese, federalese, and doublespeak. This language is full of abstractions, indirect words, and convoluted constructions; it is devoid of humanity and sensitivity. You can recognize gobbledy-gook by its meaningless pomposity and verbosity.

wds
32i

GOBBLEDYGOOK: The committee must implement the operationalizing of those mechanisms and modes of activity and strategies necessary to maintain the viability of the institution's fiscal management operations.

REVISED: The committee must take measures to ensure the institution's financial security.

The success rate of the "plain English" movement is not impressive, probably because the causes of gobbledygook have not been eliminated (and possibly cannot be). Gobbledygook flourishes for a variety of reasons: its writers have nothing substantive to say; they do not fully understand their subjects; they try to protect themselves from criticism of their ideas; they do not really want anyone to understand what they say; they believe, rightly or wrongly, that the inflated prose impresses readers.

Some of the words and phrases popular in gobbledygook follow. You should avoid them and use instead their "plain" counterparts.

GOBBLEDYGOOK	PLAIN ENGLISH
initiate	begin
terminate	end
utilize	use
discontinue	stop
transmit	send
administrate	administer
notate	note
orientate	orient
envisionize	imagine
summarization	summary
origination	origin

routinization	routine
pursuant to	according to
cognizant of	aware of
conversant with	familiar with
resultant	following
inoperative	broken
at this point in time	now
prior to	before
subsequent to	after
a majority of	most
a number of	many, some
of considerable magnitude	large
as a means of	for
as a result	so
at the rate of	at
due to the fact that	because
for the purpose of	for
in connection with	about
in the interest of	for
in such a manner as to	to
in the neighborhood of	about

**wds
32i**

When readers must struggle to glean sense from a passage, the consequences of gobbledygook are always annoyance and frustration. But when the struggle takes place in documents relating to business, medicine, insurance, and taxes, the consequences can endanger the economy and the public well-being. As William Zinsser comments in *On Writing Well,*

> What people want is plain talk. It's what the stockholder wants from his corporation, what the customer wants from his bank, what the widow wants from the Government office that is handling her Social Security. There is a yearning for human contact and a resentment of bombast. Any institution that won't take the trouble to be clear and personal will lose friends, customers and money.

❏ EXERCISE 10

Identify the gobbledygook in the following passage and rewrite in plain English.

It has been shown at this point in time that contributions to the community improvement fund have fallen short of expectations. We had envisioned reaching our goal during the course of our fund-raising drive to accumulate the optimum number of contributions. Even though we utilized all feasible resources subsequent to the initiation of the drive, the requisite amount of money has not materialized, and we find ourselves with a deficit of considerable magnitude. It is clear that a plan of action must be activated that will minimize our problems. We must be cognizant of improved techniques that can expedite our endeavors in the future.

wds
32j

32j Surplus Words

Surplus words congest prose with redundancies and meaningless clutter. Without thinking, people often use phrases like these: *past history, blue in color, playground area.* Yet, some of the words in these phrases are unnecessary. History is always in the past; "future history" is a contradiction. Blue is a color and a playground is an area, so the words *area* and *in color* are unnecessary. As the following passage demonstrates, surplus words add nothing to prose except flab.

> SURPLUS WORDS: Our future plans are to add workshops in the areas of accounting, the method of maintaining automobiles, and the process of organic gardening. Instructors will begin with the basic fundamentals and then advance forward at a rate acceptable to individual persons enrolled. The end result will be a kind of class-directed learning technique.

Cutting the surplus away allows the ideas to emerge from the flab.

> REVISED: We plan to add workshops in accounting, automobile maintenance, and organic gardening. Instructors will begin with the fundamentals and advance at a rate acceptable to the individuals enrolled. The result will be class-directed learning.

Listed are some familiar redundancies.

any and all	educational process
basic fundamentals	end result
completely finished	final outcome
consensus of opinion	4:00 P.M. in the afternoon
crisis situation	free gift
different individuals	full and complete

future plans	modern world of today
each and every	personal friend
important essentials	reduce down
in actual fact	true facts

□ EXERCISE 11

wds

32k

Remove the surplus words from the following passage.

I read the other day that in actual fact 47 percent of American adults cannot swim. The final outcome of not being able to swim could be drowning. Each and every year thousands of people drown. In my personal opinion, teaching their children to swim should be a first priority of all parents. The effort would be small in size compared with the end result—protection from drowning. Also, by means of being able to swim, any and all people can enjoy different varieties of water sports like surfing and scuba diving. Since the benefits range all the way from safety to pleasure, the ability to swim is absolutely essential.

32k Dense Noun Phrases

The compounding of nouns has long been a tendency in English. The language is full of such noun combinations as *tennis court, china cup, lawn mower,* and *garden party.* These compounds are more economic and sound more like English than *court for tennis, cup made of china, mower for lawns,* and *party in a garden.*

Three or more nouns, however, may produce a compound that is so "dense" that the reader has trouble deciding "what modifies what." For example, consider the noun phrase *campus sorority standards board.* A reader must guess at the meaning: A standards board for campus sororities? A sorority standards board located on campus? A standards board made up of members of campus sororities? Adding an adjective even further confounds readers: *new campus sorority standards board.* What is new? The campus? The sorority? The standards? The board?

You can sometimes clarify a dense phrase by the use of hyphens. Also, you can always rewrite part of the structure as a modifying phrase. The following examples demonstrate the two techniques.

DENSE PHRASE: new employee investment policy

CLARIFIED WITH HYPHEN: new employee-investment policy

CLARIFIED WITH HYPHEN: new-employee investment policy

DENSE PHRASE:	government industry regulations
CLARIFIED BY REWRITING:	government regulations for industries
CLARIFIED BY REWRITING:	regulations for government industries
DENSE PHRASE:	Nevada historical artifacts conference
CLARIFIED BY REWRITING:	conference in Nevada on historical artifacts
CLARIFIED BY REWRITING:	conference on historical artifacts found in Nevada

wds
32k

☐ EXERCISE 12

Clarify the following dense noun phrases by using hyphens or by rewriting.

1. book sales conference
2. former patient payment plan
3. baboon heart transplant
4. last chapter conclusions
5. new high school student fitness program

☐ EXERCISE 13

Read the following passages. Point out any problems such as euphemisms, clichés, sexist words, jargon, gobbledygook, surplus words, and dense noun phrases.

1.   We have an uphill battle making asbestos contamination control efforts in virtually all sectors of the environment. Our tried and true methods of cleaning up have not always made the grade. Now we need to combine together to prioritize solutions. It is in the interest of the environment and cost effectiveness to eliminate the helter-skelter removal of asbestos materials. The public is aware of the problem and demands action but opposes any revenue enhancement at this point in time. Minimizing wastes and utilizing asbestos contamination abatement procedures are easier said than done. The safest techniques, needless to say, are also the most financially demanding, but it is better late than never.

2.   In this day and age, the number of senior citizens has proliferated by leaps and bounds. The average life span was in the vicinity of fifty in 1910, but subsequent to improved quality of life, the old-timers can anticipate kicking up their heels till age seventy-five. Because of pensions and Social Security benefits, a number of these senior citizens will find rest and relax-

ation at a ripe old age in comfortable retirement villages. Lucky retirees, young in spirit, could spend their golden years in localities such as Saint Petersburg, Florida, an area where the climate is thermal.

3.   Salicylate, commonly called aspirin, has several contraindications. Yet there is no need to view the drug with alarm. Although you may utilize the drug for headaches and fever, your doctor may also prescribe it on a regular basis as an anticoagulant for prevention of transient ischemic attacks, or strokes. However, he must endeavor to prevent drug interactions during the time that the drug is ingested; and with any adverse symptoms, he must discontinue the administration of the drug itself. For inflammatory conditions such as an arthritic condition, aspirin gets the nod, but it can cause ulceration and the emission of blood from gastroenteritis. It also has the capacity to cause asthmatic conditions, retention of sodium, tinnitus, and Reyes syndrome. Although salicylate has its drawbacks, it can be a real miracle worker. Pursuant to its use, the fact still remains that it has been shown to be effectively analgesic and anti-inflammatory.

wds
32k

33

Choosing Structures

A good prose style is smooth, clear, and interesting. These qualities rarely appear in a rough draft. Instead, they result from thoughtful revising—from deliberate polishing of sentence structure to achieve variety, emphasis, and clarity; from heightening the effect with sound, rhythm, and figures of speech. In other words, good style requires finding clear and interesting structures to replace those that may be confusing or monotonous. The sections that follow offer some suggestions to help you revise prose by choosing structures that effectively express your ideas. Because many of the techniques require you to be familiar with phrase and clause structure, you may wish to review Chapter 5, "Verbals and Verbal Phrases," and Chapter 7, "Clauses and Sentences."

33a Varying Sentence Lengths, Structures, and Beginnings

Although the number of possible sentences in English is infinite, the number of possible clause patterns is limited. (See 7a, "Clause Patterns.") In fact, most sentences have the underlying pattern *subject + verb + object* or *subject + verb + complement*. If nothing is added to these basic patterns, the result is monotonous, choppy prose—one short, simple sentence after the other. In the following passage, for example, all the sentences are short and simple. To make things worse, they all begin in the same way, with the subject followed immediately by a verb.

CHOPPY: Wilson was born an aristocrat. He was brought up in a conservative family. He was trained as a Hamiltonian. He became the greatest leader of the plain people since Lincoln.

The original version, in Morison and Commager's *The Growth of the American Republic,* is vastly superior.

ORIGINAL: Born an aristocrat, bred a conservative, trained a Hamiltonian, he became the greatest leader of the plain people since Lincoln.

sent/
struc
33a

The basic pattern of this sentence is very simple: *he became leader* (subject + verb + complement). But the three introductory modifiers give the sentence an interesting structure and sound not found in the choppy passage.

Even a series of fairly long sentences can be as monotonous as choppy prose if the structures never vary. The following passage, for example, consists only of independent clauses joined by *and* or *but*. In addition, each clause begins with the subject and verb.

MONOTONOUS: George Pratt compared the horses' footfalls, and he made an interesting discovery. The two horses seemed to run at the same speed, but Secretariat covered more distance per stride. Secretariat covered 23.8 feet per stride, and Riva Ridge covered 23.2 feet.

Varying the methods of combining can eliminate the monotony. Notice that in the revised version, not only the structures but also the beginnings of the sentences are varied.

REVISED: By comparing the horses' footfalls, George Pratt made an interesting discovery. Although the two horses seemed to run at the same speed, Secretariat covered more distance per stride than Riva Ridge—23.8 feet versus 23.2 feet.

Variety in sentence structure, however, does not guarantee good writing. Prose can sound monotonous even when sentence structure is varied if each sentence begins with the subject and verb of the main clause.

MONOTONOUS: Science recognizes a number of differences between men and women. Men are physically stronger, for example, whereas women have more physical stamina. Men have more genetic defects and weaker immune systems although women are more prone to phobias and depression. Neither sex should feel superior or

> inferior. The differences fit together like the pieces of
> a jigsaw puzzle, and they create the whole picture of
> human beings.

Moving some of the modifiers to the beginnings of sentences by
rewriting and rearranging can eliminate the monotony.

> REVISED: **Science recognizes a number of differences between**
> **men and women. For example, whereas men are phys-**
> **ically stronger, women have more physical stamina.**
> **Although men have more genetic defects and weaker**
> **immune systems, women are more prone to phobias**
> **and depression. But neither sex should feel superior**
> **or inferior. Like the pieces of a jigsaw puzzle, the dif-**
> **ferences fit together to create the whole picture of**
> **human beings.**

> **sent/**
> **struc**
> **33a**

Following are some techniques for combining ideas and structures through coordination and subordination. Practicing these techniques will help you learn to manipulate—and thus to vary—
sentence structure and sentence beginnings. With a knowledge of
how to combine ideas in different ways, you can avoid simplistic and
repetitious expression of thought.

(1) Combining independent clauses through coordination

The most common ways of joining independent clauses are

- With a comma and coordinating conjunction *(and, but, or, for, nor, so, yet)*
- With a semicolon
- With a pair of correlative conjunctions *(either . . . or, neither . . . nor, not only . . . but also)*

The most effective choice depends on the relationship between the
ideas expressed in the clauses. When the ideas have a kind of equality, one clause can simply be added to the other with a comma and
the conjunction *and* or with a semicolon.

> SEPARATED: **In the early 1900s, cocaine was used**
> **in many patent medicines. It was**
> **even present in the original formula**
> **of Coca-Cola.**

> COMBINED WITH COMMA AND AND: **In the early 1900s, cocaine was used**
> **in many patent medicines, and it was**

	even present in the original formula of Coca-Cola.
COMBINED WITH SEMICOLON:	In the early 1900s, cocaine was used in many patent medicines; it was even present in the original formula of Coca-Cola.

Another way to show equality of ideas is to use the semicolon and a transitional expression such as *also, furthermore, in addition,* or *moreover.* The transitional expression can appear immediately after the semicolon or at some other appropriate place in the second clause.

SEPARATED:	The roof of the old house was full of holes. The supporting beams were rotten.
COMBINED WITH SEMICOLON AND TRANSITIONAL EXPRESSION:	The roof of the old house was full of holes; in addition, the supporting beams were rotten.

When clauses have a cause/effect relationship, they can be joined with a comma and the coordinating conjunction *so* or *for* or with a semicolon and a transitional expression such as *therefore, consequently, as a result,* or *thus.*

SEPARATED:	His two interests were medicine and children. He became a pediatrician.
COMBINED WITH COMMA AND CONJUNCTION:	His two interests were medicine and children, so he became a pediatrician.
COMBINED WITH SEMICOLON AND TRANSITIONAL EXPRESSION:	His two interests were medicine and children; consequently, he became a pediatrician.

Contrasting clauses can be joined with a comma and the coordinating conjunction *but, or, nor,* or *yet* or with a semicolon and a transitional expression such as *however, nevertheless,* or *on the other hand.*

SEPARATED:	Augustus gave the Senate control of the peaceful provinces. He kept under his authority the unstable provinces of the frontier.

COMBINED WITH COMMA AND CONJUNCTION:	Augustus gave the Senate control of the peaceful provinces, but he kept under his authority the unstable provinces of the frontier.
COMBINED WITH SEMICOLON AND TRANSITIONAL EXPRESSION:	Augustus gave the Senate control of the peaceful provinces; he kept under his authority, however, the unstable provinces of the frontier.

Other transitional expressions that express relationships between clauses are *for example, for instance, then,* and *in fact.* When clauses are joined with semicolons, these adverbs can help to clarify the connection.

sent/ struc 33a

SEPARATED:	An otherwise rational person often performs superstitious rituals. A baseball player may refuse to pitch without his favorite hat.
SECOND CLAUSE AS EXAMPLE:	An otherwise rational person often performs superstitious rituals; a baseball player, for example, may refuse to pitch without his favorite hat.
SEPARATED:	Her apartment was full of all sorts of animals. It seemed more like a pet store than a place to live.
SECOND CLAUSE AS REINFORCEMENT:	Her apartment was full of all sorts of animals; in fact, it seemed more like a pet store than a place to live.
SEPARATED:	To make the rock garden, cover the area with heavy plastic to keep out weeds. Add a layer of pea gravel for the base.
SECOND CLAUSE AS SECOND STEP:	To make the rock garden, cover the area with heavy plastic to keep out weeds; then, add a layer of pea gravel for the base.

A balanced relationship between clauses can be reinforced by the correlative conjunctions *either . . . or, neither . . . nor,* and *not only . . . but also.*

SEPARATED: The movies are getting sillier. Or I am getting more cynical.

BALANCE AND CONTRAST: <u>Either</u> the movies are getting sillier, <u>or</u> I am getting more cynical.

SEPARATED: The winds leveled trees and buildings. Also, the waters had turned a portion of the highway on its side.

BALANCE AND ADDITION: <u>Not only</u> had the winds leveled trees and buildings <u>but also</u> the waters had turned a portion of the highway on its side.

sent/
struc
33a

As these examples show, independent clauses are usually joined with conjunctions or with semicolons. Two less common devices are the colon and the dash. The colon indicates that the second clause explains or illustrates the first.

SEPARATED: The river was deceptively tranquil. Beneath the smooth, gently flowing surface were treacherous undertows.

SECOND CLAUSE AS EXPLANATION OF THE FIRST: The river was deceptively tranquil: beneath the smooth, gently flowing surface were treacherous undertows.

SEPARATED: The heat wave created a picnic atmosphere. Children played in the park fountains, while barefooted adults drank lemonade beneath shade trees.

SECOND CLAUSE AS ILLUSTRATION OF THE FIRST: The heat wave created a picnic atmosphere: children played in park fountains, while barefooted adults drank lemonade beneath shade trees.

The dash emphasizes the clause that follows. Like the colon, the dash can signal that the second clause explains the first. Also, a clause set off by a dash and a coordinating conjunction may serve as an afterthought or addition to the first. Between independent clauses, the dash is a dramatic mark of punctuation, so you should use it sparingly. Overuse defeats the purpose.

SEPARATED: Cheerleaders are the most useless addition to football games. Their frantic efforts are almost totally ignored by the fans.

SECOND CLAUSE AS EXPLANATION OF THE FIRST: Cheerleaders are the most useless addition to football games—their frantic efforts are almost totally ignored by the fans.

SEPARATED: Ice cream doesn't taste as good as it did when I was a child. Spinach doesn't taste as bad either.

SECOND CLAUSE AS AFTERTHOUGHT: Ice cream doesn't taste as good as it did when I was a child—spinach doesn't taste as bad either.

sent/ struc 33a

The different techniques available for joining independent clauses allow you to clarify the relationship between ideas as well as to vary sentence structure. To make an effective choice, consider not only the need to avoid monotony but also the relationship you want to express.

(2) Combining sentence elements through coordination

When two or more sentences share elements—such as subjects, predicates, or parts of predicates—you can avoid repetition and simplistic prose by compounding the common elements. Some of the words and phrases that allow compounding are

- Simple coordinators like *and, but,* and *or*
- Correlative coordinators like *not only . . . but also, either . . . or, both . . . and*
- Expressions like *in addition to, as well as, but not*

SEPARATED: Garlic contains natural antibiotics. Onions also contain these substances.

COMBINED SUBJECTS: Garlic and onions contain natural antibiotics.

SEPARATED: The players didn't seem to understand what had happened. And the referees didn't either.

COMBINED SUBJECTS: Neither the players nor the referees seemed to understand what had happened.

SEPARATED:	The Great Wall of China was built entirely by hand. It took hundreds of years to complete.
COMBINED PREDICATES:	The Great Wall of China was built entirely by hand and took hundreds of years to complete.
SEPARATED:	Leafy trees add beauty to your landscape. They also help lower your energy bill in the summertime.
COMBINED PREDICATES:	Leafy trees not only add beauty to your landscape but also help lower your energy bill in the summertime.
SEPARATED:	Your body requires the macronutrients (fats, carbohydrates, and proteins). It also requires the micronutrients (vitamins and minerals).
COMBINED DIRECT OBJECTS:	Your body requires the macronutrients (fats, carbohydrates, and proteins) as well as the micronutrients (vitamins and minerals).
SEPARATED:	He was willing to assume the privileges of the office. He was not, however, willing to assume the responsibilities.
COMBINED OBJECTS OF INFINITIVES:	He was willing to assume the privileges of the office but not the responsibilities.
SEPARATED:	She was a well-known jazz singer. She was also a well-respected portrait artist.
COMBINED COMPLEMENTS:	She was both a well-known jazz singer and a well-respected portrait artist.

☐ EXERCISE 1

By applying the techniques just discussed, combine each of the following into a single sentence.

1. Some species of fish live many years in captivity. Others die in a year or so, either of old age or unknown causes.
2. A serious athlete must maintain a strict physical regimen. He or she must also maintain a strict mental discipline.
3. Apathy pervades this campus. Only a fraction of the student body votes in any election.
4. Reading a good daily newspaper will help you stay informed. Reading a good weekly news magazine will help you stay informed.
5. Honey Island Swamp once served as a hideout for pirates and bandits. The swamp was also a hideout for bootleggers and their whiskey stills.
6. The flowers have vanished. The tourists have vanished.
7. The boat circled back. It dropped anchor.
8. Technically, the term "shin splints" refers to pain along the lower, inner part of the leg. The term is often used to refer to any leg pain resulting from overuse.
9. Fireworks produce colorful displays of light and sound. Firecrackers produce monotonous noise.
10. The model ships were not just matchsticks glued together. They were tiny, ornate, meticulous creations.
11. The teacher calls on us to state the facts we have learned. We are also supposed to explain their significance.
12. His eyes began to adjust to the dark. He could see a shape emerging from the trees.
13. Shakespeare created heroes with flaws. He also created villains with consciences.
14. At some point, everyone yearns for a second chance. Few ever get one.
15. Nero could not have fiddled while Rome burned. Fiddles had not been invented.

(3) Subordinating with adverb clauses

One very useful structure for combining ideas is the adverb clause, which expresses time, place, cause, purpose, condition, manner, and contrast. The nature of the information in the adverb clause is clearly signaled through the use of an introductory subordinating conjunction such as *when, until, where, because, so that, if, as though, although,* and the like. (See 6b.3 and 7c.1.) Thus, adverb clauses can improve clarity in prose by flatly stating, through the subordinating conjunction, how one idea relates to another. In addition, since most adverb clauses can introduce sentences, they provide a way to vary sentence beginnings.

SEPARATED: Billie Jean King won nineteen tournaments in 1971. She became the first woman tennis player ever to earn $100,000 a year.

COMBINED: <u>When</u> Billie Jean King won nineteen tournaments in 1971, she became the first woman tennis player ever to earn $100,000 a year.

SEPARATED: Our school system offers almost no instruction in financial planning. Few of us learn to handle our finances in an intelligent manner.

COMBINED: <u>Since</u> our school system offers almost no instruction in financial planning, few of us learn to handle our finances in an intelligent manner.

SEPARATED: Mid-afternoon drowsiness is often called the "post-lunch dip." It occurs regardless of when, or if, we eat.

COMBINED: <u>Although</u> mid-afternoon drowsiness is often called the "post-lunch dip," it occurs regardless of when, or if, we eat.

(4) Subordinating with adjective clauses

Adjective clauses can help eliminate the choppy prose that results from too much repetition of nouns and personal pronouns. In this combination, ideas are joined with relative words like *which, who/whom/whose, when,* and *where.* (See 2c and 7c.2.)

SEPARATED: The last stop on the tour was King's Tavern. This tavern was originally a hostel at the end of the Natchez Trace.

COMBINED: The last stop on the tour was King's Tavern, <u>which</u> was originally a hostel at the end of the Natchez Trace.

SEPARATED: Hamlin Garland spent his youth on farms in Wisconsin, Iowa, and South Dakota. He learned firsthand about grim pioneer life on these farms.

COMBINED: Hamlin Garland spent his youth on farms in Wisconsin, Iowa, and South Dakota, <u>where</u> he learned firsthand about grim pioneer life.

SEPARATED: I was forced to go to my first dance with Father's nephew, Talbot. His hair was longer than mine. And he danced like a trained bear.

COMBINED: I was forced to go to my first dance with Father's nephew, Talbot, <u>whose</u> hair was longer than mine and <u>who</u> danced like a trained bear.

(5) Subordinating with verbal phrases

A verbal is a verb form *(to see, seeing, seen)* functioning as a noun, an adjective, or an adverb; a verbal phrase consists of a verbal and any accompanying subject, object, complement, or modifiers. (See Chapter 5, "Verbals and Verbal Phrases.") Subordinating with verbal phrases can eliminate repetition of nouns and personal pronouns and provide a source for varying sentence beginnings.

sent/ struc 33a

SEPARATED: The wedding date was already set. She felt compelled to go through with the marriage.

COMBINED: <u>Having already set the wedding date</u>, she felt compelled to go through with the marriage.

SEPARATED: You can dust the face lightly with a white, frosted powder. This procedure will produce a faint glow.

COMBINED: <u>To produce a faint glow</u>, you can dust the face lightly with a white, frosted powder.

SEPARATED: Vines covered the entire house. They almost concealed it from the casual observer.

COMBINED: Vines covered the entire house, <u>almost concealing it from the casual observer.</u>

(6) Subordinating with appositives

The appositive, one of the most versatile structures in prose, restates or renames a word or phrase. When immediately following the word or phrase it renames, the appositive adds information. When introducing a sentence, it serves as a descriptive lead-in to the subject and an unusual beginning for a sentence. And if postponed until the end of a sentence, it lends a bit of drama and suspense. The following examples demonstrate how the appositive works to make prose more efficient and structure more interesting.

SEPARATED: This automobile is an up-to-date mechanical achievement. It has a permanently engaged, all-wheel drive system.

APPOSITIVE INSIDE SENTENCE: This automobile, an up-to-date mechanical achievement, has a perma-
nently engaged, all-wheel drive
system.

SEPARATED: The Anchor Pub is the last survivor
of the many Southwark taverns. It
was built on the site of the Globe
Theatre.

APPOSITIVE AT BEGINNING
OF SENTENCE: The last survivor of the many Southwark taverns, the Anchor Pub was
built on the site of the Globe Theatre.

SEPARATED: For the ten years of her imprisonment, Marie concentrated on re-
venge. It was the only thing that
kept her alive.

APPOSITIVE AT END OF SENTENCE: Only one thing kept Marie alive for
the ten years of her imprisonment:
the thought of revenge.

Appositives are frequently used to add ideas after an independent clause. Appositives like these can prevent short, repetitious
sentences and vague pronoun references. One way to employ the
technique is to repeat a word or words in the preceding structure, as
do these examples.

SEPARATED: Chaucer tells us of a pilgrimage to the shrine of a saint.
The pilgrimage is more social than religious.

COMBINED: Chaucer tells us of a pilgrimage to the shrine of a saint, a
pilgrimage more social than religious.

SEPARATED: Our climate is precariously balanced. This means that a
tiny variation in the earth's orbit could cause another ice
age.

COMBINED: Our climate is precariously balanced—so precariously
that a tiny variation in the earth's orbit could cause another ice age.

Another way to use the technique is to begin the appositive
with a word that summarizes the preceding idea or ideas.

VAGUE PRONOUN: Health experts recommend that we decrease fat and increase fiber in our diets. This may lower our risk of cancer.

COMBINED: Health experts recommend that we decrease fat and increase fiber in our diets—two steps that may lower our risk of cancer.

VAGUE PRONOUN: Because so much of the business world now provides information rather than goods, many adults must return to school for retraining. This will change the recruiting tactics of universities.

COMBINED: Because so much of the business world now provides information rather than goods, many adults must return to school for retraining—a trend that will change the recruiting tactics of universities.

**sent/
struc
33a**

☐ EXERCISE 2

Using some of the suggested subordinating techniques, combine each of the passages into a single sentence, eliminating choppy prose and vague pronoun reference.

1. The bird watchers all had binoculars hanging from their necks. The bird watchers climbed hills and splashed through the swamps in search of the black-throated green warbler.
2. Lincoln rode into Springfield on April 15, 1837. He carried all he owned in his saddlebags.
3. Gardeners can buy software. This supplies such information as when, where, and what to plant in particular areas.
4. Nellie Bly once pretended to be insane. She had had herself committed to a mental hospital. Her purpose was to study conditions.
5. Advancement seemed to rest on flattering the executives. This was a policy designed to promote hypocrisy.
6. The woman died. She left her house and her money to her dog, Teddy.
7. The five students were selling drugs. They were expelled from school.
8. A patient's mental attitude affects the chances for recovery. We cannot be sure that a good attitude will always effect a cure.
9. Da Vinci is recognized as one of the most versatile geniuses in history. He was a painter, a geologist, an astronomer, an inventor, a botanist, and a student of human anatomy.
10. The rock 'n' roll of the Tail Gators is often called "swampy." This refers to the warm and relaxed feeling of blues and folk music.
11. A red flag cannot anger a bull. Bulls are colorblind.

12. The man was brought to court. He claimed that someone had slipped a mysterious drug into his drink.
13. The stolen car was returned. Its owner found a note that said, "The brakes need attention."
14. Halloween used to be fun. It was ruined by the poisoned fudge and the needles in apples.
15. The Heimlich maneuver can be used on young people. Special care must be taken in using it on babies.

**sent/
struc
33a**

☐ EXERCISE 3

Improve the prose of the following passages by using the techniques for coordinating and subordinating previously discussed. With each passage, try several different ways of combining to achieve the most satisfactory results.

1.   The dinosaurs may have died out because the earth was hit by a huge asteroid. The impact of the asteroid threw dust into the atmosphere. There was enough dust to block sunlight from the earth's surface. Then plant life was killed. Then the dinosaurs starved to death.

2.   Many employers will not hire people without work experience. Perhaps employers should have apprentice programs. In apprentice programs, people could work part time. And they could work for lower pay than other workers. The apprentice program could count as job experience. The program could improve chances for employment.

3.   George Bryan "Beau" Brummell inherited a moderate estate from his father. He set up lavish bachelor quarters in London. While he was in London, he influenced the style of men's clothing and manners for almost twenty years. Gambling and extravagant living bankrupted him. He fled to France to escape creditors in 1816. He was jailed for debt in France in 1835. He died in France in a mental institution.

4.   During the seventeenth century many people were put to death. These people were accused of being witches. They were blamed for everything. They were blamed for bad weather, bad crops, diseases, and deaths. In England, Matthew Hopkins was a famous witch hunter. He called himself the "Witch Finder Generall." He claimed to have a list of witches. The list was given to him by the Devil. He and his aides went from town to town. They were searching for witches. They charged the towns money. Witch hunting was very profitable. Hopkins maintained that suspected witches should take the "swimming test." In the "swimming test" the suspects were thrown into ponds or rivers. Floaters were judged to be witches. They were put to death. Sinkers were presumed innocent. By that time, though, they had probably already drowned.

☐ EXERCISE 4

Improve the following passage by rearranging and rewriting to vary sentence beginnings.

> I have gotten together with about a dozen friends every New Year's Day for the past few years. Our day begins with a lunch of ham and black-eyed peas, the traditional symbols of good luck for the coming year. We watch the college bowl games on television then from afternoon until night. We switch to pizza and old movies after the games are over. Our day finally ends with a familiar ritual. We write down our New Year's resolutions in a faded, old notebook; date them; and sign them. Someone in the group then turns to the beginning of the notebook and reads through all our past years' resolutions. We laugh and groan over our triumphs and failures. The new year seems to begin when I share with my friends this moment between the past and the future.

33b Achieving Emphasis

The appropriate arrangement of a sentence's parts can call attention to an idea within the sentence. An exaggerated structure can even call attention to a sentence within a passage. Exaggerated structures should appear sparingly because too many will make prose seem artificial and contrived. Used occasionally, however, and in the right situations, stylistic flourishes will strengthen prose.

(1) Periodic sentences

The most common kind of sentence is the "loose" construction, which begins with the main idea in an independent clause, followed by less-important details. This order is considered normal because English speakers seem naturally to progress from subject to verb to complement, with additions and modifiers tacked on. In the periodic sentence, the normal order is reversed, and the main idea is postponed until the end. A periodic order seems to hang the reader in suspension—anticipating the outcome.

> LOOSE: This house was the last of the beautiful century-old cottages we had tried futilely to protect.
>
> PERIODIC: Of the century-old cottages we had tried futilely to protect, this house was the last.

LOOSE: **Don't order spaghetti when you go to an important business lunch, where you must present a neat, efficient, controlled image.**

PERIODIC: **When you go to an important business lunch, where you must present a neat, efficient, controlled image, don't order spaghetti.**

When exaggerated, a periodic sentence calls attention not only to the idea at the end but also to the structure itself. In the following example, the writer begins with a long, detailed modifier, postponing the main idea until a final short clause, "the realities emerged." The result is a fairly dramatic sentence that a reader will notice and enjoy.

EXAGGERATED PERIODIC: **Through the motes of cracker dust, corn meal dust, the Gold Dust of the Gold Dust Twins that the floor had been swept out with, the realities emerged.** (Eudora Welty)

In the next example, an introductory adverb clause and the parenthetical "you may ask" delay the point and thus add to the humor of the question—when it finally comes.

EXAGGERATED PERIODIC: **If Man has benefited immeasurably by his association with the dog, what, you may ask, has the dog got out of it?** (James Thurber)

In the following passage, two consecutive periodic sentences heighten the intensity of the writer's main idea: "the only difference between music and Musak is the spelling"; "it's all the same to me."

EXAGGERATED PERIODIC: **First off, I want to say that as far as I am concerned, in instances where I have not personally and deliberately sought it out, the only difference between music and Muzak is the spelling. Pablo Casals practicing across the hall with the door open—being trapped in an elevator, the ceiling of which is broadcasting "Parsley, Sage, Rosemary, and Thyme"—it's all the same to me.** (Fran Lebowitz)

☐ EXERCISE 5

Rewrite these loose sentences as periodic.

1. She finally won a beauty contest after years of practice and coaching, after rigorous diets and plastic surgery, after countless attempts that ended in defeat.

2. The reality of our loss hit us when the dawn revealed the damage, when we found a burned shell instead of a house.
3. I entered a singing contest once in the sixth grade, although I cannot imagine why, since I could barely carry a tune.
4. Just give me an A rather than encouragement, advice, and study aids.
5. The star swept into the room wrapped in furs, signing autographs, posing for photographs, followed by a throng of admirers.

(2) Cumulative sentences

The cumulative sentence is an exaggerated loose structure that begins with an independent clause and then piles up—or accumulates—structures at the end. One type of exaggeration is a long series of modifiers, like the adjective *who* clauses in the following sentences.

> CUMULATIVE: Grant was one of a body of men who owed reverence and obeisance to no one, who were self-reliant to a fault, who cared hardly anything for the past but who had a sharp eye for the future. (Bruce Catton)

A series of absolute phrases at the end of a sentence can also produce a cumulative effect. (See 5d, "Absolute Verbal Phrases.")

> CUMULATIVE: This time the sorrel mare was in the lot before he heard it at all, the rider collarless and even bareheaded, trembling, speaking in a shaking voice as the woman in the house had done, his father merely looking up once before stooping again to the horse he was buckling, so that the man on the mare spoke to his stooping back. (William Faulkner)

In the next sentence, the writer begins with two main clauses and then tacks on a series of examples after the word *say.* The length of the structure and the number of details creates an attention-getting sentence.

> CUMULATIVE: Summer will be admitted to our breakfast table as usual, and in the space of a half a cup of coffee I will be able to discover, say, that Ferguson Jenkins went eight innings in Montreal and won his fourth game of the season while giving up five hits, that Al Kaline was horse-collared by Fritz Peterson at the stadium, that Tony Oliva hit a single off Mickey Lolich in Detroit, that Juan Marichal was bombed by the Reds in the top of the sixth at Candlestick Park, and that similar disasters and triumphs befell

a couple of dozen-odd of the other ballplayers—
favorites and knaves—whose fortunes I follow from
April to October. (Roger Angell)

▢ EXERCISE 6

sent/
struc

33b

Make the loose sentences cumulative by adding structures onto
each. If the beginnings do not stimulate ideas, substitute a few of
your own.

EXAMPLE: The man was dressed like a gypsy. →The man was dressed like a
gypsy, in a red silk shirt open to the waist, tight black pants, a
bandanna on his head, gold loops in his ears, and a tight cum-
merbund circling his waist.

1. My favorite memories from childhood are summer afternoons.
2. The hamburger tasted like plastic.
3. My grammar school principal seemed frightening.
4. He wanted a wife who was like his mother.
5. I thought that college life would be fun.

(3) Climactic sentences

Another strategy for achieving emphasis is the climactic sentence, in
which the ideas move up a scale—from less important to more important, for example, or from less intense to more intense. The effect
is that the last idea expressed receives the most emphasis.

CLIMACTIC: The letter, written in pencil, expressed intense admira-
tion, confessed regrets about the past, revealed deep sor-
rows—and was never mailed.

CLIMACTIC: Like us, stars have a cycle of life from birth, through youth
and maturity, to decline and death.

CLIMACTIC: He fidgeted, took practice swings, spit, adjusted his
clothes, kissed his bat, stepped into the batter's box, and
struck out.

When the content lends itself to drama, the climactic sentence
can be particularly effective, as the following sentence illustrates.

CLIMACTIC: Thus it is that the mouse seems always to dangle so lan-
guidly from the jaws, lies there so quietly when dropped,
dies of his injuries without a struggle. (Lewis Thomas)

☐ EXERCISE 7

Combine each of the following sets of sentences into one sentence with a climactic order.

1. On the camping trip, our tent washed away in a flash flood. Also, the mosquitoes attacked us in swarms. The heat was unbearable. Our food spoiled.
2. The interviewer asked me what jobs I had held previously. She asked me if I were free for dinner. She asked me what salary I expected. She asked me what degree I held.
3. To prove he was as good a cook as my mother, my father prepared an elaborate dinner. He made Caesar salad. He concocted a flaming dessert which caught the tablecloth on fire. He fixed pork chops stuffed with raisin dressing.
4. Success is a matter of priorities. You must decide what you are willing to give up to attain your goals. You decide which goals are important to your success. You must decide what you consider success to be.
5. The child sat on Santa's lap. She pulled on his beard. She asked him for about a thousand dollars worth of toys. She said crossly, "You ain't my daddy." She stared at him hostilely.

(4) Balanced sentences

A balanced sentence creates a symmetry—a noticeable and deliberate symmetry—achieved with parallel structure and often with repetition of key vocabulary. The "echo" of structure and words emphasizes the comparison or contrast of ideas.

> BALANCED: **We have sidestepped one problem; we have stepped on two more.**

> BALANCED: **From afar, the island looked like a tropical paradise of white sand and sparkling blue sea; up close, the island looked like a garbage dump of trash and polluted water.**

When the structure and vocabulary of a sentence are perfectly balanced, the result can be quite dramatic. For example, the second sentence in the following passage has perfectly balanced independent clauses, with the subject and complement of the first clause *(seamen, gentlemen)* reversed in the second clause *(gentlemen, seamen.)*

> BALANCED: **There were gentlemen and there were seamen in the Navy of Charles II. But the seamen were not gentlemen, and the gentlemen were not seamen.** (Lord Macaulay)

Consecutive sentences can also be balanced; that is, a structure can be repeated and vocabulary carried over for two or more sentences in a row. In the next passage, the echo effect is created by the repetition of *when* clauses with *power* as the subject, followed by independent clauses with *poetry* as the subject.

BALANCED: **When power leads man toward arrogance, poetry reminds him of his limitations. When power narrows the areas of man's concern, poetry reminds him of the richness and diversity of his existence. When power corrupts, poetry cleanses, for art establishes the basic human truths which must serve as the touchstone of our judgment.** (John Kennedy)

You can exaggerate balanced structure to highlight an idea or to keep prose from sounding monotonous. Remember, however, that if overused, any kind of exaggeration will seem pretentious and will rapidly wear on your readers' nerves.

EXERCISE 8

Revise the following sentences to create balanced structures by repeating structure and, where possible, key vocabulary.

EXAMPLE: Although the plot of the mystery is ordinary, the book has unusual characters. → The plot of the mystery is ordinary, but the characters are extraordinary.

1. He knew when to give in. In addition, he also understood when he should give up.
2. Although he was friendly and outgoing in public, in private he was hostile as well as withdrawn.
3. The cost of one episode of *Miami Vice* was $1,500,000. The budget was $1,167,000 for running the entire Miami vice-squad for a whole year.
4. To young people, the absence of pleasure is painful. The lack of pain, when people get older, is a pleasure.
5. Some people say that the clothes make the man. In my opinion, however, the man can have a beneficial effect on the clothes.

(5) Cleft sentences

One way to emphasize a particular element is to create a "cleft" construction. In this technique, a sentence is cleft, or cut, into parts by a form of the verb *be* (*is, was, will be,* etc.). The construction takes the following form.

1. *It* + a form of *be*
2. the element to be emphasized
3. a *who* or *that* clause

The delay of the most important element until after the verb creates the emphasis. Notice that in the cleft examples, the elements following *be* are emphasized.

**sent/
struc
33b**

> LOOSE: **The coach lost the game for us.**
>
> CLEFT: **It was the coach who lost the game for us.**
>
> LOOSE: **The acting, not the script, distinguishes the film.**
>
> CLEFT: **It is the acting, not the script, that distinguishes the film.**

In the next example, a sentence in loose order is cleft in two different ways, to emphasize two different sentence elements.

> LOOSE: Sir Robert Baden-Powell of England started the Boy Scout movement in 1907.
>
> CLEFT TO EMPHASIZE FOUNDER: It was Sir Robert Baden-Powell who founded the Boy Scout movement in 1907.
>
> CLEFT TO EMPHASIZE DATE: It was in 1907 that Sir Robert Baden-Powell founded the Boy Scout movement.

☐ EXERCISE 9

Rewrite each sentence as a cleft structure. Point out which sentences can be cleft in more than one way.

1. The restaurant features French cuisine.
2. The magazine criticized the administration's foreign policy.
3. His insomnia causes him great distress.
4. Their ancestors migrated to Pennsylvania in 1750.
5. The quarterback was injured in the first quarter.
6. The Arabs, not the Romans, promoted bullfighting.
7. The car resembled most a miniature fire engine.
8. The ballerina Pavlova was famous for her outstanding grace.
9. Procrastination is my worst fault.
10. The harsh living conditions touched off a series of riots.

☐ EXERCISE 10

Determine whether the following sentences are periodic, cumulative, climactic, balanced, or cleft.

1. Integrity without knowledge is weak and useless, and knowledge without integrity is dangerous and dreadful. (Samuel Johnson)

2. There are, indeed, many other jobs that are unpleasant, and yet no one thinks of abolishing them—that of the plumber, that of the soldier, that of the garbage-man, that of the priest hearing confessions, that of the sand-hog, and so on. (H. L. Mencken)

3. Yet because the moth was so small, and so simple a form of the energy that was rolling in at the open window and driving its way through so many narrow and intriguing corridors in my own brain and in those of other human beings, there was something marvelous as well as pathetic about him. (Virginia Woolf)

4. It is the good reader that makes the good book. (Ralph Waldo Emerson)

5. The golf gallery is the Punchinello of the great sports mob, the clown crowd, an uncontrollable, galloping, galumphing horde, that wanders hysterically over manicured pasture acreage of an afternoon, clucking to itself, trying to keep quiet, making funny noises, sweating, thundering over hills ten thousand strong, and gathering, mousey-still, around a little hole in the ground to see a man push a little ball into the bottom of it with a crooked iron stick. (Paul Gallico)

33c Streamlining Prose

Effective writing is easy to read. It allows a reader to move smoothly through sentences without laboring to discover structure and meaning. If your prose seems cumbersome and hard to read, you may be obscuring the meaning by packing too much into single sentences, by including too many empty or passive verbs, or by clouding the connection between subjects and verbs. Practicing the following techniques can help you streamline your writing and produce crisp, clear sentences that throw no obstacles in the path of a reader.

(1) Empty verbs and nominalizations

"Empty verbs," such as *be, have, make,* and *do,* have little or no meaning themselves and must absorb meaning from their contexts.

Since these verbs do not express action, they are frequently accompanied by a "nominalization," that is, an expression of action in noun form. Using unnecessary nominalizations can result in cumbersome structures, as the following sentence illustrates.

> ORIGINAL: **Rescue teams are making attempts to uncover the mine shaft, but authorities have no expectations of success.**

Expressing the action in verbs rather than nouns tightens and streamlines the structure.

sent/ struc 33c

> REVISED: **Rescue teams are attempting to uncover the mine shaft, but authorities do not expect success.**

In revising, you should keep an eye out for nominalizations that weaken structure and pad your prose. The following pairs of sentences demonstrate how easily you can eliminate unnecessary nominalizations. Often the trick is simply to make the agent of the action the subject of the sentence (or clause) and then to express the action in a strong verb or verbal. Notice that the revised versions are shorter and crisper.

> ORIGINAL: **We had hopes that the students would vote for the abolition of the curfews.**
>
> REVISED: **We hoped that the students would vote to abolish the curfews.**

> ORIGINAL: **The basis of the achievement of your goal is the development of a positive attitude.**
>
> REVISED: **To achieve your goal, you must develop a positive attitude.**

> ORIGINAL: **To make a discovery about how many people felt a necessity for longer lab hours, I made use of a simple questionnaire.**
>
> REVISED: **To discover how many people needed longer lab hours, I used a simple questionnaire.**

◻ EXERCISE 11

Streamline the following passage by changing empty verbs and unnecessary nominalizations to strong verbs.

In this morning's meeting, the club president made note of the number of people who were participants in the recreation program. She also made comments on the club's desire to offer support for the program next year. The treasurer then made the suggestion that we conduct a survey of members to find out how many have intentions of becoming participants next year.

(2) Weak passives

Check your prose for weak passive-voice verbs. (See 4f, "Voice.") In an active sentence, the subject is the agent of the action and the direct object receives the action.

> ACTIVE: **My brother broke my guitar.**
>
> ACTIVE: **Trash litters the streets.**

In a passive sentence, the object appears in the subject position but still receives the action. The original subject can be changed to an object of the preposition *by* or *with*.

> PASSIVE: **My guitar was broken by my brother.**
>
> PASSIVE: **The streets are littered with trash.**

Or the original subject *(brother, trash)* can be left out altogether.

> PASSIVE: **My guitar was broken.**
>
> PASSIVE: **The streets are littered.**

The passive can be useful in certain situations. For example, sometimes a writer chooses passive voice to emphasize the receiver of the action. The following pair of sentences illustrates the different emphasis found in active and passive constructions.

> ACTIVE: **The Etruscans and the Greeks influenced the earliest Roman sculpture.**
>
> PASSIVE: **The earliest Roman sculpture was influenced by the Etruscans and the Greeks.**

The active sentence focuses attention on the agents *(the Etruscans and the Greeks)*, whereas the passive sentence focuses attention on the receiver of the action *(earliest Roman sculpture)*.

Other times, a writer chooses the passive because the agent is unknown or unimportant in the context. In such cases, the phrase containing *by* or *with* plus the agent is usually left out.

> PASSIVE: **The telephone lines were cut.**
>
> PASSIVE: **Equity courts in the United States are called Courts of Chancery.**

Even though the passive may be preferable in some situations, the active voice is more streamlined and more forceful because the subject acts and the verb does not require the *be* auxiliary (*am, is, are, was, were,* etc.) Furthermore, when the agent of the action figures significantly in the content, the active voice logically focuses attention on the subject-verb relationship. Compare the following two passages. The passive version obscures the important role of the host, calling attention instead to the result of his actions.

**sent/
struc
33c**

PASSIVE

> Before a Japanese tea ceremony, the tea room and surrounding gardens are cleaned by the host. Then a fire is made in the hearth and the water is put on to boil. When the guests arrive, the tea bowl, tea caddy, utensils for tending the fire, incense burner, and other necessary tools are carried in by the host. After the tea is prepared in a historical ritual, each guest is served. Finally, all utensils having been removed, the guests are bowed to, the signal that the ceremony has been completed.

In contrast, the active version is livelier and emphasizes the importance of the agent (the host) in the action (the ceremony).

ACTIVE

> Before a Japanese tea ceremony, the host cleans the tea room and surrounding gardens. Then he makes a fire in the hearth and puts the water on to boil. When the guests arrive, he carries in the tea bowl, tea caddy, utensils for tending the fire, incense burner, and other necessary tools. After preparing the tea in a historical ritual, the host serves each guest. Finally, he removes all utensils and bows to guests, the signal that the ceremony is over.

☐ EXERCISE 12

Change the following passive-voice sentences to active. When no *by* or *with* phrase exists, you will have to supply an appropriate active-voice subject.

EXAMPLE: Piles of spicy crabs and boiled corn were eaten. → We ate piles of spicy crabs and boiled corn.

1. Hypnosis has been used by psychologists for more than a century.
2. The mountains were covered with snow.
3. Almost any plant can be composted for use in the garden.
4. Cheese was used as a food source more than 4,000 years ago.

5. *Mean Streets* was filmed by Martin Scorsese in New York City's Little Italy.
6. The language in policies is being simplified by insurance companies.
7. Our lifestyles would be changed drastically by energy shortages.
8. The journal is published by a local press.
9. My bank was robbed this morning.
10. A touchdown was made in the last three seconds of the game.

(3) Unnecessary *that, who,* and *which* clauses

When revising prose, look for adjective clauses that begin with *that, who,* or *which* followed by a form of the verb *be* (*that is, who are, which were,* etc.). Frequently, these are empty words that can be deleted. The deletion converts this kind of clause to a word or phrase—a more efficient structure.

UNNECESSARY CLAUSE: The teacher had a smile that was skeptical.

REVISED: The teacher had a skeptical smile.

UNNECESSARY CLAUSE: W. C. Fields often played swindlers who were dedicated to the rule "never give a sucker an even break."

REVISED: W. C. Fields often played swindlers dedicated to the rule "never give a sucker an even break."

UNNECESSARY CLAUSE: The furniture, which is high-tech chrome and black leather, gives the room an impersonal look.

REVISED: The furniture, high-tech chrome and black leather, gives the room an impersonal look.

▢ EXERCISE 13

Streamline the following passage by eliminating any unnecessary *that, who,* and *which* clauses.

During the depression, a newspaper editor, who was from Oklahoma City, toured twenty states. In Washington, he reported his findings to a committee that was conducting hearings on unemployment. He told of conditions that were deplorable in the states that he had visited. He saw counties, which were once prosperous coal-mining regions, without a single bank. In Seattle, he saw women who were searching for scraps of food in refuse piles. He read of sheep raisers who were desperate and who were killing their sheep because they could get only a dollar a sheep. In the South, he saw bales of cotton that were rotting in the fields. He sympathized with all these people who were victims of circumstances that were uncontrollable, and he warned the committee of conditions that were worsening.

(4) Excessive verb forms

If a sentence seems congested and difficult to follow, check it to see whether it contains too many verb forms. Any verb form—main verb, infinitive, or participle—is the potential basis for a sentence. As a result, the addition of each verb form to a sentence complicates the structure. Consider, for instance, the following sentence with four verb forms.

> Residents who <u>revel</u> in the city's tradition of eccentricity <u>expect</u> 25,000 visitors <u>to join</u> in the <u>dancing</u> under the palm trees.

sent/ struc

33c

Embedded there are four potential sentences.

> Residents revel in the city's tradition of eccentricity.
>
> Residents expect 25,000 visitors.
>
> The visitors will join in.
>
> The visitors will dance under the palm trees.

Because there are only four verbs, the sentence is not unduly complicated. But when too many verb forms are packed into a sentence, the structure will groan and collapse under its own weight. For instance, consider this sentence from a government document.

> EXCESSIVE VERB FORMS
>
> After <u>conducting</u> surveys <u>concerning</u> public opinion toward <u>automated</u> highway systems, the department <u>decided to abandon</u> plans <u>to allocate</u> funds for <u>studying</u> such systems and <u>is investigating</u> mass transit systems that <u>might help to alleviate</u> congestion on highways <u>leading</u> into metropolitan areas.

Asking a reader to plow through eleven ideas in one sentence is simply asking too much. The solution is to split the sentence into smaller units and to eliminate some of the empty verbs that contribute nothing to the meaning. For example, *conducting surveys* can be expressed as *surveying; to allocate funds for studying* can be expressed as *to fund studies.* And because *decide to* and *help to* do not contribute information or clarity, they can be eliminated.

After <u>surveying</u> public opinion toward <u>automated</u> highway systems, the department <u>abandoned</u> plans <u>to fund</u> studies of such systems. Instead, the department <u>is investigating</u> mass transit systems that <u>might alleviate</u> congestion on highways <u>leading</u> into metropolitan areas.

Now the first sentence has four verb forms, and the second has three. The result is a more streamlined passage that is easier to read.

**sent/
struc
33c**

☐ EXERCISE 14

Streamline the following sentence by splitting it into more than one sentence and getting rid of any unnecessary words.

When Jones made the final shot that put the Knicks out in front just before the buzzer sounded to end the game, the excited fans were cheering and stomping so loudly that they did not realize that the official had blown the whistle to serve as a signal that someone had committed a foul and that the basket might possibly not count and the game could be lost.

(5) Obscure connection between subject and verb

To understand a sentence readily, a reader must make a swift connection between the subject and its verb. If too much intervenes between subject and verb, the vital connection is obscured, and the reader must grope for the sense. Three types of structures that can move the verb too far from its subject are long appositives, long modifiers, and involved compounds.

In the following example, a long appositive intervenes between the subject *(Second City)* and the verb *(has launched)*.

OBSCURE CONNECTION: Second City, originally a group of University of Chicago students who formed an improvisational repertory company, has launched an astonishing number of our best comic actors.

The sentence can be revised in several ways to clarify the subject-verb connection. Since the sentence has a direct object that is manageably short, shifting to the passive voice will move the original subject and appositive to the end and thus bring the new subject closer to its verb.

CLEAR CONNECTION MADE WITH An astonishing number of our best
PASSIVE VOICE: comic actors have been launched by

> Second City, originally a group of University of Chicago students who formed an improvisational repertory company.

Another alternative is to split the sentence. The original noun plus appositive construction can be made into a complete sentence by connecting the two elements with *be*. Adding a little transition between the two sentences makes their relationship clear.

sent/ struc

33c

> CLEAR CONNECTION MADE BY SPLITTING THE SENTENCE: Second City was originally a group of University of Chicago students who formed an improvisational repertory company. Since its origin, the group has launched an astonishing number of our best comic actors.

Like appositives, long adjective phrases or clauses that modify the subject can obscure the subject-verb connection. Here, the long clause separates the subject *(police officers)* from its verb *(are)*.

> OBSCURE CONNECTION: Police officers, who are apparently the only members of our society with legitimate excuses to use an assortment of deadly weapons and to drive fast with lights flashing and sirens blaring, are the favorite subjects of television writers.

In such sentences, the subject *(police officers)* and the subject complement *(favorite subjects)* are often interchangeable. Thus, when the simple subject is heavily modified and the complement is relatively short, switching the two elements can clarify the sentence.

> CLEAR CONNECTION MADE BY SWITCHING SUBJECT AND COMPLEMENT: The favorite subjects of television writers are police officers, who are apparently the only members of our society with legitimate excuses to use an assortment of deadly weapons and to drive fast with lights flashing and sirens blaring.

A further improvement is to delete the superfluous *who are,* thus shortening the adjective clause to an appositive. Then *police officers* can remain as the subject, preceded by the appositive.

CLEAR CONNECTION MADE BY INTRODUCTORY APPOSITIVE: Apparently the only members of our society with legitimate excuses to use an assortment of deadly weapons and to drive fast with lights flashing and sirens blaring, police officers are the favorite subjects of television writers.

sent/ struc 33c

If neither of those solutions seems appealing, an alternative is to rewrite the first sentence with an introductory dependent clause.

CLEAR CONNECTION MADE WITH DEPENDENT CLAUSE: Because they are apparently the only members of society with legitimate excuses to drive fast, blare sirens, flash lights, and knock heads, police officers are the favorite subjects of television writers.

A compound subject, especially one containing modifiers, can be so cumbersome that the subject-verb connection is obscured.

OBSCURE CONNECTION: Osteoclasts, dismantling cells that destroy old bone, and osteoblasts, construction cells that help form new bone, combine to create a continuous remodeling process.

The complete subject contains the simple subjects *(osteoclasts, osteoblasts)* as well as the appositives *(dismantling cells, construction cells)* and adjective clauses *(that destroy . . . , that help . . .)*. This lengthy construction overwhelms the verb *(combine)*. One way to solve the problem is to move the shorter noun phrase from the end to the subject position.

CLEAR CONNECTION MADE BY SWITCHING SUBJECTS: A continuous remodeling process results from a combination of osteoclasts, dismantling cells that destroy old bone, and osteoblasts, construction cells that help form new bone.

Another way to clarify the connection between subject and verb is visual: parentheses can help the reader isolate the subjects and "read around" the appositives. Also, this solution eliminates four commas.

CLEAR CONNECTION MADE WITH PARENTHESES: Osteoclasts (dismantling cells that destroy old bone) and osteoblasts (construction cells that help form

new bone) combine to create a continuous remodeling process.

If the sentence still sounds cumbersome, it can be split, expanding
the original subject to one sentence and the original verb to another.
Again, enclosing the appositives in parentheses reduces commas.

CLEAR CONNECTION MADE BY Dismantling cells (osteoclasts) de-
SPLITTING THE SENTENCE: stroy old bone, whereas construction cells (osteoblasts) help form
new bone. This combination creates
a continuous remodeling process.

**sent/
struc
33c**

    As the examples demonstrate, the problem with long sentences
is frequently not the length itself but rather the distance between the
subject and the verb. Thus, when you revise your writing, pay attention to the subject-verb connection; make sure it is immediately
clear. In the process, you will also streamline your prose, making it
easier to read.

❏ EXERCISE 15

**Streamline the following passage by making clear the connection
between subjects and verbs.**

    The first American mule, bred two hundred years ago by George
Washington from a Virginia mare and a Spanish jack named Royal Gift, a
present from the King of Spain, began a revolution in draft animals. The
mule, which is hardier than a horse, more resistant to disease, better able to
tolerate intense heat, more sure-footed, and more intelligent, was invalua-
ble before the Industrial Revolution. Mules cultivated cotton on southern
plantations, toiled in coal mines, and transported goods across the desert.
And of course, mules, which could carry weapons and supplies in terrain
where trucks and jeeps were helpless to move, served in both world wars.

❏ EXERCISE 16

**Using the techniques discussed in 33c, streamline the following
passage.**

    The idea that Shakespeare's plays were written not by William Shake-
speare himself but by some strange and shy genius hiding behind a pen
name is one of the silliest literary theories ever to be proposed. "Real
authors," from Ben Jonson and Christopher Marlowe to Queen Elizabeth
and the Rosicrucians, are constantly being proposed by critics and amateur

sleuths who believe that William Shakespeare was a simple-minded hick, who was possibly illiterate and did not have the background to make references to law, navigation, medicine, history, and court life, and that the records of Shakespeare's life are too scarce for someone who was so popular in his lifetime.

In fact, both of these ideas are invalid. First, Shakespeare's plays do not contain any information that would have been unavailable to any Elizabethan with a few books, and furthermore, the references made to geography and history are often mixed up and inaccurate; second, we know as much about Shakespeare's life as we know about the lives of many other famous Elizabethan authors whose work is not questioned.

The idea that some famous person would probably not have picked the name of an illiterate nobody to use as a pen name never seems to be considered by the "Shakespeare hunters."

**sent/
struc
33d**

33d Using Figurative Language

Figurative language communicates through comparison or association rather than through literal meaning.

> LITERAL: **Too many disabled people have failed to get protection from government programs.**
>
> FIGURATIVE: **Too many disabled people have slipped through the government's safety net.**

If the figurative language is effective, a reader can easily associate what is written with what is meant. For example, the familiar expression, "shed light on the matter" is not literal, but figurative. No reader would think of light in its actual sense of electromagnetic radiation. Instead readers make this association: "light" makes things clearer, more visible; therefore "shed light" means "make clear." In fact, the concreteness and vividness of effective figures of speech can communicate more directly and more intensely than abstractions and generalizations.

Although figurative language is most common in poetry and fiction, it can be used sparingly in nonfiction. The figures of speech should not, however, interfere with the information. Also, they should not seem exaggerated ("the problem is a cancer, malignant and festering, which must be excised") or trite ("he is stubborn as a mule"). But when carefully chosen, figures of speech can add depth, richness, and even clarity.

(1) Metaphor

A metaphor is a statement in which two dissimilar things are said or implied to be the same. They are not literally the same, but with a little imagination readers can make the connection. Thus, the characteristics of one item (usually unfamiliar or abstract) become clearer because of the similarity with the other item (usually familiar and concrete).

The following example illustrates how abstractions can be stated figuratively.

sent/ struc 33d

> I pass with relief from the tossing sea of Cause and Theory to the firm ground of Result and Fact. (Winston Churchill, *The Malakand Field Force*)

Here, the concrete phrase "tossing sea" stands for the more abstract "uncertainty," and "firm ground" stands for "certainty."

In the next example, two very ordinary things—fabric and jelly—are used figuratively.

> Without the support of reasoned thought the fabric of writing may collapse into a jelly of words. (Henry Seidel Canby, *Better Writing*)

Instead of "structure of the composition," the writer uses the figure "the fabric of writing" and instead of "meaninglessness," "a jelly of words."

(2) Personification

A personification is a special type of metaphor in which something not human (animal, object, place, idea) is given some human characteristic: *dancing shadow, patient forest, a marriage of flavors, the naked truth, time marching on, sister continent.* In the following quotation, two places are graphically contrasted through personification.

> The capitalist Federal Republic of Germany is a sporty blond racing along the autobahns in a glittering Mercedes-Benz. The Communist German Democratic Republic, bumping down potholed roads in proletarian Wartburgs and Russian-built Ladas, is her homely sister, a war bride locked in a loveless marriage with a former neighbor. (Michael Walsh, "Bach and Handel at the Wall," *Time*)

(3) Simile

In a simile, two dissimilar things are said to be like each other, or
one action is said to occur in the same way as another action. The key
words that distinguish a simile from a metaphor are *like* and *as*.

> SIMILE WITH LIKE: Like a monster of the sea, the nuclear-powered re-
> search submarine NR-1 prowls the twilit depth of
> the Bahamas during a practice dive. (Emory Kristof,
> "NR-1, The Navy's Inner-Space Shuttle," *National
> Geographic*)
>
> SIMILE WITH AS: Humor can be dissected, as a frog can, but the thing
> dies in the process and the innards are discouraging
> to any but the pure scientist. (E. B. White, "Some
> Remarks on Humor," *The Second Tree from the Corner*)

(4) Hyperbole

A hyperbole is an exaggeration. For example, instead of being literal
("they spend too much money"), a writer intensifies the reader's
awareness of size by writing a hyperbole ("the national defense
budget couldn't pay their bills for one month").

☐ EXERCISE 17

Identify the kinds of figurative language used in the following
quotations.

1. "The face of the sea is always changing. . . . Its aspects and moods vary
   hour by hour." (Rachel Carson, *The Sea Around Us*)

2. "Although one may fail to find happiness in theatrical life, one never
   wishes to give it up after having once tasted its fruits. To enter the
   School of the Imperial Ballet is to enter a convent whence frivolity is
   banned, and where merciless discipline reigns. (Anna Pavlova, "Pages of
   My Life," *Pavlova: A Biography*)

3. "The solar system as a whole, like a merry-go-round unhinged, spins,
   bobs, and blinks at the speed of 43,200 miles an hour along a course set
   east of Hercules." (Annie Dillard, *Pilgrim at Tinker Creek*)

4. "For a brief moment of time [clipper ships] flashed their splendor
   around the world, then disappeared with the sudden completeness of a
   wild pigeon." (Samuel Eliot Morison, *Maritime History of Massachusetts*)

5. "The fox was desperately close. Auntie Mame switched on the ignition and the car bounded forward just as a small cannon ball of black fur darted into the road. There was a terrible screech of brakes and I was thrown forward against the windshield. Then all hell broke loose. Hounds, horses, and riders descended on us like an avalanche. Nearly three dozen riders were thrown, and two big bay mares rammed into the Dusenberg so hard the front fender and hood had to be replaced. A third mount was half in and half out of the back seat, whinnying horribly. All in all, there were more horses shot that day than at the Battle of Gettysburg." (Patrick Dennis, *Auntie Mame*)

sent/ struc 33e

☐ EXERCISE 18

Use your imagination to change the literal language of these statements to figurative language.

EXAMPLE: The sentence was long and confusing. → The sentence encircled and choked the meaning like a giant boa constrictor.

1. His opponent in the tennis match was fearsome.
2. The book was boring.
3. The plane ride was extremely rough.
4. Hate made him irrational.
5. The hurricane destroyed the town.

33e Working with Sound and Rhythm

All human beings respond to the sounds of words and phrases. Children in the process of learning language constantly engage in sound play. They chant in games: *Red Rover, Red Rover, send Rachel right over; Cinderella, dressed in yellow, went upstairs to kiss her fellow.* They experiment with tongue twisters: *Peter Piper picked a peck of pickled peppers.* They show off with Pig Latin: *An-cay ou-yay eak-spay is-thay?* They delight in spoonerisms: *Mardon me padam; this pie is occupewed. Allow me to sew you to another sheet.*

Most adults rarely indulge in sound play just for fun, but they do respond to the music of the language. Television advertising, for instance, relies heavily on sound gimmicks to sell products and ensure that consumers remember brand names and slogans. Politicians use sounds and rhythmic patterns to capture the emotions of audiences. And of course, sound and rhythm help separate poetry from prose.

Although it is impossible to say exactly how or why, we respond to certain sounds and rhythms in predictable ways. In other words, some sounds seem to possess a kind of symbolism. For example, words that begin with /r/ often sound harsh *(rude, roar, riot)*, whereas words ending in /r/ after certain vowels sound soft *(purr, fur, demure)*. Repetition of /l/ can produce a liquidlike effect *(lily, lullaby, lyrical)*. Final /f/ after an /uh/ or /ih/ has a light sound *(fluff, puff, whiff)*; the addition of a /y/ can make a word seem light as air *(fluffy, puffy, whiffy)*. The /j/ and /ch/ often suggest noise *(jabber, jibberish, chime, chirp)*. Words ending in /p/, /t/, and /k/ have a popping, tapping, staccato effect *(pop, tap, pat, kit, pluck, whack)*.

In addition to the symbolism of sounds, the language has phrasal rhythms that work to wed sounds to ideas. For example, phrases with lots of unstressed syllables seem to move fast: *It's funny how rapidly phrases go running along on the page.* Phrases made up mostly of stressed syllables seem to move much slower: *Like gunmen at high noon, some words walk slow.*

In the following excerpt from *An Essay on Criticism,* Alexander Pope admirably demonstrates how sound can reinforce sense. The first two lines state Pope's thesis—that a writer must deliberately make use of sound symbolism.

(1)   'Tis not enough no harshness gives offense,
(2)   The sound must seem an echo to the sense:
(3)   Soft is the strain when Zephyr gently blows,
(4)   And the smooth stream in smoother numbers flows;
(5)   But when loud surges lash the sounding shore,
(6)   The hoarse, rough verse should like a torrent roar:
(7)   When Ajax strives some rock's vast weight to throw,
(8)   The line too labors, and the words move slow;
(9)   Not so, when swift Camilla scours the plain,
(10) Flies o'er the unbending corn, and skims along the main.

In the third line of the excerpt, the repetition of /s/ suggests the sighing of the wind. In the fourth, the /sm/ and /st/ make silklike sounds, and the long vowels in "smooth," "stream," "smoother," and "flows" make the line flow slowly. The /g/, /sh/, and /r/ sounds in lines (5) and (6) echo the noise of the surf pounding the shore. Lines

(7) and (8) have many more stressed than unstressed syllables and so seem to have "vast weight" and to "move slow." In lines (9) and (10), the predominance of unstressed syllables makes words "skim along." Thus Pope makes the sound "an echo to the sense."

Another technique writers use for rhythmic effect is repetition of words and phrases. Consider Winston Churchill's famous "Dunkirk" speech before the House of Commons during World War II. The repetition of "we shall" and "we shall fight" sets up a cadence, culminating in the bold line "we shall never surrender."

> We shall not flag or fail. We shall go on to the end. We shall fight in France, we shall fight on the seas and oceans, we shall fight with growing confidence and growing strength in the air, we shall defend our island, whatever the cost may be, we shall fight on the beaches, we shall fight on the landing grounds, we shall fight in the fields and in the streets, we shall fight in the hills; we shall never surrender.

In the next example, Adlai Stevenson not only repeats the words "rule" and "law" but also repeats a structure: compound nouns joined by "and."

> As citizens of this democracy, you are the rulers and the ruled, the law givers and the law-abiding, the beginning and the end.

To achieve this moving passage about the carrying of the Olympic flame across the country in 1984, Lance Morrow uses sound to complement sense.

> The flame came fluttering out of the darkness into an early morning light. Americans in bathrobes would sometimes stand by the sides of two-lane roads, and as a runner carried the Olympic torch toward them, they would signal thumbs up and break the country silence with a soft, startling cheer. Their faces would glow with a complex light—a patriotism both palpable and chastened, a kind of reawakened warmth, something fetched from a long way back.

The passage begins with the repetition of /f/ sounds, suggesting softness, the way the flame must have looked in the "early morning light." In the second sentence, Morrow uses a number of /s/ sounds, again suggesting softness. He ends the sentence with "a soft, startling cheer," startling the reader with an unusual idea—that something soft can also be startling. The rhythm of the last sentence is made interesting by the three appositives after the dash, which have a chantlike quality. Also, the choice of the verb "fetched" is perfect. It is a crisp word, a no-nonsense word; and it is an old-fashioned word, appropriate for something from a long way back. The passage ends with three, single-syllable words to slow the movement, "long way back." And the final word ends with the crack of a /k/.

As the examples indicate, effective writing is not merely clear and correct. It also sounds good. You may not be able to manipulate the sounds of the language with the expertise of the writers quoted here. You should, nevertheless, practice listening to what you write. Read it aloud. Try several versions. Pick the one that sounds the best, the one that is "an echo to the sense."

☐ EXERCISE 19

Rewrite the following sentences and passages to achieve better sound and rhythm. Try working with sound symbolism, repetition of words and phrases, and stressed and unstressed syllables. You may have to try several versions before you find something that sounds good.

1.   The small boy ran down the road so fast that the dust rose behind him like the wake created by a boat.

2.   The moon seemed to come up over the trees very slowly, and when it did, it threw a strange light over the garden where we were sitting.

3.   The comforter that my grandmother gave me when I was fifteen was very large, but it weighed hardly anything. I would sleep under it and stay very warm, but I didn't feel like any weight was on my body.

4.   I spent my youth on a horse. His name was Snip. He was half quarter horse and half palomino. Whenever I was not in school, we would go off and spend the day in the hills and creeks. He would seem content enough while we were out, but at the end of the ride, when he could see the barn door, he would start to run. No pulling back on the reins could stop him. His shoulders would heave. His massive head would bob. He would breathe heavily. He would frantically try to lessen the distance between himself and the barn. He would go faster and faster headed home. I feel like Snip sometimes these days.

5.   For many people, robins and jonquils are the first indications of spring. But for allergy sufferers, spring begins with an ominous cloud of yellow pollen. This pollen floats through the air. It is inside and outside. It covers cars. The pollen also gets on sidewalks and bushes. In the house it settles on bric-a-brac. As a matter of fact, it covers everything that doesn't move fast.

P A R T V

The Writing Process

No matter what the writing project, the process is essentially the same: thinking about a subject, finding an organization, producing a draft, revising until the final paper is satisfactory. This process, however, is not necessarily linear, with each stage completed before the next one begins. For instance, some writers think a subject through and then write an entire rough draft before revising. More commonly, writers think a while, write a while, think some more, revise parts of their work, think again, write again, and so on. Regardless of the sequence, it is important to work through the whole process.

34

Writing the Composition

☐ Getting Ideas

Sometimes when you prepare to write, you have a topic—by choice or by assignment—but you do not know the best angle to take or the best focus to choose. At other times, you have an angle or focus, but you cannot envision the material that will best develop and support your ideas. In any case, when considering a potential subject, you need to discover what you already know about it and what material is available through research or personal experience to fill in the gaps. The most productive procedure is not to wait for inspiration but to stimulate thought by techniques that will activate and direct ideas.

The following dozen techniques can help you generate subjects and ideas about subjects. Some of these techniques use free association to generate ideas at random; others are more structured and channel ideas in controlled directions. If a technique is not productive in one instance, it might be in another—when you are in a different mood or when you have a different subject.

34a Keeping a Journal

Keeping a journal does not mean keeping a daily record of your activities. Rather, it means writing regularly about things that happen to you; that puzzle, excite, anger, or depress you; that make you laugh; or that interest you in any way at all.

A journal can help your writing in several ways. You can structure your entries however you choose. You can try out various techniques for getting ideas. You can record impressions and anecdotes or practice answering essay tests. Journal keeping helps you get used to putting words on paper and allows you to write without stress or fear of censure. Finally, a journal can function as a source of subjects for writing.

For a journal to be useful, you must write in it regularly, preferably daily, and you should read it regularly. You may find there some revealing and productive patterns. For example, if a certain person turns up again and again in your journal, perhaps you should consider that person's role in your life and write about it. If a certain problem keeps reappearing, perhaps you should write about its cause or its solution. In this way, your journal can be a source of specific subjects for writing assignments. In your journal, you might include your impressions of a shopping mall, details of a restaurant meal, or strange habits of professors.

idea
34c

34b Meditating

In writing, the term *meditation* usually refers simply to thinking in an environment that allows you to concentrate on your innermost thoughts. When you meditate before you write, focus on a subject, if you have one. If you do not have one, begin by picking a person, a place, an object, an incident, or an idea. Then let your mind move spontaneously from that initial point. Concentrate on what you are thinking, but do not try to direct your thoughts. If you come to some particularly interesting idea, focus on it and expand it.

Meditating has the advantage of being much faster than other techniques of getting ideas, simply because you do not have to write your thoughts down. But it has the disadvantage that you may forget some of your best material. A compromise is to talk into a tape recorder. This practice will slow you down only a bit and will preserve every strand of thought.

34c Brainstorming

Brainstorming, a free-association technique, has proved successful in business, where members of a group get together to explore a topic or solve a problem—each member spontaneously contributing ideas that can stimulate other ideas.

Whether done in a group or alone, brainstorming should be completely unstructured. The theory is that structuring impedes the creative flow of ideas while brainstorming allows the subconscious to release blocked ideas, no matter how irrelevant or silly they seem to be. If you try brainstorming, remember that you cannot predict which ideas will be useful. Consequently, you should jot down the ideas in words, phrases, sentences, doodles—anything that comes to you. After about ten minutes of brainstorming, go back through what you have written—eliminating what is stupid or extraneous, linking related ideas, and thinking further about anything that strikes you as interesting.

**idea
34d**

34d Clustering

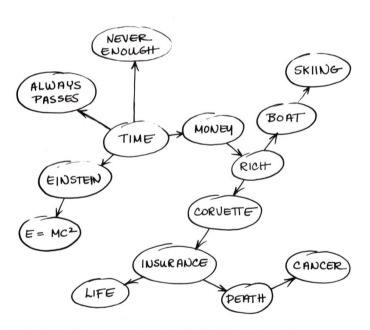

A variation of brainstorming is called *clustering*. In this system, ideas are linked through a graphic system of circles and arrows. To use this technique, start out by writing a topic, or "nucleus" word, in the middle of a blank page. Then, radiating out from the nucleus, write down words that are suggested to you by the topic. Continue to write down associations, circling each and linking it with an arrow to a related word.

The point of clustering is to release the creative element of the mind and suppress the logic and analysis that may impede productivity. Usually, the system will, at some point, produce a subject for writing. For instance, in the example in Figure 1, the writer saw in the clustering the possible subject of how the Corvette has changed over the years—suggested to him by the word *Corvette* and his nucleus word, *time*.

34e Freewriting

Freewriting is much like "talking on paper"—simply writing whatever thoughts occur, no matter how random or unimportant they may seem. Unlike brainstorming, which employs random jottings, freewriting is done in sentences or, at least, in constructions that express complete ideas. The technique serves several purposes. First, the very act of writing stimulates thinking. And many writers say that freewriting is like limbering up, like the finger exercises a pianist does before playing. Second, freewriting can turn vague ideas into visible words, thus indicating the potential of a subject.

In a typical freewriting session, you write your thoughts as fast as you can, trying not to be critical or analytical. When you have lapses, scribble or write nonsense, but do not stop the momentum of putting something down on paper. To get started, you might pick a popular issue, such as smoking in public places, television violence, or traffic and parking problems. When about fifteen minutes is up, read what you have written, and list any ideas that might serve as a subject or be useful in a paper.

34f Constructing Ladders

Subjects like "cities," "baseball," or "movies" are too broad for a good paper, and ideas such as "friendship," "warfare," or "pollution" are too abstract. If you are struggling with unmanageable subjects such as these, you might want to construct ladders—graduated scales of words or ideas, beginning with the abstract or general and moving toward the concrete or specific.

For example, the subject "cities" is too general and unfocused. But if you think of "cities" as being on the top rung of a ladder, you can place a more specific subject on the next rung and continue down the ladder until a topic strikes you as a good one for a paper. Thus you might move from "cities" to "New York" to "New York subway" and then end with the promising topic "subway graffiti." Depending on your personal viewpoint and the available information, this topic could lead to an interesting paper—maybe one classifying the kinds of messages, discussing the artistic talents on display, analyzing the techniques used, or documenting efforts to control the problem.

34g Asking Random Questions

Because asking questions is one of the most natural mental processes, you may find it a comfortable and productive technique. If you have no subject at all in mind, you might get started by asking random questions, such as these.

Who is my most peculiar relative?
What kind of car would I like to own?
What disease do I most dread?
What type of natural disaster do I think is worst?
What costs more than it ought to?
Who makes me furious? Why?
What would I like changed about my environment? my life? myself? the world?

34h Asking Journalistic Questions

The opening sentence of news stories traditionally answers the six "journalistic questions": Who? What? When? Where? Why? How? If you concentrate on just one or two of these questions, you can establish a direction for a composition. For example, the subject of corruption in college athletics might be explored with *who:* What kind of person would risk a career by betting on a game? Or with *how:* How does a basketball player "throw a game"?

34i Asking Logical Questions

Logical questions are those that grow naturally out of a subject: What caused a certain event? How does a particular device work? Use logical questions to help you explore a subject to find out how much you know about it and to help you narrow a subject sufficiently to deal with it in a concrete way.

For instance, about an object, such as a frisbee, you might ask the following logical questions.

What is it made of?
What are its parts?
How is it used?
What is it similar to?
What is it different from?
Are there categories of it?
What might be new ways to use it?
What can be substituted for it?
What are people's opinions of it?
How much does it cost?
Where did it originate?

**idea
34j**

34j The Classical Topics

To suggest lines of argument, Greek rhetoricians and orators outlined what are called the five *classical topics*.

Definition	saying what something is
Comparison	saying what a subject is like or unlike
Relationship	looking at causes and effects, antecedents and consequences
Circumstance	exploring possibility or impossibility, past or future fact
Testimony	discovering what is known, thought, and said about a subject

These topics can stimulate thought about a subject. Consider, for example, "physical fitness." The classical topic "definition" suggests a look at its components (good muscle tone, low percentage of body fat, endurance, and so forth) or its types (fitness for the average person and fitness for an athlete in training). "Comparison" suggests an analogy to emotional and mental fitness or a contrast between a physically fit person and someone who is unfit.

"Relationship" might lead to a discussion of the causes of fitness or its effects. "Circumstance" raises the question of the possible and impossible: what level of fitness is possible for, say, a person who works every day in an office.

The last classical topic, "testimony," directs attention outside personal knowledge to research and data about the subject. It suggests finding out what authorities say about fitness, conducting an opinion poll on fitness, examining statistics to discover facts about the fitness of the general public or a certain group of people, or soliciting accounts of personal experiences with fitness. Finally, these data-gathering techniques might be combined for a fairly extensive investigation.

The classical topics probably will not help you find a subject, but once you have one, they will help you narrow the subject into something manageable and interesting.

idea
34k

34k Researching

Researching is a popular method of finding a subject or gathering material about a subject. When you are just getting started on a paper, your research is not structured library work but casual exploring—looking through newspapers and magazines, conducting informal interviews, listening to radio and television news and talk shows. The advantage of finding a subject through research is that in the process you also get a head start collecting usable details.

❑ EXERCISE 1

List ten topics that might be suitable for compositions. To get ideas for these topics, use one or more of the following techniques.

1. Keep a journal for several days.
2. Meditate on people, places, and events in your life.
3. Brainstorm by writing down anything that pops into your mind.
4. Research by such techniques as observation and reading.

EXERCISE 2

List ten ideas that might be suitable for compositions. Begin with a general word such as *entertainment, pollution, employment, crime, television, cars,* or *school,* and focus it through one or more of the following techniques:

1. Clustering
2. Freewriting
3. Constructing ladders
4. Asking questions
5. Applying the classical topics
6. Researching

Making Decisions

**dec
34m**

After finding a subject and generating ideas about it, you are likely to have a jumble of facts and thoughts meaningful to you but to no one else. Now you must go beyond the subject and consider your purpose, audience, voice. Furthermore, you must narrow your subject to a thesis, or controlling idea, that can be developed into a focused composition.

34l Considering the Purpose

Normally, you write to an audience for a purpose—to create an impression, to inform, to argue, to persuade, to entertain. Of course, the purposes sometimes seem mixed: All writing informs to some extent, and an effective argument can persuade and also often entertain. Nevertheless, most writing does have an overriding or dominant purpose, and that purpose helps to unify it. Through your purpose, you transmit a message. If you have no clear purpose in mind, readers may not know whether you want them to laugh, to sympathize, to learn something, to be convinced, or to share an experience with you. If your purpose is clear to you, however, and if you keep it in mind while you write, readers stand a good chance of getting the message.

34m Identifying the Audience

No matter who your readers are, they are your audience, and you have certain responsibilities toward them. You must abide by the conventions of spelling and usage that readers expect, and you must consider the "distance" between you and your readers and make a special effort to be clear in meaning.

You must also consider the identity of your readers, a process usually called *audience analysis,* important particularly in argument and persuasion.

34n Finding a Voice

As a writer, you must adopt an effective and appropriate "voice" through which you speak to the audience. If you are writing fiction, you can invent a voice—for example, that of an all-knowing creator or of a specific character in the fiction itself. But if you are writing nonfiction, the voices available to you are projections of your own different roles or personality traits. Depending on the occasion, you might speak as a friend, a colleague, an impersonal observer, a concerned citizen, an antagonist, or an enthusiastic fan. Also, your voice may reflect traits or moods—serious, lighthearted, neutral, detached, energetic, or emotional.

For a formal paper, a third-person voice helps establish a serious tone and a polite distance between writer and reader. For an informal paper, a first-person voice helps establish familiarity, a personal relationship between writer and reader.

No matter what the writing, however, a writer's voice (sometimes called a *role, mask, stance,* or *persona*) must sound sincere. For example, if you fake the voice of a person more sophisticated than you really are, you risk sounding phony or even silly. And also, whatever voice you choose must be consistent throughout an entire paper; one voice should not intrude upon another. If you assume a distant and dignified voice in the beginning, do not insert a casual or personal remark. A technical paper is no place for a joke. Slang is inappropriate in a letter of application. Likewise, if you start out in a conversational voice, you should not suddenly become formal. For example, if you begin by calling yourself "I," do not switch to "this writer." Or if you have been using a humorous tone, do not suddenly become solemn.

☐ EXERCISE 3

Imagine a logical purpose, audience, and voice for the following subjects.

1. How to study for a history test
2. An improvement needed in your community
3. A holiday that should be added to your school's calendar
4. The safety of generic drugs
5. Steps for avoiding a mugging
6. An evaluation of a textbook
7. An overrated entertainer
8. The car you would drive if money were no object
9. The season of the year you enjoy most
10. A subject that you find through such techniques as keeping a journal, brainstorming, or research

34o Narrowing the Subject with a Thesis

After you have found a subject and put it in perspective by considering purpose, audience, and voice, you must make sure you have a thesis to control and direct your work. Sometimes this thesis, or controlling idea, is not stated in the final paper, particularly when your purpose is to create an impression or to entertain. Nevertheless, before you write, you should formulate a thesis; it narrows the subject, governs what materials you will include and exclude, and states the point of your paper. To be effective, a thesis must meet the following requirements.

- A thesis should be a complete sentence. Without a predicate, you may have a subject, but you do not have a thesis: "Muslim philosophy" is a subject; "Muslim philosophy is essentially Greek in origin and structure" is an idea.
- A thesis should not include vague words such as *good, bad,* or *nice.* The more specific the thesis, the more easily you can control your material. As an example, imagine that you have chosen the subject "study of a foreign language." Of little use is a vague statement such as "Learning a foreign language is a good idea." It is too weak to exert any control over material. It leaves too many unanswered questions: Who is studying? When? Why? Which language? A better control is a specific statement such as "Learning French helped me to understand the grammar of English."
- A thesis should narrow the subject to a manageable size, a size appropriate to the time you have and the length of the paper. You do not want a topic that requires twenty pages to develop if your assignment requires five pages. For example, if there are no strict limits on length and the amount of time available, you might undertake this thesis: "In detective novels, the settings are more important than the plots." But if you have only a week to write a 500-word paper, you will have to choose a much

less ambitious project, such as "In Elmore Leonard's *La Brava* readers learn about the Miami that tourists never see." By careful selection of a thesis, you can narrow a broad subject.

BROAD: Many Americans are poor drivers.

NARROWED: Every driver should be required to retake the driver's test every three years in order to renew a license.

BROAD: In recent years, advertising has become more and more suggestive.

NARROWED: Magazine advertisements for men's cologne rely on suggestive images to sell the product.

**dec
34o**

- A thesis must be compatible with the purpose. If you set out to convey an impression, your thesis should be vivid and interesting—for example, "The first time I saw a John Wayne western, I found my childhood hero." If you set out to entertain, your thesis should be one that promises pleasurable reading—"One of the funniest old movies on television is *The Conqueror,* starring John Wayne as Genghis Khan." If you intend to inform, your thesis should summarize the information you mean to explain—"Although people associate John Wayne with heroes, he played a few memorable villains." Finally, if your purpose is to argue or persuade, your thesis should state an opinion or a judgment. You cannot argue a fact, such as "John Wayne was a popular movie star," since there is no counter opinion "John Wayne was not a popular movie star." Also, there is little point in arguing a generally accepted opinion, such as "Except for a few roles, John Wayne usually played a strong, brave, incorruptible man of few words." On the other hand, you can produce an interesting argument with an unexpected viewpoint: "Much of John Wayne's popularity as an actor resulted from his outspoken patriotism in real life."

After you have settled on a thesis, you can start assembling materials to support it. If you have used some of the techniques for getting started, you can sort through your collection of notes and select those that are pertinent. Further, if you plan to write an argument, you can list evidence for and against your thesis. The result will be a kernel that you can develop into a complete paper.

☐ EXERCISE 4

Which of the following do not meet the requirements for a suitable thesis? For each unacceptable thesis, state which requirements are lacking.

1. Telecommunications is an interesting field of study.
2. Although Frank Lloyd Wright made his reputation as an innovator, he was actually an imitator.
3. Bystanders often fail to help people in emergencies.
4. The four types of stress are mental, physical, chemical, and thermal.
5. A rumor circulated in 1978 that a fast-food chain put earth worms in hamburger meat to increase the protein content.
6. How a sphygmomanometer measures blood pressure.
7. Astrological profiles are silly.
8. Rock stars go to extremes to be different.

struc

☐ EXERCISE 5

Write a thesis for three of the following subjects. Instead of simply turning each phrase into a sentence, narrow the subject by making a specific statement.

EXAMPLE: cooking as a hobby → Learning to cook is an effective way to improve your social life.

In search of a decent hamburger
Tarzan as a romantic hero
How computers are changing society
Status symbols in the middle class
The ultimate stereo equipment
Part-time jobs for the untrained
Magazines and their intended audiences
Self-defense for women
Unsympathetic teachers
Telephone options

☐ Structuring the Composition

In addition to finding a thesis, gathering materials to support it, and considering the logic of your ideas, you must choose a structure to frame the composition. Planning a structure helps you to develop the composition and locate any gaps that must be filled by further thought or research.

34p Considering a Structure

The ten structures described here can serve to shape either an entire paper or one section of a paper.

(1) Description

Description is the presentation of details that create a verbal picture of what something is or appears to be. Be selective in your choice of details, and be thoughtful in their arrangement. Spatial arrangement works well for descriptions of buildings or scenes in nature. Arrangement according to positive and negative features might be suitable for describing a favorite old car, and arrangement from the more obvious to the less obvious might be a way to describe your grandfather, let's say, first with those details obvious to anyone and then with subtle traits known only to people close to him.

struc
34p

(2) Narration

Narration tells a story, recounts events, or outlines the stages of a process. Narration can be strictly chronological; predominantly chronological, interrupted with flashbacks to previous actions; or episodic, with actions grouped into incidents not necessarily sequential. Narration is a good structure for recounting an experience, relating an anecdote, or for explaining a process, such as how a chemistry experiment works. Include only details that advance the story or the account of the process.

(3) Enumeration

In enumeration, details—facts, statistics, examples, precedents, or testimony—are listed to support the thesis, either of a whole paper or of the topic sentence of a paragraph. Details may be presented in order either of increasing importance or of diminishing importance.

(4) Comparison/contrast

The two most common arrangements for a comparison/contrast structure are *block* and *alternating*. In comparing downhill and cross-country skiing, for example, by block arrangement, you would first discuss one type of skiing, including each point of comparison and contrast, and then move to the other type, discussing the same points. In the alternating arrangement, you would organize the paper according to the points of comparison, with the two types of skiing under each point.

(5) Classification

In classification, items from a general category are grouped into smaller categories on the basis of selected principles. For example, campus clubs might be classified by their purpose—social, political, religious. The structure of a classification paper grows naturally out of the subject matter, with each class constituting a section (a paragraph or more) of the final composition.

struc
34p

(6) Illustration

An illustration is an example that makes a generality specific or an abstraction concrete. The illustration may be a narrative, a description, a fact, or anything that makes an idea graphic or real. An entire paper built on one extended illustration usually takes a narrative form. For example, an argument that criminals should work to compensate their victims might narrate one incident from the commission of a crime through a successful program of compensating the victim to the criminal's rehabilitation. On the other hand, a paper built on a series of illustrations usually has an enumeration pattern. A writer could enumerate the examples of Mohammed Ali, Joe Louis, and Sonny Liston to support the thesis, "Boxing should be outlawed because of the brain damage suffered by participants."

(7) Definition

A paper devoted to definition—for example, "What is a soap opera?"—must be expanded with other structures. Some of these might be classification—the types of soap operas; comparison/contrast—the ways in which soaps differ from other television forms, and illustration—the use of one popular soap opera or several to exemplify the form.

(8) Analysis

The term *analysis* means breaking a whole into component parts for the purpose of bringing a systematic understanding to a subject. An analysis of a poem could examine the theme, the voice, the figurative language, and the sound pattern. An analysis of an insect might include its physical description, its life history, its habitat, and its enemies.

(9) Problem/solution

The logic and simplicity of the problem/solution pattern make it easy to design. A paper with this pattern can either emphasize the problem or the solution or give equal time to both.

(10) Cause/effect

The cause/effect pattern is a versatile structure. A paper can begin with a cause and lead up to the effect, begin with effect and then explain cause, or shift back and forth between the two. If you decide to use the cause/effect structure, be sure that your logic is sound. A preceding event does not necessarily cause the one that follows, and many events and trends have multiple and complex causes.

34q Drafting a Working Outline

Once you are satisfied with your subject and have a structure in mind, it is wise to work from some sort of plan, whether sketchy or carefully detailed. Those writers who make structured outlines have to do much of the thinking and planning before the writing stage; those with rough outlines must usually do additional planning during the writing stage.

(1) A rough working outline

A working outline need not be formal, with a system of Roman and Arabic numerals, upper- and lower-case letters, and parallel grammatical structures. Instead, it can be "rough," with the emphasis on order and content rather than form and parallelism. A rough working outline should be finished enough to reveal the omission of necessary information, the presence of superfluous material, the compatibility of the parts of the composition, and the logic of sequences.

(2) A structured outline

If you prefer to go beyond a rough outline to make a more structured plan before beginning a draft, you can make a topic, a sentence, or a paragraph outline. The topic outline helps ensure a logical sequence, predict paragraphing, and speed up production of a first draft. In addition, a topic outline can serve as a table of contents if the assignment requires one. A sentence outline can suggest topic sentences for paragraphs and blocks in the paper. A paragraph outline, a rough draft of the paper itself, is rare because few writers are prepared to develop ideas at the same time they are organizing with an outline. Instead, most outlines develop gradually, progressing in detail and size as the subject is developed and the necessary information is accumulated.

**struc
34q**

☐ EXERCISE 6

Write working outlines to develop three of the following ideas.

1. You can tell a married man from a single one (or one who wants to be single) by the clothes he wears.
2. People can be classified by the kinds of vacations they take.
3. Seeing a movie in a theater is a different experience from seeing one on television.
4. Christmas is typically a time of stress.
5. Some college classes make me wonder what I'm paying for.
6. The problem with television is that it makes us too passive.
7. Magazine racks in stores tell us something about interests of Americans.
8. Women's clothes are designed for ultra-thin models, not for normal figures.
9. Birthday parties are among my favorite childhood memories.
10. Elaborate weddings are a waste of money.

☐ Drafting the Composition

At some point in the composition process, you must get your ideas on paper. If you should develop "writer's block," two tactics may help overcome it. First, get away from the blank paper for a while and do something else. Second, remember that you are not trying to produce a finished product in one sitting. You are simply trying to produce a rough draft. Once in rough form, the first draft can be changed, supplemented, and polished.

¶
34r

Systems for writing vary. Some writers spend most of their time on preliminaries; they think through a subject, make plans, take notes, write the entire composition, and revise it. Other writers think, write, and revise intermittently—working back and forth, weaving a composition piece by piece. When you find a system that feels comfortable and that works well for you, stick with it.

Regardless of the drafting technique you prefer, your goal is to produce a series of segments that fit together within the overall structure of the whole paper. These segments are the paragraphs, the units of information that together develop the paper's thesis. By drafting your paper paragraph by paragraph, you can focus all your attention on developing each segment of information.

34r Drafting Body Paragraphs

The "body" of a composition, between the introduction and conclusion, contains the material that supports the thesis. This material must be presented in logical segments, or paragraphs. Think of the paragraphs as "mini-compositions" with internal structures similar to the structures of full papers. Think of the details in each paragraph as supporting a central idea, just as the evidence of your whole paper supports its thesis.

(1) Constructing paragraphs with topic sentences

A useful way to construct paragraphs is to think in terms of a topic sentence, one that states the point of a whole paragraph or a block (or sequence) of paragraphs. The traditional paragraph begins with a general statement, or topic sentence, which is subsequently supported or developed by discussion, illustration, or examples. This organization works especially well for inexperienced writers; it improves coherence and unity because the details are all related to the stated idea. Furthermore, as the following paragraph illustrates, placing the thesis at the beginning ensures its emphasis.

Topic Sentence at the Beginning

Hypnosis can control people's vision. For example, if you were hypnotized and I told you a snake was slithering across the floor, you would not only believe me, you would actually perceive the snake as real. If I told you that there was no desk in the room, you could look right at it and not see it.

The topic sentence can occur not only at the beginning of a paragraph but also within a paragraph or at the end. Such variations can relieve the monotony of a series of paragraphs, each beginning with a topic sentence.

¶
34r

Topic Sentence at the End

According to a survey, 50 percent of the prisoners convicted of murders, rapes, robberies, and assaults had been drinking before committing their crimes. Sixty percent of these prisoners had been drinking very heavily. Obviously, drinking is closely related to violence.

Topic Sentence in the Middle

I see people jogging, and it looks healthful and enjoyable. But for years, whenever I tried jogging, it turned out to be a painful struggle. So I quit, tried again, quit, and on and on. But now, I have discovered the answer. I never jog alone. Jogging with others somehow makes the torture bearable. Talking gets my mind off what I'm doing, and suffering with others is better than suffering alone.

In another variation of paragraph development, writers do not state the topic sentence at all, depending on the content to indicate the central idea. For example, the idea of the following paragraph, though not stated, is obviously that baseball fans are fickle.

Topic Sentence Unstated

When a baseball team is winning, fans swarm into the stadium, enthusiastic cheers fill the air, good seats go only to those who buy tickets far in advance. When a team begins to lose, the stands are half empty, the silence broken only by catcalls, boos, and moans. With homers, high batting averages, and sparkling defensive plays, the players are magnificent heroes. In a slump, they turn suddenly into hopeless bums.

(2) Structuring paragraphs

Like an entire composition, an effective paragraph or block of paragraphs has its own logical purpose and structure. In fact, you can structure a paragraph or a block of paragraphs with the same techniques used to structure a whole paper—description, narration, comparison/contrast, classification, and so forth. Whatever the point of the paragraph, there is some effective structure for its development.

For example, to make a point about the foolish ways people treat pets, a student writer structures a paragraph by enumeration, itemizing examples found in advertisements for boarding kennels.

¶
34r

> With family vacation plans that did not include pets, I began to search for a painless way to part company with two dogs and a cat. The Yellow Pages revealed surprising choices: a ranch, a motel, an inn, an academy, a country club, and even an animal kingdom. Our pets could luxuriate at the Pet-otel, at Paradise for Pets, at Pleasant Valley, or better yet, at Rhapsody Acres. The only ominous-sounding place was the Dog House. At one of these places with "best friends" enjoying "tender loving care," the "furry four-footed companions" are provided with heated and air-conditioned accommodations, grooming, styling, and trimming. In another, they are entertained by music in "new modern facilities with a skylighted atrium." One place transports its guests in a "pet taxi" and provides "dating." While dogs enjoy a "country atmosphere," cats step into a "jungle motif." It all sounds so appealing that my family's vacation plans paled in comparison. If it weren't for the plucking and ear tattooing, I might have considered joining the animals.

To make a point about the types of people living in Venice, California, Sarah Davidson structures a paragraph by classification, dividing the people into two groups.

> The residents of Venice fall into two groups: those who work and those who don't. The latter includes senior citizens, drifters, drug addicts, would-be movie-makers, and aging hippies and surfers who have made a cult of idleness and pleasure. The other group includes lawyers, dentists, real estate brokers, accountants. Many are workaholics, attached to their jobs as they are to nothing else. They work nights and weekends, eat fast food while driving to and from their work, and live alone, longing, in the silence before falling asleep, for connection. (Sarah Davidson, "Rolling Into the Eighties," *Esquire*)

The point of a paragraph usually determines the structure. Among the possibilities are the following structures.

- Description
  A descriptive paragraph contains details that combine to create an image that the reader can envision.
- Narration
  A narrative arrangement moves from one occurrence to another, usually in chronological order.
- Enumeration
  An enumeration is similar to a list, with examples substantiating the point.
- Comparison/Contrast
  A comparison/contrast structure allows a writer to point out similarities or differences.
- Classification
  The point of classification is to organize a subject into characteristic groups on the basis of some similarity the members share.
- Illustration
  A paragraph developed by illustration supplies evidence to back up a general statement or an abstraction.
- Definition
  The point of a paragraph may be to define a key term so that readers can better understand the entire composition.
- Analysis
  A paragraph developed by analysis explores a subject by examining the units (parts, ingredients, characteristics, causes) that make up the larger whole.
- Problem/Solution
  Paragraphs developed with a problem/solution pattern usually begin with a statement of a problem and then move to a solution.
- Question/Answer
  A question/answer structure generally begins with a question and moves to an answer.
- Cause/Effect
  A cause/effect structure can begin with a cause and then move to an effect, or reverse that order. It can also describe a sequence in which one thing causes another, which in turn causes something else.

¶ **34r**

Many paragraphs use not just one of the above structures, but a combination of structures. For example, in a single paragraph Joan Didion describes the "insularity," or isolation, of the people in California's Central Valley; illustrates her point with a short narrative; and at the end, includes an ironic contrast of Modesto and Merced.

U.S. 99 in fact passes through the richest and most intensely cultivated agricultural region in the world, a giant outdoor hothouse with a billion-dollar crop. It is when you remember the Valley's wealth that the monochromatic flatness of its towns takes on a curious meaning, suggests a habit of mind some would consider perverse. There is something in the Valley mind that reflects a real indifference to the stranger in his air-conditioned car, a failure to perceive even his presence, let alone his thoughts or wants. An implacable insularity is the seal of these towns. I once met a woman in Dallas, a most charming and attractive woman accustomed to the hospitality and social hypersensitivity of Texas, who told me that during the four war years her husband had been stationed in Modesto, she had never once been invited inside anyone's house. No one in Sacramento would find this story remarkable ("She probably had no relatives there," said someone to whom I told it), for the Valley towns understand one another, share a peculiar spirit. They think alike and they look alike. *I* can tell Modesto from Merced, but I have visited there, gone to dances there; besides, there is over the main street of Modesto an arched sign which reads:

topic sentence appears beside "is the seal of these towns."

narrative appears beside the passage beginning "pitality and social hypersensitivity."

contrast appears beside "to dances there; besides, there is over the main street of Mo-"

WATER—WEALTH

CONTENTMENT—HEALTH

There is no such sign in Merced. (Joan Didion, "Notes from a Native Daughter," *Slouching Toward Bethlehem*)

(3) Arranging details

A well-structured paragraph or block of paragraphs, no matter what its purpose, contains details that require a systematic arrangement. Usually, the best strategy is a progressive order—spatial, chronological, climactic, general to particular, or particular to general. An order, however, should not be so constrictive that it forces information into an artificial mold. Instead, the order should direct the flow of ideas, provide control over details, and help the reader understand how one point leads to the next. In this paragraph on an ant colony, for example, Lewis Thomas, moves naturally from small components to the whole.

Still, there it is. A solitary ant, afield, cannot be considered to have much of anything on his mind; indeed, with only a few neurons strung together by fibers, he can't be imagined to have a mind at all, much less a thought. He is more like a ganglion on legs. Four ants together, or ten, encircling a dead moth on a path, begin to look more like an idea. They fumble and shove, gradually moving the food toward the Hill, but as though by blind chance. It is only when you watch the dense mass of thousands of ants, crowded together around the Hill, blackening the ground, that you begin to see the whole beast, and now you observe it thinking, planning, calculating. It is an intelligence, a kind of live computer, with crawling bits for its wits. (Lewis Thomas, "On Societies as Organisms," *Lives of a Cell*)

The following traditional orders suit different types of material.

¶
34r

- Spatial Order
  In paragraphs with a spatial order, the details of a specific space are arranged so that readers get a visual impression of it. The arrangement can follow the movement of the eye up, down, across, or around.
- Chronological Order
  Chronological order presents a sequence in time, arranging events in the order in which they take place.
- Climactic Order
  The climactic order moves from material of lesser importance to that of greater importance, from smaller components to larger, from the less dramatic to the more dramatic.
- General-to-Particular Order
  General-to-particular order conforms to the traditional paragraph in which the topic sentence, or general statement, appears first and is followed by support, or particular details.
- Particular-to-General Order
  Particular-to-general order begins with specifics and moves to a general statement. This order is natural when the writer wishes to postpone the topic sentence until the end of the paragraph.

☐ EXERCISE 7

Suggest strategies that you could use to develop the following subjects into paragraphs or blocks.

1. The expense of owning a dog
2. The monotony of American motels
3. American beer versus imported beer
4. Types of parents
5. The consequences of sleeping late
6. T-shirt messages

7. The problems of working students
8. A tour of your hometown
9. Effective excuses
10. The appeal of professional wrestling

34s Drafting Introductory Paragraphs

The introduction to a paper makes a commitment to the audience by establishing the subject as well as the purpose and voice. In other words, the introduction tells the audience what to expect throughout the rest of the paper. A typical introductory paragraph states or implies the thesis that the paper will support, making the point of the paper clear to the audience from the start. In the following example, the final sentence is the thesis of the entire article.

> Some call it the Dawn of a New Computer Age. Others call it the Post-Industrial Revolution. Still others call it the Age of Knowledge. Whatever the name, computers have entered another period of change in which they will be transformed, not simply improved. During the next decade or so, computers will be constructed differently and will operate differently. Most importantly, they will begin to reason and apply logic. These developments will not merely produce a dramatic change in the role of computers worldwide; they will cause a dramatic effect on society as well. (Deb Highberger and Dan Edson, "Intelligent Computing Era Takes Off," *Computer Design*)

Introductions also frequently put a subject into perspective by placing it within a larger context. For example, in an introduction to a piece on aerial acrobatics, a student writer begins with the origins of flight and then narrows the focus.

> When Orville Wright first flew in 1903, the problem was staying in the air; the first successful flight lasted only twelve minutes. To direct the plane right or left, he had to move his hips from side to side. Obviously, Wright's plane had little maneuverability. Early flights mainly moved straight ahead or wherever the winds blew the planes. Gradually, improved technology contributed speed, distance, and control. Finally, daredevils were inspired to try stunts. In 1913, a plane flew upside down. In 1914, a plane "looped the loop" one thousand times, did a tail spin, and flew inside a building. That was the beginning of aerial acrobatics.

There are many other strategies for introductory paragraphs—some brief and simple, others more complex. Whatever your strategy, remember that the introduction is the first thing the audience reads, and thus it should make a favorable impression. If you cannot think of a good start, try some of the techniques listed here, separately or in combinations.

¶
34s

- Describe a problem that the paper will address or solve.
- State a conflict that the paper will explore.
- Sketch the background of a subject.
- Give an overview of what the paper will cover.
- Surprise or shock the reader into attention.
- Identify how you became interested in a subject.
- Present the antithesis (the idea contrary to your thesis) in order to attack it.
- Define a key term.
- Relate an anecdote.
- Ask a question.
- Quote something appropriate.

☐ EXERCISE 8

Write introductions suitable for papers on two of the following subjects. If none of the subjects seem appealing, supply two of your own.

A proposal for changes in NFL rules
A formula for writing horoscopes and never being wrong
Folk remedies that work
The etiquette of coed dormitories
A classification of recreational vehicles by types of owners
Effective ways to fight depression
Types of television game shows
Body building: for men only?
Ridiculous Christmas presents
The expense of entertainment
Strange pets
Shopping by mail order catalog

34t Drafting Concluding Paragraphs

A paper should not end suddenly, as if the writer were interrupted and never returned to finish. Instead, it should come to a recognizable and logical stopping place. Papers sometimes end with the last frame in a time sequence, such as the last stage in a process or the final event in a narration. Other papers end with a concluding sentence or two. Still others end with fully developed paragraphs.

¶
34t

A typical paper begins with the thesis, or controlling idea, explores it in the body, and concludes by restating it. The major advantage of this structure is its clarity. The reader learns in the introductory paragraph what the point is, sees its development in the body of the paper, and is reminded of it again in the conclusion. In the following conclusion, the writer, without repeating the exact wording of the introduction, restates the paper's point—not only has technology made the detection of forgeries easier for criminologists, but also it has made the creation of forgeries easier for criminals.

> Detecting forgeries has moved from fingerprint powder and magnifying glasses to sophisticated analyses by such devices as ultraviolet light, infrared spectroscopy, and electrostatic detection apparatus. However, in a continuing contest with criminologists, criminals also are applying the technology, especially with copying machines and computer-generated documents. The important question is whether or not the technology of detection can keep pace with the technology of making forgeries.

While restatement is probably the most typical conclusion, many other strategies are possible. One or several of the following may be the appropriate choice.

- **Summarize the major points.**
- **Make a recommendation.**
- **End with a quotation.**
- **Warn readers against some action—or the lack of it.**
- **Make a forecast.**
- **Call for further study.**
- **Suggest applications for a study's findings.**

EXERCISE 9

Write a suitable conclusion for two of the following papers.

1. A paper that evaluates a current movie
2. A paper that develops the following controlling idea: Attitude affects one's success in school.
3. A paper that attempts to solve the problem of massive unemployment among young people
4. A paper on dictionaries and books of synonyms; the paper begins with Mark Twain's statement, "The difference between the almost right word and the right word is the difference between the lightening bug and the lightening."
5. A paper that contains evidence that acid rain is damaging our land and water life, eroding our structures, and even threatening our health

rev
34u

☐ Revising

Revising is an integral part of the writing process. Too often inexperienced writers neglect this task altogether or confuse it with proofreading for spelling and typographical errors. It is only through revising, however, that ragged drafts are transformed into a finished product.

Some writers correct and revise as they write. Others write very fast and revise the whole work afterward. Most writers, however, combine the two methods: they revise and correct glaring problems while drafting a paper and postpone careful examination until a draft is complete. Use whatever method suits you. But if possible, take a break before attempting to revise a draft you have just completed. You should find some mental or physical activity to divert your attention from the paper. This tactic helps you develop objectivity so that you can return to the manuscript as a reader rather than as the writer.

34u Checking Unity

In revising, a general rule is to begin, whenever possible, with the larger structures and then move gradually to smaller structures. This "rule" particularly applies when you check a paper's unity. First, you should look at the unity of the overall structure and then at the unity of each paragraph. Unless your paper is unified around a clear thesis, or controlling idea, there is little point in reorganizing the details that make up the paragraphs.

Is the thesis clear?

If the paper has no clear thesis, you will have to find one to pull the details together. And then you will have to structure the draft so that the thesis is apparent to readers. In the unlikely event that you cannot discover a thesis for your material, you will have to return to "Getting Ideas" (p. 336) and begin again.

Does everything in the paper relate directly to the thesis?

One of the best ways to check the overall structure is to construct an outline or to reexamine an already existing one. An outline can reveal places where a paper has diverged from its thesis. If any part of the draft might distract the reader from the thesis or is obviously irrelevant to your subject, get rid of it. Notice how the student writer of the composition-in-progress (Chapter 35) abandoned material as the paper progressed from draft to draft.

Does each paragraph have unity?

The parts of a unified paragraph should develop a single idea. A paragraph with a topic sentence expressing the central idea is less likely to contain extraneous details than a paragraph without a stated topic sentence. When you revise your paper on the paragraph level, first locate each paragraph's topic sentence or determine the central idea. Then delete any material that is unimportant or irrelevant.

34v Checking Development

Development refers to the way a whole composition or a single paragraph elaborates a thesis or topic. If an idea is developed, it is supported by a sufficient number of details, examples, illustrations, or reasons. During revision, check for the presence of these specifics.

The length of compositions or paragraphs is not a reliable indication of how well ideas are developed. A fairly long unit containing nothing but general statements usually lacks development. The same is true of a unit with irrelevant details that stray from the purpose or distort logic.

Does the paper contain enough information to develop the thesis?

Check your introduction. Does it claim that you will discuss more than your paper delivers? If you find the information in the body insufficiently developed, you can produce more ideas with tactics such as brainstorming, clustering, and asking questions. Or you can gather additional material through research—reading, interviewing, or observing.

Is each paragraph fully developed?

As you check each body paragraph, look for the topic sentence. If a topic sentence is not stated, think of what it would be. Then ask yourself if your reader would accept or understand the statement. If there is the least chance the reader would not, you probably should add supporting or explanatory information.

34w Achieving Coherence

Coherence in prose refers to a smooth and logical arrangement of the parts. Sometimes coherence is spontaneous, with the flow of ideas creating a natural sequence. More often, however, this spontaneity does not occur, and you must work to interlock the pieces smoothly and logically. The task requires the effective arrangement of the paragraphs as well as adequate connection between sentences and paragraphs. Checking your draft against the following questions will help you find weaknesses and achieve coherence.

Is the overall organization effective?

You may want to rearrange paragraphs to achieve the most logical or effective order of information. This procedure is sometimes called "cutting and pasting" and, in fact, is frequently accomplished in just this way. You can cut your paper into paragraphs and glue or tape them on paper in the desired order. Or you can write each paragraph on a separate page and then work out the best arrangement.

And, of course, if you work on a word processor, you can move whole blocks of the draft around with ease. If you have trouble deciding on the best order, you might try writing alternative outlines to see which seems most effective.

Is the organization within paragraphs effective?

Once you are satisfied with the overall scheme and the ordering of the major pieces of a paper, turn your attention to the individual paragraphs. You can treat each piece as a "mini-composition" and determine whether its structure is an effective vehicle for the information and purpose. If you are not satisfied with the structures, look over the methods suggested for organizing paragraphs in "Drafting the Composition," page 352.

Is there adequate connection between sentences and paragraphs?

After revising the arrangement of the sections, attend to the coherence between sentences and paragraphs. This kind of internal coherence is established by "links" such as the following:

- **Pronouns that refer to previous antecedents or ideas and thus help prevent repetition**

  See Chapter 2, "Pronouns."

- **Conjunctions that show the relationship between ideas**

  See 6b, "Conjunctions"; 33a.1, "Combining Independent Clauses Through Coordination"; 33a.3, "Subordinating with Adverb Clauses"; and 33a.4, "Subordinating with Adjective Clauses."

- **Transitional expressions that point to what precedes or what follows, thus indicating the relationship between sentences and paragraphs.**

  For a complete list, see TRANSITIONAL EXPRESSION in the "Glossary of Grammatical, Rhetorical, and Literary Terms."

34x Improving Style

Improving the style of a composition involves two processes: (1) ensuring that the choice of words and structures is appropriate to the purpose and audience and (2) getting rid of choppy or monotonous prose as well as awkward structures that make writing difficult to follow. The questions that follow will help you examine your prose style. The discussion under each question refers you to other sections of this text designed to address specific stylistic problems.

Is the style suitable for the purpose and audience?

If your purpose is to entertain, inspect your "delivery," that is, the timing of the sentences and the entertainment value of the vocabulary. On the other hand, if your purpose is to inform, choose vocabulary and phrasing primarily for clarity. With some audiences and purposes, you will choose informal vocabulary and sentence structure, so that you seem to be conversing with your readers. With other audiences and purposes, you will keep your distance by choosing formal words and structures. See 32c, "Formal and Informal Words"; 32a, "Considering the Purpose"; 32b, "Identifying the Audience"; and 32c, "Finding a Voice."

rev
34x

Is your prose choppy or monotonous?

When there is too little variety in the lengths, structures, and beginnings of sentences, prose will be choppy or monotonous. "Choosing Structures" can help you overcome these stylistic problems. See particularly 33a, "Varying Sentence Lengths, Structures, and Beginnings," and 33b, "Achieving Emphasis."

Are your sentences cluttered or weak?

Cluttered or weak sentences can result from both word choice and structure choice. To understand the origin of these problems and to find some solutions, consult 32e, "Clichés"; 32g "Euphemisms"; 32j, "Surplus Words"; 32b, "Dense Noun Phrases"; 33b, "Achieving Emphasis"; and 33c, "Streamlining Prose."

Is the meaning of your sentences clear?

The individual words in a sentence can obscure meaning either by being too vague or by clouding ideas with jargon and gobbledygook. Structures can also obscure meaning by creating unwieldy sentences difficult to comprehend. To clarify prose with effective choices of words and structures, see 32a, "General and Specific Words"; 32b,

"Abstract and Concrete Words"; 32c, "Denotation and Connotation"; 32h, "Jargon and Technical Words"; 32i, "Gobbledygook"; and 33c, "Streamlining Prose."

34y Editing Grammar, Punctuation, and Mechanics

rev
34y

Even when a reader understands your meaning, errors in grammar, punctuation, and mechanics are distracting; they undercut the merit of your composition. You are not likely to locate these errors with a superficial reading. When you read, your eyes jump from phrase to phrase; but when you edit, you must use some sort of scheme for focusing on every word and structure. Slow your reading down, and control your eyes by reading the manuscript aloud or out of sequence.

Are there any structural errors?

Structural errors result if phrases and clauses are not put together correctly. If you need help in editing for these errors, refer to the Table of Contents and the Index to locate discussion of such structural problems as sentence fragments, comma splices, dangling modifiers, and split constructions.

Are there any errors in the forms of words?

Nouns, pronouns, adjectives, adverbs, and verbs have a variety of forms that change or add meaning. After you have checked for structural errors, read your manuscript again to inspect the forms of individual words. This stage of the revising process involves shifting attention back and forth from individual words to the larger structures in which they fit. For example, to decide on the form of a pronoun, you must determine the case required by the sentence structure. For help in correcting the forms of words, refer to the Table of Contents and the Index for discussion of nouns, pronouns, apostrophes, adjectives, adverbs, and verbs.

Are punctuation marks and mechanics correct?

It is not usually productive to edit for punctuation and mechanical errors until fairly late in the writing process. Structures will likely change from draft to draft, and many sentences will be deleted during revision. There is no point in laboring over punctuation and mechanics until you have decided definitely on content and structure. When you have reached this stage, survey the conventions in Chapters 21 through 31.

Are there any spelling errors?

Checking for spelling errors requires reading so slowly that your eyes fall on each individual word. A trick long used by typists is to read backward, word by word. Be alert for those words that frequently cause problems—words such as *receive, occurred,* and *truly.* If you become sensitive to problem words, you can take special care to spell them correctly.

**rev
34y**

Composition-in-Progress

In this chapter, a composition is shown in all its stages of development. It represents one student's efforts from an initial freewriting through the generation of ideas, a rough outline, and several drafts. The assignment was to write in one week a 300- to 500-word composition on any subject, addressed to a general reader. Thus, the writer was relieved of making decisions about audience but was faced with finding a subject, a purpose, a voice, and a structure.

Notice that once the writer found a subject, it did not change. Its development from draft to draft, however, changed radically. Also, notice that not until the third draft did a definite purpose, voice, and structure emerge.

The student began this assignment by freewriting these notes in ten minutes.

> I don't know what to write about. This
> better work. I have a math test to study
> for. What can I eat tonight that would
> taste different? I've had it with greasy
> hamburgers, pizza, and fried chicken
> from take-out places. I need vegetables.
> Not those institutional vegetables. Like
> those green peas that look like shriveled
> marbles. Maybe if I cleaned this place
> up, it would help me think. The thing
> that would really help me think is if

that radio down the hall wasn't blasting my ear drums. Why is it that people with loud radios never consider whether everyone in ten blocks wants to hear the same music?

It's going to snow. Snow is nice when it first falls. But when it turns brown and slushy it isn't nice. It isn't romantic. It isn't a Hollywood set. It's just wet and cold.

I think I have "Math anxiety." I keep having that dream about math class. People say it's common, that dream where you have a math Test and you haven't been to class in weeks. Or maybe never. And you wander around a strange building looking for your classroom.

**comp
35**

Looking back over the freewriting exercise, the writer saw a possible subject in the question *Why is it that people with loud radios never consider whether everyone in ten blocks wants to hear the same music?* This question prompted the writer to think about the subject "background noise." Viewing background noise as a problem, the writer then asked some of the logical questions associated with problems and roughed out some answers.

What causes it?

Maybe fear of silence? Radios. Television. Stereos. Canned music.

Whom does it affect?

Me. Almost everyone in America. Families. Shoppers.

What does it affect?

Relaxation. Nerves. Stress.

Where does it occur?

Homes. Grocery stores. Department stores. Telephones. Restaurants. Elevators. Public recreation areas. Dormitories.

What is a possible solution?

Maybe education about the dangers of too much noise. Maybe

in health education classes. An individual can get away to
the country sometime to escape the noise.

What would life be like without the problem?

We could hear the sounds of nature. The normal sounds of
the city. We could relax.

The material generated by the questions and answers led to this
working outline.

1. Background noise in the home

    television

    stereos

2. Background noise outside the home

    Muzak (canned music) in stores and businesses

    radios in public areas

3. Life without background noise

Writing rapidly, without concern for grammar, spelling, or
mechanics, the writer then produced the following rough draft from
the working outline.

FIRST DRAFT

American society seems to be obsessed with background   *potential thesis*
noise. Most households have at least one television set that
plays whether anyone is watching. And many households have
several television sets that run constantly. In addition,   *details supporting
families with teenagers usually have the burden of loud stereos   obsession with
that compete with the television for your attention.   noise*

But background noise is not confined to homes.
Businesses like grocery stores, department stores, and
resterants have piped in Muzak that plays constantly in the
background. Also, individuals bring their radio to public
recreation areas and play pop music that everyone else must
listen to, whether they want to or not. It seems that if a sound
system is not provided, people bring their own.

It seems that Americans fear silence. But would life   *potential thesis*
without background music be so bad? Without the constant

blaring of local radio stations, we might be able to tune in the
sounds of nature and everyday life. We could hear the quiet
sounds of the woods, the sounds of the country side, the bustle
of the city, the sounds of children at play. We could tune into   *potential thesis*
life instead of radio and television.

comp
35

    This first draft is rather unimpressive. There are three potential
theses, and the composition lacks enough concrete details to catch a
reader's attention. Nevertheless, the draft was certainly productive. It
started the writer thinking about the subject and generating a few
potential theses, or controlling ideas.

    You will notice that the first draft has errors and misspelled
words. At this stage, however, editing for grammar and mechanics
would be a waste of time. Instead, the writer set the draft aside,
reread it the next day, and made several decisions: (1) to deal only
with music, not all background noise; (2) to expand the middle section with concrete details; (3) to expand the first idea in the third
paragraph (fear of silence) into an introduction; and (4) to expand
the description of the sounds of nature and everyday life. The second
draft incorporated these changes.

SECOND DRAFT

    Our world is filled with uncertainties and dangers, so
many that most people suffer from all kinds of fears. Some
people fear cancer; some, nuclear war; some lonliness; some,
not succeding in life. What it comes to is that people fear what
may lay ahead as an obstacle to a long and happy life. All these
fears are legitimate, I think. But there is one fear that has   *potential thesis*
swept over our country that is not only ridiculous but is
driving me crazy. The fear of one waking moment without
background music.

    Call a business and let the receptionist put you on hold;
you will be treated to a tune that sounds like a combination of
"My Beautiful Balloon" and Lawrence Welk playing a fox trot.   *details—types of*
Go the the track to jog and someone will have brought their   *background noise*

radio blaring pop music for your listening pleasure. Stop at a
traffic light in the summertime. Some person in the lane next
to you will have his car radio on so high that you could not
hear an eighteen wheeler bearing down on you from 30 feet
away. Go to a swimming pool to relax in the sun. Stereo
speakers will blast your brain with music to go crazy by.
Babies for a 10-mile radius will wake screaming from their
afternoon naps, while mothers of babies will tear their hair.
Go out for a solitery lunch during exam week and try to cram
in a few last minutes of study over your hamburger. Someone
will put dozen coins in the juke box and start a series of
country and western tunes that will wail the material you've
learned right out of your head. Or a grocery store; the Muzak
makes you feel as if you should be skating rather than walking
through the aisles.

Where did this fear of silence come from? There was a
time when people could tell where they were just from the
sounds around them. In the woods, birds chirped, crickets
sang, frogs croaked, creeks babbled. In the fields, cattle
bellowed or tractors chugged. In the suburbs, weed eaters
whirred and backyard cooks called to each other from patio to
patio. In the city horns honked, taxi drivers swore, subways
roared.

*details—
description of life
in the past.*

But no more. I know the Constitution garantees us
freedom of speech. But I don't believe it garantees freedom of
noise.

Although the second draft is much better than the first, it has a
number of problems. The introductory material on fear (which contains a potential thesis) is never developed, only mentioned briefly
again at the beginning of the fourth paragraph. Furthermore, the
voice in the introduction seems to change from serious to light.

In addition, the concrete details in the second paragraph have
no logical organization, and they are made somewhat vague by the

use of the indefinite *you*. The conclusion has no tight connection with the rest of the composition. And generally, the purpose and the structure are not clear.

The writer decided not to edit for grammar and mechanics at this point but to set the composition aside once again. Coming back later to the second draft, the writer made an important decision: to abandon the idea of fear and begin with the idea that in the past, people could hear the sounds of nature and life around them. This decision had several positive effects. It got rid of the weak introduction and the overly serious tone at the beginning. And it provided a "hook" for the conclusion: the last sentence of the next draft hooks back to the first sentence. Most significantly, the decision led the writer to a thesis: Today, people cannot hear the sounds of life and nature because of constant background music. The thesis suggested an overall chronological structure for the paper—what was in the past; what is in the present.

Another change vastly improved the composition. The writer condensed all the examples in the body of the paper into an "average day" and used a narrative in the first person (*I*). This change got rid of the vague *you* and gave chronological structure to the disjointed details. It also allowed an extension of the details to include a thwarted hiking trip—something personal and not generalized. The use of the first person allowed the writer to develop the subject in a consistent voice: the narrator is frustrated, but not irate. The purpose and structure are also clear: to inform the reader of the problem, using the "average day" as illustration.

**comp
35**

Third Draft

There was a time when people could tell where they were just from the variety of sounds around them. In the woods, birds chirped, crickets sang, frogs croaked, creeks babbled. In the countryside, cattle bellowed, tractors chugged, roosters crowed. In the suburbs, dogs barked, weed eaters whirred, and backyard cooks called to each other from patio to patio. In the city, horns honked, drivers swore, subways roared. Public parks rang with splashes of kids belly flopping in the pool, the twang of tennis rackets, the creaking of swings and see-saws.

introductory paragraph on sounds of the past

But no longer are our days filled with these sounds. That *statement of thesis*
rich variety of sounds is now masked and our lives are filled
with three audio backdrops: Muzak, country and western, and
pop music. This revelation came to me during an average day
last summer.

Early in the morning, I went to the track to jog and think *thesis supported with an illustration*
peaceful thoughts. Someone had brought a radio blaring pop
music for my listening pleasure. I went to the grocery store:
the Muzak made me feel as if I should have been skating rather
than walking down the aisles. On the way from the grocery
store, I stopped at a traffic light. In the lane next to me, a
high school boy had his car radio turned up so high that I
would have been unable to hear an eighteen wheeler bearing
down on me from 30 feet away. I went to a swimming pool to
relax in the sun, stereo speakers blasted my brain with music
to go crazy by. Babies for a 10-mile radius surely must have
waked crying from their afternoon naps, while their mothers
groan in frustration. I left the pool and went home to my little
brother and his friends glued to a television rock video
pulsating noise for several blocks around. I fled to my room
and called a local employment office to check on my job
applications. The receptionist put me on hold; I was treated to
a tune that sounded like Lawrence Welk playing "My Beautiful
Balloon." I went out for a hamburger, and the juke box was
playing pop music so loud that the waitress had to read lips to
take orders.

That night I determined to find some peace and quiet for
at least a few hours. So the next day, I got my hiking gear and
took off to the woods to rest my ears. After a few miles, I
approached the spot where I used to sit and read to the quiet
sounds of nature. But the woods were cleared, and
construction workers were building a house, hammering and
sawing to the rythms of a country and western station. Just
over the hill, a family in a camper had brought along a radio
that could pick up rock stations from Radio Free Europe.

Sadly, I walked back to my car. Wondering whether there was any escape for me in a society full of music addicts.

The mystery I am unable to solve is this: Do the people who insist on providing me with this constant background music think they are doing me a favor? Or do they feel that their own desires take precedence over the desires of others? Or is it simply that they don't want to know where they are?

conclusion "hooking" back to first sentence

Looking over the third draft, the writer found problems with the thesis: "That rich variety of sounds is now masked and our lives are filled with three audio backdrops: Muzak, country and western, and pop music." First, the metaphor is illogical; lives are not filled with backdrops. Second, the thesis suggests a three-pronged organization that is not forthcoming. The writer simplified the thesis to read "That rich variety of sounds is now masked by constant background music."

Now satisfied that the composition had a clear thesis, an appropriate voice, and a logical structure, the writer revised the paper sentence by sentence—correcting errors and improving style. The following is a final draft, complete with a title.

A Search for Silence

There was a time when people could tell where they were just from the variety of sounds around them. In the woods, birds chirped, crickets sang, frogs croaked, creeks babbled. In the countryside, cattle bellowed, tractors chugged, roosters crowed. In the suburbs, dogs barked, weed eaters whirred, and backyard cooks called to each other from patio to patio. In the city, horns honked, drivers swore, subways roared. Public parks rang with splashes of kids belly-flopping in the pool, the twang of tennis rackets, the creaking of swings and seesaws.

But no more. That rich variety of sounds is now masked by constant background music. This revelation came to me during an average day last summer.

insertion of revelation clarifies a vague this

Early in the morning, I went to the track to jog and think peaceful thoughts. Someone had brought a radio blaring pop

new thesis that more accurately predicts subject matter

music for my listening pleasure. I went to the grocery store: the Muzak made me feel as if I should have been skating rather than walking down the aisles. On the way from the grocery store, I stopped at a traffic light. In the lane next to me, a high school boy had his car radio turned up so high that I would have been unable to hear an eighteen-wheeler bearing down on me from 30 feet away. I went to a swimming pool to relax in the sun. Stereo speakers blasted my brain with music to go crazy by. Babies for a 10-mile radius surely must have waked crying from their afternoon naps, while their mothers groaned in frustration. I left the pool and went home to my little brother and his friends glued to a television rock video pulsating noise for several blocks around. I fled to my room and called a local employment office to check on my job applications. The receptionist put me on hold; I was treated to a tune that sounded like Lawrence Welk playing "My Beautiful Balloon." I went out for a hamburger, and the jukebox was playing pop music so loud that the waitress had to read lips to take orders.

That night I determined to find some peace and quiet for at least a few hours. So the next day, I got my hiking gear and took off to the woods to rest my ears. After a few miles, I approached the spot where I used to sit and read to the quiet sounds of nature. But the woods were cleared, and construction workers were building a house, hammering and sawing to the rhythms of a country and western station. Just over the hill, a family in a camper had brought along a machine that could pick up rock stations from Radio Free Europe. Sadly, I walked back to my car, wondering whether there was any escape for me in a society of music addicts.

The mystery I am unable to solve is this: Do people who insist on providing me with this constant background music think they are doing me a favor? Or do they feel that their own desires take precedence over the desires of others? Or is it simply that they don't want to know where they are?

comma splice corrected

tense shift corrected

spelling error (pulssating) corrected

spelling error (rythms) corrected

repetition of radio eliminated

sentence fragment attached to preceding sentence

comp 35

Glossary of Usage and Commonly Confused Words

This glossary provides a brief guide for commonly confused words and phrases, such as *illusion, delusion; ensure, insure; differ from, differ with.* In addition, the glossary serves as a guide for usage, that is, the acceptable use of words and phrases. Usage is sometimes determined by clarity and logic but other times merely by the preferences of influential writers and language experts. Thus, usage is subject to controversy and to change. The advice here is based on information found in current dictionaries and usage guides. However, you should bear in mind that some readers—your instructor, for example—may occasionally have other preferences.

A, An
Use *a* before words with an initial consonant sound; use *an* before words with an initial vowel sound. Remember that the sound, not the letter, controls your choice: *a thought, an idea; a heel, an honor; a unicorn, an uncle; a "k," an "s."*

Accept, Except
Accept is a verb that generally means "to receive something or someone willingly" or "to believe": *We accept your terms. Jefferson accepted the ideas of deism. Except* is usually a preposition meaning "with the exclusion of" or a conjunction (often coupled with *that*) meaning "if it were not for the fact that": *The walls of every room except the kitchen were decorated with silk screens. He is fairly well qualified for the position except that he has no experience in public relations.*

Adverse, Averse
Adverse usually describes some position or thing that is hostile or antagonistic: *adverse criticism, adverse reaction, adverse publicity, adverse re-*

port. Adverse can also refer to something unfavorable or harmful: *The pio-neers struggled against the adverse conditions of the Rocky Mountain winter. Antibiotics kill infection but can have an adverse effect on the digestive system.*

Averse is part of the idiom *averse to,* which describes someone who dislikes or opposes something: *The Mormans are averse to any kind of artificial stimulant. The editorial board, averse to all Democratic candi-dates, used the magazine as a Republican forum.*

Advice, Advise

Advice is a noun, with the *c* pronounced as an /s/ sound: *Your advice is welcome. Advise* is a verb, with the *s* pronounced as a /z/ sound: *We advise beginning students to take BASIC.*

Affect, Effect

Affect is usually a verb that means "to influence" or "to bring about a change": *The weather often affects our emotions.* Sometimes *affect* is a verb meaning "to pretend": *Although he was actually from Wisconsin, Gibbs affected a British accent.* The use of *affect* as a noun is confined to psychology, where it refers to a feeling or an emotion as opposed to a thought or action: *Although he denied feeling guilty, his affect was re-vealed in his blushing and stammering.*

Effect is usually a noun that means "a result": *The prolonged cold spell had a devastating effect on the citrus crop.* As a noun, *effect* is also used in idioms like *take effect* and *come into effect: The drug should take effect within two hours. When will the new regulations come into effect?* But *effect* occasionally is used as a verb meaning "to bring about": *Her efforts effected a change.*

Aggravate, Irritate

In formal English, the verb *aggravate* means "to make worse," "to make more troublesome or more serious": *Unusually heavy traffic aggravated the deterioration of the bridge pilings. The star's frequent lateness aggra-vated the tension among the cast members.* Irritate means "to annoy," "to exasperate," "to provoke": *Khrushchev's behavior at the U.N. irritated the Western delegates.*

Informally, some people use *aggravate* for *irritate: The dog's con-stant barking aggravated the neighbors.* This usage, however, is not ac-ceptable to many readers and should be avoided in formal writing.

Agree to, Agree with, Agree on *or* about

Used with *to, agree* means "to give consent": *The board agreed to hear the evidence on Friday.*

Agree with usually indicates accord: *He agreed with the philosophy of the transcendentalists. Agree with* can also refer to health or constitution: *Mexican food doesn't agree with many people. The desert air agrees with me.*

With *on* or *about, agree* indicates a coming to terms: *We agreed on a meeting in May. The judges could not agree about the criteria for evaluating the contestants.*

All, All of

Before nouns, especially in written English, *all* is appropriate: *All the circuits were busy. In all the excitement, I forgot where I parked the car.* However, *all of* is also acceptable: *All of the circuits. . . . In all of the excitement. . . .*

Before pronouns or proper nouns, *all of* is required: *All of us were embarrassed. In all of Europe, the plague raged.*

In the subject position, *all* takes a singular verb when the meaning is "everything": *All is forgiven. All* takes a plural verb when referring to individuals in a group: *All were refunded their money.*

All Ready, Already

All ready is pronounced with a distinct pause between the two words and means "everything or everyone in a state of readiness": *The floral arrangements were all ready for delivery. The swimmers were all ready to begin the competition.*

The single word *already* means "previously," "by this or that time," "before this or that time": *By the time dinner was served, some of the guests had already left. By January, local hotels are already booked for the summer.*

All Right

All right should always be written as two words, not run together as *alright.*

All That

Do not use *all that* in formal writing to imply comparison: *The movie was not all that bad.*

All Together, Altogether

The two-word phrase *all together* means "all at one time," "all in one place," "collectively": *They were standing all together against the menace. The students were housed all together in one run-down barracks. Altogether* means "completely," "with all counted," or "with everything considered": *Over the years fifteen engineers altogether struggled with the bridge's construction. These statistics are not altogether accurate. Altogether, I wish I had never met the man.*

Allusion, Delusion, Illusion

The noun *allusion* comes from the verb *allude,* which means "to make an indirect reference to something or someone." Thus, *allusion* means "an indirect reference" or "a hint": *Although she was never specific, she made a vague allusion to something sinister in his past.*

Deriving from the verb *delude,* which means "to mislead deliberately and harmfully," *delusion* means "a deception": *Her innocence was a delusion she cultivated cunningly.*

The noun *illusion* has no corresponding verb form. It means "a false perception of reality": *Alan Ladd's stature was an illusion; he usually stood on a box to kiss his leading lady.*

usage

Almost, Most

Most has three basic functions.

- As an adjective, *most* is the superlative of *many* and *much.* In this capacity, *most* refers to the greatest in number, quantity, intensity, degree, or size.
- As a nominal, *most* also means "the largest number or part."
- As an adverb, *most* forms the superlative of many adjectives. *(She is the most truthful of my friends. This is the most alarming development in the crisis.)* Also, *most* is sometimes used like the adverbial intensifier *very. (This is a most unusual piece of music.)*

The adverb *almost* means "not quite," "very nearly." Obviously then, *most* and *almost* have no meanings in common. Thus, you should avoid substituting *most* for *almost: We go to San Francisco almost* [not *most*] *every year. Almost* [not *most*] *all the cement has dried.*

A Lot (of), Lots (of)

These expressions are informal substitutes for such words as *much, many, frequently: You're in a lot of trouble. We went to the movies a lot that summer. He uses lots of Tabasco in his chili. I miss you lots.*

Do not write *a lot* as one word *(alot).*

Among, Between

Many guides dictate the use of *between* only with two items or persons and *among* with more than two: *Rivalry between the two teams was intense. Rivalry among the three teams was intense.*

Nevertheless, the *Oxford English Dictionary,* the most scholarly of word collections in English, states, "In all senses *between* has been, from its earliest appearance, extended to more than two. . . . It is still the only word available to express the relation of a thing to many surrounding things severally and individually; *among* expresses a relation to them collectively and vaguely: we should not say 'the space lying *among* three points,' or 'a treaty *among* three powers,' or 'the choice lies *among* the three candidates in the select list,' or 'to insert a needle *among* the closed petals of a flower.'"

Between is also used with more than two when it refers to intervals occurring regularly: *Between dances, the boys stood around sweating and the girls combed their hair. I cannot stop eating between meals.* Certainly *among dances* and *among meals* would make very little sense.

Among is more properly used to suggest a relationship of someone or something to a surrounding group: *She lived among the natives for almost ten years. There is honor among thieves.*

Amount, Number

Amount should be used with mass nouns—that is, something that cannot be counted (or made plural), such as *noise, information, linen, mud: Judging from the amount of noise inside, we expected the movie to be outrageous. Number* should be used with count nouns—that is, things that can be counted (or made plural), such as *shrieks, statistics, handkerchiefs, rocks: Judging from the number of shrieks inside, we expected the movie to be outrageous.*

And Etc.

Etc. is an abbreviation for the Latin phrase *et cetera,* which means "and other (things)." Therefore, the expression *and etc.* is redundant. See also **Et Al., Etc.**

And/Or

Writers sometimes use *and/or* to indicate three options: *Merit is rewarded by promotion and/or salary increase* means that merit is rewarded (1) by promotion or (2) by salary increase or (3) by both. Some readers, however, object to the *and/or* device outside of legal, business, or technical writing. To be on the safe side, you can write out the options.

Ante-, Anti-/Ant-

Ante is Latin for "before" or "in front of." It serves as a prefix in English in such forms as *antebellum* ("before the Civil War") and *antechamber* ("a small room in front of, or entry to, a larger room"). *Anti/ant* comes from Greek, meaning "against" or "opposite," and serves as prefix in such forms as *antibiotic* ("against bacteria") and *antacid* ("opposing acid"). A hyphen after *anti-* can clarify reading when the root word begins with a capital letter *(anti-Truman)* or an *i (anti-intellectualism).*

Anxious, Eager

In conversation, *anxious* and *eager* are often used interchangeably: *I am eager to move into my new apartment. I am anxious to move into my new apartment.* Nevertheless, in formal situations, most usage experts recommend *anxious* to convey apprehension and *eager* to convey impatient desire: *The pilot was anxious about the high winds. The Senator was anxious to avoid scandal. An eager understudy waited in the wings. The fans were eager for victory.*

Any More, Anymore

The two-word phrase *any more* is used in questions and negatives to mean "some more" or "additional": *Are any more tests necessary to confirm the presence of radiation? The department has not hired any more clerks since 1984.*

The single word *anymore* is also used in questions and negatives. It means "presently" or "from now on" and can suggest (in questions) a continuation: *The deer aren't seen in the marshes anymore. Will the shop carry imported cheeses anymore?*

Any One, Anyone

The two-word phrase *any one* refers to any person, place, thing, idea, and so on. It is followed by *of* when it precedes a noun or pronoun: *Any one of the desks will serve our purposes. Any one of you is qualified to serve. Any one* may occur without *of* if its referent has been previously stated: *Four options are available. Choose any one.*

The single word *anyone* means "anybody"; it is never followed by *of* and does not precede nouns and pronouns: *Anyone with drive and a high-energy level can succeed.*

Anyplace/Anywhere

Anyplace is usually restricted to informal situations; *anywhere* is acceptable in both formal and informal English.

Any Way, Anyway, Anyways

The two-word phrase *any way* refers to any course or any direction: *They were trapped any way they turned. Anyway* means "nevertheless" or "regardless of circumstances": *The plot is weak, but the film succeeds anyway. Anyways* is a nonstandard variant of *anyway* and should be avoided.

As, Like

In informal situations, speakers often substitute *like* for the subordinate conjunctions *as, as if, as though* to introduce dependent clauses: *Unfortunately, he dances like he sings. It looks like it's going to rain.* But most usage experts agree that in formal situations *like* should not introduce dependent clauses; the *as* conjunctions are more appropriate: *In a democracy, the government acts as the people dictate. The speaker clutched her throat as if she were gasping for air.*

As to

As to occurs frequently in published prose, particularly in journalism: *The weather service kept residents posted as to the position of the hurricane. The mayor and city council members refused to make any comment as to whether the project would require higher taxes. We consulted an efficiency expert as to how to proceed.* In all cases, *about* may be substituted and probably sounds better.

Averse, Adverse (See Adverse, Averse.)

Awful, Awfully

Awful is an adjective meaning "fearsome," "awesome," or "great"; *awfully* is the adverb form of *awful: The dragon's awful roar shook the knight's confidence. The dragon roared awfully, shaking the knight's confidence.*

usage

Informally, some speakers use *awful* and *awfully* as intensifiers equivalent to *very: The children were awful [awfully] tired.* Such use, however, should be avoided in formal writing or speaking.

A While, Awhile

The two-word phrase *a while,* consisting of an article and a noun, functions as the object of a preposition: *After a while in the city, I began to long for the quiet nights of the country. They stopped for a while in a roadside park.* The single word *awhile,* an adverb, does not occur after a preposition: *The fire will smoke only awhile.*

Bad, Badly

Bad is properly an adjective and thus should modify nouns and pronouns: *We always have bad weather this time of year. This headache is a particularly bad one. Badly* is properly an adverb of manner and should modify verbs and verbals: *She performed the piece badly. The editor soon tired of reading badly written poems.*

Confusion between the two words often occurs after a linking verb in a subject complement position, typically after the verb *feel,* in a sentence such as *I feel badly about not calling my parents.* In this sentence, the position after *feel* is a subject complement position and should be filled with an adjective modifying *I,* not an adverb modifying *feel.* Thus, the correct usage is *I feel bad about not writing my parents often enough.*

Sports announcers frequently used *bad* for *badly* in such expressions as *He's playing bad today* and *He just threw the ball bad.* Standard usage is *playing badly* and *threw the ball badly.*

Beside, Besides

The preposition *beside* means "at the side of" *(she was seated beside the guest speaker)* or "compared with" *(my game looked shabby beside his expertise)* or "having nothing to do with" *(in this case, your opinion is beside the point).*

Besides can function as a preposition meaning "other than" *(Jamison had no ambition besides doing a good job)* or as an adverb meaning "moreover" *(the restaurant was too expensive; besides, the food was only mediocre).*

Be careful not to substitute *beside* for *besides: Besides* [not *beside*] *being lazy, the new secretary could not type.*

Between, Among (See Among, Between.)

Between You and I, Between You and Me

Because *between* is a preposition, it requires an objective case pronoun. Thus *between you and I* (or *he, she, they*) is incorrect. Use *between you and me* (or *him, her, them*).

Bring, Take

In standard English, both *bring* and *take* mean "to convey." However, *bring* suggests movement toward the speaker or focal point, whereas *take* suggests movement away from the speaker or focal point: *The teacher asked the students to bring a newspaper article to class. The governor took three antique chairs from the mansion when he left office.*

In some dialects, speakers use *bring* to mean "convey away from," as when one speaker says to another in the same location, *I'll bring you to work this morning.* This substitution, however, is not acceptable in formal English.

Bunch

Conversationally, *bunch* is frequently used to mean a group: *A bunch of guys went to the ball game.* In formal English *bunch* should refer only to things growing together in a cluster—like *a bunch of grapes.*

Burst, Bust

The standard verb *burst, burst, burst* usually means "to explode" or "to fly apart suddenly": *The tank burst.* In formal English, the verb *bust, busted, busted* is inappropriate for these meanings. However, *bust* is becoming fairly widespread in passive structures, when it means "to be arrested": *Three prominent citizens were busted on drug charges.*

But However, But Yet

In informal situations, speakers sometimes combine *but* with contrastive adverbs—possibly for emphasis: *He was practicing medicine, but yet he had never been to medical school.* Such combinations are not acceptable in formal English. Write, *By 1800, the French were satisfied with wound-*

ing an opponent, but [not *but however*] *American dueling practice still demanded death.*

But That, But What

Informally, writers sometimes introduce dependent clauses with *but that* and *but what* (particularly after a negative and the word *doubt*): *No one doubted but that* [or *what*] *Miss Marple would persevere.* In formal English, the proper connector is *that: No one doubted that Miss Marple would persevere.*

Can, May

Can indicates ability *(we can meet the deadline if we work the whole weekend)* or power *(a dean can overrule a department head). May* indicates permission *(you may invite three guests).* Generally, in formal writing, *can* should not replace *may.* In negative contractions, however, most usage experts accept *can't* for permission, since *mayn't* seems stilted and archaic: *You can't* [not *mayn't*] *be excused from the graduation exercises except in dire emergencies.* Also, many experts accept *cannot* for permission in negatives: *May I have this dance? No, you cannot.*

usage

Can't Help But

This rather common idiom is appropriate only in informal situations: *I can't help but wish I had kept my old Volkswagen bug.*

Capital, Capitol

Capital usually means "head," "very serious," "principal": *capital city, capital error.* It also refers to crimes involving the death sentence: *capital offense, capital punishment.* And in finance, *capital* refers to money or property, particularly that used for investment: *capital for the venture, capital gain, capital goods. Capitol* refers to the building in which a legislature meets.

Censor, Censure

The verb *censor* means "to examine material for immoral or harmful content" or "to ban material" for those reasons: *Some state school boards appoint committees to censor textbooks.* The verb *censure* means "to criticize, blame, or rebuke": *Admiral Stanley was censured for unnecessarily endangering the lives of his men.*

Center Around

Most usage experts prefer *revolve around* to *center around: The controversy revolves* [not *centers*] *around misappropriation of funds.* This notion rests on the argument that one thing cannot logically "center around" something else; thus *centers* is more properly followed by *on* or *in: The controversy centers on* [or *in*] *misappropriation of funds.* Nevertheless, language does not follow the logic of mathematics, and *center around* is widely used by many respectable writers.

Climactic, Climatic
Confusion of *climatic* and *climactic* is not a matter of usage but rather a matter of meaning. The adjective *climatic* refers to climate, to weather; the adjective *climactic* to climax, to a turning point or high point: *Fluctuations in the earth's orbit probably affect climatic conditions. My childhood was so uneventful that the climactic moment occurred when I was chosen a bus-patrol boy.*

usage

Complected, Complexioned
Complected is a regional variation of *complexioned: She was so fair-complected [fair-complexioned] that she used number fifteen sunscreen.* In formal situations, use *complexioned.*

Complement, Compliment
Complement derives from *complete;* thus the verb *complement* usually means "something that completes or perfects": *The oriental garden complemented the architecture of the house.* The verb *compliment* means "to praise or congratulate": *She complimented the photographer on his ability to capture mood.*

Comprise, Compose
Comprise means "to embrace," "to be made up of"; *compose* means "to make up the parts": *The bureau comprises five departments. Originally the Union comprised thirteen states. Five departments compose the bureau. Originally, thirteen states composed the Union.*

Conscience, Conscious
The noun *conscience* means "moral sensibility," "recognition of right and wrong": *How could you in good conscience use my money to pay your debts?* The adjective *conscious* means "aware" or "deliberate": *She was suddenly conscious of a shadowy figure ahead. I am certainly not guilty of a conscious insult.*

Consensus
Consensus comes from Latin *con* ("together") and *sentire* ("to think" or "to feel"). Thus *consensus of opinion* is considered by many to be redundant. In any case, the phrase has become a cliché and should be avoided. *Consensus* is sufficient.

Continual, Continuous

Careful writers distinguish between these two adjectives. Strictly speaking, *continual* indicates recurring actions, repeated regularly and frequently; *continuous* indicates something unceasing, occurring without interruption: *Continual irrigation of crops is dangerously lowering the water table. The continuous motion of the sea lulled me to sleep.*

Theodore Bernstein offers a mnemonic device for remembering the difference: "Continuous ends in *o u s,* which stands for *one uninterrupted sequence.*"

Convince, Persuade

In conversation, many speakers do not distinguish between *convince* and *persuade: My advisor convinced [persuaded] me to take a course in word processing.* In formal situations, however, careful writers use the following guidelines:

usage

- *Convince* means "to cause someone to believe something" and is properly followed by *of* or a clause beginning with *that* but never by an infinitive: *He convinced me of his sincerity. The doctors finally convinced James that diet was crucial to his health.*
- *Persuade* suggests action, "to cause someone to do something by reason or argument" and is usually followed by *to* or a clause beginning with *that: He persuaded me to get back on the horse. The recruiting officer persuaded her that she should enlist.*

Could have, Could of

Could of is a misrepresentation of the way *could have* sounds in running speech. Write *I could have left* (not *could of left*).

Credible, Creditable, Credulous

Credible means "believable," "plausible": *Her account of the day's events was too amusing to be credible. Creditable* usually means "deserving commendation": *Only one of the divers gave a creditable performance. Credulous* means "believing too readily," "gullible": *Lisa was too credulous to be a probation officer.* See also **Incredible, Incredulous.**

Data

Data is the plural of the Latin noun *datum,* which means "fact." Rarely do writers use the singular *datum;* instead they use a more familiar word, such as *fact, result, statistic.* But *data* is very commonly used, traditionally with a plural verb: *The data show that most voters in this area vote for the candidate rather than the party. The data are in question; therefore, we cannot accept the conclusions of the study.*

Increasingly, however, in technical writing, *data* is considered a mass noun like *information* and is used with a singular verb: *Our data proves that the oyster beds beyond 2 miles should not be harvested. The data is inconclusive.* Outside of technical writing, the safe route is to use a plural verb with *data.*

Device, Devise

Confusion between these two words is usually a matter of spelling. *Device,* the noun, is pronounced /dee viyce/ and means "a thing constructed for a specific purpose": *We need a device for holding the jack in place. Devise,* the verb, is pronounced /dee viyze/ and means "constructing an apparatus for some specific purpose": *She devised a scheme for undermining her partner's credibility.*

usage

Differ from, Differ with

The phrases are closely related, but *differ from* usually means "to be dissimilar," and *differ with* means "to disagree": *The two dialects differ from each other mainly in the pronunciation of vowels. Most experts differed with Jones's hypothesis.*

Discreet, Discrete

Discreet means "cautious," "unobtrusive," "tactful": *The Secret Service made discreet inquiries into Mark's background. Discrete* means "separate," "distinct": *The Language Institute and the university were two discrete entities.* To help avoid confusion, you can remember that the noun forms of the two adjectives are different: *discreet, discretion; discrete, discreteness.*

Disinterested, Uninterested

Correct usage of these two words has long been disputed. Apparently, the word *disinterested* originally meant "not interested" but later took on the additional meanings of "free from self-interest" and "altruistic." *Uninterested* originally meant "impartial" but later came to mean "not interested." The best solution to the current problem of usage is to follow conservative guides. Use *disinterested* to mean "impartial," "uninfluenced by thoughts of personal gain" and *uninterested* to mean "not interested": *Some couples have a disinterested party to negotiate prenuptial financial agreements. Acting uninterested in class is likely to irritate the instructor.*

Due to

Due to means "as a result of" or "caused by" and usually appears as a subject complement after the verb *be: Many cases of depression are due to chemical deficiencies. Due to* can also occur immediately after a noun in a kind of compressed clause: *Many cases of depression due to chemical deficiency go undetected.*

So many guides caution against the use of *due to* to mean "because of" that you are probably wise to avoid a construction such as *Due to advanced technology, contemporary ball players cannot realistically be compared to those of the past.* Write instead, *Because of advanced technology. . . .*

Due to the Fact That

This bureaucratic phrase is unnecessarily wordy; *because* is the better choice.

Each and Every

This phrase is one of the favorite clichés of politicians and hucksters. Use simply *each* or *every* but not both.

Eager, Anxious (See Anxious, Eager.)

Effect (See Affect, Effect.)

Emigrate, Immigrate

Immigrate means "to enter a country"; *emigrate* means "to leave." One *immigrates* to a place, but *emigrates* from it.

Ensure, Insure

Ensure means "to guarantee" or "to make safe": *Organic gardening will ensure that produce is safe to eat. Safety goggles will ensure the worker against eye injury. Insure* means "to protect against loss, damage, injury, etc.": *Our company will insure your home against loss due to flood, fire, and nuclear attacks.*

Enthused

Enthused has not been fully accepted, although it is often substituted for *enthusiastic.* Avoid *enthused* in formal prose: *Everyone on the staff was enthusiastic* [not *enthused*] *about the new "personal shopper" service.*

Et Al., Etc.

Et al. is the abbreviation for the Latin *et allii* or *et alliae,* meaning "and other people." This abbreviation is used in some documentation systems for citing books with more than two authors: *Yanella, D., et al. Etc.* is the abbreviation for *et cetera,* meaning "and other things." *Etc.* is common in business memos and some technical documents but not in formal or literary writing. When punctuating *etc.,* put a comma before it when more than one item precedes but not when only one item precedes: *Use only the honorific and the last name—Ms. Jones, Mr. Jones, Dr. Jones, etc. Dress out completely with pads etc.* See also **And Etc.**

Every Day, Everyday

The single word *everyday* means "common" or "used on ordinary days." *He came to the dinner party in everyday work clothes.* The phrase *every day* means "each day": *Mrs. Sommes went to the hairdresser every day.*

Every One, Everyone

The two-word phrase *every one* refers to every person, place, thing, idea, and so on. It is followed by *of* when it precedes a noun or pronoun: *Every one of the candidates has an image problem. Every one of these ancient civilizations had vanished by 500 B.C. Every one* can occur without *of* if its referent has been previously stated: *Four proposals were submitted, and every one called for a budget of over $500,000.*

The single word *everyone* means "everybody"; it is never followed by *of* and does not precede nouns and pronouns: *Everyone in the audience stood and cheered Ms. Gordon for over fifteen minutes.*

usage

Except, Accept (See Accept, Except.)

Except for the Fact That

Shorten this long, bureaucratic phrase to *except that.*

Explicit, Implicit

Explicit means "not implied or suggested but stated outright": *The job description was so explicit that it even prescribed height and weight requirements. Implicit* means just the opposite, "implied or suggested, not stated outright": *Implicit in the advertisement was the notion that waxing floors is a joyful experience.*

Farther, Further

Farther usually refers to distance; *further* usually means "in addition" or "additionally": *The mountains are farther away than they appear. Regular exercise promotes weight loss, and further, increases the energy level.*

Also, as a verb, *further* means "to help to progress": *Derrick would use any means available to further his career in Hollywood.*

Fewer, Less

Fewer is used with count nouns—nouns that can be counted and made plural: *fewer files, fewer paintings, fewer letters. Less* is used with mass nouns—nouns that cannot be counted or made plural: *less software, less art, less mail.*

Further, Farther (See Farther, Further.)

Good, Well

In formal English, *good* is always an adjective, appearing either before a noun or after a linking verb like *be, seem, look, feel, sound, smell, taste: The good food lifted our flagging spirits. The newly mowed grass smelled good. That hat looks good on you.*

Well functions as an adverb when it refers to the manner in which an action is performed: *She spoke German well. He hits the ball well but his concentration is not good. Well* functions as an adjective only when it refers to health. *Don't you feel well? Get well soon.*

Had Better

Had better means "ought to." In running speech, the *had* sometimes disappears but should never be omitted in writing, except in dialogue. Write *The cabinet had better* [not *better*] *be more responsive to foreign affairs and less to partisan politics.*

Had Ought To

Had ought to is nonstandard; instead, use *ought to. We ought to* [not *had ought to*] *send a housewarming gift.*

Half

You may write *a half* or *half a,* but most usage guides do not approve *a half a: My little cabin was only a half mile from the lake* [or *only half a mile from . . .*; not *only a half a mile from . . .*].

Hanged, Hung

In every sense but one, the correct forms of the verb *hang* are *hang, hung, hung.* However, in the sense of execution, the verb is *hang, hanged, hanged: The picture was hung. The traitor was hanged.*

Hardly

Because *hardly* has a negative meaning ("insufficiency"), it should not be used with another negative—particularly, with *can't* or *couldn't.* Instead of *can't hardly* or *couldn't hardly,* write *can hardly* or *could hardly.* Also, when *hardly* means "barely," a completing clause begins with *when,* not *than: Hardly had the class started when* [not *than*] *the alarm sounded.*

Healthful, Healthy

Healthy describes people, animals, plants, and economies in a state of good health. *Healthful* describes such things as climate or food that contribute to good health. Increasingly, writers use *healthy* for both senses, but a distinction between the terms often adds clarity.

Hisself

Never use *hisself,* a nonstandard variation of *himself.*

Historic, Historical

Historic narrowly means "making history"; *historical* means "relating to history." *Uncle Tom's Cabin* is a "historic" novel, which affected history. *Gone with the Wind* is a "historical" novel, which uses history as the setting.

Hopefully

Hopefully is a generally acceptable adverb meaning "full of hope": *We watched hopefully for a change in the weather.* Many people, however, object to its use as a sentence modifier meaning "it is hoped": *Hopefully the weather will change.* Logically this second use of *hopefully* makes as much sense as *fortunately, happily, regrettably,* or *certainly,* and according to *Webster's Ninth New Collegiate Dictionary,* has been in well-established use since 1932. But as the *American Heritage Dictionary* wisely points out, "This usage is by now such a bugbear to traditionalists that it is best avoided on grounds of civility, if not logic."

usage

If, Whether

In some sentences, *if* and *whether* are equally acceptable and clear: *I do not know if* [or *whether*] *the plan is feasible.* But in some sentences *if* is ambiguous, expressing either an alternative or a condition: *Tell me if they are late.* An alternative is more clearly expressed with *whether: Tell me whether they are late.* A condition is more clearly expressed when the *if* clause is moved to the front of the sentence: *If they are late, tell me.*

Illusion, Allusion, Delusion (See Allusion, Delusion, Illusion.)

Immigrate, Emigrate (See Emigrate, Immigrate.)

Implicit, Explicit (See Explicit, Implicit.)

Imply, Infer

Imply means "to suggest"; *infer* means "to arrive at a conclusion." Words and actions can imply meaning. From them, readers, listeners, and observers can infer meaning. *The toss of her head implied a defensive attitude. From the toss of her head, he inferred a defensive attitude.*

In, Into

Into rather than *in* more clearly shows movement from outside to inside: *The fumes seeped into the room.*

Incredible, Incredulous

Incredible describes something that is hard to believe; *incredulous* describes someone who is skeptical.

Infer, Imply (See Imply, Infer.)

In Regards to

To mean "in reference to," write *in regard to, with regard to, regarding,* or *as regards*—never *in regards to.*

Insure, Ensure (See Ensure, Insure.)

Into, In to

Into, written as one word, is a preposition: *into the water, into the room, into the matter.* Sometimes *in* is a part of a phrasal verb and is followed by the word *to.* Then, *in* and *to* are not joined: *She went in to check the temperature. Turn your papers in to me.*

usage

Irregardless, Regardless

Never write *irregardless* to mean *regardless: I am going regardless of the weather* [not *irregardless of the weather*].

Irritate, Aggrevate (See Aggrevate, Irritate.)

Is When, Is Where

When refers to time, and *where* refers to place. The words are misleading in contexts that do not have these meanings. For example, do not write *A hologram is when people use a laser to create a three-dimensional photograph.* Instead write *A hologram is a three-dimensional photograph produced by a laser.* Also, do not write *A quarterback sneak is where the quarterback, with the ball, plunges into the line.* Instead write *A quarterback sneak is a play in which the quarterback, with the ball, plunges into the line.*

Its, It's

The apostrophe in *it's* shows that the word is a contraction meaning "it is" or "it has." *Its,* like the other possessive personal pronouns that end in *s (hers, his, yours, ours, theirs),* contains no apostrophe. The form *its'* does not exist.

Kind of, Sort of

The expressions *kind of* and *sort of* to mean "somewhat" or "rather" are informal. Avoid them in formal writing: *The work was somewhat* [not *kind of*] *tedious.*

Kind of (a), Type of (a), Sort of (a)

The *a* should not appear in expressions such as *this kind of a book, this sort of a plan, this type of a day.*

Later, Latter

Later (pronounced /layt r/) refers to time; *latter* (pronounced /lat r/) means "the second of two."

Lay, Lie

The forms of these two verbs are

	To Lay (To Put or Place)	*To Lie (To Rest or Recline)*
Present	lay	lie
Past	laid	lay
Participles	laid, lying	lain, lying

usage

When *lay* (present tense of *lay*) means "put" or "place," it has an object: *Lay the cards on the table.* When *lay* (past tense of *lie*) means "reclined," it has no object and either has or could have the word *down* after it: *The dog lay [down] in the mud.* Write *The valuable diamond lies* [not *lays*] *in a case unprotected. He lay* [not *laid*] *in bed all day. I was lying* [not *laying*] *on the beach all day.* When there is no object and when the meaning is "recline," the proper verb is *lie* [*lay, lain, lying*].

Lend, Loan

Some people prefer the verb *lend (lent, lent)* and scorn the verb *loan (loaned, loaned)* even though *loan* has a long history, especially in America. The verb *loan* is common in financial contexts: *The bank loaned the money.*

Less, Fewer (See Fewer, Less.)

Lie, Lay (See Lay, Lie.)

Like, As (See As, Like.)

Lose, Loose

Lose is pronounced /looz/ and means "misplace" or "get rid of." *Loose* is pronounced /loos/ and means "not tight." *If you lose your receipts, you can't be reimbursed. To hide his weight gain, he wore only loose-fitting clothes.*

May, Can (See Can, May.)

May Be, Maybe

The verb *may be* is two words. The adverb *maybe* (meaning "perhaps") is one word. *We may be late. Maybe we are late.*

Might Have, Might of

Might of is a misinterpretation of the way *might have* sounds in running speech. *I might have* [not *might of*] *picked the winning numbers.*

Moral, Morale

Moral (meaning "ethical" or "ethical lesson") is pronounced with the stress on the first syllable /mor′ al/; *morale* (meaning "spirit") is pronounced with the stress on the second syllable /mo ral′/. *The moral* [not *morale*] *of the fable is "haste makes waste." The defeat destroyed the team's morale* [not *moral*].

Most, Almost (See Almost, Most.)

Must Have, Must of

Must of is a misinterpretation of the way *must have* sounds in running speech. *They must have* [not *must of*] *left the play during the third act.*

Myself, Me or I

Confusion about whether to use *me* or *I* in compound constructions probably leads to the incorrect use of *myself: The staff and myself thank you. Myself* must refer to a previous *I* or *me: I saw the incident myself. I wrote myself a note. They told me to answer the letter myself.*

Noplace, Nowhere

Use *nowhere*, not *noplace*, in formal prose.

Number, Amount (See Amount, Number.)

Of

In formal writing

- Do not use *of* after words such as *large* and *good: That is too large a meal* [not *too large of a meal*].
- Do not use *of* after *off: The cat jumped off the ledge* [not *off of the ledge*].
- Do not omit *of* after *type: What type of car did you buy* [not *what type car*]?

O.K.

O.K., also spelled *OK* and *okay*, is informal. In formal writing use instead some expression such as *acceptable, satisfactory*, or *correct.*

Oral, Verbal

The distinction between *oral* and *verbal* can be useful, even though the two meanings are very close. Whereas *verbal* refers to either spoken or written words, *oral* refers specifically to spoken words.

usage

Orient, Orientate

As verbs, both *orient* and *orientate* can mean "to get properly adjusted or aligned." In American English, *orient* is more common: *Orient yourself to the map before you start through the unfamiliar area.*

People, Persons

Persons implies a small and specific group: *The elevator will hold only six persons. People* is more versatile and can refer to any group.

Percent, Per Cent, Percentage

When not used with a specified amount (3 percent, 75 per cent), *percentage* is preferred in formal writing: *A large percentage* [not *percent*] *of the text was destroyed.*

Persuade, Convince (See Convince, Persuade.)

Playwrite, Playwright

Even though a playwright writes plays, he or she is not called a "playwrite." The correct term is *playwright. Wright* (as in *wheelwright* and *shipwright*) means "one who makes or constructs something" and has no relation to *write.*

Plenty

In writing, avoid *plenty* as an intensifier. Instead, use words such as *very* and *quite: Legal action was quite* [not *plenty*] *appropriate.*

Plus

In formal writing, do not use *plus* to mean *and: They couldn't find summer jobs, and* [not *plus*] *they owed the school for tuition.*

Practicable, Practical

Practicable means that something is possible; *practical* means that something is sensible: *A new bridge is practicable but not practical because of the cost.*

Precede, Proceed

The root *cede/ceed* means "go." The prefix *pre-* means "before," and *pro-* means "forward"; therefore, *precede* means "go before," and *proceed* means "go forward."

Principal, Principle

Because *principal* and *principle* sound alike, they are frequently confused. *Principle* is an abstract noun meaning a "truth," "law," "rule," "code": *He advocates the principle of separation of church and state. Principal* can be both a noun and an adjective. As a noun it generally means "chief official," "main participant"; and as an adjective it means "most important," "chief": *The principal of the school insisted on a dress code. The principal role in the drama is that of the son.*

Proceed, Precede (See Precede, Proceed.)

Prosecute, Persecute

Prosecute usually means "to start legal action." *Persecute* means "to treat oppressively." *The Allies prosecuted those who had persecuted the Jews.*

Quote, Quotation

The use of the verb *quote* for the noun *quotation* is informal. *The speaker began with a quotation* [not *quote*] *from Emerson.*

usage

Raise, Rise

Raise (raised, raised) usually means "to lift" and always has an object: *They raised the Confederate ship from the muddy bottom of the Mississippi. Rise (rose, risen)* usually means "to go up" and has no object: *The sun rose before we could get good photographs of the eclipse.*

Real, Really

The use of *real* as an adverb to mean "very" is informal. Instead of *real angry,* write *really angry* or *very angry.*

Rear, Raise

One of the meanings of *rear* is "to nurture a child," although many people now use *raise* in this same sense. According to Theodore Bernstein, this meaning of *raise* is established. He comments: "At one time . . . the battle cry was, 'You raise pigs, but you rear children.' However, in this country at least . . . we raise both pigs and children, and some parents will testify that you can't always tell the difference."

Reason Is Because, Reason Is That

Instead of *reason is because,* write *reason is that: The reason for the lack of job openings is that* [not *because*] *people are retiring at the age of seventy, not sixty-five.*

Regardless, Irregardless (See Irregardless, Regardless.)

Respectfully, Respectively

Respectfully means "showing respect": *She respectfully responded to the request. Respectively* means "in a specific order": *The record and the tape cost $8.99 and $9.99, respectively.*

Right

Right as a modifier is vague; it can mean "somewhat" or "to a large degree": *right confusing, right ridiculous, right dumb.* Consequently, it should be avoided in writing.

Same

Same is a substitute for *it* or *them* in legal documents but in no other writings: *After you have written the letter, submit it* [not *same*] *for approval.*

Scarcely

In a negative construction, *scarcely* is nonstandard. Do not write *Without scarcely a notice, they moved.* Instead write *With scarcely a notice, they moved.* Do not write *I couldn't scarcely breathe.* Instead write *I could scarcely breathe.*

Scarcely When, Scarcely Than

Scarcely when is preferred over *scarcely than: Scarcely had the announcement been written, when* [not *than*] *the reporters arrived.*

Seldom, Seldom Ever

Ever is unnecessary in the phrase *seldom ever.* Do not write *We seldom ever attend movies.* Instead, write *We seldom attend movies. Ever* is acceptable in the phrase *seldom if ever: We seldom if ever attend movies.*

Set, Sit

The verb *sit, sat, sat* does not have an object: *Sit in row H.* The verb *set, set, set,* meaning "to position or place," must have an object: *Set your glass on the coaster.* A few special meanings of *set,* however, require no object: *The sun sets. The hen sets on her nest.*

Shall, Will

In the past, grammars dictated that *shall* be used with the subjects *I* and *we, will* with other subjects. These grammars also prescribed that for emphasis, promise, determination, or command, the pattern be reversed: *will* with *I* and *we, shall* with other subjects.

Attention to actual usage has shown that even in formal prose, people have never used *shall* and *will* consistently in this fashion. Instead, *will* appears commonly with *I* and *we* and also appears in emphatic statements with other subjects: *I will visit China. They repeated that they will strike if their demands are not met. Shall* seldom appears except in a question with *I* or *we* as the subject: *Shall we reject the offer? Where shall I look?* Frequently, the question is an invitation: *Shall we have lunch? Shall we dance?* In other contexts, *shall* seems extremely formal—almost stuffy.

Should, Would

Following the pattern of *shall* and *will,* many early grammars prescribed the use of *should* with the subjects *I* and *we, would* with all other subjects (see **Shall, Will**). The prescription, however, is seldom followed. *Should* is used with all subjects to indicate obligation or expectation: *The public should support the bill. He should be here shortly.* With all subjects *would* can indicate promise: *I swore that I would work out two hours every day.* Furthermore, with all subjects *would* can express a hypothetical situation: *If the schedule were more realistic, more people would fly the shuttle.* Finally, either *should* or *would* is acceptable in certain idioms expressing desire or preference: *I would [should] like to direct your attention to paragraph 3. We would [should] prefer to delay discussion until the next meeting. Would* is more common than *should* in American English.

usage

Should Have, Should of

Should of is a misinterpretation of the way *should have* sounds in running speech: *I should have written* [not *should of written*].

Sit, Set (See Set, Sit.)

Slow, Slowly

Both *slow* and *slowly* have long been used as adverbs but in special ways. *Slow* occurs only after the verb and usually in short commands: *Drive slow. Slow* also occurs frequently with the verb *run: The clock runs slow. The trains were running slow.* If the rhythm and sense are satisfied, *slowly* can occur either before or after the verb: *The cat slowly stalked the robin across the yard* or *The cat stalked the robin slowly across the yard.*

When the adverb follows a verb describing a process, either *slow* or *slowly* is acceptable, particularly with a compound adverb: *The boat drifted slow [slowly] and steady [steadily] toward the reef.*

Only *slowly* can occur as a sentence adverb. In such cases, it usually appears at the beginning of the structure: *Slowly, Earp rose to his feet, laid four aces on the table, and drew his gun.*

So, So That

So that makes the sentence structure clearer and the tone more formal than *so: Keep a record of your blood pressure so that* [not *so*] *your doctor can make an accurate interpretation.*

So, Very

In writing, do not use *so* to mean *very: The film was very* [not *so*] *maudlin.*

Some

In formal writing, do not use *some* to mean "somewhat": *The way we speak may differ somewhat* [not *some*] *in the locker room and at a cocktail party.*

Someplace, Somewhere

Someplace is more informal than *somewhere: Supposedly, there is a symbol somewhere* [not *someplace*] *in the poem.*

Sort of

Sort of is more informal than *somewhat* or *to some extent.* In formal prose, write *They are somewhat* [not *sort of*] *confused by the instructions.*

Stationary, Stationery

Stationary means "fixed"; *stationery* means "writing paper." Remember that stationERy is made of papER.

Such a

In formal writing, do not use *such a* to mean "very": *It was a very* [not *such a*] *witty play. Such a* should be used only when it is followed with a *that* clause stating a result: *It was such a witty play that I would like to see it again.*

Suppose to, Supposed to

Do not write *suppose to* for *supposed to.* Although the *d* sound often is not pronounced in running speech, it should always be written: *We were supposed to* [not *suppose to*] *attend the conference.*

Sure

Sure as an adverb is more informal than *surely* or *certainly* and should be written only in friendly correspondence and dialogue: *The book surely* [not *sure*] *is radical.*

Sure to, Sure and

Use *sure to,* not *sure and,* in a construction like *Be sure to go* [not *sure and go*].

Take, Bring (See Bring, Take.)

Than, Then

Than, a conjunction, completes a comparison; *then* indicates time: *We then learned that the matter was more serious than we had thought.*

That, Which

To be unquestionably correct, you should use *that* to introduce restrictive clauses (no commas) and *which* to introduce nonrestrictive clauses (commas): Flashman *is a book that makes a shameless cad entertaining.* Flashman, *which makes a shameless cad entertaining, is worth reading.*

Their, There, They're

Their, which shows possession, appears only before a noun: *their work, their music, their beliefs. There* indicates location *(go there)* or introduces an inverted sentence *(there are three possible answers). They're* means *they are (they're late).*

Theirselves, Themselves

Never write *theirselves* instead of *themselves: They declared themselves* [never *theirselves*] *bankrupt.*

Them People, Those People

A phrase such as *them people* or *them pencils* is considered illiterate. Instead, always write *those people* or *those pencils.*

usage

Then, Than (See Than, Then.)

This Here, That There

This here and *that there* are not Standard English. Omit the *here* and *there: this attempt* (never *this here attempt*), *that warning* (never *that there warning*).

This Kind of, These Kinds of

Use the singular *this* with *kind of* and the plural *these* with *kinds of: this kind of food, these kinds of food.*

Thusly

An *-ly* added to *thus* is unnecessary; *thus* is already an adverb. *We will thus* [not *thusly*] *cancel plans.*

Till, Until

These words are both correct and interchangeable. The spelling *'til* is incorrect.

To, Too

To can be a preposition *(to them, to school)* or an infinitive marker *(to go, to win). Too* is an adverb meaning "excessively" *(too tired, too much)* or "also" *(we too left): The news was too* [not *to*] *disappointing.*

Toward, Towards

These words have the same meaning; however, the sound of *toward* is usually preferable: *The camera faced toward* [or *towards*] *the crowd.*

Try to, Try and

Write *try to,* not *try and: You should try to understand* [not *try and understand*].

-type

The suffix -*type* can be used to create adjectives: *A-type personality, European-type clothes, a Playboy-type publication*. If you use an adjective with a -*type* suffix, be sure that the suffix creates the right meaning. *A Bogart hero* refers to one of the characters Humphrey Bogart made famous. *A Bogart-type hero* only resembles those characters. In some constructions the addition of -*type* is illogical: *compact car* (not *compact-type car*), *spy novel* (not *spy-type novel*), *suspension bridge* (not *suspension-type bridge*).

Type, Type of

Do not omit the *of* after the noun *type: It is the type of computer they recommend* [not *type computer*].

Uninterested, Disinterested (See Disinterested, Uninterested.)

Unique

Some people object to phrases like *more unique, somewhat unique, almost unique,* or *very unique*. They argue that *unique* is absolute and thus cannot be compared, modified, or intensified. According to *Webster's Ninth New Collegiate Dictionary, unique* is absolute when meaning "without like or equal"; but when meaning "distinctively characteristic" or "unusual," *unique* can properly appear in phrases such as *a very unique region* and *a somewhat unique school*.

Until, Till (See Till, Until.)

Up

Omit *up* in verb phrases where it adds no meaning, as in *join up, check up, end up, fold up, call up, divide up, lift up*.

Use, Utilize

The verb *use* means "to put to use." Utilize means "to find a special purpose for something." Although these verbs are sometimes thought of as synonyms, *utilize* actually has a narrower meaning than *use: They used the detergent for washing clothes. They utilized the detergent as an insecticide*.

Use to, Used to

Do not leave the *d* out of *used to: The family used to* [not *use to*] *believe in flying saucers*.

Verbal, Oral (See Oral, Verbal.)

Wait for, Wait on

Some people say *wait on* to mean "await." But the expression is not Standard English; write instead *wait for: He waited for me* [not *on me*] *under the clock at Holmes'.*

Way, Ways

Write *They have a long way to drive,* not *They have a long ways to drive.*

Well, Good (See Good, Well.)

Whether, If (See If, Whether.)

Which, That (See That, Which.)

Which, Who

Do not use *which* to introduce a relative clause modifying a person or people: *They reprimanded the doctor who* [not *which*] *prescribed the drug.* Do not use *who* with animals and things: *The plate pictured an eagle, which* [not *who*] *clutched an olive branch.*

Who's, Whose

Do not confuse *who's* and *whose. Who's,* which is somewhat informal, means *who is: Who's going? Whose* is the possessive form of *who: Whose responsibility is the statistical analysis?*

Will, Shall (See Shall, Will.)

Would, Should (See Should, Would.)

Would Have

In *if* clauses, use *had,* not *would have: If they had* [not *would have*] *checked the engine, the accident would not have occurred.*

Would Have, Would of

Would of is a misinterpretation of the way *would have* sounds in running speech: *Except for the Vietnam War, in 1968 Lyndon Johnson would have* [not *would of*] *run for President.*

Your, You're

Your is the possessive form of *you: your idea, your order, your assignment. You're,* which is somewhat informal, is a contraction of *you are: You're indecisive. You're trapped.*

Glossary of Grammatical, Rhetorical, and Literary Terms

This glossary provides a quick reference to terms—some useful and some essential for writers to know. Many definitions provide all the necessary information. Other definitions may require supplementary information from the text.

Absolute Phrase

An absolute phrase—usually a participial or infinitive phrase—modifies the whole sentence to which it is connected: *Speaking of problems, have you seen our new assignment? To be blunt, Jones has no sense of rhythm.* An absolute phrase that begins with a subject is sometimes called a nominative absolute: *The reservation confirmed, we called a cab. The climbers struggled up the mountain, their lungs aching.* (Section 5d)

Abstract Noun

An abstract noun names something with no physical existence: *beauty, fury, dishonesty.*

Acronym

An acronym is a word formed from the initial letters or syllables of the words in a phrase: *awol* ("absent without leave"), *COBOL* ("common business-oriented language"), *CINCPAC* ("Commander in Chief, Pacific"), *Fiat* ("Fabrica Italiana Automobili, Torino").

Active Voice

A verb is in the active voice when its subject acts or controls the action and its object receives the action or is acted upon: *Harry bet thirty dollars. The jury convicted him.* See also **Passive Voice**. (Section 4f)

404

Ad Hominem Attack

An argument that involves an attack on an individual's character rather than on ideas and positions is called an ad hominem attack.

Adjective

An adjective is a word that describes, limits, or qualifies a noun or a noun equivalent: *a tart apple, a foolish remark, a successful opening.* (Section 3a)

Adjective Clause

An adjective clause modifies a noun or pronoun. These clauses are introduced by relative pronouns (*who/whom/whose, which, that*) or relative adverbs (*when, where, why*): *The game, which will be televised, is a sell-out. I returned to Pocatello, where I had spent my first ten years.* (Section 7c.2)

terms

Adverb

An adverb modifies an adjective (*fairly complex*), adverb (*very carefully*), verb (*moved backward*), or whole sentence (*Certainly, we want to go.*).

Adverb Clause

An adverb clause modifies a verb, adjective, adverb, or whole sentence. Adverb clauses are introduced by subordinate conjunctions (*when, until, because, since, if, unless, although,* etc.): *After they left Vermont, they moved to Quebec. He thought he was a woodsman, just because he bought clothes at L.L. Bean.* (Section 7c.1)

Adverbial Conjunction (See Conjunctive Adverb.)

Agreement

The term *agreement* refers to the correspondence of both verbs with subjects and pronouns with antecedents. A verb must agree in number with its subject, and a pronoun must agree in number with its antecedent (singular verb with singular subject, singular pronoun with singular antecedent; plural verb with plural subject, plural pronoun with plural antecedent): *The raccoon washes its food.* [*Raccoon, washes,* and *its* are all singular.] *Raccoons wash their food.* [*Raccoons, wash,* and *their* are all plural.] (Chapters 10 and 13)

Alliteration

Alliteration is the repetition of the initial sounds of words to create a musical effect: "sunless sea," "the weary, way-worn wanderer," "the hunter home from the hill," "dusty death."

Analogy
An analogy compares two dissimilar things to show that what is true of one is also true of the other. For example, language is analogous to a river; both have branches, and both constantly change. A false analogy distorts the points of similarity and arrives at an invalid conclusion.

Analysis
In an analysis, a subject is broken into parts or segments in order to clarify the whole.

Antagonist
In a literary work the antagonist is the force that opposes the main character; the antagonist can be another character or characters, society, nature, or even some trait within the main character. (See also **Protagonist.**)

terms

Antecedent
An antecedent is the noun or noun phrase that a pronoun refers to: *In the 1960s Bob Dylan was at the height of his success.* [*Bob Dylan* is the antecedent of *his.*] *Mosquitoes filled the air; they ruined the entire picnic.* [*Mosquitoes* is the antecedent of *they.*]

Antithesis
In rhetoric, an antithesis is an opposing idea—an idea contrary to the thesis. A writer may state the antithesis to an argument in order to attack it.

Appositive
An appositive renames, restates, or explains the word or words it refers to: *She bought an expensive car, <u>a BMW luxury model</u>.* (Section 21d.2)

Argument
Argument is one of the purposes of writing. In an argument, a writer tries to move readers to act or to agree.

Article
An article is a word (*a, an, the*) that signals the presence of a noun.

Audience
In rhetoric, the audience is the anticipated reader or readers of a composition.

Auxiliary Verb
An auxiliary verb combines with a main verb to form a verb phrase: *is burning, <u>did</u> stand, <u>has been</u> grown, <u>could have</u> watched.* (Section 4b)

Balanced Sentence

A balanced sentence has a noticeable symmetry of structure and often vocabulary. This kind of sentence heightens comparison or contrast: *What is true about losing weight is not magic, and what is magic about losing weight is not true.* (Section 33b.4)

Begging the Question

Begging the question is a logical fallacy in which a writer argues in a circle. The writer "begs" the audience to accept as true the very point at issue.

Bibliography

A bibliography is a list of sources on a particular subject. A bibliography most often appears at the end of a research paper as a record of the sources referred to in the text. Annotated bibliographies list and also describe writings relating to a subject.

terms

Brainstorming

In rhetoric, brainstorming involves jotting down anything that comes to mind in order to stimulate ideas. Brainstorming should be unstructured and spontaneous so that blocked ideas can come into consciousness. (Section 34c)

Case

Case refers to the special forms of nouns and pronouns that indicate their function. Some pronouns have three cases.

Subjective (or nominative) case—used for subjects and subject comple-
    ments: *I, we, he, she, they, who*
Objective case—used for objects: *me, us, him, her, them, whom*

Possessive (or genitive) case—used to show ownership, authorship,
    source, and description: *my/mine, our/ours, his, her/hers, their/
    theirs, whose*

Nouns and all other pronouns have two cases.

Common case—used for all functions except possession: *Linda, everyone,
    friends, actors*
Possessive (or genitive) case—used for the same functions as the posses-
    sive pronouns and formed by adding *'s* to singular forms and *'* to
    most plural forms: *Linda's, everyone's, friends', actors'.* (Chapter 14)

Cause/Effect

Writers can structure a composition or a paragraph by explaining to readers the cause of a particular effect or the effect of a particular cause.

Characterization

Characterization refers to the way an author depicts characters. Characters may be "flat," not developed in any depth; or they may be "round," developed with lifelike complexity. Also, characters may be "static" (unchanged by experiences) or "developing" (changed by experiences).

Chronological Order

The actions narrated in a composition are in chronological order when arranged according to the same time sequence in which they occurred, do occur, or should occur.

Classical Topics

The classical topics, formulated by Greek rhetoricians and orators, reflect typical ways of thinking (definition, comparison, relationship, circumstance, and testimony). Writers can use these "topics" to find and develop a subject for a composition. (Section 34j)

terms

Classification

When a composition is structured according to classification, a general category is divided into smaller groups on the basis of some selected principle.

Clause

A clause is a grammatical construction with both a subject and predicate. Independent (main) clauses may stand by themselves as sentences: *My car had a flat.* Dependent (subordinate) clauses must be attached to independent clauses: *I was late because my car had a flat.* (Chapter 7)

Cleft Sentence

A cleft sentence is a construction that emphasizes an element that follows a form of *be.* The construction occurs when an ordinary sentence with a subject-verb-object pattern is changed to one with this pattern: *it* plus a form of *be* plus the element to be emphasized plus a *who, which,* or *that* clause. The term *cleft* refers to the fact that the ordinary sentence is cleft, or cut, into parts. The ordinary sentence *The pitcher hit the home run* can be changed to these cleft sentences: *It was the pitcher who hit the home run. It was a home run that the pitcher hit.* (Section 33b.5)

Cliché

A cliché is an expression made stale and boring by overuse: *quick as a wink, last but not least, hour of need.* (Section 32e)

Climactic Order

The parts of a composition may be arranged in climactic order, from the less important to the more important or from the small to the large.

Climactic Sentence

The ideas in a climactic sentence move up a scale from less important to more important, from less intense to more intense, or from ordinary to extraordinary: *Once, in the early days before the buffalo herds had dwindled, Grinnel saw a Cheyenne Indian noiselessly ride his horse close to the side of a huge bull, and springing gracefully on his back, ride the beast for some distance, and then, with his knife, give it its death stroke.* (Section 33b.3)

Coherence

Coherence literally means "the quality of sticking together." A composition whose parts fit together logically is said to have coherence. Coherence can be achieved by logical sequences, transitional devices, pronouns, connecting words, and repetitions.

Collective Noun

A collective noun refers to a group that forms a unit: *family, team, army, audience.* (Section 10h)

terms

Comedy

Comedy is usually lighthearted entertainment. In drama, comedies end happily or at least with justice done.

Comma Splice

A comma splice, a punctuation error, occurs when two independent clauses are connected, or spliced together, with only a comma: *Alcohol enhances confidence, at the same time, it impairs judgment.* Two independent clauses must be joined with a comma and a coordinating conjunction or with a semicolon: *Alcohol enhances confidence, but at the same time, it impairs judgment. Alcohol enhances confidence; at the same time, it impairs judgment.* (Chapter 9)

Comparative Conjunction

A comparative conjunction is a subordinate conjunction with two parts: *as . . . as, so . . . that, such . . . that,* a comparative modifier *. . . than,* a superlative modifier *. . . that.* These conjunctions express comparisons: *He laughed so loud that we got embarrassed. The train was more comfortable than we had expected. She was the hardest teacher that I ever had.* (Section 6b.4)

Comparative Degree

The form of an adjective and adverb used to compare two items is called the "comparative degree." An *-er* ending and the words *more* or *less* usually indicate the comparative degree: *May was wetter than June. Cod is more plentiful than flounder. This paper is less expensive.* See also **Superlative Degree.** (Section 3c)

Comparison/Contrast

In rhetoric, a comparison/contrast structure examines the similarities and differences between people, ideas, and things.

Complement

In a clause, a complement "completes" the meaning of the predicate. A complement may be

- The object of a transitive verb: *They ate pizza.*
- The indirect object of a transitive verb: *He told me a lie.*
- The object complement of a transitive verb: *They called the storm Frederic.*
- The subject complement following *be* or a linking verb: *The book is a challenge. The water felt hot.*

Complex Sentence

A complex sentence contains one independent clause (ind.) and at least one dependent clause (dep.): *The bus filled* [ind.] *until even the aisle was jammed with people* [dep.]. *When the bell rang* [dep.], *the students raced from the room* [ind.]. (Section 7d.3)

Compound-Complex Sentence

A compound-complex sentence contains two or more independent clauses (ind.) and at least one dependent clause (dep.): *In New England earthworms are called nightwalkers* [ind.]; *in the Midwest, where they are best known as bait* [dep.], *they are called fishing worms* [ind.]. (Section 7d.4)

Compound Sentence

A compound sentence contains two or more independent clauses (ind.): *English has a phonetic alphabet* [ind.]; *Chinese has a pictographic system* [ind.]. (Section 7d.2)

Concrete Noun

A concrete noun names a material object that can be seen, touched, heard, tasted, or smelled: *rock, hamburger, wallet.*

Conflict

In literature, a conflict involves a clash of forces. The usual plot pits the main character against an opposing force—another character or characters, society, nature, or some personal trait.

Conjugation

A conjugation is a list of all the forms of a particular verb—its tenses (present, past, future, present perfect, past perfect, and future perfect), its voices (active and passive), its moods (indicative, imperative, and subjunctive), its persons (first, second, and third), and its numbers (singular and plural).

Conjugation of *Write, Wrote, Written*

INDICATIVE MOOD

PRESENT TENSE—ACTIVE VOICE: I/You/We/They write.
He/She/It writes.

PRESENT TENSE—PASSIVE VOICE: I am written.
He/She/It is written.
You/We/They are written.

PAST TENSE—ACTIVE VOICE: I/You/He/She/It/We/They wrote.

PAST TENSE—PASSIVE VOICE: I/He/She/It was written.
You/We/They were written.

FUTURE TENSE—ACTIVE VOICE: I/You/He/She/It/We/They will write.

FUTURE TENSE—PASSIVE VOICE: I/You/He/She/It/We/They will be written.

PRESENT PERFECT TENSE— I/You/We/They have written.
ACTIVE VOICE: He/She/It has written.

PRESENT PERFECT TENSE— I/You/We/They have been written.
PASSIVE VOICE: He/She/It has been written.

PAST PERFECT TENSE—ACTIVE I/You/He/She/It/We/They had written.
VOICE: ten.

PAST PERFECT TENSE—PASSIVE I/You/He/She/It/We/They had been
VOICE: written.

FUTURE PERFECT TENSE— I/You/He/She/It/We/They will have
ACTIVE VOICE: written.

FUTURE PERFECT TENSE— I/You/He/She/It/We/They will have
PASSIVE VOICE: been written.

terms

SUBJUNCTIVE MOOD

PRESENT TENSE—ACTIVE VOICE:	I/You/He/She/It/We/They write.
PRESENT TENSE—PASSIVE VOICE:	I/You/He/She/It/We/They be written.
PAST TENSE—ACTIVE VOICE:	(same as indicative mood)
PAST TENSE—PASSIVE VOICE:	I/You/He/She/It/We/They were written.
PRESENT PERFECT TENSE— ACTIVE VOICE:	I/You/He/She/It/We/They have written.
PRESENT PERFECT TENSE— PASSIVE VOICE:	I/You/He/She/It/We/They have been written.
PAST PERFECT TENSE—ACTIVE AND PASSIVE VOICE:	(same as indicative mood)

IMPERATIVE MOOD

PRESENT TENSE—ACTIVE VOICE:	Write.
PRESENT TENSE—PASSIVE VOICE:	Be written.

See also **Progressive Forms.**

Conjunction

A conjunction is a grammatical connector that links sentence elements—words, phrases, or clauses. See also **Coordinating Conjunction, Correlative Conjunction,** and **Subordinating Conjunction.** (Section 6b)

Conjunctive Adverb (Adverbial Conjunction)

A conjunctive adverb serves as a transitional expression to link ideas: *however, therefore, thus, in addition, on the other hand,* and so on. See **Transitional Expression** for a more complete list.

Connotation

Connotation refers to the feelings and memories evoked by a word. See also **Denotation.** (Section 32c)

Controlling Idea

The controlling idea, or thesis, of a composition is central to the meaning to be conveyed. Everything included should contribute to the development of this idea.

Coordinating Conjunction
Coordinating conjunctions (*and, but, or, nor, for, so, yet*) connect grammatically equal structures—words, phrases, clauses. (Section 6b.1)

Coordination
Coordination is the process of combining two or more grammatically equal structures—for example, two or more nouns, verbs, predicates, prepositional phrases, dependent clauses, or independent clauses. For techniques that use coordination, see Sections 33a.1–33a.2.

Correlative Conjunction
A correlative conjunction is a coordinating conjunction that consists of a pair of words or phrases: *both . . . and, not . . . but, not only . . . but also, either . . . or, neither . . . nor*. (Section 6b.2)

Count Noun
A count noun names something that can be counted. Thus, count nouns have plural forms. *Desk* and *bracelet* are count nouns with the plural forms *desks* and *bracelets*. *Furniture* and *jewelry* with no plural forms are not count nouns. See also **Mass Noun**.

terms

Critical Review
A critical review helps readers understand and evaluate some form of scholarship, art, or entertainment.

Cumulative Sentence
A cumulative sentence begins with an independent clause and then piles up—or accumulates—structures at the end in order to create a dramatic effect.: *Last night I had very discomforting dreams—full of evil creatures, plunges down precipices, and prolonged re-creations of embarrassing moments from my past.* (Section 33b.2)

Dangling Modifier
A modifier with nothing nearby to modify is called "dangling." A dangling modifier is usually a verbal or elliptical clause that appears at the beginning of a sentence: *Despising the habit, a resolution was made to quit smoking tomorrow.* The word modified should appear close to the modifier and should be the agent of the action expressed by the verb or verbal in the modifier: *Despising the habit, she resolved to quit smoking tomorrow.* (Section 15a)

Deduction
Deduction is a method of logical reasoning whereby a conclusion follows accepted premises. In a classic example, the two premises "All men are mortal" and "Socrates is a man" are joined to produce the conclusion "Therefore, Socrates is mortal." A conclusion that does not follow logically is called a non sequitur.

Definition

The definition of a word can be a synonym or a formal explanation that puts the word in a general class and then differentiates it from other members of that class. In rhetoric, definition can be extended to a paragraph or a whole composition. A writer can explore the meaning of a word by a variety of methods: description, classification, comparison, illustration.

Demonstratives

The demonstrative pronouns are *this* and *that,* along with their corresponding plurals, *these* and *those.* These demonstratives fill a noun position or precede a noun and function as a determiner: *this pen, that tape, these marks, those noises.* (Section 2b)

Denotation

The denotation of a word is its literal and explicit meaning independent of any emotional association. See also **Connotation.** (Section 32c)

Dependent Clause

A dependent clause (also called a subordinate clause) has a subject and predicate but must be tied to an independent clause as a modifier or noun element: *When I noticed the menu's eight dollar hamburger, I quickly left. They insisted that I stay for the weekend.* (Section 7c)

Description

In description, a writer uses concrete details to create a representation of what something is or appears to be.

Determiner

A determiner is a word like *a, the, our, this,* or *Susan's* that signals the presence of a noun. (Section 6c)

Direct Address

Words in direct address (set off from the rest of the sentence with commas) name whoever or whatever is being spoken to: *This time, Ed, I'll pay. Get in the car, old dog.* (Section 21h)

Direct Object

A direct object is a word, phrase, or clause that receives or is affected by the verb's action: *Jessica likes historical romances. He said that he felt dizzy.*

Direct Quotation

A direct quotation, enclosed in quotation marks, duplicates the exact words of a speaker or writer: *"The first rule for taxi drivers,"* Mr. Geno *said, "is to be sure the passenger is in the car." The* London Times *called it "the lastest American humbug."* See also **Indirect Quotation.** (Section 27a)

Double Negative

No, not, nothing, hardly, scarcely, and barely are considered negatives in English. Use only one of these words to create a negative statement: *I have no cash. They have hardly begun.* A double negative is redundant and incorrect: *I don't have no cash. They haven't hardly begun.*

Elliptical Construction

In an elliptical construction, a word or several words are omitted, but their sense is clearly understood: *The bus takes an hour; a taxi, only thirty minutes.* [*Takes* is omitted in the second clause.] (Section 7c.4)

Emphatic Pronoun

An emphatic pronoun (also called an intensive pronoun) ends with *-self* or *-selves* and emphasizes a noun or another pronoun: *The Constitution itself says so. We were reprimanded by the conductor himself.* See also **Reflexive Pronoun.** (Section 2a)

Enumeration

Enumeration is a structural pattern for a paragraph or an entire composition. Details are listed to support the central idea.

Equivocation

In logic, *equivocation* refers to the use of an expression to mean more than one thing in a single context.

Escape Literature

The purpose of escape literature is to entertain, not to provide insights into human existence. See also **Interpretive Literature.**

Essay

An essay is a short composition written from a personal point of view.

Etymology

The etymology of a word is its origin and development.

Euphemism

A euphemism, an expression such as *revenue enhancers* for *taxes* or *passed away* for *died,* is used for evading or glorifying reality. (Section 32g)

Evidence

Evidence is the material used to support an opinion. Effective kinds of evidence are facts, details, and expert testimony.

Expletive

An expletive is a meaningless word (*there* or *it*) that fills out a sentence's structure and allows its subject to be delayed: *There is a fly in the room. It is hard to translate the story.* (Section 6d)

terms

Exposition

The purpose of exposition is to explain by supplying information. The main techniques used in exposition are description, narration, enumeration, comparison/contrast, classification, illustration, definition, analysis, and cause/effect.

Fallacy

A fallacy in logic is any kind of faulty reasoning—primarily avoiding the real issue and making an error in the reasoning process.

Figurative Language

Figurative language is not literal, straightforward language. Instead, it uses comparisons and associations to communicate meaning. Common figures of speech are the metaphor, simile, personification, and hyperbole. (Section 33d)

terms

Finite Verb

A finite verb serves as the main verb of a clause or sentence. Unlike non-finite verbs (infinitives, participles, and gerunds), finite verbs do not serve as modifiers and nominals.

Fragment

A fragment is an incomplete sentence punctuated as if it were a complete sentence: *When the team lost eighty-two games.* A fragment can be corrected by incorporation into another sentence: *When the team lost eighty-two games, no one was playing well.* A fragment can also be rewritten as a complete sentence: *The team lost eighty-two games.* (Chapter 8)

Freewriting

Freewriting, writing down whatever thoughts occur, is a technique for stimulating ideas and generating material for a composition. (Section 34e)

Function Word

A function word is a preposition, conjunction, determiner, or expletive that creates structure. (Chapter 6)

Fused Sentence

A fused sentence (sometimes called a run-on sentence) contains two independent clauses not separated by a conjunction or proper punctuation: *The students take regular classes however, all the subjects are taught in French.* The clauses must be separated: *The students take regular classes; however, all the subjects are taught in French.* For other ways of correcting fused sentences, see Chapter 9.

Gender
In English, *gender* refers to the sex represented by third-person singular pronouns: masculine *(he, him, his)*, feminine *(she, her, hers)*, and neuter *(it, its)*. A few nouns reflect gender: masculine *(actor)* and feminine *(actress)*.

General-Particular Order
In general-particular order, an entire composition or a paragraph begins with a general statement and moves to explain or develop that statement with particular details.

General/Specific Words
General words refer broadly to categories: *food, book, person.* Specific words refer more narrowly to a member or members of a category: *burrito, telephone directories, Joe.* (Section 32a)

terms

Genitive Case
Genitive case is a term for possessive case or for an *of* phrase showing possession: *the coach's rule, the rule of the coach.* See also **Possessive Case.**

Genre
Genre refers to a category of literature such as fiction, poetry, and drama.

Gerund
A gerund is a verb form (the present participle, or *-ing* form) functioning in a sentence as a noun. A gerund phrase is a gerund plus another element—an object, subject, or modifier: *Writing well can be important in getting a good job.* [*Writing* is a gerund subject; *getting* is a gerund object of preposition. *Writing well* and *getting a good job* are both gerund phrases.] (Section 5b)

Gobbledygook
Gobbledygook (also called bureaucratic language, double talk, officialese, and doublespeak) is the abstract and confusing language used by officials who think simple, direct prose will not impress readers. (Section 32i)

Hasty Generalization
A hasty generalization is a logical fallacy that involves jumping to a conclusion on the basis of too little evidence.

Helping Verb
Helping verb is a name sometimes given to an auxiliary verb. See also **Auxiliary Verb.**

Hyperbole

A hyperbole is a figure of speech that uses exaggeration rather than a literal statement to make a point: *We must have walked a thousand miles on this shopping trip.* (Section 33d.4)

Idiom

An idiom is an expression peculiar to a language or dialect. The meaning of idiomatic speech is not always clear from the meaning of each word: *put up with his foolishness, carry on about the problem, make off with the loot.*

Illustration

In a paragraph or a composition developed by illustration, an idea is supported with one or more examples.

Image

An image is a vivid description that appeals to the sense of sight, sound, smell, taste, or touch.

Imperative Mood

Verbs in the imperative mood are those used to give commands. *You* is always the understood subject: *Look out! Answer the roll. Delete the conjunction.* (Section 4g.2)

Indefinite Pronoun

An indefinite pronoun (*anyone, everybody, each, either, both,* etc.) does not require an antecedent and need not refer to a specific person or thing. (Section 2f)

Independent Clause

An independent clause, sometimes called a main clause, is a structure with a subject and predicate. It need not be connected to any other structure: *We drove to Atlantic City.* (Section 7b)

Indicative Mood

Verbs in the indicative mood make statements and ask questions: *I saw the movie. Was the movie good?* (Section 4g.1)

Indirect Object

An indirect object, usually a noun or pronoun, appears between a transitive verb and a direct object. The indirect object may be converted to a prepositional phrase with *to, for,* or *of* and moved after the direct object: *They gave the school an award. [They gave an award to the school.]* (Page 59)

Indirect Quotation

In an indirect quotation, the exact words of a source are paraphrased. No quotation marks surround an indirect quotation: *Soren explained that he was curious about their everyday life.* See also **Direct Quotation.** (Section 27a)

Induction

Induction is a method of logical reasoning whereby a conclusion follows the study of a representative group. For example, if every tap water sample contains chlorine, one can conclude that the source of the water also contains chlorine.

Infinitive

An infinitive is a verbal made of *to* plus a verb: *to live, to listen, to appear.* An infinitive may function as a noun or as a modifier; it may appear alone or as part of an infinitive phrase: *To finish was his dream.* [*To finish* is an infinitive noun subject.] *She had the determination to finish the assignment.* [*To finish the assignment* is an infinitive phrase used as a modifier.] Though *to* is called the "sign" of the infinitive, it may be omitted after a few verbs like *let, make,* and *hear.* (Section 5a)

terms

Inflection

An inflection is a change in the form of a word that signals a change in meaning or in grammatical relation to another word. The parts of speech, or word classes, that have inflection are nouns *(bird, birds, bird's, birds')*, verbs *(go, goes, went, gone, going)*, pronouns *(it, its)*, adjectives *(tall, taller, tallest)*, and adverbs *(badly, worse, worst)*.

Intensifier

An intensifier is a modifier that adds emphasis: *very ill, extremely successful, really hopeful.* See also **Qualifier.**

Intensive Pronoun (See Emphatic Pronoun.)

Interjection

An interjection is an expression of emotion or exclamation (such as *oh, well,* or *wow*) structurally unconnected to a sentence: *Well! it's about time. Oh, I forgot the key.* (Sections 21h and 25g)

Interpretive Literature

The purpose of interpretive literature is to comment on human existence in a meaningful way. See also **Escape Literature.**

Interrogative Pronoun

An interrogative pronoun (*who, whom, whose, which,* or *what*) introduces a question that asks for information. *Whose, which,* and *what* can function as a pronoun or as a determiner: *Whose is this? Which job is available?* (Section 2d)

Intransitive Verb

An intransitive verb expresses action but has no object: *The substance vanished. The package arrived quickly.*

Irregular Verb

The past tense and past participial forms of an irregular verb do not follow the predictable pattern of adding *-d* or *-ed*. Following is a list of most of the irregular verbs in English and their principal parts.

terms

Base	Past	Past Participle
arise	arose	arisen
awake	awoke	awakened, awoken
be	was	been
bear	bore	borne
beat	beat	beaten
become	became	become
befall	befell	befallen
begin	began	begun
behold	beheld	beheld
bend	bent	bent
bet	bet	bet
bid*	bade, bid	bidden, bid
bind	bound	bound
bite	bit	bitten, bit
bleed	bled	bled
blow	blew	blown
break	broke	broken
breed	bred	bred
bring	brought	brought
build	built	built
burn	burnt, burned	burnt, burned
burst	burst	burst
buy	bought	bought
cast	cast	cast
catch	caught	caught
choose	chose	chosen

* When the verb refers to offering a price, *bid* is appropriate for both the past and past participle. Otherwise, either *bade* or *bid* is appropriate for the past; either *bidden* or *bid* is appropriate for the past participle.

Base	Past	Past Participle
cling	clung	clung
clothe	clothed, clad	clothed, clad
come	came	come
cost	cost	cost
creep	crept	crept
crow	crowed, crew	crowed
cut	cut	cut
deal	dealt	dealt
dig	dug	dug
dive	dived, dove	dived
do	did	done
draw	drew	drawn
drink	drank	drunk
drive	drove	driven
eat	ate	eaten
fall	fell	fallen
feed	fed	fed
feel	felt	felt
fight	fought	fought
find	found	found
flee	fled	fled
fling	flung	flung
fly	flew	flown
forbid	forbade, forbad	forbidden
forecast	forecast, forecasted	forecast, forecasted
forget	forgot	forgotten
forgive	forgave	forgiven
freeze	froze	frozen
get	got	got, gotten
give	gave	given
go	went	gone
grind	ground	ground
grow	grew	grown
hang	hung, hanged*	hung, hanged*
have	had	had
hear	heard	heard
hide	hid	hidden
hit	hit	hit
hold	held	held
hurt	hurt	hurt
inlay	inlaid	inlaid
keep	kept	kept
kneel	knelt	knelt
knit	knitted, knit	knitted, knit

* When the verb refers to execution, *hanged* is preferred for both past and past participle. Otherwise, *hung* is preferred.

terms

Base	Past	Past Participle
know	knew	known
lay	laid	laid
lead	led	led
leap	leaped, leapt	leaped, leapt
learn	learned, learnt	learn, learnt
leave	left	left
lend	lent	lent
let	let	let
lie	lay	lain
light	lit, lighted	lit, lighted
lose	lost	lost
make	made	made
mean	meant	meant
meet	met	met
melt	melted	melted, molten
mistake	mistook	mistaken
mow	mowed	mowed, mown
pay	paid	paid
prove	proved	proved, proven
put	put	put
quit	quit	quit
read	read	read
rid	rid, ridded	rid, ridded
ride	rode	ridden
ring	rang	rung
rise	rose	risen
run	ran	run
saw	sawed	sawed
say	said	said
see	saw	seen
seek	sought	sought
sell	sold	sold
send	sent	sent
set	set	set
sew	sewed	sewn, sewed
shake	shook	shaken
shave	shaved	shaved, shaven
shear	sheared	sheared, shorn
shed	shed	shed
shine	shone	shone
shoe	shod	shod
shoot	shot	shot
show	showed	shown, showed
shrink	shrank, shrunk	shrunk, shrunken
shut	shut	shut
sing	sang	sung
sink	sank	sunk, sunken

Base	Past	Past Participle
sit	sat	sat
slay	slew	slain
sleep	slept	slept
slide	slid	slid
sling	slung	slung
slink	slunk	slunk
slit	slit	slit
sow	sowed	sown, sowed
speak	spoke	spoken
speed	sped, speeded	sped, speeded
spell	spelled, spelt	spelled, spelt
spend	spent	spent
spill	spilled, spilt	spilled, spilt
spin	spun	spun
spit	spat	spat
split	split	split
spread	spread	spread
spring	sprang	sprung
stand	stood	stood
steal	stole	stolen
stick	stuck	stuck
sting	stung	stung
stink	stank, stunk	stunk
stride	strode	stridden
strike	struck	struck, stricken
string	strung	strung
strive	strove	striven
swear	swore	sworn
sweep	swept	swept
swell	swelled	swollen, swelled
swim	swam	swum
swing	swung	swung
take	took	taken
teach	taught	taught
tear	tore	torn
tell	told	told
think	thought	thought
throw	threw	thrown
thrust	thrust	thrust
understand	understood	understood
upset	upset	upset
wake	woke, waked	woken, waked
wear	wore	worn
weave	wove	woven
weep	wept	wept
win	won	won
wind	wound	wound

terms

Base	Past	Past Participle
withdraw	withdrew	withdrawn
withhold	withheld	withheld
withstand	withstood	withstood
wring	wrung	wrung
write	wrote	written

Jargon

Jargon is the specialized vocabulary of a group such as lawyers, sociologists, and linguists. Jargon should be avoided when it obscures meaning or overburdens style. (Section 32h)

terms

Journalistic Questions

The journalistic questions, which can generate ideas about a subject, are *who? what? when? where? why?* and *how?* (Section 34h)

Linking Verb

A linking verb requires a subject complement to complete its meaning. An adjective complement modifies and a noun complement renames the subject of the clause. Common linking verbs are *be, become, seem, look, feel: The discussion was painful. The supplies grew scarce.* (Pages 61–62)

Loose Sentence

A loose sentence begins with the main idea and then adds modifiers: *Computer chess programs allow stronger play because new methods of searching have improved the evaluation of positions and moves.* See also **Periodic Sentence.**

Main Clause (See Independent Clause.)

Mass Noun

A mass noun names something that cannot be counted. Thus, mass nouns have no plural form. In their normal senses, *clothing, money, water, garbage,* and *equipment* are examples of mass nouns. See also **Count Noun.**

Metaphor

A metaphor is a figure of speech that conveys information in a nonliteral way by stating or implying that two things are similar: *The book is a passport into exotic, untrodden lands.* (Section 33d.1)

Misplaced Modifier

A misplaced modifier seems to relate to the wrong element in a sentence: *The delivery service brought the package to the house in a van.* [seems to modify *house*] Modifiers should be positioned so that they clearly modify the intended word: *In a van, the delivery service brought the package to the house.* [clearly modifies *brought*] (Section 16b)

Modal Auxiliary

A verb auxiliary that cannot undergo conjugation is called a modal auxiliary: *can, could, shall, should, will, would, may, might,* and *must.* Modals express such ideas as ability, advisability, necessity, and possibility. (Page 26)

Modifier

A modifier is a word, phrase, or clause that describes, limits, or qualifies some other word, phrase, or clause. Adjectives and adverbs (and words functioning as such) are modifiers: *The tribe had no written language. Without warning, the horse stumbled. I got a unicycle, which I could never learn to ride.*

terms

Mood

The mood of a verb is shown by form and meaning. The indicative mood expresses a fact or a question: *I attended. Was the problem solved?* The imperative mood expresses a command: *Buy bonds. Get help.* The subjunctive mood expresses desire or possibility: *I wish I were there.* See also **Indicative Mood, Imperative Mood,** and **Subjunctive Mood.** (Section 4g)

Narration

Narration tells a story, recounts events, or outlines the stages of a process.

Nominalization

A nominalization is an expression of action in noun form: *contribution, development, failure, inclusion.* Unnecessary nominalizations can sometimes be changed to more forceful verb equivalents: *contribute, develop, fail, include.* (Section 33c.1)

Nominative Absolute (See Absolute Phrase.)

Nominative Case (See Case.)

Nonfinite Verb (See Finite Verb.)

Nonrestrictive Element

A nonrestrictive element does not restrict or limit the word or phrase it modifies. Commas should surround a nonrestrictive element to indicate its loose connection with a sentence: *I heard someone called a "dork," which can't refer to anything complimentary. The research has led to the CD GUIDE, a successful software product.* (Section 21d)

Non Sequitur

A non sequitur is a logical fallacy in which the conclusion does not follow from the evidence: *If one pill is good, then two must be twice as good.*

Noun

A noun names things in the physical and nonphysical worlds: *Jim, sister, novel, field, generosity, grief,* and so on. (Chapter 1)

Noun Clause

A noun clause is a dependent clause that functions in the same ways that all nouns do—as subjects, objects, and complements: *What you should do is quit. I know that cheval means "horse." The winner will be whoever spends the most money.* (Section 7c.3)

Number

Number refers to the form of a noun, pronoun, or verb that shows singularity (one) or plurality (more than one): singular—*car, it, sings;* plural—*cars, they, sing.* (Section 1c)

Object (See Direct Object, Indirect Object, and Object of Preposition.)

Object Complement

An object complement, either an adjective or a noun, completes a clause's structure by modifying or renaming the direct object: *The drought made water scarce. She named her dog Josh.* (Page 59)

Objective Case (See Case.)

Object of Preposition

An object of a preposition, usually a noun, noun phrase, or pronoun, combines with a preposition to form a prepositional phrase: *at school, after washing the car, in front of them.* (Section 6a)

Paradox

A paradox is the linking of seemingly contradictory ideas or feelings to express a truth: *arming for peace, spending money to make money, listening to silence.*

Paragraph

A paragraph in a composition is a unit of thought or information set off by an indentation of the first line. Most paragraphs develop a topic sentence, stated or implied.

Paragraph Block

A paragraph block is a group of paragraphs that together develop a single thought or unit of information.

Parallelism

In grammar, *parallelism* refers to the use of the same grammatical structure for items in a compound structure, a series, a list, or an outline. (Chapter 20)

Paraphrase

A paraphrase is a rewording of a passage without changing its meaning.

terms

Parenthetical Element

A parenthetical element in a sentence is set off with commas, dashes, parentheses, or brackets to show its loose, interruptive, or nonessential nature: *A robot, at least to most people, is a manlike creature. The production—how can I put it politely?—lacks interest. In the story, Zeus had a child by Pluto (not to be confused with the god of the underworld). The islands were named the Canary Islands from the wild dogs [Latin canes] found there.* (Sections 21g.1, 24d–24g)

Participle

A participle is a verb form used as an adjective. Participles have two basic forms—the present participle (*-ing* verb form) and past participle (the form that follows *have* in a verb phrase). A participial phrase is a participle plus another element—an object, subject, or modifier: *Remembering, Eugene started over. Meat cut very thin is called scallopini.* [*Remembering* and *cut* are both participles modifying the subjects of both sentences. *Cut very thin* is a participial phrase.] See also **Absolute Phrase.** (Section 5c)

Particular-General Order

In particular-general order, an entire composition or a paragraph begins with specifics and moves to a general statement—the topic sentence or thesis.

Part of Speech

Part of speech refers to the grammatical classification of a word based on its form, function, or meaning. Traditionally, a word is classified as a noun, verb, adjective, adverb, pronoun, preposition, conjunction, or interjection.

Passive Voice

A verb is in the passive voice when its subject receives the action. The verb consists of a form of *be* plus a past participle: *The purse was stolen. Your account has been credited.* See also **Active Voice.** (Section 4f)

Past Participle

The past participle is the form of a verb that normally follows *have.* The past participle of regular verbs adds *-d* or *-ed* to the base form: *called, increased, pitched, assumed.* Irregular verbs do not have predictable past participles. The forms for the past participles of irregular verbs can be found in dictionaries and in appropriate lists. See also **Irregular Verb.**

Perfect Tenses

The perfect tenses are formed by combining *has/have/had* or a modal and *have* with the past participle: *has escaped, had rebuilt, will have withdrawn, could have read.* (Sections 4d and 4e)

Periodic Sentence

In a periodic sentence the main idea is postponed until the end: *Just at the height of his power when he could have become an American monarch, Washington went home to farm.* See also **Loose Sentence.** (Section 33b.1)

Person

For pronouns, the term *person* refers to the form that indicates whether a reference is to the speaker or spokesperson (first person: *I, we*), to the person(s) spoken to (second person: *you*), or to the person(s) or thing(s) spoken about (third person: *he, she, it, they*). All other pronouns and nouns are in the third person. For verbs, the term refers to the form that goes with each of the three persons. (Section 4c)

Persona

Persona, a term that first meant "mask worn by an actor," refers to the voice an author uses to address the audience. The voice should sound natural whether it is or not.

Personal Pronoun

A personal pronoun refers to a specific person or people (*I, you, she, they,* etc.) or to a specific thing or things (*it, them,* etc.). For a complete list of the personal pronouns, see Section 2a.

Personification

Personification is a figure of speech in which something nonhuman is given a human characteristic: *The printer ate the paper. The unplugged TV stared blankly.* (Section 33d.2)

terms

Phrase

A phrase is a group of related words that together have a single function (as a noun, verb, or modifier). Unlike a clause, a phrase has no subject and finite verb: *a heavy eater, has been applied, in a rural town, tending to be jealous, to close the letter, the meal over.*

Plot

Plot refers to the sequence of events that occurs in a work of literature.

Point of View

Point of view refers to the way the narrator relates the action of a work of literature. The point of view may be omniscient (the narrator knows everything), limited omniscient (the narrator knows the thoughts of one character), first person (the narrator speaks as *I*), or objective (the narrator describes only what is seen and heard).

terms

Positive Degree

Positive degree refers to the simple, uncompared form of adjectives and adverbs: *crazy, evenly, complex, quick, angrily.* See also **Comparative Degree** and **Superlative Degree.** (Section 3c)

Possessive Case

The possessive case is the form of a noun or pronoun that indicates ownership (*Sue's job, their vacation*), authorship (*Poe's story, her essay*), source (*paper's headline, teacher's assignment*), measurement (*a mile's distance*), and description (*a child's bike*). See also **Case.** (Chapter 14)

Post Hoc Fallacy

In a post hoc fallacy, one reasons that whatever immediately preceded an outcome also caused it. For example, if a landing on the moon preceded bad weather, one cannot assume correctly that the landing caused the problem.

Predicate

The predicate joins with the subject to form a clause. A predicate consists of at least one finite verb and may also include modifiers and completing words: *The dress was cut low in the front and lower in the back. He sent his grandmother a poinsettia for Christmas.*

Predicate Adjective

A predicate adjective, also called a subject complement, follows *be, seem, appear, become, grow, remain, taste, look, smell, sound,* or *feel* and modifies the subject: *The topic was boring. He remained angry.*

Predicate Noun

A predicate noun or nominative, also called a subject complement, follows *be, become, remain, seem,* and *appear* and names or refers to the subject: *The topic was euthanasia. He remained an enemy.*

Prefix

A prefix is a syllable that attaches to the beginning of a root to add or alter meaning: *pre-* in *preview* means "before"; *de-* in *devalue* means "reduce"; *mal-* in *malfunction* means "badly."

Preposition

A preposition is a function word like *in, to, from, by,* and *through* that connects its object to the rest of the sentence. The preposition plus its object is called a prepositional phrase: *Over the past year, the school in our neighborhood has deteriorated to the point of needing extensive repairs.* (Section 6a)

Present Participle

The present participle is the form of a verb that ends in *-ing: surviving, making, breathing, lying.* See also **Participle, Gerund,** and **Progressive Forms.**

Principal Parts

The principal parts of verbs are the base form (*see, step*), the past form (*saw, stepped*), and the past participle form (*seen, stepped*). (Section 4a)

Process Analysis

A process analysis is a composition that traces, usually in chronological order, the steps of an event or an operation.

Progressive Forms

The progressive forms of a verb indicate actions in progress. These forms appear in all six tenses and are made with a form of *be* plus the present participle (*-ing* form): *is looking, was looking, will be looking, has been looking, had been looking, will have been looking.* (Section 4e)

Pronoun

Pronouns are words that appear in the same positions as nouns. A pronoun usually substitutes for a previously stated noun or noun phrase, called its antecedent: *The language was easy to learn because it had many words similar to Latin. Pigs were used in the research; they were fed large amounts of sugar.* See also **Personal Pronoun, Interrogative Pronoun, Relative Pronoun, Demonstrative Pronoun, Indefinite Pronoun, Reciprocal Pronoun, Reflexive Pronoun,** and **Intensive Pronoun.** (Chapter 2)

terms

Proper Noun and Adjective

Proper nouns and adjectives are specific names that begin with a capital letter: *Churchill, Xerox, Crimean War, Natchez Trace, Florida vacation, Easter service, October weather.* (Section 31b)

Protagonist

In literary works, the protagonist is the main character. See also **Antagonist.**

Purpose

Purpose is the writer's intention—to entertain, to explain, to win an argument, to move the audience to action.

Qualifier

A qualifier is an adverb that serves to intensify or restrict an adjective or adverb: *very tired, highly motivated, somewhat bitter, rather large.*

terms

Quotation (See Direct Quotation and Indirect Quotation.)

Reciprocal Pronoun

The reciprocal pronouns, *each other* and *one another,* are only used as objects: *The two always give each other help. The noise was so loud we could not hear one another.* (Section 2e)

Red Herring

A red herring is a logical fallacy in which a writer diverts the reader from the issue by switching to another, vaguely related subject.

Reflexive Pronoun

A reflexive pronoun, ending in *-self* or *-selves,* is always an object that refers to, "reflects," the subject of the clause: *I wrote myself a note. They couldn't imagine themselves as losers.* See also **Emphatic Pronoun.** (Section 2a)

Regular Verb

A regular verb adds *-d* or *-ed* to the base to form the past tense and the past participle: *use, used, used; warn, warned, warned.*

Relative Pronoun

A relative pronoun (*who, whom, whose, whoever, which, whichever, what, whatever,* and *that*) introduces a dependent clause: *No one was injured by the tank that exploded. You can't trust whoever looks honest.* (Section 2c)

Restrictive Element

A restrictive element restricts, limits, or identifies the word or phrase it modifies. A restrictive element is not set off by commas: *The coach created an offense that used a variety of sets.* See also **Nonrestrictive Element.** (Section 21d)

Rhetoric

Rhetoric is the effective use of language.

Root

The root of a word provides its base, or primary, meaning. For example, the root of *telegraphy* is *graph,* which means "write"; the root of *amorphous* is *morph,* which means "shape."

Run-on Sentence (See Fused Sentence.)

terms

Satire

Through satire, an author ridicules a subject and exposes weaknesses and vices.

Sentence

A sentence is an independent statement, question, or command beginning with a capital letter and ending with some terminal punctuation. Except for exclamations like "Oh!" and idioms like "The more, the merrier," sentences contain a subject and predicate, usually with modifiers and complements: *A man wearing sweaty, seedy clothes pushed his way in. Why did he enter a race that he was sure to lose?*

Sentence Fragment (See Fragment.)

Sentence Modifier

A sentence modifier is an adverbial that has an independent or parenthetical meaning. Sentence modifiers, sometimes called absolutes, relate to whole sentences rather than to particular words or phrases: *Obviously, she would like a job. Without a doubt, I will be there. She is fasting, although I don't know why.*

Setting

The setting of a work of literature is the time and place in which the story occurs.

Shift

A shift is an unnecessary change from one kind of construction to another. Shifts can occur in tense, voice, number, person, and structure. (Chapter 17)

Simile

A simile is a figure of speech in which two dissimilar things are said to be alike. The words *like* or *as* distinguish a simile from a metaphor: *problems sprouting like weeds, the moon round like a Concord grape, a plot as complicated as an acrostic puzzle.* (Section 33d.3)

Simple Sentence

A simple sentence has one independent clause (main clause) and no dependent clause (subordinate clause): *The smell of the food reminded me of my childhood.* (Section 7d.1)

Slang

Slang is a kind of informal language that develops when people invent new expressions or change the meaning of existing expressions to create an individual and unique way of speaking: *pinkie* for *little finger, whirlybird* for *helicopter, cop out* for *refusal to commit oneself, yak* for *chat.* (Section 32d)

terms

Spatial Order

In descriptions with a spatial order, details are arranged so that readers can follow the eye's path.

Split Infinitive

A split infinitive has a modifier between the *to* and the base form of the verb: *to slowly stroll, to desperately yell, to at the last second fall.* In most split infinitives, the modifier should be moved: *to stroll slowly, to yell desperately, to fall at the last second.* (Section 18d)

Squinting Modifier

A squinting modifier appears between two words both of which it might modify: *The woman he called reluctantly made an appointment.* [*Reluctantly* could modify *called* or *made.*] Squinting modifiers must be repositioned: *The woman he called made an appointment reluctantly.* (Section 16c.4)

Straw Man

In an argument, a straw man is an opponent whose position is distorted or invented to make it easier to attack.

Subject

The subject joins with the predicate to form a clause. A subject consists of a noun (or a noun substitute) plus any modifiers. A simple subject is the subject minus its modifiers. *The interior of the car lit up.* [The subject is *the interior of the car;* the simple subject is *interior.*] (Sections 5a, 7a, 7c)

Subject Complement

A subject complement follows *be* or another linking verb and renames or modifies the subject of the clause: *He was a scrawny kid.* [*Kid* renames *he* and can be called a predicate noun or nominative.] *The conversation became serious.* [*Serious* modifies *conversation* and can be called a predicate adjective.] See also **Linking Verb.**

Subjective Case (See Case.)

Subjunctive Mood

The subjunctive mood primarily indicates that something is not a fact or that something should happen: *If I were qualified, I would apply for the job. The doctor insisted that Jack get a second opinion.* Unlike the indicative mood (*I was qualified* and *he gets*), the subjunctive mood has only one form for each tense and person. (Section 4g.3)

Subordinate Clause (See Dependent Clause.)

Subordinating Conjunction

A subordinating conjunction introduces a dependent clause and expresses relationships such as cause, contrast, condition, manner, place, and time. Common subordinating conjunctions are *because, although, if, as if,* and *when.* (Section 6b.3) For a more complete list, see 7c.1. See also **Adverb Clause.**

Subordination

Through subordination, writers show that one idea is dependent on another. Subordination can be achieved through dependent clauses, verbals, and appositives. For techniques that use subordination, see 33a.3–33a.6. See also **Adverb Clause, Adjective Clause, Noun Clause, Infinitive, Participle, Gerund,** and **Appositive.**

Suffix

A suffix is a syllable or sound that attaches to the end of a word to alter the word's meaning, to change the word from one class to another, or to change the word's form. The suffix *-itis* ("inflamed") added to the root *appendix* creates the word *appendicitis.* The suffix *-ly* changes the adjective *sad* to the adverb *sadly.* The suffix *-ed* changes the present tense verb *call* to the past tense *called.*

Superlative Degree

The form of an adjective and adverb used to make a comparison among three or more items is called the *superlative degree.* An *-est* ending and the words *most* and *least* indicate the superlative degree: *This is the largest hotel in the city. The video you selected is the one most frequently pur-*

chased. This brand of yogurt is the least fattening of all. See also **Comparative Degree.** (Section 3c)

Symbol
A symbol is an image that stands for an idea or a complex of ideas. A vulture might symbolize death; spring might symbolize a new beginning; a closed door might symbolize lost opportunity.

Synonym
A synonym is a word with approximately the same meaning as another—for example, *accord* is a synonym for *agreement; stagnation* for *inaction; derision* for *ridicule.*

Syntax
Syntax refers to the arrangement of words to form structures—phrases, clauses, and sentences.

terms

Tag Question
A tag question appears at the end of a statement and asks for verification. It is composed of an auxiliary verb and a pronoun: *The car has been repaired, hasn't it? You read the book, didn't you?* (Section 21h)

Tense
Tense is the feature of verbs that indicates a meaning related to time. English is said to have three simple tenses (present, past, and future) and three perfect tenses (present perfect, past perfect, and future perfect). (Section 4d)

Theme
A theme is the central idea of a work, primarily a work of literature.

Thesis
The thesis is the central, or controlling, idea of a nonliterary composition. The content of the composition should support and develop the thesis.

Topic Sentence
The topic sentence of a paragraph is the main idea developed. If a paragraph has no stated topic sentence, one should be clearly implied.

Tragedy
Tragedy does not end happily. In the plot of a dramatic tragedy, the main character suffers a "fall," the loss of something dear, as the result of events and human weakness.

Tragic flaw
In drama, a tragic flaw is the human weakness that combines with circumstances to ruin the main character.

Transitional Expression
A transitional expression indicates the relationship between ideas. Sometimes called conjunctive adverbs or conjuncts, transitional words and phrases serve to link independent clause to independent clause, sentence to sentence, and paragraph to paragraph. The following list illustrates the linking characteristic of these expressions:

accordingly	eventually	in fact	otherwise
actually	finally	in other words	regardless
after all	first	instead	similarly
again	for example	last	sometimes
all in all	for instance	likewise	still
also	for this reason	moreover	surely
as a result	furthermore	nevertheless	that is
basically	however	next	then
besides	in addition	on the contrary	therefore
certainly	in conclusion	on the other hand	thus
consequently	indeed	on the whole	

Transitive Verb
A transitive verb expresses action and requires an object: *She wrote the letter. Mr. Williams speaks Japanese fluently.* (Pages 59–61)

Verb
A verb is a word that indicates action (*swim*), occurrence (*happen*), or existance (*be*). (Chapter 4)

Verbal
A verbal is one of three verb forms functioning in a sentence as a noun or a modifier: infinitive (*to write*), present participle (*writing*), past participle (*written*). A verbal alone never functions in a clause as a finite verb. A verbal with a subject, object, complement, or modifier is called a verbal phrase. See also **Infinitive, Participle,** and **Gerund.** (Chapter 5)

Verb Phrase
A verb phrase is a verb made up of more than one word: *is calling, will consider, have been reading.*

Voice
The voice of a verb indicates whether the subject acts (active voice) or receives the action (passive voice). See also **Active Voice** and **Passive Voice.** (Section 4f)

Index

Numbers in **boldface** refer to sections of the Guide; other numbers refer to pages.

index

437

index

index

index

index

index

index

index

index